Prophecy in the New Millennium

When Prophecies Persist

D1741446

Edited by

SARAH HARVEY
Inform, UK

SUZANNE NEWCOMBE
Inform, UK

ASHGATE

Published by
Ashgate Publishing Limited
Wey Court East
Union Road
Farnham
Surrey, GU9 7PT
England

Ashgate Publishing Company
110 Cherry Street
Suite 3-1
Burlington, VT 05401-3818
USA

www.ashgate.com

British Library Cataloguing in Publication Data
Prophecy in the new millennium : when prophecies persist.
  -- (Ashgate Inform series on minority religions and spiritual movements)
  1. Prophecy--History--21st century. 2. Prophecy--Social aspects.
  I. Series II. Harvey, Sarah. III. Newcombe, Suzanne.
  203.2-dc23

The Library of Congress has cataloged the printed edition as follows:
Prophecy in the new millennium : when prophecies persist / edited by Sarah Harvey and Suzanne Newcombe.
      p. cm. -- (Ashgate inform series on minority religions and spiritual movements)
  Includes bibliographical references and index.
  ISBN 978-1-4094-4995-9 (hbk) -- ISBN 978-1-4094-4996-6 (pbk) --
  ISBN 978-1-4094-4997-3 (ebook) 1. Eschatology. 2. Prophecies. 3. Prophecy. 4.
  Religions. I. Harvey, Sarah. II. Newcombe, Suzanne.
  BL500.P76 2013
  202'.117--dc23

                                                                        2012031450
ISBN 9781409449959 (hbk)
ISBN 9781409449966 (pbk)
ISBN 9781409449973 (ebk – PDF)
ISBN 9781472400611 (ebk – ePUB)

Printed and bound in Great Britain
by MPG PRINTGROUP

PROPHECY IN THE NEW MILLENNIUM

This is a rich text full of significant insights for both new comers to the field of study and established experts. Uniquely combining the views of scholars and participants in prophetic movements, the essays in this volume make important contributions to our theoretical and empirical grasp of why and how prophecies generate, sustain, and sometimes strain religious movements, ranging from the lengthy legacy of Christian apocalypticism to the recent preoccupation with the Mayan 2012 prophecy and many other contemporary revelations.

Lorne Dawson, University of Waterloo, Canada

Seasoned scholars are joined by new researchers in this rich and lively collection. Coverage is broad and comparative, chapters are written in an accessible yet scholarly style, and a sure editorial hand is evident throughout. The volume as a whole makes a persuasive case for restoring prophecy to a central place within the comparative study of religion.

Steven J. Sutcliffe, University of Edinburgh, UK

Secular and spiritual prophets of doom abound in the information-rich twenty-first century – as they have for millennia. But there has yet to be worldwide floods, meteor impact, global computer failure, obvious alien contact, or direct intervention from God to end the world as we know it. Considering the frequency with which prophecy apparently fails, why do prophecies continue to be made, and what social functions do they serve?

This volume gives a concise, but comprehensive, overview of the rich diversity of prophecy, its role in major world religions as well as in new religions and alternative spiritualties, its social dynamics and its impact on individuals' lives. Academic analyses are complemented with contextualized primary source testimonies of those who live and have lived within a prophetic framework. The book argues that the key to understanding the more dramatic, apocalyptic and millenarian aspects of prophecy is in appreciating prophecy's more mundane manifestations and its role in providing meaning and motivation in everyday life.

Ashgate Inform Series on Minority Religions and Spiritual Movements

Series Editor: Eileen Barker,
London School of Economics, Chair and Honorary Director of Inform

Advisory Board:
Afe Adogame, University of Edinburgh, UK,
Madawi Al-Rasheed, King's College, London, UK,
François Bellanger, Université de Genève, Switzerland,
Irena Borowik, Jagiellonian University, Krakow, Poland,
Douglas E. Cowan, University of Waterloo, Ontario, Canada,
Adam Possamai, University of Western Sydney, Australia,
James T. Richardson, University of Nevada, Reno, USA,
Fenggang Yang, Purdue University, USA

Inform is an independent charity that collects and disseminates accurate, balanced and up-to-date information about minority religious and spiritual movements. The Ashgate Inform book series addresses themes related to new religions, many of which have been the topics of Inform seminars. Books in the series will attract both an academic and interested general readership, particularly in the areas of Religious Studies, and the Sociology of Religion and Theology.

Other titles in this series:

Spiritual and Visionary Communities
Out to Save the World
Edited by Timothy Miller

Contents

Notes on Contributors   *ix*
Acknowledgements   *xv*

1   From the Extraordinary to the Ordinary:
        An Overview of Prophecy   1
        Suzanne Newcombe and Sarah Harvey

PART I: PERSPECTIVES ON PROPHECY

2   Messages from Beyond: Prophecy in the Contemporary World   17
        Michael Barkun

3   Prophecy: Social Scientific Perspectives and Lubavitch   27
        Simon Dein

4   Prophecy on the Margins: A Case Study of the Apocalypse in
        Later Seventeenth-Century England   43
        Warren Johnston

5   Prophecy: A Perspective from the Early Church and the
        Contemporary Experience of a Methodist Minister   57
        Andrew Maguire

PART II: PERENNIAL PROPHECY IN MAINSTREAM TRADITIONS

6   The New Apostolic Reformation:
        Main Street Mystics and Everyday Prophets   75
        Margaret M. Poloma and Matthew T. Lee

7   The Mahdi and the End-Times in Islam   89
        Hugh Beattie

8   The Coming Golden Age: On Prophecy in Hinduism   105
        Luis González-Reimann

9   Divination, Prophecy and Oracles in Tibetan Buddhism   123
      Christopher Bell

10   Chasing the Horizon: Prophecy in Secular Contexts   137
      Wendy M. Grossman

PART III: CONTEMPORARY CASE STUDIES

11   Living in the Time of the End: A Personal Commentary from
      My Experiences with the Children of God and the
      Family International   155
      Abi Freeman May

12   Mormonism and The Family International:
      Toward a Theory of Prophecy in the Development of
      New Religious Movements   165
      Gordon Shepherd and Gary Shepherd

13   The Dispensation of Providence:
      Growing Up as a Blessed Child in the Unification Church   185
      Hani Zaccarelli

14   Waco: Living Prophecy   195
      Livingstone Fagan

15   (Always) Living in the End-Times:
      The 'Rolling Prophecy' of the Conspiracy Milieu   207
      David G. Robertson

PART IV: 2012 PROPHECIES

16   From Mushrooms to the Stars: 2012 and the Apocalyptic Milieu 225
      Andrew Fergus Wilson

17   Viral Email and the 2012 Apocalypse Contagion:
      Seven Reasons Why the World WON'T End in 2012   239
      Kristine Larsen

18   Remembering the Future: 2012 as Planetary Transition   255
      Suzanne Rough

19   2012 and the Revival of the New Age Movement:
     The Mayan Calendar and the Cultic Milieu in Switzerland   261
     Jean-François Mayer

20   Looking into the Future: Why Prophecies Will Persist   277
     J. Gordon Melton

Index   *285*

Notes on Contributors

Professor Michael Barkun is Professor Emeritus of Political Science in the Maxwell School at Syracuse University. His books on millennialism include *A Culture of Conspiracy* (2003), *Religion and the Racist Right: The Origins of the Christian Identity Movement* (1997), and *Disaster and the Millennium* (1974). His most recent book, *Chasing Phantoms: Reality, Imagination, and Homeland Security Since 9/11* was published in 2011. He edits the Religion and Politics series for the Syracuse University Press and sits on the editorial boards of several journals.

Dr Hugh Beattie is Lecturer in Religious Studies at The Open University. After reading history at Cambridge, he moved into social anthropology at SOAS (the School of Oriental and African Studies), and undertook field research in Afghanistan in the late 1970s. Subsequently he has conducted extensive research in the British Library's Oriental and India Office archive. His interests include Islam, state and society in Afghanistan and KhyberPakhtunkhwa, the history of Sikhism, and end-times religion. Author of *Imperial Frontier Tribe and State in Waziristan* (2002), he is currently working on religious leadership in Waziristan in the twentieth century.

Christopher Bell received a BA in English Literature and Religious Studies (2003), and an MA in Asian Religions (2006), both from Florida State University. His Master's thesis focused on the cult of Tsiu Marpo, one of the central protector deities of Samyé, Tibet's first Buddhist Monastery. He is currently a doctoral candidate at the University of Virginia, concentrating on Tibetan and Buddhist History. His dissertation research will examine the seventeenth-century rise and ritual systematization of the Nechung protective deity cult under the auspices of the Fifth Dalai Lama's burgeoning government.

Dr Simon Dein is a Senior Lecturer in Anthropology and Medicine at University College London and Honorary Professor at Durham University. He is also Visiting Professor in Psychology at Glendwyr University, Wales and is a part-time psychiatrist working in the NHS. He has written extensively on religion and health and on millennialism in Judaism and is the author of *Religion and Healing among the Lubavitch Community of Stamford Hill: A Case Study in Hasidism* (2004) and *Lubavitcher Messianism: What Really Happens When Prophecy Fails?* (2010). He is one of the editors of the journal *Mental Health, Religion and Culture*.

Livingstone Fagan was born in Jamaica. As a young child he was taken to England in 1965. He first met David Koresh while completing a post-graduate degree at a theology seminary west of London in 1988. He subsequently visited the Mount Carmel community on several occasions prior to the assault in 1993. Fagan was there when the initial shootout occurred on 28 February. During the ensuing 51-day siege he came out to serve as theological spokesperson for the group. The majority of the members perished in the flames on 19 April, including Fagan's wife and mother. A year later Fagan was among a small number of survivors detained and tried in what he claims was an obvious political trial. Although acquitted of the false charges brought against them the survivors were nevertheless given 40-year prison terms. After serving almost 15 years Fagan was returned to England in the summer of 2007.

Dr Luis González-Reimann received his MA in South Asian studies from El Colegio de México, and his PhD in South Asian studies from the University of California, Berkeley, where he teaches. He is the author of *The Mahābhārata and the Yugas* (2002), *Tiempo cíclico y eras del mundo en la India* (1988), and *La Maitrāyanīya Upanisad* (1992) as well as many scholarly articles.

Wendy M. Grossman is a freelance writer primarily but not solely covering technology and science. She is the founder (in 1987) and twice former editor of the UK's *The Skeptic* magazine, and co-editor of the 2010 book *Why Statues Weep: The Best of The Skeptic*. She has covered the Internet and related technology for more than 20 years and writes a weekly column, *net.wars*, covering the border wars between cyberspace and real life. Her website is at www.pelicancrossing.net.

Sarah Harvey is a Research Officer at Inform where she has worked since 2001. She is also a PhD candidate in the Religious Studies Department at the University of Kent, researching 'natural' approaches to pregnancy and childbirth.

Dr Warren Johnston is an Associate Professor at Algoma University in Ontario, Canada. His research focuses on religious, political and social thought in early modern England. He has published a number of articles and essays on apocalyptic thought, and is the author of *Revelation Restored: The Apocalypse in Later Seventeenth-Century England* (2011). He is currently working on a project examining sermon literature in seventeenth- and eighteenth-century England.

Dr Kristine Larsen is Professor of Physics and Astronomy at Central Connecticut State University. The author of *Stephen Hawking: A Biography* (2007) and *Cosmology 101* (2007), her research focuses on the myriad intersections between science and society, including science and pseudoscience. She has spoken on the 2012 Apocalypse Hysteria at various professional meetings and has published articles on the topic in numerous journals. She is also a contributor to the 2012hoax.org website.

Dr Matthew T. Lee is Professor and Chair of Sociology at the University of Akron. He has published in journals such as *Criminology*, *Sociological Quarterly*, *Social Problems* and *Social Psychology Quarterly*. His books include *The Heart of Religion* (co-authored with Margaret Poloma and Stephen Post), *A Sociological Study of the Great Commandment in Pentecostalism* (co-authored with Margaret Poloma, 2009), *The Science and Theology of Godly Love* (co-edited with Amos Yong, 2012); and *Godly Love: Impediments and Possibilities* (co-edited with Amos Yong, 2012).

The Revd Andrew Maguire has, over the last 30 years, served as a Methodist Minister in East Anglia, South London, Bristol and Hertfordshire. His studies included 'Greats' at Oxford in the mid-1970s followed a little later by a postgraduate Bachelor of Divinity degree at the University of Manchester while training for the Methodist Ministry. The opportunities given to a Methodist Minister for a three-month sabbatical every seven years have enabled him to develop an interest in early Christian studies with reference to original language texts. He created and runs the website www.earlychurchtexts.com. Since around 1990 he has been nominee of the UK Free Churches Group on the Board of Governors of Inform and is also a member of Inform's Management Committee.

Abi Freeman May grew up in England in an Orthodox Jewish family, and converted to Christianity in her teenage years. She joined what was then the Children of God, later The Family International. She lived in communities in England, Iran, Turkey, the Indian Subcontinent and Eastern Europe until 2007. She initially trained as a Montessori teacher, and later taught English to Speakers of Other Languages. She has a PGCE in Lifelong Learning from Staffordshire University. She compiles and edits devotional books, with nine in print.

Dr Jean-François Mayer received both his master's degree (1979) and his doctorate in history (1984) from the University of Lyon. Since the 1980s, he has paid special attention to new religious movements. He is the author of 10 books and numerous articles dealing with those topics as well as other religious developments in the contemporary world. In 2007, he founded the Religioscope Institute. He is the editor of Religioscope, an independent, bilingual website offering news and analyses on the role and place of religion in our world. He is associate editor of *Religion Watch*, a New York-based newsletter monitoring trends in contemporary religion. Webpage: www.mayer.info.

Professor J. Gordon Melton is Distinguished Professor of American Religious History at Baylor. He is also the founder and director of the Institute for the Study of American Religion and the author of hundreds of scholarly articles and more than 25 books, including several encyclopaedias, handbooks and almanacs on American religion and new religious movements. His internationally acclaimed *Encyclopedia of American Religions* has now reached its eighth edition.

Dr Suzanne Newcombe is a Research Officer at Inform where she has worked since 2002. She is also an Associate Lecturer for the Open University in the East of England and has lectured in the field of new and alternative religions at Kingston University. Her PhD research at the University of Cambridge explored the popularisation and development of yoga and Ayurvedic medicine in Britain.

Dr Margaret M. Poloma, Professor Emeritus of Sociology at the University of Akron, has written extensively about religious experience in contemporary American society, including pioneering studies of prayer and divine healing. Many of her publications have focused on Pentecostal spirituality, including the following books: *Charismatic Movement: Is There a New Pentecost?* (1982), *The Assemblies of God at the Crossroads: Charisma and Institutional Dilemmas* (1989), *Main Street Mystics: The Toronto Blessing and Reviving Pentecostalism* (2003), *Blood and Fire: Godly Love in a Pentecostal Emerging Church* (with Ralph Hood, 2008), *A Sociological Study of the Great Commandment in Pentecostalism: The Practice of Godly Love as Benevolent Service* (with Matthew Lee, 2009), *The Assemblies of God: Godly Love and the Revitalization of American Pentecostalism* (with John Green, 2010) and *The Heart of Religion* (with Matthew Lee and Stephen Post, 2013).

David G. Robertson is a PhD candidate in the Religious Studies department of the University of Edinburgh. His research examines how UFO narratives became the bridge by which ideas crossed between the conspiracist and spiritual milieus in the post-Cold War period. More broadly, his work concerns contemporary alternative spiritualities, and their relationship with popular culture. He is co-founder and presenter of the podcast series and blog at www.religiousstudiesproject.com.

Suzanne Rough is a philosophy graduate and has been a full-time practicing astrologer and teacher since 1989. In 1998 she established the DK Foundation School of Astrology with the aims of producing the next generation of astrology practitioners and making astrology available as a resource to practitioners in a range of other alternative disciplines. She has written several works for serious students of astrology: *Understanding the Natal Chart: An Esoteric Approach to Learning Astrology* (2008), *Transitional Astrology* (2008), *Working with Time: Recognising and Using Opportunity* (2008), *Understanding Relationship: Relationships and Conscious Living* (2008). In 2009 the DK Foundation became DKF-Koruna, an educational project based in Lapland.

Gary Shepherd is Professor of Sociology at Oakland University (Michigan) where he teaches courses in research methods, social psychology, social theory and the sociology of religion.

Gordon Shepherd is Professor of Sociology at the University of Central Arkansas where he teaches courses in statistics, social movements, social theory and the sociology of religion.

Together, the Shepherds have co-authored four books and numerous scholarly articles on both Mormonism and The Family International. Their books include *A Kingdom Transformed: Themes in the Development of Mormonism* (1984), *Mormon Passage: A Missionary Chronicle* (1998), *Talking with the Children of God: Prophecy and Transformation in a Radical Religious Group* (2010) and *Binding Earth and Heaven: Patriarchal Blessings in the Prophetic Development of Early Mormonism* (2012).

Andrew Fergus Wilson is Senior Lecturer in Sociology and Assistant Subject Head of Social Studies at the School of Education, Health and Sciences at the University of Derby. He has published widely on the themes of apocalypse in popular culture and the role of media and communication technologies in the contemporary 'cultic milieu'. Recent publications are 'Beyond Reason: The Exotic Millennium in English Culture', *Journal of Religion and Popular Culture*, 23(2) (summer 2011), and 'On the Outskirts of the New Global Village: Computer-mediated Visions of the End', in *Network Apocalypse: Visions of the End in an Age of Internet Media*, edited by Rob G. Howard (2011).

Hani Zaccarelli was raised and schooled in exclusive communes of the Unification Church near Swindon until he was nine. Then, after three years of moving between secular schools, he was sent to Seoul until his expulsion from the Unification-owned Little Angels school at the age of 14. A philosophy degree on the north coast of Ulster enabled his ultimate departure from the Unification Church. He now lives in New Jersey with his wife and two children, where he works in computing.

Acknowledgements

This book was a truly collaborative venture and could not have happened without the help and support of many individuals. The editors would wish to thank Eileen Barker, in particular, for providing both the methodological grounding and specific inspiration from which this volume originated. We wish to acknowledge our gratitude to all the current staff and management committee at Inform, who have read drafts and tolerated the time away from our routine responsibilities that was necessary for us to edit this volume. In particular we wish to acknowledge the support of Jim Beckford and Andrew McGuire on the Inform Management Committee for their many subtle contributions to making this work a success. In the office, Amanda van Eck, Duymaer van Twist and Silke Steidinger read various drafts of material relating to prophecy and kept our moral high. Special mention should also be made of the administrators at Inform who organised the two Inform seminars which fed into this volume: Sibyl Macfarlane who organised 'Prophecy in the New Millennium: When Prophecies Persist' in May 2012 and Charlotte Alton who organised the seminar on 'New Religions and Prophecy' in November 2008. We would also like to thank all the participants and speakers at these events, as fruitful discussions at these events directly contributed to the conceptualisation of the present volume. Of course this volume could not have existed without the enthusiasm and generosity of chapter contributors, to whom we are very grateful.

There are a number of other individuals outside Inform who deserve special mention: Lois Lee at the Non-religion and Secularity Research Network for her practical help and enthusiasm in finding contributors to this discussion from non-religious perspectives; David Lorimer, Programme Director at the Scientific and Medical Network; and Martin Redfern, Senior Producer in the BBC Radio Science Unit who invited Inform to events around the theme of 2012 prophecy which helped extend our perspective. Thanks are also due to the organisers and participants of the December 2010 inter-disciplinary conference on 'The Apocalypse and Its Discontents' held at the University of Westminster. The positive encouragement of Lorne Dawson at early stages of this project was also greatly appreciated.

Above all, the editors would also like to thank their families for their support and encouragement.

Chapter 1

From the Extraordinary to the Ordinary: An Overview of Prophecy

Suzanne Newcombe and Sarah Harvey

Apocalyptic images fascinate and terrify; at the dawn of the new millennium, end-times prophecy can be found everywhere. Images of the world destroyed – overwhelmed by water, ice or fire – have inspired both the religious and artistic imagination for millennia. Popular imagination acknowledges a kind of incomprehensibility of this scale of disaster, inviting an image of a 'hand of God'. In modern times we worry about the possibility of a human-created end of time – through nuclear war (Strozier 2002) or environmental mismanagement. Recent action films like *Armageddon* (1998), *The Day after Tomorrow* (2004), *I Am Legend* (2007) and *2012* (2009) testify to the lucrative popularity of the end-times scenario. More visibly, there continues to be a proliferation of newspaper headlines, books, music, disaster movies and other media activity relating to 'end of the world as we know it' – prophecies of Christ's imminent return, the 'end' of the Mayan calendar cycle on 21 December 2012, and the possibility of a cataclysmic disaster such as a meteor-impact or a nuclear attack by terrorists.

There are several good academic volumes that focus on violent and volatile millennialism (Landes 2011, Wessinger 2000, Wessinger 2011). This volume aims to bring about a more comprehensive understanding of the wider effects of the spectrum of prophetic expression.[1] The founder of Inform, Professor Eileen Barker, often states that the only dependable generalisation one can make when considering the scope and variety of contemporary religious expression is that you cannot make generalisations. Of course, as a social scientist, one can and must make a variety of limited generalisations about the groups studied, seeking to discover trends and patterns as well as putting religious beliefs and behaviour into context. But the idea of always being open to the exception, another way of

---

[1] This volume emerges from the method and aims of Inform, an independent charity based at the London School of Economics and supported by the British government and mainstream Churches, among other grants. Inform was founded in 1988 with the aim to help enquirers by providing as reliable, balanced and up-to-date information as possible about minority religious, spiritual and esoteric movements, as well as fringe political groups. Inform has held thematic, bi-annual seminars since its founding. A major purpose of these seminars is to bring together a variety of people and perspectives to consider important issues, topics and controversies involving minority religions.

considering the situation, the other points of view, is central to Inform's approach. Likewise, we hope that the reader of this volume will be able to consider the variety of insights provided by the contributors to this volume as challenges to conventional generalisations and assumptions about the nature of prophecy.

The End of the World: A New Millennium for Prophecy

The minority who fervently believe the 'end is nigh' attract avid voyeuristic attention from the popular press. Predictions are sometimes made on a grand scale, such as Family Radio's 2011 prediction of the imminent Rapture and End of Times in the United States which gained extensive press coverage (mentioned by Barkun, Johnston and Melton in this volume. See also Bartlett 2012). There is also reoccurring media attention to individual 'survivalists', quietly stockpiling supplies or preparing for the End of the social order as we know it 'just in case'. For example, in the United States both the National Geographic and the Discovery television channels have run weekly 'reality' series on 'Preppers' – individuals actively preparing for an 'end-times' scenario (Genzlinger 2012) – and media reports in June 2012 state that Spike TV will run a reality TV series called 'Last Family on Earth' in which contestants compete in various disaster scenarios (see *Daily Mail*, 5 June 2012). The press typically positions the reader as a sceptical outsider. There is an assumption that prophecy is something of a marginal activity. The observer is asked – how could these people believe so strongly in something so unlikely? Their visions of the future seem irrational and fantastic. How can people base their life decisions on a belief in such divergence from the general consensus?

Although images of a dramatic end enjoy widespread visibility, those who irrevocably change their lives in response to prophecy – who refuse employment and the accumulation of wealth, who choose not to educate their children for future employment in anticipation of an immediate end – are small in number. Some religious movements have inspired people to sell assets and await the arrival of the new kingdom, but others have taken more direct, violent action, such as the group suicides of 37 members of Heaven's Gate in 1997 or the active attempt to trigger the end-times by releasing deadly Sarin gas into the Tokyo underground by Aum Shinrikyo (now known as Aleph) in 1995. These examples push the boundaries of the general public's comprehension, provoking anxiety and concern about those who ascribe to millennial beliefs.

Also provoking social anxiety are the few individuals who decide to take their own life, or other drastic action on the basis of an idiosyncratic interpretation of these apocalyptic themes. Examples of this include the tragic case of a British schoolgirl who decided to pre-empt the inevitable destruction of humanity due to nuclear meltdown in 2012 by hanging herself (*Daily Mail*, 18 May 2012), or the case of Peter Gersten who has vowed to jump into a space-time portal that he believes will open up on the 21 December 2012 at Bell Rock near Sedona, Arizona.[2]

In social contexts of relative peace and prosperity, these numbers will probably always be small – but some of the contributors to the volume have personally organised their lives around the belief of an imminent 'end'. Suzanne Rough (Chapter 18) does not consider herself a prophet, but rather an 'auditor' who helps bring messages of the 'Hierarchy' and the Ascended Masters Kuthumi and Serapis Bey to a wider audience.[3] In anticipation of natural disasters in 2012, she has established an educational community in Lapland where she hopes that those prepared for worldwide flooding will avoid the worst effects of the disaster. Likewise Livingstone Fagan (Chapter 14) does not consider himself a prophet directly, but considers himself as called upon to continue to spread the prophecies of David Koresh, who was the leader of the Branch Davidian community in Waco, Texas and one of the 75 killed in the conclusion of a siege initiated by the United States government's Bureau of Alcohol, Tobacco and Firearms on the community in 1993. Hani Zaccarelli (Chapter 13) writes from the perspective of someone who was raised within a religious culture that believed the last days were near, whilst Abi Freeman May (Chapter 11) writes from the perspective of someone who joined such a group as a young adult. These personal accounts can add an insight into the lived experience of prophecy and the effects of belief.

But prophecy is not just about apocalyptic, end-times scenarios. It is also about more mundane predictions. It can provide narratives for envisioning a future world, for critiquing contemporary society and for fixing the problems of the current world, as well as methods of personal divination and accessing what might be considered 'divine guidance' for everyday life.

What Is Prophecy?

Prophecy is often thought of in the context of its more extreme millenarian aspects. But prophecy is a much further-ranging spectrum of human behaviour than its extreme form might suggest: a prophecy usually provides information about something beyond normal human ability to predict. While it is often assumed that prophecies are predictive – foreseeing something which has not yet occurred,

---

[2]   Peter Gersten has invited those who are 'seeing' 11:11 symbolism to join him when this portal opens; his main website for propagating these views is http://web.archive.org/web/20111219034021/http://www.1111invitation2012.info/1111Invitation2012/Welcome.html and his older articles are archived http://www.pagenews.info/ (accessed: 21 May 2012).

[3]   Ascended Masters are often believed to be spiritually enlightened beings, existing in other dimensions, who were once incarnated on earth as humans. They are believed to be the spiritual teachers of humanity, helping humans on their own paths to 'ascension'. Suzanne Rough, however, understands the Masters not as discarnate entities but as mental constructs which help people to access the Planetary consciousness.

prophecies can also be used as a retrospective explanation as to why something occurred. Damian Thompson, in his study of the millennial expectations of members of the Kensington Temple in London, makes a useful distinction between 'predictive millennialism', associated with the date-setting, end-of-world type scenarios and the less personally risky 'explanatory millennialism' which uses a millennial narrative to critique the current social situation (2005: 9).

A prophecy can manifest in many different ways: the source of the unique insight might be attributed to God, or a channelled source like an 'Ascended Master' or someone in the 'spirit world', or it may just be an inherent 'gift'. Sometimes a prophecy is experienced by an individual or group; sometimes it takes the form of a voice, other times a physical apparition or dream. At other times, prophecies are understood to have been given by channelled entities during a purposefully induced trance. Sometimes apparatuses, such as a crystal ball or tarot cards, are used to see the future. Others look for insight into the future from a more systematic approach which could range from studying arrangements of numbers or looking for hidden codes in sacred books to studying the movement of the stars or tracing symbolic meaning on the landscape.

Prophecy could be considered to be a fundamental expression of religious experience. This is the approach taken by Margaret Poloma, a contributor to this volume. Based on her research on contemporary Christian prophecy, she argues that: 'Prophecy is a particular type of religious experience that can be regarded as an extension of prayer experiences familiar to most pray-ers. One of the first encounters with the prophetic appears to be God offering guidance and personal direction' (Poloma 2001: 173). This insight into the more mundane level of prophecy is essential in coming to terms with the persistence of prophecy. It is also important to note that the language, rhetoric and imagery of prophecy prevalent in the media also affects those who are not prophets and do not seek a personal religious experience.

Prophets, those who have unique access to prophecy, are often considered to have a special quality that some find authoritative. In many contexts, the social role of prophets can be described by Max Weber's concept of charisma:

> … a certain quality of an individual personality, by virtue of which s/he is 'set apart' from ordinary people and treated as endowed with supernatural, superhuman, or at least specifically exceptional powers or qualities. These as such are not accessible to the ordinary person, but are regarded as divine in origin or as exemplary, and on the basis of them the individual concerned is treated as a leader (Weber [1920] 1968: 241).

But conversely, those who claim unique prophetic insight are often not believed and are subject to ridicule, an archetypal example being the figure of Cassandra in Greek mythology. Contemporary prophets often find a small audience which recognises them as a charismatic leader while being a subject of contempt and derision from the greater population. Contemporary prophets are no exception to the more familiar historical expressions. One example of this from the secular milieu is the figure of Alex Jones, a well-known radio presenter and 'conspiracist' in the United States who is considered prophetic by some of his audience and ridiculed by his antagonists. Jones' form of prophecy is explored in this volume in the chapter by David G. Robertson (Chapter 15).

Prophecy in the New Millennium: Trends and Patterns

Far from being exclusive to the domain of minority and 'new' religious movements, the prophetic finds ambivalent expression in a broad spectrum of contemporary cultures. This volume aims to demonstrate how prophecy can be found in most global religious movements, and even popular scientific thinking. It hopes to make the extreme beliefs of the apocalyptic end more understandable by showing continuity with the more mundane functioning of prophecy within religious movements, both new and old. The extremes of belief can be illuminated with the more mainstream elements of the prophetic; conversely the more mundane expressions of prophecy can be better understood in the context of its more radical expressions.

Fascination with apocalyptic visions is not limited to Christian and post-Christian nations. One recent poll suggested that around 14 per cent of the global population actively believe that the world will end within their lifetime (Ipsos 2012). The nature and global accessibility of modern communication technology and the expansion of literacy and leisure time has meant that more people are exposed to a wider range of prophetic narratives. One of the chapter authors, Christopher Bell (Chapter 9), describes how he met a Tibetan monk in India who reported to have been somewhat influenced by publicity for the *2012* (2009) movie.

Interest in apocalyptic narratives extends beyond those who literally believe that they will form an imminent future for humanity. In some ways prophesying 'end times' and/or the establishment of a new, righteous world order, serves as a theodicy for the dispossessed. A feeling of 'knowing' the future can give a sense of power in a situation where an individual feels very little agency. With the pervasive influence of global economic systems, where income disparity is great, the perception of being 'oppressed' could also include the populations of the developed world. Andrew Fergus Wilson (Chapter 16) argues that it is through these 'end-times' stories, through images of utopias and dystopias, that some are actively trying to create an understanding of the modern world. It is a world where our personal experience remains localised, but the effects of technology and the extent of mass communications are felt on a global scale.

As contemporary 24-hour news channels broadcast tragedies of disasters – tsunamis, earthquakes, volcanic eruptions, terrorist attacks, nuclear accidents and more – in real-time across the globe, an individual can identify with both the personal tragedies of the lives lost, but also with an idea of humanity as having a single, globalised future. The drama and emotion of these events, fuelled by access to minute-by-minute commentary on the extent of damage and known information, forces individuals who have any contact with a news source to confront their emotions about the event. It is these images that often make their way into religious narratives of 'end-times' scenarios as described by Abi Freeman May in Chapter 11.[4] The rise of 24-hour and Internet news has also contributed to the process of 'mainstreaming the fringe', described by Michael Barkun in Chapter 2, in which ideas once the domain of 'insular subcultures', including prophetic beliefs, become accessible to a wider audience.

Prophecy in Established Traditions

Prophecy takes specific forms in specific religious traditions: the language and imagery of Judeo-Christian prophecy – including a belief in the return of Jesus as the Messiah, 'trials and tribulations' of natural disaster and warfare, and the eventual establishment of a paradise on earth – are pervasive within European and North American cultures. However, it is perhaps less well known that prophecy is an important part of the Islamic, Hindu and Buddhist traditions, as well as many indigenous religions. Zoroastrianism, one of the world's oldest extant religions, emphasises cycles of time during which there will be a great destruction and then a rebuilding of the world in a purer form.

The idea of cyclical time is also common in many Indian religions. Although Jains believe that the universe exists without beginning or end, they do believe that time is marked in cycles that are either progressive or regressive in nature. Beliefs in Hindu traditions often encompass an idea of a cyclical system of time, each age of which is characterised by varying degrees of morality and prosperity. The most pervasive interpretation of Hindu belief is that we are currently in an age of *Kali-Yug*, a time of spiritual degeneration often described as lasting 432,000 years in total. Luis González-Reimann (Chapter 8) explores both Indian scripture and some of the more influential modern manifestations of these time cycles so frequently used in prophecy both within the Indian traditions and, more popularly, in contemporary Western 'spiritual' narratives.

Judaism has the concept of a '*moshiach*' who will be anointed as king at the 'end of time'. After the coming of the *moshiach* a utopian age of Judaism is envisaged in which all is peace and prosperity and the Jewish people have returned to Israel, the Temple is rebuilt and the Jewish God is recognised as the only true God (see Simon Dein, Chapter 3). This theme also resonates with the messianic beliefs of Christianity, Islam and Baha'ism.

The Book of Revelation specifically mentions that when Christ returns he will reign for a millennium, 1,000 years. Because millennialism has been a historically significant element of doctrine and continues to influence contemporary prophecy, it is worth noting some of the forms of Christian millennialism.

---

[4]   This point was raised in the general discussion at the Inform seminar on the theme of prophecy held on 12 May 2012.

Pre-millennialism is the belief that we are currently awaiting the 'millennium' reign of Christ. In most forms, a seven-year period of 'Tribulation' is expected before the return of Jesus. This time of tribulation will culminate in the battle of Armageddon. Many pre-millennialists believe that those already 'saved' through their faith will be 'raptured' – or taken directly to heaven before the Tribulation. Pre-millennialism is particularly popular among evangelical Protestants in North America and has entered popular culture with bestselling novels like Tim LaHaye's *Left Behind* series (2003–07). It also informs the theology of groups influenced by the Adventist tradition.

Pre-millennial Dispensationalism focuses on several cycles of differing relationships with God. The first dispensation was in the Garden of Eden, then from Adam to Noah, and so on. This theological grouping believes that Jesus will return before the seven-year Tribulation; after the defeat of the anti-Christ, there will be an additional return of Christ with his saints, which will initiate the millennium of Christ's reign on Earth. This doctrine was popularised by John Nelson Darby (1800–1882) and was then further propagated by the nineteenth-century American theologian Dwight Moody (1837–99) (see Gordon Melton, Chapter 20).

Post-millennialism is associated with the belief that only after everyone in the world has been reached with the Gospel will Jesus return and inaugurate the millennium of peaceful rule. It is believed that the forces of Satan will gradually be defeated by the expansion of the Kingdom of God throughout history up to the second coming of Christ.

Amillennialism or *Nonmillennialism* teaches that the Kingdom of God is present in the contemporary world and that we are currently living in the time of both the millennium and Tribulation which are to be understood symbolically – not in terms of literal periods of years. This is perhaps an underlying belief in the majority of 'mainstream' Christian denominations.

In Islam it is generally believed that there will be a day of judgment at which time individual souls will be sent to heaven or hell. In the oral tradition associated with the life and teachings of Mohammad (the *hadith*), there are specific predictions about the signs that may precede the Day of Judgment. Some Muslims believe that various 'normal' social structures will become inverted as the return of the Mahdi (the redeemer of Islam) becomes imminent, including: slaves giving birth to their masters, and women and men 'rubbing shoulders' in business as well as dressing in the same way. As discussed further by Hugh Beattie in Chapter 7, it is believed that in the 'end times' an anti-Christ-like figure (the *Dajjal*) will rule in the East and Jesus will return and rule with the Mahdi to preside over a time of peace and prosperity.

In some Buddhist teachings there is an understanding that the historical Buddha was not unique; one prophecy predicts that after the Buddha's teachings are 'forgotten' or ignored a new Buddha will reincarnate. This 'future Buddha' is usually called Maitreya or Ajita Bodhisattva (Sponberg and Hardacre [1988] 2011). The myth of Maitreya has been evoked historically to found the creation of numerous sects and inspire rebellions, particularly in China (Shek 2004).

The idea of Maitreya – a future world saviour from the East – was borrowed by the Theosophical Society in the late nineteenth century and has entered into popular culture and sections of the 'New Age' movement. There is also a wider context for prophecy within some forms of Buddhism, particularly in East Asia, and Christopher Bell's contribution in Chapter 9 discusses the example of Tibetan Buddhism.

As for indigenous religions, Norse mythology, revived by some contemporary Pagans and in the operas of Richard Wagner, includes the myth of Ragnarök – usually translated from the ancient Icelandic as the 'final destiny' or 'twilight of the gods'. It is described as a battle between the gods and a race of giants, and it involves many natural disasters including a great flood and finally the destruction of the world. According to the myth, some of the gods will survive and help the two remaining humans to repopulate the world, which will then experience a time of prosperity and peace. Some Native American cultures include prophetic beliefs which have been appropriated by contemporary 'Westerners', who often have a degree of involvement in the 'New Age' milieu (as discussed by Jean-François Mayer in Chapter 19). The Mayan calendar is a case in point and is discussed further below. Hopi prophetic beliefs about the coming destruction of the Fourth World (the world humans currently inhabit) and a transition to the Fifth World also feed into popular contemporary prophecies (see Loftin 2003 and Mumm 2002).

Although it is often assumed that prophecies are intimately related to religion and the supernatural, this is not necessarily the case. The scientific community also makes predictions, and sometimes these may include apocalyptic consequences. In 2008 for example, there were a variety of concerns picked up by the popular press that the Large Hadron Collider experiments at the European Centre for Nuclear Research (CERN) in Switzerland might create a 'black hole' which might cause the universe to implode (Plaga 2008).

Secular apocalyptic scenarios also often focus on the human ability to either self-destruct or avert possible self-destruction. An example is 'Y2K', the worldwide panic in anticipation of the year 2000 and the problems this might cause to computer systems designed in the twentieth century. At least $300 billion was spent to prevent anticipated computer failures which, it was feared, may cause disasters in a variety of systems that rely on computers – from aircraft to banking (*BBC*, 1 January 2000). The essential role of prophecy in technological advancement and secular culture is explored further by Wendy M. Grossman in Chapter 10. These secular predictions, like the religious prophecies, tap into anxiety about humans' limited control of the world and our uncertainty about the full consequences of our activities. Some scientists have argued that the lack of public understanding of scientific results and the process by which scientific theories advance underlies public 'panic' generated by media headlines and Internet activity. This subject was the focus of the 2011 Royal Society Annual

Lecture by Jocelyn Bell Burnell[5] and is covered in this volume by Kristine Larsen in Chapter 17; both scientists emphasise the importance in promoting 'scientific literacy' in popular culture to reduce misinterpretation and unnecessary emotional reactions which could have serious consequences.

Synchronistic Prophecies: 2012 as a Case Study

More recently, the year 2012 has become a focal point for millennial expectations. Interest in 2012 became popular in the 'New Age Movement' around 1987, largely due to the teaching of a Mexican-American spiritual author and artist named José Argüelles (1939–2011) who organised a 'Harmonic Convergence' (mass meditation) in that year. Argüelles drew on the work of both Tony Shearer (1975), who argued that 1987 marked the start of a new world age, and Terence McKenna (1985), who was involved in interpreting the Mayan 'Long Count' calendar to suggest that 2012 marked a transformation. Argüelles claimed that 1987 marked the start of a 25-year period, the end of which (in 2012) would usher in a period of greater enlightenment. Steven Sutcliffe and Kevin Whitesides have argued that Argüelles combined these two dates into a single eschatological narrative stating that the Harmonic Convergence, if enacted properly (that is by 144,000 people), would eliminate Armageddon and instead set humanity on the correct path to the 'New Age', which would begin in 2012 (Sutcliffe and Whitesides 2012).

As has been widely noted in the media, 2012 marks the end of the 'Long Count' calendar used by the Mayans in what is termed the 'Classical Period' of their culture, roughly 250–900 CE. In particular, the date of 21 December 2012 marks the end of the current *b'ak'tun* cycle (a *b'ak'tun* is a period of 144,000 days, roughly equivalent to 394 years). More significantly, it marks the end of the thirteenth *b'ak'tun*, the end of a far larger calendar cycle that began in August 3114 BCE. However, according to scholars of ancient Mayan civilisations, this 'Great Cycle', in which 2012 represents the 'end-date', is part of a calendar system that could extend infinitely both backwards and forwards in time with no fixed beginning or end (Ritter 2012). It is worth noting that contemporary Mayans, to whom the dating system of their ancestors remains largely unknown, attribute little significance to this date. The 'Long Count' calendar was abandoned before the sixteenth-century Spanish invasion and was only rediscovered in more recent times (Sitler 2006).

Thus far, the majority of prophets and the largest amount of publishing activity around the 2012 date appears to have come from the United States of America, with a significant amount of 2012 'prophecy' generated in the New Age circles of the United Kingdom, elsewhere in Europe, and Australasia (Gelfer 2011b, St John 2011). However, the developing world might be a significant consumer of 2012 beliefs. A 'Google Trends' search in November 2011 provided information

───────────

[5] A video of this talk is available on the Royal Society website http://royalsociety.org/events/2011/end-world/ (accessed: 18 June 2012).

that '2012 end of the world' is most frequently searched for in India, followed by the Philippines, United Arab Emirates, Pakistan, South Africa, New Zealand, Singapore, Malaysia, Australia; the USA is ranked number 10. The languages in which this search is most often conducted are Tagalog (used in the Philippines), English, Indonesian, Arabic, Dutch, French and Spanish (Google Trends Search Results, November 2011).[6]

The idea of the Mayan calendar marking the end of the world also seems to have entered public consciousness in China, with a recent poll suggesting that 20 per cent of Chinese believed that 2012 marked the end of the world in the Mayan calendar (Ipsos 2012). Likewise, Harold Camping's 2011 Rapture prophecy was translated and broadcast in Vietnam, where it was taken up by some Christians in the Hmong ethnic group. Camping's prophecy was interpreted to add weight to a belief that the Hmong would inherit some land and contributed to a clash between government forces and believers (Bruner 2011). The Internet, social-network sharing and Google predictive searching shapes the landscapes of prophetic thinking in the global context and points towards one of the ways the prophetic might enter a new phase in the new millennium.

Although much of the information on the Internet and in the mass media about exactly what might happen in 2012 is contradictory, some express a belief in the synchronicity of associations leading to the conclusion that 'something big' must happen in 2012, even if it is not clear exactly what. In particular the 2012 phenomenon has strong cultural influences from both the apocalyptic pre-millennialism of the Judeo-Christian traditions (which require a period of 'tribulation' before Jesus can found paradise on earth) and the more optimistic Hindu prophetic traditions which focus on the coming 'golden age', which have in turn influenced the Theosophical movement and the individuals and groups deriving from it such as Alice Bailey, the I Am movement of Guy and Edna Ballard, and the 'New Age' milieu more generally (see González-Reimann Chapter 8, Gelfer 2011a, Lewis and Melton 1992, Sutcliffe and Whitesides 2012). The way the 2012 date has been adopted by different groups is explored more fully by Andrew Fergus Wilson (Chapter 16), Kristine Larsen (Chapter 17), and Jean-François Mayer (Chapter 19).

---

[6]   Google Trends searches 'all years to date' (from its public launch in August 2004) and claims to provide 'insights into broad search patterns' while warning that 'several approximations are used when computing these results'. The same search conducted in early June 2012 showed the ranking of regions as: 1. India, 2. Philippines, 3. United Arab Emirates, 4. South Africa, 5. New Zealand, 6. Singapore, 7. Malaysia, 8. Australia, 9. Ireland and 10. United Kingdom, and the most frequently used languages for the search as: 1. Tagalog, 2. English, 3. Greek, 4. Indonesian, 5. Arabic, 6. Dutch and 7. Spanish.

Prophecy: Why Does It Persist?

One of the strengths of approaching the topic of prophecy from a variety of perspectives (including academics and members and former members of prophetic groups) is that it challenges some typical definitional assumptions about millennialism, for example, that communities with apocalyptic expectations are necessarily 'voluntary' associations of adults (Landes 2011: 15). As several examples from contemporary new religions show, if a movement persists with its apocalyptic expectations for at least a decade, children will most likely be raised having the expectation of an imminent end to their world. In the case of the Family International (see May, Chapter 11 and Shepherd and Shepherd, Chapter 12) the first generation of children were encouraged to believe that they would have access to superpowers during the end times including the ability to fly, walk through walls and shoot fire from their finger tips (Thompson 2002). The Unification Church prophesised that its 'Blessed Children' would be more perfect and free from sin than the children born outside the movement, and hence able to form the foundation for the Kingdom of Heaven on Earth (Zaccarelli, Chapter 13).

　　Another important theme of the book as a whole is a continuity between more mundane prophecies and inspired messages with the more dramatic narratives of the end of the world. A theoretical chapter by Shepherd and Shepherd (Chapter 12) offers new insights into different models of how prophecy might be organised and 'routinised' as a religious movement matures into several generations. Simon Dein (Chapter 3) challenges the traditional focus on failed prophecy with the model of 'cognitive dissonance', emphasising the more affective, ritual elements in the maintenance of belief for the Lubavitchers, while Gordon Melton's conclusion to the volume (Chapter 20) offers some demographic insights on why prophecy is poised to remain a significant social force for the foreseeable future.

　　There is an important connection between the foretelling of the future and the 'forth-telling' of divinely inspired directives. Both situate the individual as holding a special place in the grand story of the world. The embodied experience of the prophetic invites the possibility of the individual as part of a myth – becoming the hero, the prophet or at least an indispensable tool of divine action. Meaning and purpose to life can be reified and crystallised with the belief that the end is near, the 'end' being imagined as more cataclysmic than the prosaic (and obviously inevitable)[7] death of the individual amplifies the significance of the individual's life story.

　　As in a good book of fiction where 'the sweep of prediction was more compelling than the predicted ...' (Lerner 2011: 20), the actual content of the

---

　　[7]　Although there are a few new religious movements which claim immortals including People Unlimited Inc. and Life Unlimited Research Institute, and others which are working towards this goal including the Raelians, Summum (both of which have an interest in cloning) and various Transhumanist groups (whose interest lies in the potential of various new technologies to overcome mortality).

prediction and whether or not it comes to pass perhaps misses some of the central functions of prophecy. The social significance of prophecy does not necessarily lie in what is predicted, it can be found in the prophecy's effect in the present – as an organisational or motivational force – and how this creates the future. It is our hope that the essays in this volume will help elucidate the social appeal of prophecy by drawing attention to the complex and far-reaching effects that the prophetic continues to have in the twenty-first century.

References

Bartlett, T. 2012. A Year after the Non-Apocalypse: Where Are They Now? *Religion Dispatches* [Online 18 May 2012]. Available at: http://www.religiondispatches. org/archive/atheologies/5983/a_year_after_the_non-apocalypse%3A_where_ are_they_now [accessed: 21 May 2012].

Bay, M. (dir.) 1998. *Armageddon*.

British Broadcasting Corporation (BBC). 2000. Y2K Bug Fails to Bite [Online 1 January 2000]. Available at: http://news.bbc.co.uk/1/hi/sci/tech/585013.stm [accessed: 3 January 2009].

Bruner, J. 2011. The Other, Forgotten Apocalypse of 2011. *Religion Dispatches* [Online 20 October 2011]. Available at: http://www.religiondispatches.org/ archive/atheologies/5035/the_other%2C_forgotten_apocalypse_of_2011 [accessed: 21 May 2012].

Daily Mail. 2012a. Girl, 16, Kills Herself after Researching Doomsday Disasters and Becoming Convinced the World Was about to End [Online 18 May 2012]. Available at: http://m.dailymail.co.uk/mobile/news/article. html?articleID=2146179 [accessed: 18 May 2012].

——. 2012b. New TV Series to Air with Survivalist Families Competing to Win a Fortified Bunker … to Protect Them at the End of the World [Online 5 June 2012]. Available at: http://www.dailymail.co.uk/news/article-2155070/Last-Family-Earth-New-TV-series-survivalist-families-compete-fortified-bunker. html [accessed: 6 June 2012].

Emmerich, R. (dir.) 2004. *The Day after Tomorrow*.

——. (dir.) 2009. *2012*.

Gelfer, J. (ed.) 2011a. *2012: Decoding the Countercultural Apocalypse*. Sheffield: Equinox.

——. 2011b. In a Prophetic Voice: Australasia 2012, in *2012: Decoding the Countercultural Apocalypse*, edited by J. Gelfer. Sheffield: Equinox, 144–62.

Genzlinger, N. 2012. Doomsday Has Its Day in the Sun. *The New York Times*, Television [Online 11 March 2012]. Available at: http://www.nytimes. com/2012/03/12/arts/television/doomsday-preppers-and-doomsday-bunkers-tv-reality-shows.html?_r=1 [accessed: 21 May 2012].

Ipsos. 2012. One in Seven (14%) Global Citizens Believe End of the World Is Coming in Their Lifetime / One in Ten Believe Mayan Prophecy Is True (10%), Fear World Will End in 2012 (8%). Press Release, 1 May 2012. Available at: http://www.ipsos-na.com/news-polls/pressrelease.aspx?id=5610 [accessed: 20 May 2012].

Landes, R. 2011. *Heaven on Earth: The Varieties of Millennial Experience.* Oxford: Oxford University Press.

Lawrence, F. (dir.) 2007. *I Am Legend.*

Lerner, B. 2011. *Leaving the Atocha Station.* Minneapolis, MN: Coffee House Press.

Lewis, J.R. and Melton, J.G. 1992. *Perspectives on the New Age.* New York: SUNY Press.

Loftin, J.D. 2003. *Religion and Hopi Life.* Bloomington, IN: University of Indiana Press.

Mumm, S. 2002. Aspirational Indians: North American Indigenous Religions and the New Age, in *Belief Beyond Boundaries: Wicca, Celtic Spirituality and the New Age*, edited by Joanne Pearson. London: Ashgate/Open University Press, 103–31.

Plaga, R. 2008. On the Potential Catastrophic Risk from Metastable Quantum-Black Holes Produced at Particle Colliders [Online 11 November 2008]. Available at: http://arxiv.org/abs/0808.1415v2 [accessed: 3 January 2009].

Poloma, M. 2001. The Millenarianism of the Pentecostal Movement, in *Christian Millenarianism: From the Early Church to Waco*, edited by S. Hunt. Bloomington, IN: Indiana University Press, 166–84.

Ritter, M. 2012. New Mayan Records Ruin the 2012 End-of-the-World Theory. *Hamilton Spectator* [Online 10 May 2012]. Available at: http://www.thespec.com/news/article/721943--new-mayan-records-ruin-the-2012-end-of-the-world-theory [accessed: 6 June 2012].

Shek, R. 2004. The Heterodoxy of Buddhism, Maitreyanism, and the Early White Lotus, in *Heterodoxy in Late Imperial China*, edited by K.-C. Liu and R. Shek. Honolulu, HI: University of Hawaii Press, 73–108.

Sitler, R.K. 2006. The 2012 Phenomenon: New Age Appropriation of an Ancient Mayan Calendar. *Nova Religio*, 9(3), 24–38.

Sponberg, A. and Hardacre, H. (eds) [1988] 2011. *Maitreya, the Future Buddha.* Cambridge: Cambridge University Press.

St John, G. 2011. The 2012 Movement, Visionary Arts and Psytrance Culture, in *2012: Decoding the Countercultural Apocalypse*, edited by J. Gelfer. Sheffield: Equinox, 123–43.

Strozier, C. 2002. *Apocalypse: On the Psychology of Fundamentalism in America.* Eugene, OR: Wipf & Stock Pub.

Sutcliffe, S. and Whitesides, K. 2012. New Ages 'Hard' and 'Soft': An Epidemiological Approach to the Transmission of a Modern Millenialist Trope. Paper presented at the Inform Seminar, Prophecy in the New Millennium. London. 12 May 2012.

Thompson, D. 2002. They Told Us We Might Have to Die. *The Telegraph* [Online 28 February 2002]. Available at: http://www.exfamily.org/cgi-bin/gf.pl?fmt= dyn&t=articles&m=1&s=&r=art/exmem/andrewmcmillion.shtml   [accessed: 21 May 2012].

——. 2005. *Waiting for the Antichrist: Charisma and Apocalypse in a Pentecostal Church*. Oxford: Oxford University Press.

Weber, M. [1920] 1968. *Economy and Society: An Outline of Interpretive Sociology*, Vol. 1, edited by G. Roth and C. Wittich. New York: Bedminster Press.

Wessinger, C. 2000. *How the Millennium Comes Violently: From Jonestown to Heaven's Gate*. New York and London: Seven Bridges Press.

—— (ed.) 2011. *The Oxford Handbook of Millennialism*. Oxford: Oxford University Press.

PART I
Perspectives on Prophecy

This section of the book is a collection of papers written by academics from different disciplines; political science, anthropology and history, as well as a paper written by a practising Methodist minister. The papers bring different disciplinary perspectives to the issue of the persistence of prophecy in the contemporary world.

In Chapter 2, Michael Barkun considers why there has been a recent return of prophecies which involve date-setting. He provides three examples of such prophecies which have received relatively widespread media attention: the prediction of the Rapture on 21 May 2011 and the end of the world on 21 October 2011 by the American Evangelist Harold Camping; the 'Earth Changes' predictions of Gordon Michael Scallion and others which have been taken up by some within 'New Age' circles; and the apocalyptic predictions around the date 21 December 2012 which come largely from a 'New Age' interpretation of the Mayan calendar, particularly the work of José Argüelles. Barkun suggests that an increased pessimism in America fuelled by the economic crisis and difficult international relations, alongside the transformations in the contemporary communications milieu, contribute to the popularity of these prophecies. He describes a process of 'mainstreaming the fringe' in which 'stigmatised knowledge', knowledge once contained within sub-cultures, has reached a mass audience through the Internet, rolling news channels and popular cultural forms including films, novels and television programmes. He argues that the prophetic voices of this 'stigmatised knowledge' might speak to both rising anxiety and the increasing need for new explanatory narratives.

Simon Dein, in Chapter 3, takes up the challenge of providing an overview of the literature on 'failed prophecy' within the social sciences. Following Festinger et al.'s seminal text, *When Prophecy Fails* (1956), much social scientific writing about prophecy has focused on the concept of 'cognitive dissonance', i.e. the discomfort caused by holding competing cognitions simultaneously, and on what happens to the religious group and the prophetic belief when the prophecy 'fails'. Dein traces the development and critique of Festinger's theory by other authors including Zygmunt (1972), Melton (1985), Dawson (1999), Stone (2000), O'Leary (2000) and Thompson (2005) amongst others. He then provides his own critique of Festinger illustrated with a case study of the Lubavitch, a Jewish religious group which he has studied for over 20 years. Dein argues that the social science literature on prophecy over-emphasises the cognitive construction of religious life-worlds whilst neglecting the embodied and experiential material practices which simultaneously construct reality. He describes the ways in which the Lubavitcher Rebbe, Menachem Schneerson (who died in 1994) is maintained as the living *Moshiach*, the Jewish Messiah, by some of his followers, through specific ritual practices in which he is rendered present.

In Chapter 4, historian Warren Johnston, provides a counter-point to Michael Barkun's contemporary focus. He reminds us that there have been other periods in history in which there have been a plethora of date-specific prophecies. To make this point, Johnston uses a case study of seventeenth-century England to argue that understanding the social and political context is fundamental to an understanding of the formation of religious prophecies, their popularity and appeal. This insight is also applicable to an understanding of the appeal of contemporary prophecies, as Barkun also suggests.

Thus Johnston focuses not on the period leading up to 1660 (the restoration of the Monarchy and the Anglican Church following the Civil War of 1642–48), which is usually taken as the high point and then the end of millennial expectation in seventeenth-century England, but rather on the years 1660–1700, in which prophecies were reinterpreted to suit the new political and religious conditions. Johnston argues that the most vocal exponents of prophecy in these years were those who opposed the restored monarchy and Anglican Church. He goes on to provide a case study of both the 'radical' and the nonviolent religious nonconformists in this period. In line with Barkun, and other authors in this volume, such as David G. Robertson in Part III, Johnston suggests that prophecy might provide a particular function within the life-worlds of those who feel socially marginalised; it offers hope and assurance that their situation will change for the better in the near future.

Andrew Maguire is a Methodist minister and member of Inform's Management Committee, and has a particular interest in early Christian texts. In Chapter 5, Maguire combines these interests by looking first at early Christian writings and then at some of the debates and controversies around prophecy in contemporary Christianity. Within early Christianity, prophets were not only considered 'fore-tellers' (predictors of the future) but also 'forth-tellers' (as uttering a word from God, as one of the gifts of the Holy Spirit) (Poloma and Lee, in Chapter 6, discuss this distinction in contemporary Pentecostal Christianity). Fore-telling or predictive prophecy, Maguire argues, initially took the form of interpreting the Hebrew Scriptures to predict the coming of Christ and discerning predictions of the imminent end-times in Scripture, in the utterances of Jesus and in the messages of prophets found in the Christian community after the death of Jesus. Maguire also offers examples of prophetic texts which did not make it into Canonical Scripture and gives a short case study of the second-century Montanists, to illustrate how the practice of prophecy was marginalised in early Christianity. He concludes his chapter by noting that certain prophetic beliefs, such as those associated with Christian Zionism, remain a challenge to contemporary Church Councils.

Chapter 2

Messages from Beyond:
Prophecy in the Contemporary World

Michael Barkun

While only a few people explicitly present themselves as prophets, many more engage in prophetic behaviour. That is, they purport to transmit a message of transcendent importance that is not available to the population at large. Utterances perceived as prophetic have sometimes been institutionalised in religions with relatively deep roots. Thus we find it in Pentecostalism, where it is identified with gifts of the Spirit, and in the Afro-Cuban religion, Santeria, where it occurs during celebrants' trance states. But it may also be found outside ritualised contexts, as well as in new and alternative religions.

For present purposes, we can discern four varieties of potentially prophetic behaviour. The most obvious and conventional conception is the individual who claims that a deity has communicated a message directly and that he or she is merely the amanuensis or spokesperson for the deity. The contents of the message are thus divine, and the prophet is merely the vehicle for its transmission. Second is the person who discovers divine messages concealed or encoded in events or attributes of society. This search for 'signs of the times' frequently involves the correlation of what occurs in the outer world with scriptural passages in order to supply the correct meaning for events. Those involved in such activities, particularly in Christianity, often claim that their abilities are not unique and that anyone could do the same thing, although at the same time they may claim special authority for their own interpretation. The purpose of such efforts is often to establish the timing of such end-time events as the Rapture and Second Coming. Third, there are those who claim knowledge from a transcendent source, but not necessarily directly from God. This category includes the many occult and New Age prophets who use channelling and dream techniques to access Ascended Masters and other spiritual entities associated with Theosophy and its offshoots. As in the first form of prophecy, the result is usually a specific message. Finally, it would be a mistake to exclude some secular analysts of society who, although they do not claim transcendent knowledge, predict apocalyptic futures. Despite their secular empiricism, these prophets of environmental disasters, nuclear war and other calamities deserve a place in the prophetic fold for two reasons: first, they often have a powerful influence on public opinion; second, even religionists may see them as reinforcing and/or 'proving' more conventionally religious apocalyptic prophecies even though they employ an entirely different epistemology.

Thus warnings of catastrophic climate change can be at once secular, apocalyptic and prophetic.

A common error in discussions of prophecy is the assumption that prophecies always involve date-setting. There have, of course, been dramatic cases of this kind, such as William Miller's 1843 prediction of the Second Coming, later revised to 1844, prophetic failures that believers referred to as the 'Great Disappointment' (Numbers and Butler 1987). Generally, however, prophet figures have skirted predictions that centre on specific dates, perhaps out of an abundance of caution and a desire to avoid the kind of embarrassing disconfirmation that the Millerites suffered. Yet the equation of prophecy and date-setting continues. Many people assumed, for example, that the millennial year 2000 would possess a prophetic significance. In the late 1990s, the Federal Bureau of Investigation produced a report about the year 2000, 'Project Megiddo', that suggested religionists might greet the millennial year with violent outbursts (Barkun 2002). The Canadian Security Intelligence Service produced a similar document. Yet, of course, we passed into the 2000s with scarcely a ripple. Remarkably few religionists invested the year 2000 with the significance that observers expected. However uncommon as date-setting has been, as we shall see, it has made a dramatic recent appearance among the prophetically inclined.

By way of demonstrating both the profile of contemporary prophecy and its propensity for date-setting, let us look at three recent examples: the predictions of the Rapture by Harold Camping, beginning in May 2011; the so-called 'Earth changes' predictions that have achieved currency in New Age circles; and, finally, the rising tempo of speculation about millenarian/apocalyptic developments that are supposed to take place in 2012. They have been chosen precisely because they constitute non-institutionalised examples, cases that would not occur, for example, in the routine course of worship. By virtue of their abrupt emergence and often dramatic content, they cast an especially strong light on the phenomenon of contemporary prophecy.

Harold Camping

The radio preacher Harold Camping was no stranger to prophecy. He had previously predicted the Rapture for 7 September 1994, a prediction that gained relatively little attention. His 2011 prophecy, however, was another matter. Although Camping's Family Stations, Inc. claim to own 140 radio stations, and his small band of followers worked strenuously to spread his message, these resources could scarcely have made his teachings a national news story.[1] Rather, his belief that the events of divine judgment would commence on 21 May 2011 came to general public notice because a wide array of mainstream media decided

---

[1]   A Brief Biography of Harold Camping. http://www.familyradio.com/english/connect/bio/haroldcamping_bio.html (accessed: 31 January 2012).

it was newsworthy. In fact, in a society of great religious diversity, it may be safely said that at any given time some group is likely to be making an eschatological prediction of some kind, yet it was Camping's that came to be widely publicised.

Camping's brief celebrity may be attributed to several factors. In the first place, he used theological categories, such as the Rapture, that were at least somewhat familiar to many Americans, although Camping does not subscribe to the dispensational premillennialism common among many Protestant evangelicals. The dispensationalist scheme involves an elaborate end-time chronology that requires the Jewish re-settlement of biblical Palestine before the saved can be Raptured and the battle of Armageddon can take place. In addition, Camping made a splendid interview subject, since he presented his position with a certainty and an absence of doubt that might evoke a variety of reactions ranging from ridicule to envy. Thus, in responding to an interviewer from *New York Magazine*, Camping stated:

> God has given *sooo* [sic] much information in the Bible about this, and so many proofs, and so many signs, that we know it is *absolutely* going to happen without any question at all …. I would be absolutely in rebellion against God if I thought anything other than *it is absolutely going to happen without any question.*'[2]

From this, one may draw two inferences beyond those that might speak to Camping's temperament: first, he is among those prophets who derive a message from the close examination of a text, and, second, by implication anyone else who examines the text as closely as he would come to the same conclusion. In both, he closely resembles his nineteenth-century counterpart, William Miller.

When the predicted events failed to occur, Camping responded in the same manner as predecessors. He went into brief seclusion and then first announced a new date of October 21st, much as William Miller had done; and then proclaimed that the end-time events had in fact occurred, but in an invisible manner, an explanation that had also been used by post-Millerite Second Adventists in the nineteenth century. In an essay, 'What Happened on May 21?', Camping asserted that 'earthquake' and 'rapture' had not been properly understood. They were not physical acts, but spiritual phenomena connected with God's judgment of the world. He concluded that what had happened was that anyone not saved by 21 May could not be saved, but that the physical manifestations of God's judgment would eventually be seen five months later.[3] Thus the calculations might have been wrong, but on the other hand, they were probably correct but only the faithful had eyes to see. Camping suffered a stroke in June. However, he recovered sufficiently

---

[2]   A Conversation With Harold Camping, Prophesier of Judgment Day, *New York Magazine*. Emphasis in original. http://nymag.com/daily/intel/2011/05/a_conversation_with_harold_cam.html (accessed: 31 January 2012).

[3]   What Happened On May 21? http://www.familyradio.com/x/whathappened.html (accessed: 31 January 2012).

to make yet another prediction of the end, the conclusion of the five month period, 21 October 2011. No doubt chastened by earlier failures, his initial certainty was replaced by a new conditional 'probably'.[4] In any case, by this time the media had gone on to new fancies, and neither the prediction nor its disconfirmation was reported by most media. He did get a glimmer of attention when, in March 2012, he announced not only that his 21 May prediction had been in error but that 'We must also openly acknowledge that we have no new evidence pointing to another date for the end of the world … Family Radio has no interest in even considering another date.'[5]

As strange as Harold Camping's predictions may have seemed to many people, he was working within a well-established religious tradition. Others, such as Miller, had announced similar prophecies in earlier periods and, like Camping, had relied upon close analyses of Biblical texts. Even though Camping was shunned by all of the major denominations, his reliance upon scripture placed him in a thought world to which even non-believers could relate. That, however, was not the case with the far more exotic prophecies known as 'Earth changes'.

Earth Changes

Prophecies about imminent, cataclysmic geological changes can be traced back to the Kentucky psychic, Edgar Cayce (1877–1945). Between the 1920s and his death, Cayce gave thousands of 'readings' while in a trance state, and although many concerned healing and esoteric themes, many others dealt with predictions of calamitous changes in the very fabric of the planet, foretelling momentous alterations in the planet's geography. This style of prediction did not, however, become widespread until the 1960s and 1970s, when similar claims began to be made by others in New Age circles. They sometimes come to their prophets in dreams, as has been the case with Gordon Michael Scallion, a self-proclaimed prophet who began to produce Earth changes predictions in 1979 and now disseminates them through his Matrix Institute. But others are channellers, the terrestrial avenues through which spiritual beings communicate messages to humanity in a manner not unlike mediumship.

Although styles of communication may differ, the messages are remarkably similar. Earth changes predictions fall into two major categories. The most common are quite specific predictions of mountain ranges rising where none existed before and inundations flooding previously dry areas either to increase the size of existing bodies of water or to create new lakes or bays. One of the most

4   Harold Camping: World 'Probably' to End Oct. 21, 2011. http://www.washingtonpost.com/blogs/under-god/post/harold-camping-world-probably-to-end (accessed: 31 January 2012).

5   An Important Letter from Mr. Camping – March 2012. http://www.familyradio.com (accessed: 31 January 2012).

famous of such predictions, the flooding of Chicago, was the subject of the social science classic, *When Prophecy Fails* (Festinger et al. 1964), but despite that prophetic failure, which took place in 1954, more sweeping claims continued to be made. The prophetess involved in the Chicago case, Dorothy Martin, claimed to have received messages from extra-terrestrials who would rescue her and her followers before the disaster. Despite the humiliating disconfirmation of her predictions, which was widely reported in local newspapers, Martin went on to a long career as a channeller under the name 'Sister Thedra' (Barkun 2003) although she avoided similar predictions in this new persona.

Subsequent Earth changes prophets tended to be somewhat more circumspect about dates but far more specific about consequences. Their prophecies have often come complete with maps of what the new Earth will look like, specifying where new mountain ranges will rise, where new lakes and bays will flood large areas, and how shorelines will be modified. The latter are often radical, with large areas destined to be submerged.

The second type of Earth changes prediction involves so-called 'pole shift', in which the locations of the north and south poles will suddenly change, altering the Earth's rotation by changing the position of its axis. The more radical the shift, the greater the catastrophes that are said to ensue as a result. A widely advertised pole shift prediction was made for 5 May 2000, in the book, *5/5/2000* (Noone 1986), part of the apocalyptic literature generated by the turn of the millennium. Gordon Michael Scallion is best known for his 'Future Map of North America'.[6] Great inundations will turn California into a collection of islands and flood much of the Great Basin. Phoenix and parts of Nebraska will now be on the new West Coast, while a flooded Mississippi Valley will virtually split the rest of the country. Scallion is banking on a pole shift and climate change to do the job, but he is careful to hedge his predictions: 'I … believe that no event or prediction is final. Predictions are given as probabilities. Even at this time, consciousness can alter an event, modify changes in a particular area or at the very least, help us to prepare for what is to come.'[7]

The Year 2012

The prophecies of the moment are, of course, those that centre on the year 2012, and even more specifically on 21 December 2012. The 2012 literature, whatever its content, ultimately derives from the Mayan calendar studies of the late José Argüelles (1939–2011). Argüelles first came to widespread public notice in the summer of 1987 when he proclaimed the quasi-millenarian 'harmonic

---

[6]   Future Map of North America Virtual Tour. http://www.earthchanges.com (accessed: 31 January 2012).

[7]   Gordon Michael Scallion's Future Maps. http://www.earthchanges.com/future-maps/gmss-future-maps (accessed: 31 January 2012).

convergence'. He promised that 'if 144,000 persons could respond to the call of meditating at dawn, on 16th and 17th August 1987, the world would be renewed and humanity would enter a "new age".'[8]

In a 2006 statement of his ideas, Argüelles again emphasised the importance of the number 144,000 and specifically noted that although it appeared in his numerical calculations of Mayan calendar cycles, it was the same number as those that were sealed in the Book of Revelation. In a like manner, he noted that he found a correspondence between the number 1,260 in the Mayan calendar and the same number in Revelation.[9] Somewhat coyly, Argüelles implied that the parallelisms could not be accidental.

However, by the time his final work, *Manifesto for the Noosphere*, appeared in 2011, published posthumously, all references to the Book of Revelation had disappeared. The numbers were still there – 144,000 and 1,260 – but Argüelles made no attempt to connect them with their Christian counterparts. Whatever his motives for abandoning the quest for parallels, the change came too late. By the time *Manifesto for the Noosphere* appeared, it was lost in a vast 2012 literature written by others, much of which had only the most tenuous connection to Argüelles's original conception. His final statement of the significance 21 December 2012 might have was surprisingly free of apocalyptic expectations. Rather, he saw it as a moment of potential spiritual liberation. However, once Argüelles had placed the date of 21 December 2012 in public view and attached a millenarian significance to it, anyone was free to hang any agenda on it, and that is precisely what occurred. It has become the focus of sensational motion pictures, tracts and websites, most of which have nothing to do with Argüelles's ideas.

The Fad for Date-setting

In all three of the contemporary examples we have looked at – Harold Camping, Earth changes and 2012 – some prophetic message is often linked to dates. Yet in general those with prophetic messages, especially end-time messages, avoid specifying dates, lest they fall into the embarrassing trap of prophetic disconfirmation. So we need to ask, why now? Why the concentration on dates, when the messages could so easily have been cast in vaguer, more general terms? There is also a subsidiary issue: why did these three cases, all clustering in the very recent past, reach such high levels of public visibility? Camping's predictions were a major news story. The Earth changes ideas spread very widely in the large New Age community. And, of course, '2012' has become a virtual element of

[8]   José Argüelles, 1939–2011. Issued Global Call to New Agers. http://articles.latimes.com/print/2011/apr/10/local/la-me-jose-arguelles-20110410 (accessed: 31 January 2012).

[9]   The Meaning of the 2012 Prophecy: A Galactic Meditation Program for the Whole Planet Synthesis – the Noosphere. http://www.lawoftime.org/archives/mastery.html (accessed: 31 January 2012).

popular culture, still in play not only among devotees of the New Age and the esoteric but in the mass media.

Several factors appear to be involved in this set of concerns. First, this is a period characterised by what might be termed 'mainstreaming the fringe'. At one time, a clear distinction could be made between ideas regarded as deviant and those that received the approbation of significant social institutions – government, religion and the academy, among others. Deviant ideas, including the prophetic, remained within insular subcultures. They rarely had access to avenues of communication that might bring them to the attention of mass audiences. It was as though a boundary lay between ideas considered acceptable and those deemed false, dangerous, heretical or outmoded. These I have elsewhere termed 'stigmatised knowledge' (Barkun 2003).

'Mainstreaming the fringe' is the process by which this stigmatised knowledge – the ideas once confined to insular sub-cultures – has reached mass audiences traditionally denied to it. Put another way, the boundary that once clearly distinguished the fringe from the mainstream and prevented fringe ideas from becoming generally known is no longer a firm barrier. What used to be a wall is now a kind of permeable membrane. That permeability is a function of the radical changes that have occurred in the system of communications.

Beginning in the mid-1990s, the Internet has, as it were, 'levelled the playing field' as far as communications is concerned for those espousing fringe ideas. With minimal capital investment and no need to worry about gatekeepers, believers in stigmatised knowledge can now promote their ideas in the same way as those in the mainstream. By the 2000s, the Internet began to overtake other media as a source of information, and ideas first broached on websites often make the jump to 24/7 cable news channels, where they are legitimised and spread even more broadly. These channels, hungry for material to feed their mass audiences and drawn to sensational material in their competitive struggle for ratings and advertising dollars, have often found fringe material irresistible. At the same time, similar motifs penetrated popular culture. The *X-Files* television programmes and films, and Dan Brown's novels and the motion pictures made from them, are examples of the kind of mass entertainment products that have drawn on stigmatised knowledge themes that were sometimes of the most esoteric kind.

In this transformed communications milieu, it is hardly surprising that date-driven prophecies would have been widely disseminated. In an earlier period, only print media or late night radio might have been available as outlets, but now the Internet has provided a unique platform. Not only is the timing propitious in terms of the available means of dissemination, but the timing is right because of a large cultural factor.

Date-Driven Prophecies and the New Declineists

Much of this prophetic material – particularly the accelerating interest in a 2012 apocalypse – coincides with a rising concern about the fate of America in the world. Many Americans see the future in increasingly pessimistic terms. The United States, once the sole superpower after the collapse of the Soviet Union, now seems to be losing both power and prestige. Long, unpopular and relatively indecisive wars in Iraq and Afghanistan, the continuation of the economic crisis that began in 2007–2008, and the rise of China to great power status, all seem to signal an end to American pre-eminence. At the same time, Europe is experiencing its own form of pessimism as the integrity of the euro has come into question and with it the future of the European Union. Such fears have arisen before, notably in the 1970s, when they were triggered by the oil crisis and the rise of Japan. Then, too, they were accompanied by a spate of apocalyptic warnings by both religious and secular figures. It was in that fevered atmosphere that Hal Lindsey's apocalyptic tract, *The Late Great Planet Earth* (1970), became a best-seller.

However, to many the present situation seems both more dire and more perplexing. The collapse of the Soviet Union and the end of the Cold War in the early 1990s ended a whole set of widely shared narratives about good and evil predicated on a bifurcated world. During the intervening 20 years, no single explanatory narrative about the distribution of good and evil has taken the place of those that reigned during the Cold War. Hence when troubling events began to multiply, beginning with the 9/11 attacks and continuing through the Iraq and Afghanistan wars, the economic crisis and the rise of China, there has been both an increase in anxiety and an explanatory vacuum. Typical of the sense of malaise, an influential columnist in the *Financial Times* wrote in the autumn of 2011 that 'America must manage its decline' (Rachman 2011: 11). Prophetic voices speak to both rising anxiety and the increasing need for new explanatory narratives.

In an earlier period many of these voices would doubtless have been exiled to the fringe, heard only by tiny coteries of believers. But, as we have seen, massive changes in the communications environment have made them accessible to vast new audiences, made receptive to their message by the flow of world events. Harold Camping made one end-time prediction just after the collapse of the Soviet Union and the end of the Cold War, and he made his last prediction in 2011, in time to coincide with the fears of American decline. The Earth changes literature reached a peak as the millennial year 2000 approached and received indirect reinforcement from the pervasive concerns about climate change. Immediately after, the United States and to some extent the larger Western world were consumed by the anxieties and fears associated with the 11 September 2001 attacks. As to the year 2012, expectations concerning events that might occur towards its end began to increase as early as 2009, along with the rise of China and the seemingly endless economic crisis.

Thus there seems no reason to think that the appetite for prophecy will decline any time soon, and given the desire for messages that bear the stamp of transcendent authority, individuals will almost certainly continue to bring them. If the Earth changes and 2012 cases are any indication, the future is likely to hold increasing prophecies that exist outside historic religious traditions. In that sense, Harold Camping's predictions, redolent of Millerite date-setting, seems a charming anachronism rather than an indication of the resilience of old-time religion.

References

Amira, D. 2011. A Conversation with Harold Camping, Prophesier of Judgment Day. *New York Magazine* [Online 11 May 2011]. Available at: http://nymag. com/daily/intel/2011/05/a_conversation_with_harold_cam.html [accessed: 31 August 2011].

Arguelles, J. 2006. *The Meaning of the 2012 Prophecy: A Galactic Meditation Program for Whole Planet Synthesis – the Noosphere*. [Online 1 November 2006]. Available at: http://www.lawoftime.org/archives/mastery.html [accessed: 28 November 2006].

——. 2011. *Manifesto for the Noosphere: The Next Stage in the Evolution of Human Consciousness*. Berkeley, CA: Evolver Editions.

Barkun, M. 2002. Project Megiddo, the FBI and the Academic Community, in *Millennial Violence: Past, Present and Future*, edited by J. Kaplan. London: Frank Cass, 97–108.

——. 2003. *A Culture of Conspiracy: Apocalyptic Visions in Contemporary America*. Berkeley, CA: University of California Press.

Camping, H. [no date]. A Brief Biography of Harold Camping. Available at: http://www.familyradio.com/english/connect/bio/haroldcamping_bio.html [accessed: 31 August 2011].

——. 2011. What Happened on May 21? Available at: http://familyradio.com/x/ whathappened.html [accessed: 19 October 2011].

——. 2012. An Important Letter from Mr. Camping – March 2012. Available at: http://www.familyradio.com [accessed: 12 March 2012].

Festinger, L. et al. 1964. *When Prophecy Fails: A Social and Psychological Study of a Modern Group That Predicted the Destruction of the World*. New York: Harper.

Lindsay, H. with Carlson, C. 1970. *The Late Great Planet Earth*. Grand Rapids, MI: Zondervan.

Little, J. 2011. Harold Camping: World 'Probably' to End Oct. 21, 2001. *Washington Post* [Online 18 October 2011]. Available at: http://www. washingtonpost.com/blogs/under-god/post/harold-camping-world-probably-to-end-oct-21-2011/2011/10/05/gIQAmxMMuL_blog.html [accessed: 19 October 2011].

Noone, R.W. 1986. *5/5/2000. Ice: The Ultimate Disaster*. New York: Harmony.

Numbers, R.L. and Butler, J.M. (eds.) 1987. *The Disappointed: Millerism and Millenarianism in the Nineteenth Century*. Bloomington, IN: Indiana University Press.

Rachman, G. 2011. America Must Manage Its Decline. *Financial Times* [Online 17 October 2011]. Available at: http://www.ft.com/cms/s/0/0c73f10e-f8aa-11e0-ad8f-00144feab49a.html#axzz1pfopnnpk [accessed: 18 October 2011].

Scallion, G.M. [no date]. *Gordon Michael Scallion's Future Maps*. Available at: http://www.earthchanges.com/future-maps/gmss-future-maps [accessed: 4 November 2011].

———. 2011. Future Map of North America Virtual Tour [Online 23 March 2011]. Available at: http://www.earthchanges.com [accessed: 4 November 2011].

Woo, E. 2011. Obituaries: Jose Arguelles, 1939–2011. Issued Global Call to New Agers. *Los Angeles Times* [Online 10 April 2011]. Available at: http://articles.latimes.com/print/2011/apr/10/local/la-me-jose-arguelles-20110410 [accessed: 6 September 2011].

Chapter 3
Prophecy:
Social Scientific Perspectives and Lubavitch

Simon Dein

Introduction

In June 1994 the Lubavitcher Rebbe, Menachem Schneerson, died. For many years his faithful followers had maintained that he was *Moshiach*, the Jewish Messiah who would usher in the Redemption. The Lubavitch had invested much time and money publicising this idea through newspapers, billboards and radio broadcasts. Not only were they bereft of their spiritual leader but more importantly his 'unexpected' death at the age of 92 created a crisis of belief among Lubavitchers: how could the promised Jewish Messiah die? Unlike Christian messianism, it is believed that the Jewish Messiah will usher in the Redemption during his lifetime. Menachem Schneerson's death should therefore invalidate his messianic status. And in fact, nearly 17 years after his death the majority of Lubavitchers no longer assert that he is *Moshiach*. However, a small but significant group – the Messianists – maintain that he is *Moshiach*. For them his death was purely illusory and they proclaim 'Just open your eyes and you can see him.'

With a focus on the example of the Lubavitch, this chapter will outline the major social-scientific theories of prophecy, which have historically focused on the idea of cognitive dissonance. Moving beyond the cognitive perspective I will then develop the role of ritual and experiential factors in the maintenance of belief and exemplify my argument by describing a number of rituals that Lubavitchers have deployed to keep the dead Rebbe 'alive'. The conclusion of the essay will highlight the experiential and ritual role prophecy has within the Lubavitch and underline more recent thinking which emphasises the wider role prophecy plays in the group dynamics and coherence of religions.

Social-Scientific Thinking on Prophecy: Festinger and Beyond

Almost all the work in the social sciences has framed the 'problem' of prophecy around the concept of 'cognitive dissonance' – a discomfort caused by holding conflicting cognitions (including ideas, beliefs, values, emotional reactions) simultaneously. From the perspective of the social scientist, it appears that religious believers should have a difficult time reconciling a prophecy about, say the end of the world (or another specific empirical event) with the fact that empirical reality – as observed by those outside the group – appears not to support what was prophesised. So according to this understanding, in the example of the Lubavitchers, with the belief that the *Moshiach* is immortal, the physical death of Rebbe Menachem Schneerson should cause 'cognitive dissonance'.

The classic theory for understanding dissonance resolution was formulated by Leon Festinger, Henry Riecken and Stanley Schachter (1956) whose empirical study of 'a flying saucer cult', was published in *When Prophecy Fails*. For members of this group called the Seekers, unequivocal disconfirmation of a prophesised event, in this instance, the prediction of a destructive flood and the subsequent rescue of believers by flying saucers, culminated in what Festinger and colleagues asserted was 'a crisis of belief'. As these authors assert, while the best course of action for believers would have been to discard these 'incorrect' beliefs and continue with their former lives, 'frequently the behavioural commitment to the belief is so strong that almost any other course of action is preferable [to discarding the "erroneous" beliefs]', and they go on to argue that 'it may even be less painful to tolerate the dissonance than to discard the belief and admit that one had been wrong' (1956: 27). Festinger's seminal contribution was to underscore the fact that failure of prophecy does not always cause a group to break up nor does it necessarily diminish a members' faith.

To reduce psychological dissonance, Festinger et al. theorised two main responses to reducing feelings of dissonance – 1) by expanding on the beliefs most resistant to change and 2) by increasing proselytisation and spreading the message: 'If more and more people can be persuaded that the system of belief is correct, then clearly it must, after all, be correct' (1956: 28). In fact Festinger et al. argued that in response to disconfirming evidence, believers may actually intensify rather than abandon their beliefs. Festinger et al. argued for five criteria that allowed intensification of belief to occur: there must be firm conviction; there must be public commitment to this conviction; the conviction must be amenable to unequivocal disconfirmation; such unequivocal disconfirmation must occur; and lastly social support must be available to the believer subsequent to the disconfirmation. The final condition – social support – is the only truly sociological component of the theory. Although Festinger's theory has been criticised on both empirical and theoretical grounds, a number of studies conducted in diverse religious contexts have supported the basic tenets of cognitive dissonance (see Bainbridge 1997, Dein 2001, Dein and Dawson 2008, Gager 1975, Poloma 1982, Wardie 2000).

The sociological literature on prophecy is replete with studies demonstrating how individuals cling tenaciously to their convictions in the wake of failed prophecy. Sociologist Lorne Dawson (1999) in his comparative study of prophetic movements underscores the fact that whether or not a group survives the failure of prophecy is decisively influenced by the degree of in-group social support available for validating the rationalisations of a failure. He argues that it is not the size of the group but rather its degree of solidarity or cohesiveness that impacts upon the group's survival. However Dawson also notes that proselytisation is only one among a number of possible responses to reducing dissonance and is certainly not the most common response. Likewise in his overview of the sociological literature on prophecy, Jon Stone (2000) maintains that studies on failed prophecy post-Festinger demonstrate that active proselytisation is a relatively uncommon occurrence. Believers reaffirm their faith by reinterpreting both its substance and its meaning, an idea that has largely remained underdeveloped in social science literature on prophecy.

Festinger's original work on failed prophecy was further developed by Joseph Zygmunt (1972) who notes three modes of adaptation to prophetic failure: adaptation, reaffirmation and reappraisal. First, believers may acknowledge a minor human error in the prophecy, such as in calculating the date of a significant event. Second, the blame may be attributed to some force inside or outside the group which interferes with the cosmic plan. Finally, believers may postulate that the event in fact occurred, but that it did so not on the material plane, but rather on the spiritual plane, that it was, therefore, unobservable to believers.

J. Gordon Melton has argued with Festinger et al. that 'the denial of failure of prophecy is not just another option, but the common mode of adaptation of millennial groups following a failed prophecy' (1985: 21). But Melton reframes responses into two general modes of adaptation: cultural/ 'spiritualisation' or social. His first mode – 'the cultural or spiritualisation mode' – means the groups tend to reinterpret the promise of a visible verifiable event into the acceptance of a non-verifiable, invisible event. The prophecy has been fulfilled, albeit on a spiritual plane. The second mode – 'the social mode' – ameliorates emotional distress by placing an emphasis on renewing group ties after disconfirmation. Following disconfirmation of prophecy Melton argues that groups tend to turn inwards, engaging in a process of group building.

Melton (1985) also took issue with Festinger's assertion that millennial groups are organised around the prediction of prospective events. Melton sees this as a one-dimensional view of millennialism which neglects the presence of a complex cosmology and rightly asserts that prediction often springs from a broad context of belief and disconfirmation provides a 'test' which generally strengthens the group concerned. Furthermore the researcher's standard for logic (and thus 'disconfirmation') might not necessarily be consistent with the internal definitions of the group studied. For outsiders, who by definition do not adhere to the worldview of the group, specific prophecies and their failures are often the sole items of concern, and they may view failure of a major predicted event as the sign of invalidating the group's convictions. This is not the case for members of that group who hold a much broader perspective.

I have argued elsewhere (Dein 2001) that Festinger's approach is too positivistic and he presents his subjects as irrational and driven by forces beyond their comprehension. Festinger et al. fail to pay sufficient attention to the perspectives and interpretations of followers and the way they try to reason their way through facts and doctrine in pursuit of understanding. Others point out that

Festinger et al. impose secular-empirical modes of thought on the research field while at the same time displaying condescending attitudes towards their subjects (Baumgarten 2000, Tumminia 1998). Bem (1970: 29) even goes so far as arguing that cognitive dissonance may be less of a problem for the believer than for the researcher. Unlike scientific beliefs, many believers do not require consistent and frequent confirmatory evidence. Beliefs may withstand the pressure of disconfirming events not because of the effectiveness of reducing strategies, but because disconfirming evidence may simply go unacknowledged (Snow and Machalek 1982).

O'Leary (2000) similarly argues that in order to make sense of the growth and continued vitality of millennial and apocalyptic groups, even following failed predictions, we must note that such groups do not operate from the same premises or worldviews of scientists, and therefore researchers must not impose their modernist scientific epistemology that valorises falsification onto apocalyptic subjects. He underscores the need to reconstruct the group's own logic and assumptions and belief systems may feature validation logic that helps ensure their persistence.

For O'Leary the functional significance of a prediction in an apocalyptic movement cannot be understood in scientific terms; he argues that we need to conceptualise the whole process of apocalyptic conversion and organisational development as a communicative, or more specifically an argumentative process. While prophecies may 'fail' in the scientific sense following their disconfirmation, they may simultaneously be successful from the perspective of the prophet and his followers who gain a wide variety of benefits – economic, sexual and psychological – in the new social structure created by the prediction and its aftermath.

Other researchers have emphasised that a focus on prophecy disconfirmation is too narrow and fails to take account of the subjective life worlds of believers and the power of religious meaning systems to construct social realities that are able to support illogical and incompatible religious beliefs (Bader 1999, Kravel-Tovi and Bilu 2008, Tumminia 1998, Zygmunt 1972). Kravel-Tovi (2009) for instance asserts that social scientists need to move beyond the existing social psychological paradigm of cognitive dissonance to examine cultural strategies for reinventing and reviving meaning in a ruptured religious world including rituals. Processes of defining and constructing reality occur constantly and the vitality of a movement depends on the modes of reality that are provided to believers directly and indirectly.

Sociologist Damian Thompson (2005) underscores a point neglected by Festinger: in many instances millennialists steer clear of time specific prophecies or at least become more cautious of them. Given the fact that millennialists always have to square their convictions with empirical reality, it is therefore unsurprising that in some movements, millennial convictions have shifted from predictive to explanatory. In the former, believers make specific predictions which can easily be disconfirmed. In the latter, millennialism fulfils a rhetorical function in providing an explanation of the current state of evil and how this state can be remedied.

He notes that in contemporary Pentecostalism 'predictive' millenarianism – with its risky time-specific predictions of the end – has been substantially replaced by 'explanatory' millenarianism, which deploys apocalyptic narratives to explain features of the contemporary world. Most apocalyptic believers, he asserts, are more comfortable with these 'lower-cost' explanatory narratives that do not require them to sell their possessions and give up their everyday lives.

Much post-Festinger research on prophetic groups affirms that despite the fact that cognitive dissonance may provide a useful strategy for explaining certain dynamics of apocalyptic sects, it obscures or distorts other aspects. The theory of cognitive dissonance (and its emphasis on tension reduction and balance) and subsequent theories of rationalisation are not sufficient for explaining the complexities, contradictions and ambiguities involved in dealing with a failed prophecy.

This is not to ignore the fact that these strategies outlined by Festinger et al. are sometimes employed by members of religious groups in the short term as 'first aid' measures enabling followers to deal with the anguish of failed prediction. For example anthropologist Tanya Luhrmann remarks in relation to cognitive dissonance: 'The important feature of this theory is that the effort to straighten out inconsistencies in experience and belief resemble an odd-job-man's repairs. If people notice a mismatch of ideas and experience they do something to make them fit' (1991: 272). A few lines later she goes on to point out: 'Festinger's subjects do not act to promote long term consistency, or even long term self-interest; they act to avoid current cognitive embarrassment, and they do in ways which are sometimes quite damaging to long term self interest.'

Ritual, Performance and Belief Maintenance

The literature on 'failed' prophecy has to date emphasised cognitive factors to the neglect of other social practices which construct alternative realities. Ritual plays a key role in the maintenance of belief. I have argued with Dawson (Dein and Dawson 2008: 175) that: 'The authoritative provision of a plausible rationalisation, communicated promptly and persuasively, can offset the cognitive dissonance initially experienced by individuals. If further actions are taken at this juncture to reaffirm the group's cohesion, such as special rituals, ceremonies, and educational events, the dissonance can be significantly dissipated.' This point is echoed by Palmer and Finn (1992) who argue that the ritual context in which the 'disconfirmation' occurs is at least as important in determining the continuation of the movement as the commitment to the belief. In examining the Ottawa-based Institute of Applied Metaphysics, these authors postulate that if millenarian activity is approached not as a set of beliefs, but rather as a collective ritual of initiation into a new type of religious organisation, then an important factor in the survival of millenarian movements is the quality of the ritual experience:

'waiting for world's end is a symbolic act and it requires the presence of ritual actors and the organisation of sacred time and space' (1992: 409).

The academic study of rituals has moved towards seeing rituals as processes of practice and performance; rituals are effective on account of their non-discursive, dramaturgical and rhetorical characteristics (Schechner and Appel 1990, Schieffelin 1985). As Rappaport notes 'Performance as well as formality is necessary for ritual' (1996: 428). According to this perspective rituals not only reflect everyday and cosmological realities, they construct these realities in the first place. Ritual performance creates a sense of presence and verisimilitude, which influence moods, attitudes, social states and states of mind. Performance is made compelling through the ways in which the symbolic materials emerge in interactions between actors and the audience.

Huizinga (1995: 14) asserts:

> The sacred performance is more than an actualization in appearance only, a sham reality; it is also more than a symbolical actualization – it is a mystical one. In it, something invisible and inactual takes beautiful, actual, holy form. The participants in the rite are convinced that the action actualizes and effects a definite beautification, brings about an order of things higher than that in which they customarily live.

As Wagner (2012: 3) argues in her study of ritual and virtual reality, for Huizinga rituals evoke in us and are reflections of our desire for purpose and meaning, instantiated through engagement in temporary 'worlds' that make sense, allowing us to escape from our everyday mundane lives.

Bell (1997) has described the general characteristics of ritual-like activities which facilitate the production of a sense of an authoritative order that lies beyond the mundane world: multi-sensory experience, framing, formalism, traditionalism and invariance. Rituals are multi-sensory performances involving visual imagery and dramatic sounds in which not only is seeing believing, but doing is believing (Moore and Meyerhoff 1977, Wagner 2012). The power of performance originates from the heightened multi-sensory experience it provides: participants are pulled into a complex sensory experience that can also communicate a variety of messages and generate specific religious experiences by eliciting emotions. Diverse aspects of ritual, such as music, dancing and monotonous repetition, suppress commonsense perspectives on the world by facilitating the experience of 'trance' (Rouget 1985). They enable counterintuitive beliefs to be more readily accepted.

Bell's second characteristic of ritual is framing – a term referring to the ways in which some activities or messages construct an interpretive framework for understanding other subsequent or simultaneous acts or messages. Framing permits performance to be understood as other than mundane reality, and in turn shapes people's experiences and cognitive ordering of the world. The third characteristic – formalism – relates to the fact that rituals often employ more formal, or restricted, codes of speech and action than people use in everyday life. This may enhance the 'power' of ritual. Bell's fourth element is that ritual emphasises traditionalism – the attempt to make a set of activities identical to or consistent with cultural precedents. Traditionalism is a powerful tool of legitimation and involves the near-perfect repetition of activities from an earlier period, the adaptation of such activities in a new setting or the creation of practices that simply evoke links with the past. The final characteristic discussed by Bell is invariance – a disciplined set of actions marked by a precise repetition and physical control. While traditionalism emphasises the authority of the past, and subordinates the present, invariance, in contrast, ignores the passage of time altogether and emphasises the timeless authority of the group, its doctrines and its practices. These elements work together to construct an understanding of reality that is not as reliant on the cognitive assumptions that Festinger et al. and the social-science literature generated in response to his seminal study have suggested.

After a brief description of the Lubavitch Movement, I will go on to discuss how performative aspects can be used to understand the persistence of Lubavitcher Messianism.

Introducing the Lubavitch

Over the past 20 years, I have been conducting ethnographic fieldwork among Lubavitcher Hasidim in Crown Heights, Brooklyn, USA and Stamford Hill in London. Lubavitch is a worldwide movement of Hasidic Jews, whose main centre is in Brooklyn, New York. The organisation is also called Chabad, an acronym deriving from the first three Kabbalistic *sefirot*, *Chochma*, *Binah* and *Daath*. It is estimated there are about 200,000 members of Lubavitch worldwide, the main communities being in Israel, Great Britain, the United States and Belgium. This group differs from other Hasidic groups by its efforts to return secular Jews to religious observance, an activity which Lubavitchers maintain will hasten the messianic Redemption. Recently, Lubavitch has become known for its messianic fervour and the conviction that their 'current' Rebbe is *Moshiach* – the Jewish Messiah (see Dein 2001, 2010, 2011, Dein and Dawson 2008, Ehrlich, 2004).

A unique facet of Hasidism, and the way in which Hasidim differ from other ultra-Orthodox groups, is the idea of the *zaddik* or Rebbe, a perfectly righteous man who is the spiritual leader of the group. The recent Rebbe, Menachem Schneerson, was born in 1902 and became the leader of Lubavitch in 1954; he lived in 770 Crown Heights, Brooklyn until his death in 1994 (this location is referred to by his followers as simply '770'). He is the seventh Lubavitcher Rebbe and the successor to his father-in-law, Rabbi Yosef Yitzchak Schneerson. During his lifetime Menachem Schneerson was seen by his followers as a miracle worker and he was regularly consulted on issues related to health, wealth, education and marriage. His gravesite in Queens, the *Ohel*, has become a major site of pilgrimage by his followers who continue to petition him for miraculous interventions in their lives.

Lubavitcher Messianism and the Rebbe as Prophet

The concept of the Messiah in Lubavitcher Hasidism is defined in the writings of the founder of the sect, Schneur Zalman of Liady (1745–1812), and is ultimately based on the writings of Maimonides, the great Jewish philosopher and codifier. According to the former, the Messiah is no more than a successful *zaddik* who will return Jews to Judaism. In accordance with traditional Jewish teachings, there is an obligation for all Jews to hope for and await the Messiah and to demand his coming. Waiting for *Moshiach* and anticipating his coming is not simply a virtue, but a religious obligation akin to following the other commandments. According to Maimonides' Twelfth Principle of the Faith: 'I believe with complete faith in the coming of Masiach. Though he tarry, nonetheless, I await him every day, that he will come' (Maimonides, *Kol Menachem Rambam*, Thirteen Principles of Faith: Principle 12).

In popular understanding, the term prophecy typically connotes the prediction of a future event. However within Judaism a prophet is basically a spokesman for God, a person chosen by God to speak to people on God's behalf and convey a message or teaching; prophets set the standards for the entire community. The Jewish philosopher and physician Maimonides counts it as one of the 13 foundations of the Jewish faith that 'G-d communicates to mankind through prophecy' (*Shloshah Asar Ikkarim*) (Maimonides, *Kol Menachem Rambam*, Thirteen Principles of Faith: Principle 6). Prophets were traditionally role models of holiness, scholarship and closeness to God. Prophecy indicates a close relationship with the Divine and as such it can bolster the charisma of those who express it; the Rebbe was well known for his prophetic utterances.

There are many stories in the Lubavitch community documenting the Rebbe's prophetic ability. For instance, a week and a half before the Six Day War in 1967, he predicted a great victory and asked that this victory be publicised (Schneerson 1967: 20). In 1985 he announced that the fall of communism was imminent, and two years later he asked his followers to build homes and prepare jobs in Israel for the masses of Jews who would be leaving Russia (Schneerson 1985: 96). His predictions were subsequently confirmed when in 1989 the Iron Curtain fell. During the first Gulf War in 1991 he predicted that Israel would be the safest place to be, that there would be no need for gas masks, and that the war would be over by Purim (Schneerson 1991). He advised people to travel confidently to Israel, and assured them that they would be unharmed. His predictions on each occasion were subsequently confirmed.

According to Maimonides, two correct prophecies are sufficient for a person to be considered a true prophet (Russell and Cohn 2012: Basic Principles of the Torah, 10:5). His followers hold that *Moshiach* must be a proven prophet, just like the Rebbe. It was a short step for his followers to use the Rebbe's supposed powers of prophecy to affirm his messianic status (Katchen 1991, Shaffir 1993). As one rabbi said during one of my interviews:

The Rebbe has told us as a prophet that *Moshiach* is here and that the Redemption is now. All we need to do is to open our eyes and see the changes that are taking place and how these changes fulfil the ancient prophecies of redemption from the written and oral Torah.

For his followers, Rabbi Schneerson possessed all the qualifications for being the Messiah. And this idea was reinforced by the Rebbe's own statements concerning the imminence of the Messiah.

For many years his followers held the Rebbe to be the Jewish Messiah and much time and effort was devoted to various campaigns proclaiming his messiahship (see Dein 2001, 2010, 2011). From 1991 until the Rebbe's death in 1994 there was increasing messianic excitement throughout Lubavitch communities in the USA, the UK and in Israel. The publication of messianic literature increased, more advertisements appeared in national newspapers, and public meetings were held where Schneerson's followers propagated the idea that Rabbi Schneerson was *Moshiach*.

There is little doubt that the Lubavitcher messianic campaign has benefited greatly from the use of modern media technology from the arrival of the sixth Lubavitcher Rebbe in the United States in 1940, through to the death of the 'current' Rebbe and continuing into the present. Shandler (2009) notes that Lubavitch has forged a new spiritual relationship with the Rebbe through innovative and provocative media practices: print advertising, photography, radio, the internet and television. Unlike other Hasidic groups in the USA, Lubavitch has a commitment to visibility in the public sphere and this commitment is central to their mission of fostering increased religious observance and propagating their messianic ideas.

The Death of the Rebbe

The Rebbe suffered from two strokes prior to his death. After his first stroke in 1992, when the Rebbe was paralysed and unable to speak, there was increased proselytisation. Far from dissuading his followers of the Rebbe's messianic status, discourse about Rabbi Schneerson being *Moshiach* increased in Lubavitch communities worldwide, thus supporting Festinger's prediction that with cognitive dissonance increased proselytising may occur.

The Rebbe experienced a second stroke in June 1994 at the age of 92 years and died several weeks later. Shortly after his death Lubavitchers appealed to a number of *post hoc* rationalisations to account for the fact that their expected Messiah had died before fulfilling his messianic mission and ushering in the Redemption. Some admitted that they had been wrong in asserting the Rebbe's messianic status – only God could know this status they claimed. For others, however, the fact that the Rebbe had left his physical body rendered him even more powerful. However, shortly after his death the majority view amongst his followers was that he would be resurrected. This view was seen by outsiders, primarily other Jewish groups, as heretical and quickly raised assertions of a Christian influence on Lubavitch.

Within a few years Lubavitch had divided into two groups: anti-Messianists and Messianists. While the former maintain that Rabbi Schneerson could have been *Moshiach*, they accept that he is dead and that his death invalidates his messianic status. The latter however hold the contrary view. For them the Rebbe's death was illusory, and he is *Moshiach* and still lives. This group is largely based in Crown Heights and comprises young Lubavitchers, many deriving from Sefad in Israel. Significantly, this group continues to sing the *Yechi* – a statement asserting the fact that the Rebbe is alive – and act as though he is still present. To date there have been tensions between the two factions of Lubavitch which at times has resulted in physical skirmishes.

Keeping the Rebbe Alive through Cultural Performance[1]

In the Rebbe's synagogue, the Rebbe is repeatedly brought into existence by the enactment of stylised, repetitive and stereotyped performances which literally embody the Rebbe. In recent years the Messianists have taken over ownership of the '770' synagogue, hanging messianic banners inside and in several instances physically attacking anti-Messianists who tried to remove them. Hundreds of Lubavitcher Hasidim gather there to commune with the Rebbe on a daily basis. Since the Rebbe's death things have hardly changed in the synagogue; everything is as it was during the Rebbe's life. The physical appearance of the basement synagogue has changed little since Rabbi Schneerson's death. The situation appears stage-managed to create the living presence of the Rebbe. Pictures of the Rebbe are prominently displayed everywhere, his staring eyes signifying the fact that the Rebbe can see into his followers' innermost selves, a fact commonly mentioned by those who visited him while alive. In the entrance hall, a DVD plays showing the Rebbe distributing 'dollars' – a weekly ceremony attended by thousands of people during his life who would petition him for blessings and who would receive a dollar from him symbolising charity. This visual signifier gives the sense that everything continues just as it had always done when the Rebbe was alive.

'770' is a continuous hive of activity and many of the Rebbe's followers study religious texts, pray and even sleep in the synagogue. The sound of men reciting tracts from the Rebbe's books and other discussions on Jewish literature continues throughout the day and night only to be interrupted by a sudden eruption of loud repetitive clapping and singing of 'Long live our master, our teacher and our rabbi, King Messiah for ever and ever', signifying the start of the thrice daily public prayer. At these times his followers appear to enter a state of ecstasy as the singing intensifies. They are easily recognisable by the fact that they wear yellow lapel

---

[1]   I have addressed this issue extensively in Dein (2010, 2011, Dein in press) and here I provide a brief summary of this work.

pins with the word *Moshiach* inscribed on them; these signify their conviction that the Rebbe is *Moshiach*.

The Rebbe's empty chair is prominently displayed at the front of the synagogue; its cushions unruffled for more than 15 years. The chair is kept as it was while the Rebbe was alive. Before the daily afternoon prayers, several men perform the ritual of opening out a Persian rug, moving the Rebbe's chair out from under a desk, and fiddling with his prayer shawls and books as if Rabbi Schneerson were about to enter and take his seat. At the start of the service the Rebbe's followers stand on either side of a red carpet creating a pathway leading from the stairs to the podium. His Hasidim stare towards a balcony in the distance as if expecting the Rebbe to emerge and take up his place on a platform as he did when he was alive. These activities are accompanied by loud singing of Hebrew prayer. In major rituals the Rebbe is honoured with uttering the first verse of the prayer and the gaze of the congregation is focused upon the vacant chair. The congregation then recites the subsequent verses. At the conclusion of the service the carpet is rolled up and the Rebbe's chair is again covered: these activities are accompanied by song and dance while the Rebbe 'exits'. Then the dancing stops abruptly and a sudden hush silences the room. Four young boys, each carrying a large yellow flag bearing the Rebbe's crest, part the dancers and move alongside the platform that supports the Rebbe's chair and desk. Raising the flags high in the air they chant in unison: 'We want *Moshiach* now! We want *Moshiach* now! We want *Moshiach* now!' The movements of the Hasidim, their making a symbolic pathway for the Rebbe, their deferential posture create a symbolic space in which the Rebbe appears. Their gestures, words and physical delineations of space and time actually accomplish what a ritual ought to do, namely shape religious life-worlds, in this instance providing a sense of the Rebbe's presence.

Other rituals continue as if nothing has changed in the synagogue. On the Sabbath and High Holidays there is a *farbrengen* – a ceremonial gathering of Hasidim – where prior to his death, the Rebbe presided and regularly gave his discourses on Hasidic matters, frequently alluding to the 'imminent' Redemption. Since his death the setting has been kept intact. The Rebbe's table remains covered with a white tablecloth and is set with *halla* (Sabbath bread), a bottle of wine and a wineglass. The Rebbe's armchair is brought to the table and his Hasidim sit in front of it as if celebrating with the Rebbe. At the conclusion of the meeting, a Hasid cuts the *halla* and pours wine from the wineglass. These are then distributed among the Hasidim. On the Day of Atonement (Yom Kippur) a mobile staircase is placed upon the podium enabling the Rebbe to 'watch from above' and direct the traditional singing as he had done in previous years. During the Harvest festival (Succoth) a tabernacle is built for the Rebbe with the 'four species' (citron, palm branch, myrtle branch, willow branch) laid out for him inside. Some eagerly extend their hands to receive the Rebbe's *lekah* (cake), a custom which was carried out when he was alive.

Imhoff (2009) notes that the use of modern audio-visual media technology has strengthened the convictions and the practices of the Messianists by making the claim that Rabbi Schneerson is *Moshiach* more credible, and has created novel ways of interacting with him through allowing his body and voice to be present and renewed. Not only can his followers feel his spirit, but through media technology they can also see his body and hear his voice. Furthermore, by creating a sense of presence in his physical absence, these media practices are essential to the continuing survival of Lubavitch, and serve as sources of inspiration and instruction for future generations of Lubavitchers. Like ritual, the power of media derives from its ability to mediate the rhetorical and psychological power of performers and in turn to persuade by argument and suggestion.

At the Rebbe's Tomb

Just as Rebbe once visited the *Ohel* (tomb) to commune with his deceased father-in-law when he was alive, his followers continue to travel to the *Ohel* to commune with him and ask for his intercession for life issues: marriage, business, health and education. It has become a place of prayer, contemplation and communal bonding for them. Typically women who experience infertility will petition him for children. Others plead that a sick relative will recover from their illness or that a marriage will be successful. Paradoxically, although they maintain that the Rebbe is alive, many Messianists regularly visit the Rebbe's grave. Although some vehemently deny that he lies there, and do not visit him there, others will still go to the graveside to communicate with him and ask for his intercession.

In close proximity to the Rebbe's gravesite is a centre which includes a video room, a library, a small synagogue, a quiet room for visitors to compose the prayers they will say in the *Ohel*, and refreshments. The entrance to the *Ohel* is through the back door of this house and down a pathway. Men and women enter the *Ohel* through separate doors. Two fax machines constantly churn out a stream of requests from people requesting the Rebbe's blessings. On an hourly basis, one of the Rebbe's assistants collects them and takes them to the Rebbe's grave, where he reads them and deposits them on top of the pile of notes. Approximately 1,000 faxes arrive each day, each from someone hoping that the Rebbe will intercede on his or her behalf in heaven. Lubavitchers maintain that their deceased Rebbe's spirit hovers over the gravesite and that his spiritual interaction with his followers increases after his death. As the Lubavitcher mystical text *Tanya* explains, the benefit of the *zaddik* to the world increases after his death because his spirit is freed from his body and is shared with all humanity. Despite its freedom, the spirit is believed to reside closer to the body than anywhere else, and therefore proximity to the grave is considered meritorious and spiritually beneficial (Ehrlich 2004: 265).

There are numerous ritual observances related to visiting the Rebbe's resting place, such as refraining from food (though not drink) before the visit and removing leather shoes before entering the mausoleum (as did Moses before nearing the burning bush). But most important is the mental preparation of charity, learning and spiritual stock-taking. Prior to entry visitors wash their hands and light candles. After removing their shoes they enter the gravesite surrounded by walls and take their place among the assembly of people fervently praying and requesting the Rebbe's intercession. As a sign of respect some visitors perform the custom of knocking on the door before entering. While leaving visitors walk backward for similar reasons. Though *Ohel* means 'tent', the *Ohel* itself is like an inverted *chuppah* (canopy): closed on all sides but open to the heavens. Inside, there is a second inner wall about waist high that dozens of people lean on as they say prayers over the graves themselves.

These ritualistic aspects create a sense of the Rebbe's presence within the sacred space of the *Ohel*. The hand washing, taking off of shoes, and the lighting of candles render this site special. This is reinforced by the sense of formality. The fact that the sixth Lubavitcher Rebbe is buried there next to Schneerson signifies a link with tradition when the Rebbe would regularly visit his father in law; this ritual evokes both the past and the present. At the *Ohel* the Messianists are 'cut off' from everyday reality. Their sense of being inside the tomb creates a feeling of separateness from the outside world. The solemn atmosphere reinforces a sense of separation from the joviality of the outside world. The walls of the *Ohel* create a symbolic space; the fact that the *Ohel* has no roof further provides a space in which the Rebbe can literally come in from above. The singing at the graveside creates a heightened sensory experience in which the Rebbe appears.

Conclusion

This chapter introduced social-scientific theories of how groups deal with prophetic 'failure'. It argued that existing literature largely framed the subject in cognitive terms emphasising cognitive dissonance. But this has serious limitations and does not reflect the complex sociocultural processes involved in belief maintenance, nor does it reflect the insider's perspective which may be far more rational than is traditionally assumed by social scientists.

It then discussed how the Lubavitch has adapted to the death of their spiritual leader whom they held to be *Moshiach*. Aspects of the Lubavitch reaction to the death of the Rebbe support cognitive dissonance theory: there was increased proselytisation as well as a number of *post hoc* rationalisations. As I have pointed out, cognitive dissonance theory might account for short-term changes in cognition. But I argue that longer-term belief maintenance requires the use of cultural strategies and in this sense ritual is a useful framework for understanding how the Rebbe continues to be embodied. To date the function of ritual in maintaining belief in prophetic groups has been under-researched. This should be a focus for future work in this area including the complex links between ritual, religious experience and embodiment.

References

Bader, C. 1999. When Prophecy Passes Unnoticed: New Perspectives on Failed Prophecy. *Journal for the Scientific Study of Religion*, 38(1), 119–31.

Bainbridge, W. 1997. *The Sociology of Religious Movements*. New York: Routledge.

Balch, R., Farnsworth, G. and Wilkins, S. 1983. When the Bombs Drop: Reactions to a Disconfirmed Prophecy in a Millennial Sect. *Sociological Perspectives*, 26, 137–58.

Baumgarten, A.I. (ed.) 2000. *Apocalyptic Time*. Leiden: E.J. Brill.

Bell, C. 1997. *Ritual: Perspectives and Dimensions*. New York: Oxford University Press.

Bem, D. 1970. *Beliefs, Attitudes and Human Affairs*. Belmont, CA: California Brooks/Cole.

Brierley, P. 1999. *UK Christian Handbook: Religious Trends 2000/2001*, no. 2. London: Christian Research.

Dawson, L. 1999. When Prophecy Fails and Faith Persists: A Theoretical Overview. *Nova Religio*, 3(1), 60–82.

Dein, S. 2001. What Really Happens When Prophecy Fails: The Case of Lubavitch. *Sociology of Religion*, 62(3), 383–401.

——. 2010. A Messiah from the Dead: Cultural Performance in Lubavitcher Messianism. *Social Compass*, 57(4), 537–54.

——. 2011. *Lubavitcher Messianism: What Really Happens When Prophecy Fails*. London: Continuum.

——. [in press]. Cognitive Dissonance, in *Brill Dictionary of Religion*, edited by Kocku von Stuckrad. Leiden: Brill.

Dein, S. and Dawson, L. 2008. The Scandal of the Lubavitch Rebbe: Messianism as a Response to Failed Prophecy. *Journal of Contemporary Religion*, 23(2), 163–80.

Ehrlich, A. 2004. *The Messiah of Brooklyn: Understanding Lubavitch Hasidism Past and Present*. Jersey City, NJ: KTAV Publishing.

Festinger, L., Riecken, H. and Schachter, S. 1956. *When Prophecy Fails*. New York: Harper and Row.

Gager, J. 1975. *Kingdom and Community*. Englewood Cliffs, NJ: Prentice Hall.

Geertz, C. 1973. *The Interpretation of Culture*. New York: Basic Books.

Huizinga, J. 1955. *Homo Ludens: A Study of the Play Element in Culture*. Boston, MA: Beacon Press.

Imhoff, S. 2009. The Rebbe's Body [Online]. Available at: http://divinity.uchicago.edu/martycenter/publications/webforum/022009/Imhoff%20response%20to%20Shandler.pdf [accessed: 17 April 2012].

Katchen, M. 1991. Who Wants Moshiach Now? Pre-millennialism and Post-millennialism in Judaism. *Australian Journal of Jewish Studies*, 5(1), 59–76.

Kravel-Tovi, M. 2009. To See the Invisible Messiah: Messianic Socialization in the Wake of a Failed Prophecy. *Chabad Religion*, 39(3), 248–60.

Kravel-Tovi, M. and Bilu, Y. 2008. The Work of the Present: Constructing Messianic Temporality in the Wake of Failed Prophecy among Chabad Hasidism. *American Ethnologist*, 35(1), 64–80.

Luhrmann, T. 1991. *Persuasions of the Witch's Craft: Ritual Magic in Contemporary England*. Boston, MA: Harvard University Press.

Maimonides, M. 2009. *Kol Menachem Rambam*, edited by C. Miller. Brooklyn, NY: Kol Menachem Publishers.

Melton, J.G. 1985. Spiritualisation and Reaffirmation: What Really Happens When Prophecy Fails. *American Studies*, 26(2), 17–29.

Moore, S. and Meyerhoff, B. 1977. *Secular Ritual: A Working Definition of Ritual*. Assen: Van Gorcum.

O'Leary, S. 1994. *Arguing the Apocalypse: A Theory of Millennial Rhetoric*. Oxford: Oxford University Press.

———. 2000. When Prophecy Fails and When It Succeeds: Apocalyptic Prediction and the Re-Entry into Ordinary Time, in *Apocalyptic Time*, edited by A.I. Baumgarten. Leiden: Brill, 341–62.

Palmer, S. and Finn, N. 1992. Coping with the Apocalypse in Canada: Experiences of End Time in La Mission de L'Esprit Saint and Institute of Applied Metaphysics. *Sociological Analysis*, 53, 397–415.

Poloma, M. 1982. *The Charismatic Movement*. Boston, MA: Twayne.

Rappaport, R. 1996. The Obvious Aspects of Ritual, in *Readings in Ritual Studies*, edited by R. Grimes. Upper Saddle River, NJ : Prentice Hall, 173–221.

Rouget, G. 1985. *Music and Trance: A Theory of the Relations Between Music and Possession*, translated by Brunhilde Bie-buyck. Chicago, IL and London: University of Chicago Press.

Russell, J. and Cohn, R. 2012. *Mishneh Torah*. [No place]: Book on Demand Ltd.

Schechner, R. and Appel, W. 1990. *By Means of Performance*. Cambridge: Cambridge University Press.

Schieffelin, E. 1985. Performance and the Cultural Construction of Reality. *American Ethnologist*, 12(4), 707–24.

Schneerson, M. 1967. *Kfar Chabad Magazine*, 762 [self-published].

———. 1985. *Sefer Hisvaduyos*, 5745(3) [self-published].

———. 1991. *Kfar Chabad Magazine*, 442 [self-published].

Shaffir, W. 1993. Jewish Messianism Lubavitch-Style: An Interim Report. *The Jewish Journal of Sociology*, 35, 115–28.

Shandler, J. 2009. *Jews, God and Videotape: Religion and Media in America*. New York: New York University Press.

Snow, D. and Machalek, R. 1982. On the Presumed Fragility of Unconventional Beliefs. *Journal for the Scientific Study of Religion*, 21(1), 15–26.

Stark, R. 1991. Normal Revelations: A Rational Model of 'Mystical' Experiences, in *Religion and the Social Order*, Vol. 1, edited by D.G. Bromley. Greenwich, CT: Jai Press, 225–38.

Stone, J. 2000. *Expecting Armageddon: Essential Readings in Failed Prophecy*. New York: Routledge.

Thompson, D. 2005. *Waiting for Antichrist: Charisma and Apocalypse in a Pentecostal Church*. Oxford: Oxford University Press.

Tumminia, D. 1998. How Prophecy Never Fails: Interpretive Reason in a Flying Saucer Group. *Sociology of Religion*, 59(2), 157–70.

——. 2005. *When Prophecy Never Fails: Myth and Reality in a Flying Saucer Group*. Oxford: Oxford University Press.

Wagner, R. 2012. *Godwired: Religion, Ritual and Virtual Reality*. London: Routledge.

Wardie, E. 2000. Cognitive Distance and Proselytism: An Application of Festinger's Model to Thirteenth Century Joachites, in *Apocalyptic Time*, edited by A.I. Baumgarten. Leiden: Brill, 269–82.

Zygmunt, J. 1972. When Prophecies Fail: A Theoretical Perspective on the Comparative Evidence. *American Behavioural Scientist*, 16, 245–67.

Chapter 4

Prophecy on the Margins:
A Case Study of the Apocalypse in
Later Seventeenth-Century England

Warren Johnston

Introduction

Imagining, predicting and fearing the end of the world is a prevalent aspect of early twenty-first-century thought and popular culture. Nuclear annihilation, environmental disaster or global pandemic – to name just a few – are common themes in film, literature and even in daily newscasts. Such concerns not only demonstrate people's apprehension with the end of life, on a personal and universal level, but also reflect anxiety about the current and future state of human society – the ways of living and the values of the world.

Religious prophecies about an approaching End also continue to spark popular interest. In 2011, the American evangelical minister Harold Camping predicted that the Rapture – the gathering-up of true Christian believers that precedes the destruction of the World – would occur on 21 May 2011. In the weeks leading up to this date, major print and television media outlets in both Canada and the United States reported on the apocalyptic convictions of Camping and his followers, including their efforts to advertise the impending doom on billboards throughout the United States and other parts of the world (see, for example, Breen 2011, Mahoney 2011, Whitaker 2011). And the passing of that date did not signal an end to such prognostication: the *New York Times* published an interview with Camping two days after his failed prediction in which he stated that there had been 'an invisible [spiritual] judgement day' in May, and that the End would now arrive in October; he promised that new billboards would be coming soon (McKinley 2011; see also Berg 2011).

The aspect of Camping's movement that differs from representations of apocalypticism in popular culture is that, while the latter often present the End of the World as an existential abyss to instil dread, and from which last-minute brinksmanship must heroically pull us back, for Camping's followers, and others who share similar beliefs, this End is something eagerly anticipated. Of course the question that must be asked is: Why?

This chapter will attempt to answer that question through a case study of the apocalyptic beliefs of both radical and nonviolent religious nonconformists in the last four decades of the seventeenth century in England.[1] Though at their core these convictions were founded in Christian ideas and theological doctrine, of more interest here is what they say about the political and social cultures within which they were developed. This can provide some insight into what attraction and power such beliefs had, and continue to have.

Civil Upheaval and Radical Apocalyptic Beliefs

England in the 1600s was a place and period of great civil, social and religious turmoil. Developing ideas of subjects' political rights clashed with the apex of royal absolutism; the ongoing concerns of the Protestant Reformations ran headlong into a reinvigorated and resurgent European Catholicism. These anxieties culminated in Civil War throughout the British Isles from 1642 to 1648, a conflict that would eventually lead to the overthrow of established religious institutions and, more shockingly, the trial, conviction and execution of a sitting king, Charles I, for treason in January 1649. This, in turn, brought about the abolishment of monarchy in Britain, and the establishment of England as a republic ruled by Parliament.

These radical events not only shook the English political and religious establishment, but also signalled, for some, the onset of more universally significant affairs. Many who lived in England thought that they must be living in the End Times, the period that would see Christ's return to earth to establish a worldly kingdom ruled by his faithful followers. With this in mind, those who had supported the overthrow of monarchical and ecclesiastical government looked to the images and symbols found throughout the biblical Book of Revelation as prophecies with immediate and particular effect. Monarchical government and the Church of England were equated with the various beasts found in the prophecies of Revelation, which in turn were seen to represent Antichrist (see, for example, Hill 1971: chapters 2–3). Parliament and Protestant denominations were the faithful witnesses of chapter 11 of Revelation, who would hold out against corrupt worldly powers and, eventually, be raised into heaven by God. The destruction of worldly political and religious enemies, in turn, was interpreted as the prelude to the Millennium, a thousand-year period spoken of in Revelation 20 that would see Satan bound in chains and the godly ruling the world with Christ.

These predictions from the mid seventeenth century, like Harold Camping's from the early twenty-first, did not materialise: significant religious and social change did not occur, and English politics devolved into chaos in the late 1650s. This resulted in the end of the republican experiment and the Restoration of monarchical government in the person of Charles II, son of the executed king,

---

[1]   This chapter is a case study in the sense that it examines some examples of a specific set of prophetic convictions. The study is not intended to be exhaustive, neither within this particular group of beliefs nor beyond it. For a fuller account of the wider range of apocalyptic ideas during this period see Johnston (2011).

in 1660, accompanied by the re-establishment of the Anglican Church as the sole legal religious institution shortly thereafter. All of this also indicated the failure of millenarian hopes that had been so high from the mid 1640s to the mid 1650s.

These developments, however, did not mean the end to beliefs that apocalyptic prophecies would be accomplished. Though the civil and ecclesiastical settlements of the Restoration were incompatible with most of the millennial visions of the Civil War and the Interregnum, the period from 1660 to 1700 saw the adaptation of prophetic predictions to suit the altered political and religious conditions. While supporters of monarchy and the Church of England did use prophetic imagery to endorse the newly restored institutions, the most vocal and prolific exponents of apocalyptic beliefs in the later seventeenth century in England were those who opposed the restored civil and ecclesiastical authorities: having pinned their hopes upon the overthrow of monarchical government, radical groups and religious nonconformists were sorely disappointed with its return. Their interpretations of prophecy remained an important way for them to understand the societal circumstances they faced in the later seventeenth century.

The most violent response to the restored monarchy came less than a year after Charles II took the throne. On 6 January 1661, a radical preacher named Thomas Venner led a band of followers on an armed rampage through the streets of London in an attempt to occupy St Paul's Cathedral and, three days later, to kidnap the Lord Mayor. Venner and his supporters were part of the Fifth Monarchy movement that had been prominent during the late 1640s and the 1650s (see, for example, Capp 1972). Named after the prophecy in Daniel 2:31–45 (see especially verse 44) that was interpreted as referring to the thousand-year reign of Christ, the Fifth Monarchists were motivated by the belief that their rebellion would lead the way for Christ's return to earth, and that they would become the vanguard for the millennial government of the godly 'saints'. Venner's beliefs were a critique not only of the political and religious circumstances of England, but of the social ones as well: the written tract that accompanied his rebellion declared that the apocalyptic kingdom would see a series of reforms, including equal justice for the poor and wealthy alike, employment for all and an end to taxation (Anonymous 1661: 4–5). The millennial government would become the foundation of 'all Civill Liberty, and Rights of men … [that] shall rise alone upon the Root of the Visible Kingdom of our Lord Jesus Christ, which … may from henceforth take place among us according to the Prophecies of the Scriptures' (Anonymous 1661: 10). Such millenarian visions were not meant to be: Venner's small army was defeated, and he was executed with a group of his followers in the street outside their meeting house.

Venner's movement was the most notorious outbreak of millenarian violence in the early 1660s, but similarly subversive ideas are found in other publications. *The Panther-Prophesy* told of a vision, with a soldier, a lawyer, a citizen and a clergyman who refused an invitation to the 'Marriage Supper', an allusion to Revelation 19:7. These four marvel at a panther emerging from the forest, which then eats them; as this is happening, others flee, adhering to God's warning to withdraw from Babylon in Revelation 18:4 (Anonymous 1662: 1–3). The four men who had been eaten were excreted from the panther in different forms: the soldier became a duke, the lawyer an earl, the citizen a baron and the clergyman a bishop, and these four lifted and carried the panther (the animal clearly a thinly-veiled reference to the Restoration regime). With the 'poor People' hiding in the forest, the panther seizes a 'Godly Man' by the throat, causing Christ to descend from heaven, shooting the beast with arrows. The tract ends with the panther's supporters running away, the people emerging from the woods saying 'The Lord Reigns'; a voice then announces that Babylon has fallen [Revelation 14:8, 18:2], and there is a conflagration (Anonymous 1662: 4–6). Although the 'prophecy' it describes bears no similarity in its details to any biblical account, the scriptural references within the story and inserted in its margins suggested the apocalyptic consequences for those who submitted to the Restoration religious and civil settlements. In addition, the characters and their actions anticipated radical social and political change, as well as insinuating that the Restoration government would soon meet a sudden and violent collapse.

The intent to violently bring down monarchy and the Church of England were not simply the stuff of the imagination. Like Venner's rising, some apocalyptic beliefs were directly connected to plans to revolt against the government. *A Treatise of the Execution of Justice* was published to coincide with a planned rebellion that was foiled by the English government in October of 1663 (Greaves 1986: 222). This tract argued that rulers were to adhere to divine law, and that their subjects were responsible for holding them accountable. The connection to apocalyptic fulfilment is made clear, noting that 'the Beast or Antichristian Tyrants were overcome by the Saints' in Revelation 13:7, and that God's people were commanded 'to reward Babylon as she rewarded them, Rev. 18:6. That is, as the Antichristian Tyrants have led the saints into captivity, and killed them with the sword; so shall the Saints lead them into captivity, and kill them with the sword' (Anonymous 1663a: 29). In addition to these opinions of the existing civil government, the work condemned Anglican worship as 'no better than that poisonous Cup of Abomination and filthiness of Fornication which the Whore gives her lovers to drink [Revelation 17:4]' (Anonymous 1663a: 17).

Radical expressions of apocalyptic beliefs were largely a product of the early 1660s, when resentment toward the restored monarchy and Church of England was fresh. Yet there were still those who held out into the last years of the decade. *The Saints Freedom from Tyranny Vindicated* followed in the spirit of earlier tracts, asserting the saints' responsibility to seek reform of Church and state, as well as describing current circumstances as antichristian and the period of the beast, but 'under promise of the Last Times' (Anonymous 1667: A2v, 8, 9). Although underpinned by an entirely different validation, this tract foreshadowed Lockean political theory by arguing that rulers who broke from the original basis of their power were not to be obeyed because 'they answer not the ends of Political Government, as Ordained by God … and the People are disingaged, on their part from Subjection', concluding that 'a People Opposing or Deposing a wicked or oppressing King ... is no Opposition to Magistracy ... when they seek to ... remove a wicked man in the place of a Magistrate' (Anonymous 1667: 23). While this work affirmed traditional Protestant identification of the Roman Catholic Church and the papacy with Antichrist, it also asserts a specifically English interpretation, arguing that the beast arising from the earth in Revelation 13:11 was an 'abruption or breaking off from the former Beast, and so assuming absolute Jurisdiction Civil and Ecclesiastical in his own Kingdom, as Hen. 8 did', referring to Henry VIII's establishment of royal supremacy over the Church of England (Anonymous 1667: 28). This prophetic connection to English monarchs' claims of authority over religious matters demonstrated the work's condemnation of the political and ecclesiastical establishment in the later seventeenth century.

Moderate Nonconformity's Apocalyptic Response to Oppression

Radical resistance provided the most obvious threat to the government in England during the 1660s, as well as the most dangerous application of prophetic ideas. However, it was not the only form of opposition to the restored state and church: moderate Protestant nonconformists were also disappointed with the return of the Church of England's monopoly over religious worship and the secular government's enforcement of it. Unlike their radical brethren, however, moderate nonconformists eschewed violent action against civil and ecclesiastical authorities. Instead, Presbyterians, Baptists, Congregationalists (Independents) and Quakers, among others, sought ways of living within the Restoration state without violating their consciences, demonstrating their dissent from Anglican worship through passive disobedience. The circumstances that nonconformists faced after 1660 were understood within a prophetic framework, and the expression of these convictions proved to be the most prominent representation of apocalyptic beliefs in the later seventeenth century. Nonconformist response to the religious conditions of the Restoration included the justification of passive resistance to unacceptable ecclesiastical policies and the acclamation of their suffering under religious oppression, understanding these things as necessary elements in the fulfilment of prophecy.

The distinction between radicalism and moderate nonconformity is most readily apparent in the latter's renouncing of violent resistance. In the aftermath of Venner's revolt in 1661, nonconformist groups quickly moved to make clear that their non-Anglican stance did not equate with rebellious actions against the government. Congregational and Baptist ministers, as well as Quaker leaders, each published condemnations of Fifth Monarchist beliefs and each affirmed their obedience to the 'lawful' commands of temporal rulers (see Caryll et al. 1661, Fox et al. 1661, Kiffen et al. 1661). While such responses were an obvious immediate reaction against the violence and bloodshed of Venner's millenarian uprising, nonconformist denunciation of active resistance to the English government continued long after these events had passed. The Baptist John Tombes devoted an entire book to this topic. In *Saints No Smiters* Tombes characterised radical millenarian ideas on the overthrow of government as a threat to society itself. Instead, he argued that the promised defeat of 'Babylon' in apocalyptic prophecy required the cooperation and compliance of the saints with secular rulers (Tombes 1664: 57–8). William Sherwin, a Presbyterian minister who was ejected from his pulpit when legislation mandated a reinstatement of Church of England services in the summer of 1662, wrote over a dozen works expounding apocalyptic prophecy in the 1660s and 1670s. In these, Sherwin denied the opinion that the saints were to actively attempt to take power themselves (Sherwin 1665a: a2v), calling it a 'bold presumption and scandalous wickedness of our latter times, for any, under pretence of Christs Kingdom ... to go about by the Sword, or any unlawful means, to divest Magistrates and Governors of their Offices' (Sherwin 1665b: 15). Such confirmation of the non-violent and non-radical nature of apocalyptic beliefs persisted into the 1680s and 1690s. Christ's kingdom would be accomplished not by 'Seditious, Turbulent, or Rebellious Commotions', but 'by purest and most unblemish'd Instruments, and by Princes of Great Brittain' (Beverley 1684: 73). Authors continued to deny that apocalyptic prophecy posed any danger, with those who held radical beliefs denounced as 'ignorant turbulent People' who would be punished by God for their 'Disquiet of the Publick Peace' (Anonymous 1690: c2r).

Even with this denunciation of active resistance against secular authority, moderate nonconformists did not simply acquiesce to the religious policies and laws of England in the later seventeenth century. Finding various aspects of Anglican worship and doctrine unpalatable, members of dissenting denominations often chose to passively resist compliance to religious policies of the Restoration state rather than violating their consciences. Baptist pastor Hanserd Knollys maintained that, though God mandated obedience to civil authorities, if rulers command their subjects 'to do anything, which God hath forbidden, or ... forbid them to do any thing, which God hath Commanded, they ought to obey God rather than Men ... and patiently suffer for Righteousness sake' (Knollys 1679: 43). Benjamin Stonham, a Congregational minister, affirmed this principle by asserting that the 'Saints ... owe no Obedience unto Man, in Gospel-matters' unless those laws were confirmed by biblical authority. These actions of passive disobedience and suffering also became part of nonconformists' prophetic understanding.

Several passages and images in Revelation provided fitting representations of nonconformist noncompliance with the government's religious dictates. One of the most used was the account of the two prophesying witnesses who were killed by the beast, lay dead in the street, and were then brought back to life by God [Revelation 11:3–12]. The Presbyterian minister Edward Bagshaw, himself imprisoned during the mid 1660s for his nonconformity, reminded his readers to avoid 'all manner of Communion with false and Adulterous Churches ... during the whole time of Antichrist in opposition to whom ... they are called Witnesses' (Bagshaw 1669: 31). The death of the witnesses became a convenient metaphor for the exclusion from public worship and for the persecution of nonconformists in the later seventeenth century. For one author the year 1660 marked the slaying of the witnesses, and their lying dead [Revelation 11:8–9] symbolised the subsequent passing of legislation outlawing non-Anglican worship (Anonymous 1692: A2r, 8). As the Congregationalist William Hooke explained, the death of the witnesses was a figurative one, symbolising a denial of legal and spiritual rights from nonconformists (Hooke 1681: 5–6, 41). Similarly, Hanserd Knollys regarded the witnesses' death as a deprivation 'of their civil Liberties, and the Exercise of their Religion ... taken away by the tyrannical Power of the Beast ... whereby the Witnesses shall be deprived of that Zeal, Vigor, and Courage ... they had formerly manifested ... openly for Christ' (Knollys 1667: Part I, 20). Yet, though the period preceding the destruction of the beast would be 'a time of trouble to the Saints' and the witnesses would be killed, it was also observed that 'a Beast never bites more furiously, and deadly then when dying' (Anonymous 1664: A2r). Not only did the prophecy of the witnesses provide a means to explain and understand the persecution of English Protestant dissent in the later seventeenth century, but it also encouraged the expectation of redemption in the (near) future 'resurrection' of the witnesses, along with their worship forms.

Other prophetic imagery was also suitable to the expression of religious disobedience. Apocalyptic figures like Babylon and the whore were useful in depicting false religious beliefs and persecuting powers. Quaker authors criticised their opponents' beliefs as 'the Waters on which the Whore ... sits' (Bayly 1664: 2r) and as 'Mystery Babylon the Mother of Harlots' (Roe 1666: 11). Over 25 years later, Sebastian Ellythorp still viewed his Quaker convictions as a call 'to come out of Babylon, the false Spirit, the Mother of Harlots ... in whose Skirts is found the Blood of the Saints' (Ellythorp 1692: 11). Presbyterian ministers identified the imposition of religious conformity by force as evidence that the national church was 'that woman drunken with the blood of the Saints [Revelation 17:6]' (Monck et al. 1661: 7). The call to come out of Babylon [Revelation 18:4] was often seen as a warning against participation in corrupt worship forms (see, for example, Anonymous 1664: 15, Beverley 1688, Rosewell 1665: 14). False religious worship was also equated with the mark of the beast, without which no one could buy or sell [Revelation 13:17]. Again, this passage was interpreted figuratively: the mark of the beast was generally seen as being received through 'publick Worship' (Anonymous 1680: 4). The beast's stipulation regarding buying and selling was understood as the religious conditions imposed upon nonconformists, calling for people 'either to joyn with him ... [and] manifest their Conformity, or else they should ... not so much as exercise any civill Commerce or Society with men' (Bagshaw 1661: 24).

Inherent in these interpretations, of course, were criticisms of the Church of England's worship practices, as well as the government that enforced the Anglican monopoly on worship. The Quaker leader George Fox described the beast as 'all these Pulpits, Priests, Tythes, Churches with Crosses in the Church-yards ... and all this making of Ministers by the will of men, by their Schooles and Colledges' (Fox 1660: 8). Another Quaker, Thomas Lawson agreed, finding 'Man-made Ministers' in the locusts of the fifth trumpet [Revelation 9:3] and criticising the 'Antichristian exaction of Tythes' (Lawson 1680: 36, 109). Other nonconformists made similar comparisons. Ejected from his pulpit in 1660, the Baptist minister Robert Brown not only denounced Anglican clergy as the beast and false prophet [Revelation 19:20], but also the kings that implemented the Church's laws as 'drunk by the Whores intoxicating-cup' and 'cruel Butcherers of the Saints' (Brown 1664: 52, 11). In the politically volatile period of the early 1680s, when concerns over papal conspiracy and absolute government were rampant, the Congregational pastor Christopher Ness went further, linking civil and spiritual power together under the influence of the whore of Babylon, and then, more specifically, connecting the beast to 'royal Prerogative' which, in turn, 'brings forth Monstrous Tyranny' (Ness 1681: 29, 30). After the Glorious Revolution, nonconformists could still criticise Anglican submission to royal authority as 'Spiritual Whoredom' (Morland 1690: B1r).

Despite these apocalyptic condemnations of the religious and civil policies of later seventeenth-century English government, moderate nonconformist responses remained true to the stance of nonviolence, with the punishment inflicted upon religious dissenters due to their passive disobedience explained as part of the fulfilment of prophecy. Advising separation from worship practices of 'Babylon', a pamphlet entitled *The Voice of the Shepherd* promised that the time of redemption was approaching, as revealed by the efforts of the beast to 'bitterly vex and oppress the Lord's people with … cruelties' (Anonymous 1663b: 38). Another tract likened the sufferings of nonconformists to the labour pains in the prophecy of the woman who gave birth to a child that would rule all nations [Revelation 12:2–5] (Stuckley 1667: A5r).

Authors reminded nonconformists not only that persecution was a sign of coming prophetic fulfilment, but also that their response to this was detailed in Revelation. The patience of the saints [Revelation 13:10 and 14:12] was held up as the exemplary reaction to affliction. The Presbyterian Thomas Rosewell encouraged his readers to follow the example of patient suffering, promising them that they would 'out-live Antichristian rage and tyranny' (Rosewell 1665: 143, 230). The poet George Wither stressed the purgative quality of suffering, affirming that 'when the Saints have drunk so much of this bitter Cup, as will suffice to cleanse them; Then shall the Scarlet Whore … swallow down the Dreggs' (Wither 1666: C1r). Even at the end of the century *The Great Signs of the Times* argued that the time 'for the Trial of the Faith and patience of the Saints, is not yet ended', and a terrible time of suffering would precede the establishment of Christ's millennial kingdom (Anonymous 1699: B1v, 6).

While the fulfilment of prophecy in the establishment of Christ's earthly kingdom may have been enough justification for English nonconformists' patient suffering, there was, in fact, hope of an even greater reward. As one author put it, those who had suffered for true Christianity would reign with Christ during the thousand-year kingdom, and the saints would serve as 'Officers and Vice Roys … to Rule and Govern there' (Anonymous 1672: 96–7). The ejected minister William Alleine went so far as to depict the saints' millennial rule as absolute, 'above ordinances in the New Jerusalem' (Alleine 1677: 51–2). It was only within the context of this final Christian polity that nonconformists gave voice to their opposition to the earthly governments that had persecuted them. Thomas Brookhouse declared that the defeat of the king and the Church of England in the 1640s was a prelude to their complete destruction in the Millennium. He interpreted the harvest depicted in Revelation 14 [verses 14–20] as a symbol of the 'Rejection and Abolition' of monarchy and the episcopal church, and criticised any understanding of Christ's future earthly kingdom that was based on 'such rotten and weak [political and religious] Foundations' (Brookhouse 1696: 23, 55–6). The Baptist Benjamin Keach went even further: determining that the saints would be rewarded by making them 'Rulers over Cities, over all Nations', they would also 'bind Kings in Chains, and Nobles in Fetters of Iron; and dash them in pieces like Potters Vessels' (Keach 1681: Book II, 261). So, despite nonconformists' inhibitions about commenting on the alteration of existing contemporary political structures, it seems that their perceptions of future reward in the millennial kingdom did allow for punishment of those powers that had been responsible for their persecutions.

The prospect of political change in the accomplishment of apocalyptic prophecy also included the possibility of social changes. Though its premise was a critique of Catholicism as the Babylon mentioned in Revelation, the pamphlet entitled *The Rise and Fall or Degeneracy of the Roman Church* warned the 'Rich' to be generous and charitable toward the poor in order to 'escape the Wrath to come' (Anonymous 1680: 22). The Quaker William Bayly condemned those who were responsible for 'Scoffing and deriding the poor and harmless', and he determined that such people 'by what names or flattering titles soever you are called' were among those who would be punished as Babylon and the whore (Bayly 1662: 4–5). For William Hooke, the 7,000 men slain at the resurrection of the witnesses [Revelation 11:13] would be specifically from among the elite, 'Dukes, and Earls, and Lords, and Knights, and Esquires, and Prelates, and Judges, and Counsellors, and Magistrates, officers &c.' (Hooke 1681: 37). In language reminiscent of the social and political upheavals of the mid seventeenth century, the mystic Jane Lead described the coming Millennium as a time when God's power would 'turn the World upside down' (Lead 1694: 32).

Conclusion

Though the circumstances, world views and language of later seventeenth-century apocalyptic thought is far removed from an early twenty-first-century context, there is still much in it that can explain the continued attraction and power of prophetic beliefs today. The radical and violent apocalyptic beliefs of the 1660s demonstrate that such ideas can motivate and justify resistance to existing civil and religious authorities, as well as validate convictions purposefully cultivated to challenge the orthodoxies of the day. The prophetic interpretations of moderate religious dissenters, whose opposition to existing power structures was less bellicosely inclined, but not necessarily any less resolute, show how perceptions of political, legal and religious oppression can be rationalised by giving that kind of treatment a scriptural validation. The promise of future divine satisfaction – and perhaps even millennial ordination – for patience and suffering under persecution demonstrates why believers in prophecy are willing to tolerate such conditions, as well as accept their placement on the margins of society. Finally, though it has not been emphasised in the preceding examination, it is readily apparent that those who studied and interpreted apocalyptic scripture could claim access to an inspired understanding of the meaning of enigmatic sacred texts. The attraction of such convictions to those who perceive themselves as powerless or unjustly subjugated should not be surprising. The examples of later seventeenth-century apocalyptic justifications for resistance to government confirm that these beliefs can supply powerful inspiration for the critique of and resistance to worldly powers that are judged to be corrupt or misguided, as well as supplying a source of assurance for those who suffered under such authorities. Apocalyptic prophecy provides confirmation for those who appear defeated, evidence that God is still with them and that their reward would come.

There is one final parallel between the later seventeenth-century variety of apocalyptic utterance and those of the twenty-first century. From 1684 to 1702, the Congregational minister Thomas Beverley published over 40 books and pamphlets containing his interpretations of the meaning of the prophecies of the Book of Revelation. Each of these works contained assurances that the fulfilment of apocalyptic prophecy, including the death of the beast and the beginning of the Millennium, would occur in 1697. When his predictions failed to come true, Beverley was forced to admit his mistake from a public pulpit. Though this acknowledgement of his failure must have been humiliating, Beverley, like his early twenty-first-century counterpart, was not finished: after announcing his mistake, Beverley concluded by asserting Christ's return, nonetheless, 't'was not farr off' (Luttrell 1857: 269). It is certain that, had they been available, new billboards would have followed.

References

Alleine, W. 1677. *The Mystery of the Temple and City, Described in the Nine Last Chapters of Ezekiel, Unfolded*. London: B. Harris.

Anonymous. 1661. *A Door of Hope: or, a Call and Declaration for the Gathering Together of the First Fruits unto the Standard of Our Lord Jesus*. [No place]: [no publisher].

Anonymous. 1662. *The Panther-Prophesy, Or, a Premonition to All People, of Sad Calamities and Miseries Like to Befal These Islands*. [No place]: [no publisher].

Anonymous. 1663a. *A Treatise of the Execution of Justice, Wherein is Clearly Proved, That the Execution of Judgement and Justice, is as Well the Peoples as the Magistrates Duty*. [No place]: [no publisher].

Anonymous. 1663b. *The Voice of the Shepherd Through the Clouds to His Lambs on Earth, Shewing Them a Way of Escape from the Dragon's Subtilities.* [No place]: [no publisher].

Anonymous. 1664. *Antipharmacum Saluberrimum; Or, a Serious and Seasonable Caveat to All the Saints in This Hour of Temptation.* [No place]: [no publisher].

Anonymous. 1667. *The Saints Freedom from Tyranny Vindicated: Or, the Power of Pagan Caesars, and Antichristian Kings Examined.* London: [no publisher].

Anonymous. 1672. *Theopolis, or the City of God New Jerusalem, in Opposition to the City of the Nations Great Babylon.* London: T. Ratcliff and N. Thompson.

Anonymous. 1680. *The Rise and Fall or Degeneracy of the Roman Church ... and a Call ... to Come Out of Her.* London: Benjamin Billingsley.

Anonymous. 1690. *Remarks on Dr. Henry More's Expositions of the Apocalypse and Daniel, and upon His Apology: Defended against His Answer to Them.* London: T.M.

Anonymous. 1692. *An Enquiry into the Vision of the Slaying and Rising of the Witnesses, and Falling of the Tenth Part of the City.* London: [no publisher].

Anonymous. 1699. *The Great Signs of the Times.* London: J. Nutt.

Bagshaw, E. 1661. *A Discourse about Christ and Antichrist.* London: Simon Miller.

——. 1669. *The Doctrine of the Kingdom and Personal Reign of Christ Asserted and Explained.* [No place]: [no publisher].

Bayly, W. 1662. *Iacob is Become a Flame and the House of Esav Stubble. Or the Battail Betwixt Michael and the Dragon, in Which the Seed of the Woman is Bruising the Serpents Head.* [No place]: [no publisher].

——. 1664. *The Great and Dreadful Day of the Lord God Almighty.* [No place]: [no publisher].

Berg, E. 2011. Radio Prophet Gone from Airwaves on New Judgment Day Eve. *Reuters* [Online 21 October 2011]. Available at: http://www.reuters.com/article/2011/10/21/us-doomsday-prophet-idUSTRE79K07Z20111021 [accessed: 27 February 2012].

Beverley, T. 1684. *A Calendar of Prophetick Time, Drawn by an Express Scripture-Line; From the Creation to the New Jerusalem.* London: [no publisher].

——. 1688. *The Command of God to His People to Come Out of Babylon, Revel. 18.4.* [No place]: [no publisher].

Breen, T. 2011. End of Days in May? Believers Enter Final Stretch. *MSNBC* [Online 3 January 2011]. Available at: http://www.msnbc.msn.com/id/40885541/ns/us_news-life/t/end-days-may-believers-enter-final-stretch/#.TmDqM83ItcI [accessed: 2 September 2011].

Brookhouse, T. 1696. *The Temple Opened: or, the Great Mystery of the Millennium, and the First Resurrection, Revealed.* London: George Larkin.

Brown, R. 1664. ΜΑΡΤΥΡΙΟΝ ΧΡΙΣΤΙΑΝΟΝ, ... *Or, a Christian and Sober Testimony against Sinfull Complyance.* [No place]: [no publisher].

Capp, B. 1972. *The Fifth Monarchy Men: A Study in Seventeenth-century English Millenarianism.* London: Faber and Faber.

Caryll, J. et al. 1661. *A Renuntiation and Declaration of the Ministers of Congregational Churches and Publick Preachers of the Same Judgement, Living in, and about the City of London: Against the Late Horrid Insurrection and Rebellion Acted in the Said City*. London: Peter and Edward Cole.

Ellythorp, S. 1692. *A Testimony Wherein is Shewed Certain Weighty Reasons Why the National Ministers, Their Way and Practice is Conscientiously Disowned*. London: T. Sowle.

Fox, G. 1660. *The Pearle Found in England*. London: Robert Wilson.

Fox, G. et al. 1661. *A Declaration from the Harmles and Innocent People of God Called Quakers. Against All Plotters and Fighters in the World*. London: Robert Wilson.

Greaves, R. 1986. *Deliver Us from Evil: The Radical Underground in Britain, 1660–1663*. Oxford: Oxford University Press.

Hill, C. 1971. *Antichrist in Seventeenth-Century England*. Oxford: Oxford University Press.

Hooke, W. 1681. *A Discourse Concerning the Witnesses, Relating to the Time, Place, and Manner of Their Being Slain*. London: J. Astwood.

Johnston, W. 2011. *Revelation Restored: The Apocalypse in Later Seventeenth-Century England*. Woodbridge: Boydell Press.

Keach, B. 1681. Τροπολογια: *A Key to Open Scripture-Metaphors*. London: John Richardson and John Darby.

Kiffen, W. et al. 1661. *Apology of Some Commonly Called Anabaptists, on Behalf of Themselves and Others of the Same Judgement with Them: With Their Protestation against the Late Wicked and Most Horrid Treasonable Insurrection and Rebellion Acted in the City of London*. London: Henry Hillis.

Knollys, H. 1667. *Apocalyptical Mysteries, Touching the Two Witnesses, the Seven Vials, and the Two Kingdoms, to Wit, of Christ and of Antichrist Expounded*. London: [no publisher].

——. 1679. *An Exposition of the Eleventh Chapter of the Revelation*. [No place]: [no publisher].

Lawson, T. 1680. *A Treatise Relating to the Call, Work and Wages of the Ministers of Christ; as Also to the Call, Work and Wages of the Ministers of Antichrist*. London: Benjamin Clark.

Lead, J. 1694. *The Enochian Walks with God, Found Out by a Spiritual-Traveller, Whose Face Towards Mount-Sion Above Was Set*, second edition. London: D. Edwards.

Luttrell, N. 1857. *A Brief Historical Relation of State Affairs from September 1678 to April 1714*, Vol. IV. Oxford: Oxford University Press.

Mahoney, J. 2011. Marketers of the Apocalypse: Christian Group's Ads Warn the Second Coming Is Near. *The Globe and Mail* [Toronto], 10 May, A3.

McKinley, J. 2011. An Autumn Date for the Apocalypse. *The New York Times*, 24 May, A18.

Monck, T. et al. 1661. *Sions Groans for Her Distressed, or Sober Endeavours to Prevent Innocent Blood, and to Stablish the Nation in the Best of Settlements.* London: [no publisher].

Morland, I. 1690. *A Short Description of Sion's Inhabitants from the Days of Abel the Righteous; as Also of the Inhabitants of the Bloody City and Harlot-Church, from the Days of Cain the Murderer.* London: [no publisher].

Ness, C. 1681. *The Signs of the Times: Or, Wonderful Signs of Wonderful Times ... All Which Have Hapned Within the Compass of This Last Year.* London: [no publisher].

Roe, D. 1666. *God's Judgments Still Threatned against Thee O England.* [No place]: [no publisher].

Rosewell, T. 1665. *The Causes and Cure of the Pestilence.* London: [no publisher].

Sherwin, W. 1665a. Ειρηνικον: *Or a Peaceable Consideration of Christ's Peaceful Kingdom on Earth to Come.* [No place]: [no publisher].

——. 1665b. Προδρομος: *The Fore-Runner of Christ's Peaceable Kingdom Upon Earth.* London: [no publisher].

Stuckley, L. 1667. *A Gospel-Glasse, Representing the Miscarriages of English Professors ... Or, a Call from Heaven to Sinners and Saints.* London: Randolph Tayler.

Tombes, J. 1664. *Saints No Smiters: Or, Smiting Civil Powers Not the Work of Saints.* London: R.D.

Whitaker, B. 2011. How Harold Camping Marketed the Rapture. *CBS Evening News* [Online 20 May 2011]. Available at: http://www.cbsnews.com/stories/2011/05/20/eveningnews/main20064856.shtml [accessed: 2 September 2011].

Wither, G. 1666. *Ecchoes from the Sixth Trumpet.* [No place]: [no publisher].

Chapter 5

Prophecy: A Perspective from the Early Church and the Contemporary Experience of a Methodist Minister

Andrew Maguire

It should be stated at the outset that the early Christians did not see a prophet simply as somebody who predicted the future. The definition of the New Testament Greek word 'προφήτης / prophētēs' in the Greek lexicon widely used by New Testament scholars (the Bauer/Danker BDAG lexicon) is, 'A proclaimer or expounder of divine matters or concerns that could not ordinarily be known except by special revelation'. This does not explicitly mention the future. I will reflect further on that later.

Nevertheless there can be little doubt that the early Christians did feel that their prophets (and those of the Hebrew Scriptures) could indeed sometimes predict the future. So in the book of Acts of the Apostles Agabus is described as a prophet, and in Acts 11:27–8 he predicts a famine. This was a fairly straightforward prediction of a future event.

There were at least two ways in which early Christians used predictive prophecy with significant reference to their faith:

1. Christocentric interpretation of the Hebrew Scriptures as predictive of Christ;
2. discerning predictions of the 'end times' in passages from the Hebrew Scriptures, in some of the utterances of Jesus and in some of their own writings.

I will discuss each of these categories of prophecy with reference to canonical and non-canonical early Christian writings. I will show that prophets were also seen as 'forth-tellers', not simply 'fore-tellers'. With reference to a second-century controversy I will explore how authority in the early church transitioned from that of prophets and apostles to that of a canon of scripture interpreted through ecumenical councils and bishops. The literature referred to comes from a period which was formative for the Christian tradition when Christianity itself was a 'new religious movement'.

The second part of the chapter will consider areas of contemporary controversy and debate about prophecy and the Christian churches where there is some resonance with the issues dealt with in the first part.

Prophecy and Early Christianity

The Hebrew Scriptures Interpreted as Predictive of Christ

There is a profound sense in which the early Christians felt that their faith was the fulfilment of prophecy, particularly the prophecies which, from their faith perspective, they discerned in the Hebrew Scriptures. A sermon preached by the Apostle Peter on the day of Pentecost is recorded in Acts. The central point of this sermon is that the venerable King of Israel, David, had looked ahead and prophesied the resurrection of Christ. Peter quotes some words from a psalm: 'My body also will live in hope, because you will not abandon me to the grave, nor will you let your Holy One see decay'[1] (Acts 2:26–7: Psalm 16:9–10).

Not all expounders of the Hebrew Scriptures would interpret it in this way, but for Peter, as the sermon is presented in Acts, the meaning is clear. The sweet singer of Israel, King David the psalmist, foresaw the resurrection of Christ.

Many other examples could be given. The 'suffering servant' passages from the book of Isaiah (for example, Isaiah 53) are a classic case where the servant described there is seen as a foreshadowing or a prophecy of Christ. So in the second chapter of the First Epistle of Peter, verses 24 and 25, it is written: 'He himself bore our sins in his body on the tree, so that we might die to sins and live for righteousness; by his wounds you have been healed. For you were like sheep going astray, but now you have returned to the Shepherd and Overseer of your souls.' If you read Isaiah 53 alongside that then the resonance and the parallel are clear. Isaiah writes that 'We all, like sheep, have gone astray' and says of the servant 'By his wounds we are healed' and 'he bore the sins of many' (verses 6, 5 and 12).

It is also interesting to note how several commentators, ancient and modern, have discerned similarities between, for example, the way the Jesus story is told in the Gospels and some of the narratives in the Hebrew Scripture. A case in point is how there are similarities between the Hebrew Scriptures' description of the life of Moses in the book of Exodus and Matthew's gospel's description of the life of Jesus (see Table 5.1).

---

[1]   The translation is from the *New International Version*, as are all scripture quotations in this chapter.

Table 5.1   Biblical description of the lives of Jesus and Moses

Hebrew Scriptures	Matthew's Gospel
Pharaoh, who enslaved the people of Israel, was ruler in Egypt when Moses was born. (Exod. 1:8–11 and 2:1–2)	When Jesus was born (Matt. 1:18–25), a wicked king was on the throne. (Matt. 2:1–12)
Pharaoh ordered Hebrew children to be killed. (Exod. 1:22)	King Herod, upon learning of Christ's birth, ordered infants to be slaughtered. (Matt. 2:13–18)
Moses had an amazing escape. (Exod. 2:1–10)	The Holy Family received angelic guidance and fled to Egypt. (Matt. 2:13)
Moses was hidden in the bulrushes by the river. (Exod. 2:3–4).	Jesus descended into the waters of baptism. (Matt. 3:13–17)
Moses spent time in the wilderness. (Exod. 3:1–2)	Jesus spent time in the wilderness. (Matt. 4:1–11)
Moses received the divine law on Mount Sinai. (Exod. 19:20–21:1)	Jesus delivered the sermon on the mount. (Matt. 5–7)
Moses led his people from slavery to freedom. (Exod.)	Jesus is to save people from their sins. (Matt. 1:21)

The rough correlation with the story of Moses and the exodus is patent. There are differences too: Moses fled *from* Egypt, Jesus *to* Egypt; Moses was an adult when he fled, Jesus a child. So we have to be careful not to overplay this. But there has been a long tradition of seeing this kind of typology in Matthew – from fourth-century Persian and Syrian Church fathers like Aphraates and Ephraim, up to present day commentators (Allison 2008).

What is going on here? For Matthew, did Moses somehow prefigure Jesus? Is he saying that Jesus is the new Moses who will lead his people to a new freedom? He seems to be suggesting that the hints of divine glory glimpsed in Moses are seen fully in Jesus: this might be seen as a kind of prophecy. It has not been uncommon in Christian tradition to see Moses, in his teaching role and in his reflecting the glory of God, as foreshadowing Jesus. For Moses reflecting God's glory see Exodus 34:29 and 35 and Matthew 17:1–3.

Discerning Christ in the Hebrew Scriptures could be taken to intriguing extremes in some of the non-canonical early Christian literature. An instance of this is found in the *Epistle of Barnabas* (Holmes 2007: 380). This epistle is generally dated between 70 and 135. Authorship by the Barnabas who appears several times in the New Testament book of Acts is unlikely. The epistle commends an 'allegorical' approach to the interpretation of Hebrew Scriptures. I will give an example that sees the first two letters of the name of Jesus and also the cross in the number 318. In Greek (and the author of *Barnabas* was clearly working with the

Septuagint Greek[2] translation of the Hebrew Scriptures) the letters of the alphabet can have numerical value (alpha to iota = 1–10, kappa to rho = 20–100, sigma = 200, tau = 300. So eta = 8, iota = 10, tau = 300) and Iota and Eta are the first two letters in Greek of the name Jesus. In *Barnabas* chapter 9 we read,

> Abraham, who first instituted circumcision, looked forward in the spirit to Jesus when he circumcised, having received the teaching of the three letters. For it says: 'And Abraham circumcised ten and eight and three hundred men of his household.' What, then, is the knowledge that was given to him? Observe that it mentions the 'ten and eight' first, and then after an interval the 'three hundred'. As for the 'ten and eight', the Iota is ten and the Eta is eight; thus you have 'Jesus'. And because the cross, which is shaped like the T, was destined to convey grace, it mentions also the 'three hundred'. So he reveals Jesus in two letters and the cross in the other one (Holmes 2007: 409).

Barnabas says that nobody has ever learned from him a more reliable word. I have already observed that the entire argument rests on the Greek version of the Hebrew Scriptures, the Septuagint, often used by the early Christians, and not the original Hebrew. Barnabas gives here what is a striking example of an approach to scripture which was also followed by other early Christian writers. One of the most prolific commentators on the Bible was Origen in the third century. Robert J. Daly, writing in the *Encyclopedia of Christianity* (1988: 836), says in relation to him: 'Every word of scripture is sacred because, beyond the literal or historical meaning, which is not always present in every passage, stands always a *spiritual meaning*, which is Christ, if not literally then at least metaphorically, typologically, or allegorically.'

End Times Prophecies

For early Christians the Hebrew Scriptures were inspired scripture, just as they had been for Jesus. When the writer of the Second Letter to Timothy speaks of all scripture being inspired (2 Timothy 3:16) he is talking of Hebrew Scripture. As well as containing passages which spoke to them of Christ, the Hebrew Scriptures also contained passages speaking of how God would act in the world in future. Some of these passages are beautiful visionary passages of a time of peace when swords will be beaten into ploughshares (Isaiah 2:1–4). Others are more mysterious visions belonging to a genre of literature known as apocalyptic (for example, chapter 7 and following in the book of Daniel). Such literature contains strange visions of beasts and creatures. When the visions are interpreted (in Daniel itself) they are said to refer to kingdoms that are to appear on the earth.

---

[2]   According to legend this translation was made by 72 Jewish elders (hence the name 'Septuagint', meaning 'seventy') at the request of Ptolemy II Philadelphus (283–246 BCE). Note based on article in *Encyclopedia of Early Christianity*, second edition, 1048–9.

In the New Testament passages of a somewhat similar nature are found, for example, in the book of Revelation, in parts of Paul's epistles such as 2 Thessalonians 2:2 and in the gospels on the lips of Jesus in passages such as Mark 13, Matthew 24 and Luke 21.

This literature raises difficult issues of interpretation. In the cases of Daniel and Revelation some maintain that the 'prophecies' are actually a kind of code referring to events going on at the time of writing, while others prefer to see detailed prophecies of the future, potentially being fulfilled in their own times. A brief and helpful account of the former relating both to Daniel and to Revelation can be found in *The Revelation of Saint John The Divine* (Preston and Hanson 1949: 12–17). The writers argue that, although Daniel might appear to be detailed prophecy of the future written during exile in Babylon (586–536 BCE) it is actually a 'tract for the times' written in the second century BCE when the Syrian king, Antiochus Epiphanes, tried to suppress the Jewish religion and erected a heathen altar in the temple at Jerusalem. Revelation, it is argued, is also a tract for the times. 'Just as in *Daniel* Nebuchadnezzar stands for Antiochus Epiphanes, so in *Revelation* Babylon stands for Rome' (Preston and Hanson 1949: 14). The veiled and cryptic language might help the Christians not to get into trouble, but for those who had ears to hear it encouraged them to recognise that their time of persecution would not last forever.

Prophets in the Writing of St Paul and Prophecy as 'Forth-telling'

In 1 Corinthians 12, verses 27 and 28 St Paul gives a list of some of the important offices in the Church.

> Now you are the body of Christ, and each one of you is a part of it. And in the church God has appointed first of all apostles, second prophets, third teachers, then workers of miracles, also those having gifts of healing, those able to help others, those with gifts of administration, and those speaking in different kinds of tongues.

It is noteworthy that the prophets have a very high place. They are second in the list, but are not quite on a par with the apostles. Space does not permit a long digression on apostles[3] and who they were and what it meant to be an apostle, but the prophets were up very close with them.

In 1 Corinthians 14 Paul says a little more about prophets in the Church as he writes about the relative value of 'speaking in tongues' (ecstatic utterance in an unfamiliar language) and 'prophecy'. It is clear that Paul has a preference for prophecy, particularly if there are visitors in the congregation. In 14:2–3 he speaks

---

[3]   Primarily the 12 disciples chosen by Jesus were 'apostles', but the title could be extended to others. St Paul insisted that he was an 'apostle' to the Gentiles. For a helpful brief article see *Encyclopedia of Early Christianity*, second edition, 88–90.

of tongues and prophecy thus: 'For anyone who speaks in a tongue does not speak to men but to God. Indeed, no-one understands him; he utters mysteries with his spirit. But everyone who prophesies speaks to men for their strengthening, encouragement and comfort.'

In his commentary on 1 Corinthians Nigel Watson states that by 'prophecy' Paul means 'primarily a Spirit-inspired declaration of the will of God for this congregation at this present time' (1992: 144). This is very much in the territory of the definition of prophecy given in the BDAG Greek lexicon, with no necessary reference to the future. It is very different from the apocalyptic visions of the book of Revelation. The different styles of 'prophecy' can, however, exist alongside each other. While the book of Revelation is full of passages in an apocalyptic genre which, as has been seen, are interpreted by some as giving clues to the 'end times' it also has, in chapters 2 and 3, letters to seven churches which can be seen as prime examples of this style of prophecy described by Paul in 1 Corinthians. Paul himself in the Thessalonian epistles has passages in a more apocalyptic style (1 Thessalonians 4:13–15:11 and 2 Thessalonians 2:1–12). If it is accepted that apocalyptic literature can itself be a 'tract for the times' then the two come even closer together.

Other Non-Canonical Early Christian Writings Relevant to the Theme of Prophecy with Reference to Their Acceptance or Otherwise into the Canon of Scripture

The Shepherd of Hermas (Holmes 2007: 454) is a long work full of prophetic teaching and visions – it probably dates from the late first century to early second century. It begins with 'visions' which are mediated and explained by an angelic figure. The reason why the work has the rather strange title is because a key figure in the book, the 'angel of repentance' appears to Hermas in the form of a shepherd.

It is full of 'divine matters that became known by special revelation' – to refer back to the BDAG lexicon definition of 'prophet'. Hermas begins with five visions of things heavenly, and then the shepherd, the angel of repentance, commands him to write down the commandments. Michael Holmes says of the Visions in *The Shepherd* that their genre is that of a Jewish-Christian apocalypse except that their contents refer not to the end times but rather to the 'possibility of repentance because the end is not yet' (2007: 445).

The Shepherd is extremely well attested in the early literature so demonstrating its popularity. Several of the early Church fathers treated it as scripture.[4] Most of it is found at the end of the important fourth-century biblical manuscript – *Codex Sinaiticus*. This is the earliest surviving complete copy of the New Testament and it contains at the end both *The Epistle of Barnabas* and *The Shepherd*.

---

[4] Irenaeus and Clement of Alexandria accepted it as scripture, as did Origen and Tertullian for a while. Athanasius quoted and used it in the fourth century and his contemporary Didymus the Blind included it in his canon of scripture.

So this genre of literature was evidently popular and held in high esteem, but we should note that it did not actually finally make it into the canon of scripture. Eusebius (*Historia Ecclesiastica*, 3.25) in the early fourth century rejects it, and although Athanasius quotes from it and gives it a favourable mention, it does not make it into his official list of 27 books given in his 39th *Festal Letter* of 367 – the first time all 27 books of the New Testament are included in a canonical list together.

So there was clearly debate about the place of such prophetic literature among the trustworthy books to be read by Christians.

The book of Revelation, which did make it into the canon, is another case in point. Here too, as we have seen, we have divine revelations – and the contents of the book are described at the beginning as 'the words of this prophecy'. The classic thing to say here would be that the book of Revelation made it into the canon because in it the Church perceived God's true word and revelation. It may also have been because it was thought to be associated with the apostle John, while poor old Hermas could claim no such status. But even with Revelation the journey into the canon was not straightforward. Eusebius, Bishop of Caesarea, probably writing in the early fourth century, says, in describing the canonical books, that some reject the apocalypse of John (*Historia Ecclesiastica*, 3.25). Gregory of Nazianzus, the distinguished Cappadocian Father writing towards the end of the fourth century, wrote a catalogue of the canonical books in iambic verse.[5] He does not include Revelation and concludes by saying 'If there is any besides the ones in my list, it is not among the genuine books.'[6]

Another piece of early Christian literature, *The Didache* (Holmes 2007: 344), talks, as did St Paul, about the apostles and the prophets almost in the same breath. With many Christian documents the dating can be controversial. *The Didache* is probably from the latter part of the first century. When describing itinerant apostles and prophets it says in chapter 11: 'He is not to stay for more than one day, unless there is need, in which case he may stay another. But if he stays three days, he is a false prophet' (Holmes 2007: 363). Clearly you could have too much of a good thing!

Prophets were not to pursue their calling with a view to financial gain. 'If he asks for money he is a false prophet' (Holmes 2007: 363). Nor were the prophets supposed to ask for their food. A rather odd passage has this: 'Any prophet who orders a meal in the spirit shall not partake of it; if he does, he is a false prophet' (Holmes 2007: 363). So the prophets were not supposed to ask for money or food, and yet the Church was to respond to them with generosity. 'Take all the first

---

[5]   *Poemata Dogmatica*, Book I, Section I, Carmen XII, which can be found in Migne, *Patrologiae Cursus Completus*, vol. 37, cols 471–4.

[6]   Some also argue that another reason for the apparent reluctance to include Revelation among the canonical books was its coded criticism of Rome which from the time of Constantine in the fourth century (except during the reign of Julian 'the apostate') was a strong supporter of 'Catholic' Christianity.

fruits of the produce of the wine press and the threshing floor, and of the cattle and sheep, and give these first fruits to the prophets, for they are your high priests' (Holmes 2007: 365). So there was a fascinating relationship between the Christian people and their apostles and prophets.

Transition from Emphasis on the Authority of Prophets to Emphasis on the Canon of Scripture Interpreted through Ecumenical Councils and Bishops

We have seen that in the fourth century Eusebius and Gregory of Nazianzus expressed concerns about prophetic literature. Concerns about the writings and utterances of prophets were also expressed much further back. By the time of Ignatius in the early second century, at least in the area of his activity, we sense a transition from the leadership of 'apostles and prophets' to the leadership of 'bishops, presbyters and deacons'; from that kind of approach which valued the direct divine revelation mediated through the prophet, to a more established form of church life where officially appointed local ministers, and particularly bishops, became the focus of authority. Ignatius below is writing to Christians in Smyrna:

> Let no one do anything pertaining to the Church apart from the bishop. Let that eucharist be considered valid which is under the bishop or him to whom he commits it. Wheresoever the bishop appears, there let the people be, even as wheresoever Christ Jesus is, there is the Catholic Church. It is not lawful apart from the bishop either to baptize or to hold a love-feast. But whatsoever he approves, that also is well-pleasing to God, that everything which you do may be secure and valid (J.H. Srawley translation [*Epistles of St Ignatius*, 1919: 96–8] – slightly altered).

We cannot say that this was the pattern of church life everywhere in the early second century, but it was certainly how Ignatius of Antioch saw things.

As ever things were not monochrome. The prophets were not going to be so easily silenced. So let me conclude the section of the chapter about early Christianity with reference to a second-century movement that attracts quite a lot of interest. That is 'Montanism'.[7]

The Montanists got their name from a Christian named, unsurprisingly, Montanus, a figure about whom we do not know a great deal. Montanus was said to have come from the town of Pepuza, a small and rather insignificant place in the province of Phrygia, in what is now west-central Turkey. He saw himself as a prophet who received revelations directly from God. Associated with him were two prophetesses Maximilla and Prisca. We know of their prophetic utterances

---

[7]   Sources for information on Montanism and the Church's concerns about it are: Eusebius, *Historia Ecclesiastica*, 5.3.4, 5.14–18; Epiphanius, *Panarion*, 48; Jerome, *Letter* 41.

almost entirely from quotations in the writings of later, mainly hostile authors. None of their own writings survive.

Ethically, the Montanists were strict, insisting, for example, that a Christian should not remarry after the death of a spouse but should be completely devoted to the Church instead. These strict ethics may have derived from the Montanists' view that the end of all things was near and that people needed to prepare for it. The Montanists urged people to prepare to meet their maker, fully recognising that this might be a prospect arousing considerable anxiety. In particular, Montanus believed that the new Jerusalem was to descend from heaven to Pepuza. That is where the Kingdom of God would arrive and Christ would then reign. Christians should devote themselves to its coming, standing up for their faith, even to the point of being martyred if necessary. Moreover, this end of the age was to arrive very soon. In the words of the prophetess Maximilla, 'After me there will be no more prophecy, but the End' (Epiphanius, *Panarion*, 48.2.4).

The faith of Montanism was in many ways orthodox, and the great Latin Christian writer Tertullian became associated with the Montanists. But alongside the apparently orthodox faith there were these claims to personal divine revelations and the prophecy of the end. The end, however, did not come and that created problems. What do you make of prophets whose predictions about the future do not come true? And what do you make of somebody who claims direct divine revelation but whose credentials you are inclined not to trust completely?

Probably because of issues and questions like these the prophets became marginalised. Montanism was condemned (for example by Eleutherus, Bishop of Rome 174–89). Such claims to personal divine revelation could be seen as dubious and risky. The future for 'orthodox' Christianity lay more with an authoritative canon of scripture interpreted through ecumenical councils and bishops. The trustworthiness of claims to direct personal divine revelation has been a recurring topic for discussion and controversy in the life of the Church which continues to wrestle with the question of where true authority lies. At one end of the spectrum are churches (for example Independent Evangelical Churches) who believe that each individual congregation can have authority for its own life (though often within a traditional, strictly defined statement of faith) and where individual members may be encouraged to share a word of prophecy in the spirit of 1 Corinthians 14:1. At the other end of the spectrum are churches like the Roman Catholic Church with its strong central 'magisterium' focused on the Pope and with its emphasis on the central importance of remaining in communion with the Pope and the Church of which he is the earthly head.

Related Themes and Issues in the Life of the Contemporary Church

Discerning Christ in the Hebrew Scriptures

It is interesting to reflect on how some of these themes are played out in more contemporary discussions. For the early Christian writers it was important to demonstrate that the Hebrew Scriptures pointed to Christ. While most Christians today might not be as ingenious as the *Epistle of Barnabas* in so perceiving Christ, there is no doubt that there is a presumption that the Hebrew Scriptures point to and are fulfilled in Christ. One only need attend a service of nine lessons and carols with the traditional readings or attend worship during Passiontide, when one is likely to hear about the Suffering Servant in Isaiah 53, to be reminded that this is so. There is little sense of there being any 'polemic' in this and hundreds of years of often uneasy co-existence have made each tradition very much aware of the other's interpretative traditions.

Christians have been reminded through the work of scholars like Geza Vermez (1973) of the 'Jewishness' of Jesus and a lot of work has been done in Jewish–Christian dialogue to emphasise that the Hebrew Scriptures can and should be understood and interpreted in their own integrity. Two examples from a Roman Catholic perspective are given below:

> It is true then, and should be stressed, that the Church and Christians read the Old Testament in the light of the event of the dead and risen Christ and that on these grounds there is a Christian reading of the Old Testament which does not necessarily coincide with the Jewish reading. Thus Christian identity and Jewish identity should be carefully distinguished in their respective reading of the Bible. But this detracts nothing from the value of the Old Testament in the Church and does nothing to hinder Christians from profiting discerningly from the traditions of Jewish reading (Vatican 1985: II.6).

> The misguided interpretations of the prophets as directly foretelling the coming of Christ is really part of a general Christian misuse of the Hebrew Scriptures. We in the Church have tended to look on the Hebrew Scriptures only as prelude, only as giving us glimpses of the New Testament message. We have generally failed to appreciate its spiritual richness in its own right. There exists a mandate for Catholics to move away from this narrow approach to the Hebrew Scriptures which not only leads to negative portrayals of Judaism but hampers our own spiritual development (Pawlikowski and Wilde 1991: 3).

'End Times' Prophecy

If 'Discerning Christ in the Hebrew Scriptures' is an area of discussion less controversial than it once was, there is an area related to 'end times' prophecy where discussion can become heated – not only theologically but also politically.

Christian Zionism, for example, has become and remains something of a hot potato. We have seen that 'end times' prophecies have featured in Christian discourse from early days. Many others have followed the Montanists in expressing in different generations and in different ways the conviction that the end is nigh. The Christian preacher haranguing people in the high street and wandering up and down with a placard proclaiming 'the end is nigh' has become something of a figure of fun, but there can be a more serious side. Christian Zionism sees biblical prophecies fulfilled in the return of the Jews to the Holy Land and the establishment of the state of Israel. There is a variety of ways in which biblical texts are presented and interpreted to 'prove' this, although there is not space in this chapter to explore this in detail. Significant figures include the Irish-born evangelist John Nelson Darby (1800–1882), the founder of dispensationalism, and David Pawson (born 1930) who has written the books *When Jesus Returns* (1995) and *Defending Christian Zionism* (2008). An underlying concern on the part of critics of Christian Zionism is that a sense of the inevitability of certain prophesied events occurring in divine providence undermines the search for peace and the possibility of a two state solution in the Middle East.

The National Council of Churches in the USA has been to the fore in a critique of a narrow form of Christian Zionism. A leaflet, *Why We Should Be Concerned About Christian Zionism?* was issued in December 2008. The leaflet sees Christian Zionism as 'a dangerous movement that distorts the teachings of the Church, fosters fear and hatred of Muslims and non-Western Christians, and has negative consequences for Middle East Peace'. Concerns expressed are:

1. an excessive focus on the movement's own 'end time' hopes;
2. the promotion of negative stereotypes of Muslims and Middle Easterners, including Middle Eastern Christians;
3. a vision of Israelis and Palestinians not as neighbours to be loved, but as pawns in a cosmic drama;
4. that the theology of Christian Zionism is not based on traditional Christian doctrine but on nineteenth-century innovations.

Discerning the 'True' Prophets (Forth-tellers)

Prophecy as 'forth-telling' continues to be manifested in the life of the Church, but sometimes shows up deep divisions. In churches of a Pentecostal tradition where expression of the 'gifts of the spirit' is encouraged it is expected that a 'divine' word may be given through a member of the congregation (as in 1 Corinthians 14 referred to above).

In other churches there may be a sense of the rightness of responding to an eloquent preacher who challenges the congregation to seek God's justice. A good instance of the latter still in recent memory was when mainstream churches took up the cause of the anti-Apartheid movement inspired by men like Trevor Huddleston and Desmond Tutu. In this case there was consonance between the voice of the preacher and the wider councils of the Church. The same might be said in regard to the challenge to care for the environment where in general the call to be 'good stewards' of God's creation is heeded.

But there is not always happy agreement between the voice of the individual prophet and the wider councils of the Church. It is well known that in formulating its approach towards ethics in the area of human sexuality the Church struggles. One 'prophetic' voice, drawing attention to verses from books such as Leviticus (18:22 and 20:13) and Romans (1:27–8), stresses that the physical expression of gay sexuality cannot be considered within acceptable norms of Christian behaviour. Another 'prophetic' voice might remind us of how Jesus accepted all kinds of people and how he often came into conflict with the legal and moral rigorists of his day and emphasised the importance of compassion. The different prophetic voices tend to find affirmation and reinforcement from within their own like-minded communities, but attempts at dialogue across theological and cultural divides can be very frosty with little meeting of minds.

Such prophetic voices draw inspiration from the canon of scripture and may both challenge and be challenged by the councils of the Church as the Church seeks to express the '*sensus fidelium*', i.e. doctrinal truth recognised by the whole body of the faithful. For better or worse the faithful are not infrequently divided into blocks, '*sectae fidelium*' maybe, who eye each other with caution and suspicion. The Church is here challenged by its own scriptures which speak of the God who 'was in Christ reconciling the world to himself' (2 Corinthians 5.19) and of the Christ who destroys the 'dividing wall of hostility' (Ephesians 2.14). It often feels as though prophetic voices are still needed to call the Church to be faithful in its life and practice to principles and insights which are central in its scriptures.

References

Allison, D.C. Jr. 2008. Matthew and the History of Its Interpretation. *The Expository Times*, 120(1), 1–7.

Athanasius. 367. The 39th *Festal Letter* can be found at: Greek text in Migne, J.P. 1857. *Patrologiae Cursus Completus, Series Graeca* vol. 26, col. 1436. Belgium: Turnholti. Translation in Schaff, P. and Wace, H. 1892. *Nicene and Post-Nicene Fathers, Second Series, Volume 4, Athanasius: Select Works and Letters*. Peabody, MA: Hendrickson, 551.

Danker, F.W. and Bauer, W. 2001. *Greek-English Lexicon of the New Testament and Other Early Christian Literature*. Chicago, IL: University of Chicago Press.

Darby, J.N. 1800–1882. Many of the works of Darby can be found online. Available at: http://www.plymouthbrethren.org/byauthor/5/john_nelson_darby [accessed: 5 March 2012].

Epiphanius. Fourth century. *Panarion (Adversus Haereses)*. For the Greek text see Holl, K. 1915, 1922, 1933. *Epiphanius, Bände 1–3: Ancoratus und Panarion [Die griechischen christlichen Schriftsteller]*. Leipzig: Hinrichs. For an English translation see Williams, F. 1997 (two volumes). *The Panarion of Epiphanius of Salamis*. Leiden: Brill.

Eusebius. c. 260–340. *Historia Ecclesiastica*. The Greek text and English translation can be found in Lake, K. and Lawlor, H.J. 1926 and 1932. *Eusebius, The Ecclesiastical History*. London: Heinemann. Cambridge, MA: Harvard University Press.

Ferguson, E. (ed.) 1988. *Encyclopedia of Early Christianity*, second edition. New York and London: Garland. Articles on 'Apostle' (Everett Ferguson), 'Origen' (Robert J. Daly, S.J.) and 'Septuagint' (Claude Cox) are cited in the chapter and footnotes.

Holmes, M.W. 2007. *The Apostolic Fathers*. Grand Rapids, MI: Baker Academic.

Jerome. c. 347–420. For the Latin text of *Letter 41* see Migne, J.P. 1845. *Patrologiae Cursus Completus, Series Prima* vol. 22, col. 474. For an English translation see Schaff, P. and Wace, H. (eds) 1893. *Nicene and Post-Nicene Fathers, Second Series, Volume 6, Jerome: Letters and Select Works*. Peabody, MA: Hendrickson, 55.

National Council of Churches (USA). 2008. *Why We Should Be Concerned about Christian Zionism*? [Online]. Available at: http://www.ncccusa.org/pdfs/christianzionismbrochure.pdf [accessed: 5 March 2012].

Pawlikowski, J.T. and Wilde, J.A. 1991. *When Catholics Speak about Jews*. Chicago, IL: Liturgy Training Publications.

Pawson, J.D. 1995. *When Jesus Returns*. London: Hodder and Stoughton.

——. 2008. *Defending Christian Zionism*. Bristol: Terra Nova Publications.

Preston, R.H. and Hanson, A.T. 1949. *The Revelation of Saint John the Divine*. London: SCM.

Srawley, J.H. 1919. *The Epistles of St Ignatius Bishop of Antioch*. London: SPCK.

Vatican Commission for Religious Relations with the Jews. 1985. *Notes on the Correct Way to Present the Jews and Judaism in Preaching and Catechesis in the Roman Catholic Church*. Vatican, Holy See: Commission for Religious Relations with the Jews.

Vermez, G. 1973. *Jesus the Jew*. London: Collins.

Watson, N.W. 1992. *The First Epistle to the Corinthians*. London: Epworth Press.

PART II
Perennial Prophecy in
Mainstream Traditions

One of the intentions of this volume is to highlight the pervasiveness of prophetic beliefs throughout human cultures. This section contains chapters on prophetic beliefs in contemporary Pentecostal Christianity, in Islam, Hinduism and Tibetan Buddhism (and there is a case study on Judaism in Chapter 3). It also includes a chapter on prophecies deriving from secular sources. While this section could have been expanded almost infinitely, including, for example, chapters on Ancient Greece or Rome and on contemporary Chinese 'folk' religion, we have decided to focus on some of the major world traditions to illustrate our point. Through looking at aspects of how prophecy is used within the main world traditions illustrated in this volume, we also hope to demonstrate a continuum between group millennialism and more mundane, prophetic inspiration. We argue that one of the reasons millennial groups can appeal to a minority of the population is because there is a wider experience of prophecy in many belief systems, both sacred and secular.

Margaret Poloma and Matthew Lee, in Chapter 6, trace the divergent interpretations of prophecy within the Christian tradition over its 2,000-year history. Covering similar ground to Maguire in Chapter 5, but from an etic, academic perspective, they trace the way in which prophecy had a central place in early Christianity (represented by Paul's statement in 1 Corinthians 14) but increasingly came under the control of religious authorities. Until the early twentieth century, they argue, prophecy remained the domain of the marginalised (as Johnston argues was the case in late seventeenth-century England in Chapter 4). However, from the development of Pentecostalism from the 1900s onwards (tracing its origin to the Asuza Street Revival in Los Angeles, 1906–1909), prophecy is once again in the 'mainstream' of Christianity, as this style of Christian worship has emerged as the fastest growing approach to Christianity with an estimate of over half a billion followers globally.

Poloma and Lee provide a case study of the New Apostolic Reformation, which is at the forefront of the 'Five Fold Ministry' which seeks to raise up apostles and prophets to complement the more widely accepted roles of teachers, evangelists and pastors, and which emphasises the charismata, or gifts of the spirit, to a greater extent than other traditions. Within this tradition, they argue, emphasis is not on prophecy as fore-telling but as forth-telling, as an encouraging word that God has given to them in order to 'edify, encourage and bless others' (p. 82). These words are not accompanied with the drama of fore-telling prophecies; they are spoken, either in public or private, and are experienced as an interaction of God and individual, frequently leading to benevolent service, as Poloma and Lee's interview data suggests. Poloma and Lee thus emphasise the 'everyday' role of prophecy in an individual's experience of and relationship with God and the changes in behaviour and relationality that can lead on from this.

In Chapter 7, Hugh Beattie explores the origins of Mahdist belief in the first centuries of Islam, traces its interpretations in the medieval and early modern periods and its contemporary manifestation, especially amongst Shia Muslims in Iran. Beattie explains how Mahdist beliefs became more central in the Shia traditions (which emphasised the period of peace and justice that the Mahdi would usher in) than the Sunni traditions. However, interpretations of the belief became important in both traditions in particular political and social contexts (emphasising Johnston's argument in Chapter 4 that the context in which religious prophecies are formed and maintained must be recognised). Beattie considers the resurgence of Mahdist beliefs in revolutionary political movements in a broad range of specific contexts, considering tenth-century North Africa; early twelfth-century North-West Africa and Spain; late fifteenth- and sixteenth-century Iran and India; and nineteenth-century Africa. Beattie then goes on to consider some of the roles Mahdist beliefs have played in contemporary Iran and Iraq, from the Iranian Revolution of 1978–79, to the Iraqi 'Me(a)hdi Army' which clashed with US forces in 2004, to the rhetoric of the Iranian President Mahmoud Ahmadinejad. Beattie concludes that whilst millennialism might be most popular or visible as a 'vehicle for discontent' in the political sphere, it has also been used by those in power to legitimate their rule. Mahdism is not always oppositional, he reminds us. Theodicy can tie in to political action and confrontation, and other forms of engagement, but may also encourage withdrawal and acceptance of suffering.

In Chapter 8, Luis González-Reimann traces the development of a particular form of prophetic belief within the Hindu traditions of India. González-Reimann suggests that whilst there is no direct equivalent of the Abrahamic 'End-times', a Hindu idea that has some parallels is the belief in the succession of four declining world ages called *yugas*. The *yugas* are understood to characterise society by its degree of *dharma* (proper social and religious conduct) and each marks a decline in conduct before reaching the *Kali Yuga*, the lowest age, and then beginning again with the *Kṛta Yuga* or *Satya Yuga*. González-Reimann shows how belief in the *yugas* emerged in the centuries surrounding the beginning of the Common Era, when the *Kali Yuga* was seen as an explanation for current events including foreign incursion into the subcontinent and internal religious transformations. He illustrates how this interpretation was continued in later centuries, in certain time periods in Indian history which were marked by political and social upheaval, including the introduction of Islam and Christianity into India. González-Reimann also shows how the idea of a saviour-type figure (Kalki) became combined with *yuga* beliefs early on, and was again invoked under these particular historical circumstances; how this saviour-figure was expected to arrive during the difficult *Kali Yuga*, defeat the foreign invaders and heretics and introduce the new 'Golden Age'. González-Reimann highlights the renewed impetus of this idea in the nineteenth and early twentieth centuries by new Hindu and Hindu-inspired groups and individuals, including the Theosophical Society, Swami Vivekananda and Mahatma Gandhi. These beliefs thus inspired some of the movements for Indian Independence. They have continued to be a rallying point for expectations of a better future, and have become part of global 'New Age' ideas.

Christopher Bell, in Chapter 9, highlights the importance of divination, prophecy and oracles in Tibetan Buddhism. Bell shows that from the pre-Buddhist religious tradition of Tibet, the Bön religion, through the founding of Buddhism in Tibet in the seventh century, into the present day, prophecy has been central. Not only is the landscape considered to be replete with hidden texts and objects (termed 'treasures') waiting to be discovered through prophetic revelations, but various material objects are used in contemporary divination practices. Bell traces the diversity of these practices before noting that religious authorities have often considered them to be superstitious. These authorities have placed greater emphasis on the prophetic nature of the Buddhist canon, using Buddhist scripture to find predictions, often to legitimate the establishment of a sect, monastery or political ruler. Oracles, Bell writes, span the continuum of the divination of the laity and the monastic's focus on textual prophecy. This chapter shows then not only the great diversity of prophetic practice in Tibet but also that in this context, as in Pentecostal Christianity, prophecy is not a dramatic anomaly but is part and parcel of everyday religious life, guiding individuals' behaviours and relationships.

In Chapter 10, Wendy M. Grossman, a technology and science writer and founder and editor of *The Skeptic* magazine, considers some of the science-based prophecies circulating in contemporary UK and US contexts. Providing examples drawn from science, science-fiction, futurology and marketing material, Grossman points out that it is difficult to assess such prophecies: Have they failed? Have they just not happened yet? Or will they never happen? With Y2K, for instance, the belief that all computer systems would fail as the date ticked over to 1 January 2000, there was a great deal of hype and panic and yet, Grossman argues, it was also a real problem which needed some action. The prophecy was successful on one level in that it led to action on the issue, a reactionary change in behaviour. This is an important aspect of prophecy which is also raised in other chapters in this volume, especially in 'Part IV: 2012 Prophecies'; Suzanne Rough for instance, who is expecting a planetary transformation in December 2012 and is creating a community in Lapland in anticipation of major climatic upheaval, writes that the primary importance of the prophecy lies in individuals' spiritual preparations leading up to this date.

Chapter 6

The New Apostolic Reformation:
Main Street Mystics and Everyday Prophets

Margaret M. Poloma and Matthew T. Lee

Prophecy has played a major historic role in the founding of religions of the Abrahamic tradition. Judaism, Christianity and Islam – and the countless sects found within each – trace their roots to Abraham, the patriarch of the Israelites who lived over 4,000 years ago. Abraham was the father of Isaac, through whom Jews and Christians claim lineage; he was also the father of Ishmael, through whom Muslims trace their history. Abram heard God tell him to leave his country and his people, and travel from the land of the Chaldeans (present day Iraq) to the land of Canaan (later known as Israel). In response to his obedience, Abram received a prophetic promise as reported in Genesis 17:5: 'No longer will you be called Abram; your name will be Abraham, for I have made you a father of many nations.'[1] For Jewish, Christian and Muslim sons and daughters of Abraham, this prophecy has long been fulfilled.

   Noted prophets and their prophecies are found throughout the history of ancient Judaism and generally are accepted (albeit often with different interpretations) by most Christian groups. The early Jews were not alone, however, in their experiences of the prophetic. Scholars have noted that prophecy was widespread in the ancient Mesopotamian region with prophetic activities similar to and concurring with those of the Israelites. Israel's prophetic activity differed from those of their polytheistic neighbours, claiming to be unique 'for it was derived solely from Yahweh, Israel's God' (Robeck 2002a: 1001). Prophetic practices are also found in the history of Greece and Rome, but like those of other Mesopotamian countries, they too were regarded by the monotheistic followers of Abraham as inauthentic. Although the early Christian church would condemn Greco-Roman prophetic works, the Christian Testament suggests that consulting oracles and seers had been part of the culture at the time of Jesus and his disciples. Greco-Roman prophecies would be rejected, but prophecy inspired by the Hebraic tradition and its key prophets was believed to come from the one true God. Hebrew Testament prophecies continue to be used in orthodox Christian denominations and sects, significantly in support of proclaiming Jesus to be the promised Jewish messiah (Robeck 2002a). On the first Christian Pentecost (regarded as a fulfilment of Jesus' prophecy to send the

---

[1]   http://www.aboutprophecy.com (accessed: 15 October 2011).

Spirit to his early followers), the apostle Peter would quote the Jewish prophet Joel
to explain the paranormal occurrences that had mystified onlookers:

> In the last days, God says, I will pour out my Spirit on all people. Your sons and
> daughters will prophesy, your young men will see visions, your old men will
> dream dreams. Even on my servants, both men and women, I will pour out my
> Spirit in those days, and they will prophesy (Acts 2:12–17, NIV).

Judging from the Acts of the Apostles and the Pauline epistles, the early Christian
church presented prophecy as charismata or spiritual gifts to be sought by all
believers. The practice of prophecy was no longer for only the few gifted men and
women heralded as prophets. In writing on the 'spiritual gifts', especially speaking
in tongues (glossolalia) and prophecy, the Apostle Paul admonishes,

> Follow the way of love and eagerly desire spiritual gifts, especially the gift of
> prophecy. For anyone who speaks in tongues does not speak to men but to God
> … He who speaks in a tongue edifies himself, but he who prophesies edifies the
> church. I would like every one of you to speak in tongues, but I would rather
> have you prophesy (1 Corinthians 14: 1–5, NIV).

Like the charismata of glossolalia and divine healing, prophecy had a significant
place in early Christianity, but it would lose ground as the church grew in power
and became the established religion of the Western world. Church historian
C.M. Robeck notes that 'the church [in the first several centuries AD] was no
stranger to continuing prophetic activity' and that 'room was made within the
church structure for prophets to function on both itinerant and local levels' (2002a:
1007).[2] History suggests that the leaders of early Christianity learned that whatever
else they may be, prophecies are institutionally dangerous. The heresy label would
be levelled against the Gnostics and their 'exclusive revelations' that did not
conform to orthodox Christian beliefs, while criticisms were levelled against the
Montanists, who although orthodox, taught that the Spirit used prophecy to guide
believers in specific situations. Prophecy in both groups was potentially a threat
to established authority and was eventually silenced by the church. There were
still others within the early Christian community, who while professing belief in
prophecy, put strict reins on its definition and practice. Some mainstream Christians
would come to identify prophecy with teaching/preaching; however, 'the revealed
understanding of the (biblical) text was a prophetic word' (Robeck 2002a: 1008).
In sociological language, the charismata were becoming routinised within the

---

2   Robeck (2002a) describes a prophetic experience of Ignatius, bishop of Antioch,
in the second century and the writings of the Shepherd of Hermas on prophecy (first third
of the second century). Hermas was concerned about the potentially negative effects of
prophecy on young believers and was critical of 'personal' prophecies which he described
as 'empty words'. See also Andrew Maguire, Chapter 5.

established church as religious experience lost ground to religious text, emergent authority structures and more controlled rituals. Robeck succinctly described the state of prophecy found in the Middle Ages as follows: 'On the whole, however, there is clear evidence that the regular church understood the *charismata* as being present in a more or less routine way with the order of Christian leadership … those called to Christian leadership were assumed to stand in the prophetic tradition' (2002a: 1009). This was clearly the position of the leading theologian of the medieval church, Thomas Aquinas, whose teachings remained the bedrock of Roman Catholic theology for over seven centuries. Although theologically open to prophecy, for Aquinas there was no room for any trace of falsehood in the word spoken. If the prophecy were defective in any way, it would be deemed false.

Neither Roman Catholic teaching that proscribed prophecy in favour of doctrine and church authority nor the cautionary stance of the Protestant Reformers toward the phenomenon, however, could totally silence prophetic speech. Marginal groups would continue to rise up over the centuries, including the Quakers, the Shakers, the Ranters and the Mormons, in which prophecy would play a significant (if temporary) role. Also among those experiencing the prophetic were 'marginal' Catholics, often founders of Catholic religious orders (for example Francis of Assisi) and common visionaries of nineteenth- and twentieth-century Catholicism (for example Fatima [Portugal] in the early twentieth century and Medjugorje [Bosnia-Herzegovina] beginning in 1981).[3] For the most part, however, Catholics were taught that God spoke through church doctrines and proclamations while Protestants equated the Bible and often preaching to the prophetic word of God.

In sum, prophetic activity, where it existed at all in the history of post-Constantinean Christianity, has been circumscribed, marginalised and often demonised. Few traditions seemed to be able to sustain the experiential practices described in the second chapter of Acts. Yet within the past 100 years as Pentecostalism has emerged as a major face of Christianity, prophecy has become a focal point of theology and practice within this rapidly growing movement – a movement that has infiltrated major Christian denominations, birthed new denominations and spawned countless independent organisations and networks. Based on Peter's Pentecost sermon cited earlier, on accounts found in the Acts of the Apostles and on the Pauline writings on prophecy, contemporary Pentecostals have laid a foundation for both populist Pentecostal prophetic practices and in the hierarchical 'office of the prophet' believed to function as a medium through which God speaks to the larger church. Prophets are seen to work in tandem with those holding the 'office of the apostle' that embodies the pinnacle of church authority. Apostles and prophets are regarded as messengers of God, with the distinction that prophets are interpreters of specific utterances while apostles are

---

[3]   See for example the website for the ongoing prophetic Marian apparitions in Medjugorje http://www.medjugorje.org/ (accessed: 10 May 2011).

vested with the authority to represent God's will in a more general sense in the larger church.[4]

At the forefront of promoting the so-called 'five-fold ministry', which proposes apostles and prophets be raised up to complement existing teachers, evangelists and pastors for church ministry, is the New Apostolic Reformation (NAR). The NAR is not a single organisation but rather consists of multiple relational networks that are amorphous, fluid and reticulate (Wagner 2011). In the summer of 2011 the NAR came to the attention of the US news media because of reported connections that a few of its leaders had with the Republican presidential candidate Governor Rick Perry of Texas. Filtered through the eyes of reporters interested in an intersection of faith and politics, the NAR has been defined as 'a little known movement of radical Christians and self-proclaimed prophets' who seek 'to infiltrate government'.[5] The political facet of the NAR is derived from popular teachings on the 'seven mountains of culture', one of which is government (but the most important of which is commonly acknowledged to be business).[6] In fact, talk about the 'infiltration of government' plays but a small part, arguably among the radical fringe of the movement who take the stance that Christians should 'take dominion over' cultural institutions (Enlow 2008, Silk 2009).

The NAR might better be described at its centre as a movement that proposes to use 'supernatural gifts' of the Spirit (including prophecy) to serve others in the 'seven cultural mountains' of society – education, government, media, arts and entertainment, religion, family and business. Although there is talk about 'dominion' and 'take-over' of these mountains (especially business which is said to 'fill and fuel the other mountains'), many in the NAR have translated this prophetic call to faithful service in whichever mountains the believer is involved.

---

[4]   Those who propose that the offices of 'apostle' and 'prophet' be restored to the contemporary church base their theology on Ephesians 4:11 in which Paul writes 'It was he who gave some to be apostles, some to be prophets, some to be evangelists, and some to be pastors and teachers, to prepare God's people for works of service.' According to populist theologian Mike Bickle (2008: 39) the passage is better understood as being about *ministries* practised by members of the church rather than *offices* held by select and often self-proclaimed individuals. Just as pastors, teachers and evangelists are widely recognised as common ministries within Protestantism, so too should prophetic and apostolic ministries be encouraged within the church.

[5]   See Forrest Wilder, 'Rick Perry's Army of God', *The Texas Observer*, 12 July 2011. See also C. Peter Wagner's statement on the New Apostolic Reformation (http://globalspheres. org/ [accessed: 2 September 2011]) and an interview conducted by NPR's Terry Gross with C. Peter Wagner on the Apostolic Reformation http://www.npr.org/2011/10/03/140946482/ apostolic-leader-weighs-religions-role-in-politics#commentBlock (accessed: 2 September 2011).

[6]   The 'seven mountains of culture' are derived from a vision of Youth With a Mission founder Loren Cunningham and affirmed by evangelical writer Francis Schaefer and evangelist Bill Bright in 1975. Cunningham presented it as a 'way to reach people for God' – in other words, for personal evangelism.

Thus mainstream Pentecostals are likely to seek to usher in the Kingdom of God as empowered by the charismata in daily living rather than as militant rhetoric and political strategy.[7]

The Rise of New Apostolic Reformation in Pentecostalism

As we have seen in our abridged history of prophecy, there has been an ebb and flow of the prophetic throughout Christian history. It tends to flow with the birth of new (and often marginalised) religious sects, but it appears to ebb with the development of institutionalised authority structures. The rise of historic Pentecostalism in the first decade of the twentieth century broke a theological stronghold against the contemporary use of prophecy and experiences of other charismata that had been in danger of being relegated to history. The Wesleyan Holiness movement of the last half of the nineteenth century, itself a revivalist movement against an increasingly institutionalised Methodism, provided fertile ground for the Azusa Street Revival in Los Angeles (1906–1909) that is commonly regarded as the birthplace of the Pentecostal movement (Robeck 2002b). Thousands from across North America and beyond who participated in Azusa Street experienced the charismata (especially speaking in tongues and divine healing) that were familiar to some extent to those involved in the Holiness movement. Spiritual gifts of glossolalia, divine healing and prophecy would become important hallmarks as Pentecostalism made its way around the globe (Robeck 2006).

Early Pentecostals claimed to experience prophecy, but ongoing revival was required to keep this highly experiential approach to Christianity in practice beyond the first generation. Three major 'waves' have been commonly identified that revitalised American Pentecostalism during its 100-year history in America, each having effects on prophecy as a social practice. The first wave began at Azusa Street (Los Angeles) and in its wake birthed Pentecostal sects both in America and abroad. Two of these sects (Church of God in Christ and Assemblies of God) would become major Pentecostal denominations that are presently found in the top 10 in terms of number of congregants of all religious denominations in the United States. The second wave, often known as the charismatic renewal, occurred within mainline Christianity and marginally touched most Protestant denominations,

---

[7]   'To know God's love and to give it away' was the epigram of the Toronto Blessing that continues to be reflected in the popular literature of many tributaries of the NAR in writing about the transformation of society and culture. Kris Vallotton (2007: 111) succinctly describes this common theme that runs through his and other works cited throughout this article that instruct followers on how to usher in the kingdom of God: 'I finally figured out that prophetic ministry, like every other ministry in the Kingdom, should be the love language of God. ... Every expression of the gifts of the Spirit should come from love and work to bring the love of the Father to the person receiving them. That is what the supernatural ministry of the New Covenant is all about. Love *never* fails!'

Roman Catholicism and Eastern Orthodoxy. In the late 1960s and 1970s a form of Pentecostalism commonly known as the 'charismatic renewal' would make headlines as Pentecostal experiences swept through countless mainline congregations (Poloma 1982). While this second wave had yet to crest and recede, another – the so-called 'third wave' – was already forming in southern California.

The third wave, labelled as such by Fuller Theological Seminary professor C. Peter Wagner in the early 1980s, singled out those Pentecostals who chose not to identify (or ceased to identify) with the theology of denominational Pentecostals of the first wave or the charismatics of the second wave. Wagner writes: 'The desire of those in the third wave is to experience the power of the Holy Spirit in healing the sick, casting out demons, receiving prophecies, and participating in other charismatic-type manifestations without disturbing the current philosophy of ministry governing these congregations' (2002: 1141). Some congregations of the third wave would become independent American megachurches; others would remain small congregations commonly linked to one or more emerging and ever-changing loose networks. A few churches would become epicentres for the Pentecostal revivals of the 1990s and the rise of the New Apostolic Reformation (NAR), with emphases on the revived five-fold ministry and transforming the seven mountains of culture that took hold within these revivals.

Prophecy and the Toronto Blessing

British Pentecostal scholar William K. Kay observes that the NAR began in the second wave charismatic movement of the 1970s and developed steam during the third wave Toronto Blessing Revival (1994–2006), a revival that affected both North American and British Pentecostalism. Whatever else may be fruits of the 1990s revivals, for which the so-called 'Toronto Blessing' became the epicentre (see Poloma 2003), the revival ushered in a new eschatology that also marked changes in the prophetic. Kay describes this shift as follows:

> Whatever variation there was among them in the 1970s, restorationists rapidly developed a preferred postmillennial eschatological scheme. This removed many of the prophecies of pain and persecution from the timeline of current events. Postmillennialism allowed restorationists to diffuse the blessings of the millennium into the present age of the church and to argue and preach that the reign of Christ upon the earth, which many pentecostals had placed within the millennium, could be seen here and now (2007: 29).

In other words, emerging NAR leaders 'believed that the kingdom of God was going to advance against all opposition and that the kingdom had an earthly and political dimension and was not simply a distant spiritual benefit or an internal blessing to be invisibly enjoyed by the believer' (Kay 2007: 29).

By the 1980s changes were well underway within the Pentecostal organisations birthed by the Azusa Street revival as the most successful of the established sects grew in number and social class and assumed their place among established American denominations (see Poloma 1982, 1989). Signs of charismatic activity diminished as congregational rituals increasingly succumbed to the 'routinization of charisma' with prophecy being silenced in many Pentecostal churches (Poloma 1989, Poloma and Green 2010, Poloma and Pendleton 1989). Among the newly emerging independent congregations that made up much of the third wave of the Pentecostal movement, however, the seeds were sown for what has come to be known as the New Apostolic Reformation with a stronger emphasis on the prophetic. Prophets (specifically the so-called 'Kansas City Prophets', whose key players included Mike Bickle, Bob Jones and Paul Cain) briefly found a platform in the mid 1980s among some third-wave congregations, especially those that were part of John Wimber's Association of Vineyard Churches (AVC). However, failed prophecies would soon cause Wimber to rethink his alliance with the prophets, including his relationship with prophet Mike Bickle.

At the time he connected with Wimber, Mike Bickle was a fledgling prophet who had been drawn into the world of the prophets by a dramatic experience he had in Cairo, Egypt in 1982. This experience would leave him open to the influence of Kansas City prophets Bob Jones and Paul Cain when he returned to the United States. After Cain's prophecies about a major revival that he predicted would take place in England in 1989 failed to materialise, Wimber began to back away from the Kansas City prophets (KCP) – even to regret his brief involvement with them. In a surprise move in 1990, however, Bickle would bring his church into the AVC and submit himself to Wimber's leadership. James Beverley (1995: 126), a theologian who studied the KCP and its relationship to the Toronto Blessing, reported that when he interviewed Wimber in September 1991, Wimber indicated that 'the prophets would not be loose cannons on the Vineyard ship. They would be bolted down to the deck, or they would be told to exercise their gifts elsewhere.' The AVC, however, was already a house divided about the prophetic star performers who made up the KCP. Wimber himself estimated that 25 per cent of the pastors were against the KCP, 25 per cent were in favour, and 50 per cent were neutral (Jackson 1999: 200). Despite these divisions, the KCP exerted a strong influence on the neopentecostal revivals of the 1990s.

It was not long before a revival would wash up on Great Britain's shores, but it would come from Canada and in 1994 (not in 1989 as the prophet Paul Cain had predicted to AVC founder John Wimber). The revival that came to be known as the 'Toronto Blessing' erupted in the Toronto Airport Vineyard (TAV), a member of Wimber's AVC. The level of charismatic activity and accompanying physical manifestations found in the new revival was too much for Wimber, and the TAV would be soon ousted from the AVC to become the Toronto Airport Christian Fellowship (TACF) in the beginning of 1996. As a member of the AVC, TAV was not a stranger to the Kansas City prophets or to prophetic foretelling. Unlike Wimber's experience with failed prophecy, however, prophetic words foretelling the revival in Toronto seemed to come true at this small church then located in a strip mall across from the Toronto Airport (see Poloma 2003). As the Toronto Blessing would spread to churches across North America, the United Kingdom and soon across the globe, prophets and their prophecies would find new platforms to disseminate their teachings, tapes and books in which they largely presented positive and encouraging messages of prophetic forth-telling that were available to all believers.

What Is Prophecy?

Thus far in our discussion we have given descriptive historical information on prophecy in Christianity and its ebb and flow in contemporary Pentecostalism, but we have not yet provided a working definition. Clearly nuances in the definition of prophecy and its practice in Christianity have shifted over time depending on the prominence of the charismata or spiritual gifts. Prophecy has been understandably controlled, if not totally blocked, by religious institutions. Certain general definitional points can be made, however, about prophecy as it is found in all three waves of the American Pentecostal movement. Although dictionaries favour defining prophecy as foretelling or prediction,[8] this face of prophecy applies primarily to the relatively few men and women who self-designate and are recognised by others to hold the 'office of prophet'. Prophecy as understood by many Pentecostals (and as taught by the 'prophets' to those in the pews) is more commonly expressed as a charisma or gift of divine grace available (at least in some degree) to all believers, enabling them to speak or act out messages from God that edify, encourage and bless others.

Thus, it is important to emphasise that most Pentecostals do not practice prophecy as 'foretelling', including the prediction of future cataclysmic events, but rather as 'forth-telling' an encouraging word they believe God has given to them. Although the prediction of future events remains a recognised prophetic form, it tends to be a practice that has been subject to criticism (especially by evangelicals outside the movement) and often comes with disclaimers by those inside the movement. As a result, self-proclaimed prophets of both the foretelling and forth-telling varieties are more likely to be found in sectors of the NAR where leaders tend to 'push the envelope' in order to open up new experiences of the charismata rather than in established Pentecostal denominations and congregations influenced by the second wave of Pentecostalism with their more routinised rituals.

Prophecy has changed in style and often is found in today's spiritual marketplace with cautionary labels of the possibility of error or 'mistakes'. In days before the Internet, these 'mistakes' were more likely to involve back-peddling with statements of what was 'really' said and what the prophet 'really

---

[8]   See for example, http://www.thefreedictionary.com/prophecy and http://dictionary. reference.com/browse/prophecy (both accessed: 25 October 2011).

meant' when prophecy failed (see Beverley 1995). Furthermore the delivery style of public prophetic words has changed significantly from a generation or two ago. In traditional Pentecostal churches, prophecies once would have been delivered with great emotion – ending with the dogmatic proclamation 'thus saith the Lord'. Today, as we will demonstrate in the section that follows, the proclamation of prophecy is commonly less dramatic. Prophetic words are spoken simply, whether the setting is public or private, creating an atmosphere that allows the receiver(s) to discern whether it is in fact a word from the divine. In a world filled with easy access to information and critique, prophets have had to assume a more humble stance than many did in decades past. In sum, prophecy as commonly understood and practised by prophets on Main Street consists in hearing from God and then 'speaking and acting on God's behalf as a result of the prompting of the Holy Spirit'. The message is generally one of forth-telling encouragement, edification and support rather than foretelling hellfire and brimstone (Poloma 2003, Tyra 2011).

Having provided this general definition, there still is variation in the form, frequency and content of prophetic messages. In general it is safe to say that as historic Pentecostalism has experienced institutionalisation of doctrine and rituals, prophetic voices have been tamed – even silenced. Within established Pentecostal denominational churches, prophecy – both public and private – is decidedly less practised than it once was, with some ministers equating prophecy with preaching. For example, among adherents of the Assemblies of God (AG), the ninth largest denomination in the United States and second-largest Pentecostal one, Poloma has noted that prophecies are less commonly given in today's AG services than in the congregations she observed a generation earlier (Poloma and Green 2010). This muting of the prophetic stands in contrast to the high level of prophetic activities found in many third-wave congregations, especially those affiliated with the NAR, where conferences, books, websites and other teachings on prophecy abound. As AG theologian Gary Tyra writes:

> Pentecostal and charismatic Christianity around the world in recent years can be attributed, as least in part to the dynamic of prophetic activity taking place in the lives of rank-and-file church members. This realization offers hope that a similar missional faithfulness can be experienced in Western, industrialized nations should the dynamic of prophetic activity be rediscovered by the evangelicals living within them (2011: 35).

In other words, the purpose of prophetic activity is not fame, fortune or winning a political election, but the advancing of the kingdom of God through divinely-led service. Sermons and teachings about how to accomplish the goal of bringing heaven to earth generally steer clear of partisan politics, focusing rather on learning to listen for God and allowing God to empower believers in whatever is their life calling and destiny (see Johnson 2006). Whether it be on the 'mountains' of business and finance, education, administration or the arts, the message is to rely on the Holy Spirit to direct and empower the worker to bring a piece of heaven to the situation.

Prophetic Interactions and Benevolence

Prophecy, whether practised publically by one believed to be holding the office or privately by a prophet on Main Street, involves ritual built around a perceived interaction with God and with others (Lee and Poloma 2009, Lee, Poloma and Post 2013). This insight has guided an international research team comprised of theologians and social scientists involved in a multidisciplinary study of perceived experiences of God and their effect on human benevolence. In this research, prophecy was found to play a significant role in experiencing God's love, which in turn affects benevolence (Lee and Poloma 2009, Lee, Poloma and Post 2013, Lee and Yong 2012, Poloma and Green 2010, Poloma and Hood 2008). Responses to questions on prophecy from a recent national random survey of 1,208 US respondents (including both religious and non-religious adults) suggest that interpersonal interaction with God (sometimes involving others) was surprisingly common among American adults (Lee, Poloma and Post 2013). They included sensing a divine call to perform a specific act (experienced, at least on occasion, by 51 per cent of all respondents); experiencing God 'providing direction to do something through another person' (65 per cent of all respondents); 'giving a word from God to another person' (59 per cent) and receiving 'revelations directly from God' (41 per cent). Although the prevalence of prophecy is striking, it is also important to note that prophecy is not a monolithic construct. Mike Bickle, for example, describes the prophetic relationship at three levels: strong and primarily the voice of God (regardless of whether this voice is sensed directly or through other people); average ('mature') with a weaker mix of divine and human voices; or weak ('immature') consisting primarily of human impressions intertwined with a divine mandate. According to Bickle, '… prophecy today has a degree of mixture in it. Sometimes this yields "mature" word that reflects more ideally what God would like to communicate, and sometimes it is communicated in a much-less-than-ideal fashion, yielding a "weak" word of lesser value, but still one that should not be despised' (2008: 37). Books like Bickle's, conferences and Internet materials abound to guide neophytes into the world of prophetic experiences complete with guidance on how to discern the voice of God from other voices, while reminding them that 'we know in part and we prophesy in part' (1 Corinthians 8:2). Even those well seasoned with prophetic experiences make mistakes.

Our research data also includes countless qualitative reports by the 120 men and women whose in-depth interviews cast light on the interpretation of our US national survey statistics. We select one account from an exemplar – a church pastor who lectures and conducts prophetic workshops – to describe the interactive process at the heart of third-wave prophecy. Poloma first met Steve Witt in 1995 as she was just beginning her research on the Toronto Blessing revival.

Steve – who is loosely affiliated with the NAR – was at that time an AVC pastor in eastern Canada and a native of Cleveland. Poloma learned that Steve had moved from Cleveland some 10 years earlier under church-related circumstances that left him with no desire to return. It was on a flight back from Japan that a friend with whom he had been travelling – a man known for 'hearing from God' – leaned over and said, 'You're about to be called back to Cleveland, Ohio.' Steve reported his reaction: 'My heart sank. This would not have been my first choice. Don't get me wrong; Cleveland is an excellent city. It's just that for me it was connected to many memories of pain and rejection that I preferred not to face again.' Steve did not move on that word; he waited to see what would happen next. A month earlier a prophet in Florida who did not know him told him that a 'geographical relocation' was coming, but Steve reasoned that 'relocation' could be 'in sunny Florida or North Carolina just as easily as Cleveland'. Several days after the prophecy about Cleveland, Steve would receive an unexpected call from a long-time acquaintance in Cleveland inviting him to come to do a conference in that city. While doing the conference, Steve received a strange call from another minister who spoke to him 'In a parabolic tone that left you guessing as to what he really meant'. The minister then 'went on to talk about my future in the city of Cleveland. I had not shared that possibility with anyone because I had not come to that conclusion myself. He used words that God had used in my life before.' Four months later, Steve and his family were living in Cleveland where he planted a new church and developed a prophetic vision for 'supernaturally' being an instrument of change for this decaying city. Steve finished this account saying, 'In hindsight, I cringe to think where I might be had I not listened to the multiple hints from God. He used a disparate group of people from several countries in a variety of circumstances to corral me into His purpose' (Witt 2007: 39–41).

Implied in such terse accounts of prophetic interactions are various 'levels' or channels through which the voice of God is heard. It is generally acknowledged that most of it is what prophet Rick Joyner (1997: 97) describes as 'the lowest level of prophetic revelation', namely impressions or 'generally revelations that we put into our own words'. Prophecies may also commonly come through visions that can range from 'those you see with the eyes of your heart to "open" visions which are like watching a movie screen'. Dreams are another common form of revelation, also having different levels of clarity. Joyner describes trances, 'the highest form of revelation', as 'like having a dream while you are awake. All of a sudden, you are caught up into a vision that is so real it seems as though you are literally there.'

Prophecy – as understood in the Pentecostal third wave and by those associated with the NAR – can take a variety of forms that represent different levels of intensity and discernment of God's will. Prophetic acts and utterances are given meaning in interaction with God and other people. Research that we have conducted suggests that the media's emphasis on the language of 'dominion' over social and political institutions misses the emphasis within the NAR on bringing heaven to earth in a process of benevolent service. It is generally the case that there is an affinity between NAR practices and conservative politics, but there is also significant variation. Another of our interviewees – American missionary Heidi Baker – is a case in point. Her benevolent service has been directed at the poorest of the poor. She and her husband Rolland have endured many hardships in their work, including exposure to life-threatening disease and physical violence, yet they have experienced many successes that are perhaps best described as miraculous.[9]

In the mid 1990s Heidi Baker had just defended her PhD in Systematic Theology from King's College in London, and she and her husband Rolland were 'burned out' from their 17 years of missions work, most recently in war-torn Mozambique. They had run out of money, they were sleep-deprived because Marxists were keeping them up all night by shooting their machine guns. Heidi reported that she had begun to feel that she should work at a retail store (K-Mart) and leave her vocation (and life of stress) behind. Tired and discouraged, she left Mozambique for her first visit to the Toronto Airport Christian Fellowship and showed up at a sermon being preached by Randy Clark, the AVC minister credited with sparking the Toronto Blessing. At this particular sermon, Randy was admonishing people to 'press in' for God, at which point Heidi ran up to the stage and felt the power of God. Randy began to 'prophesy' over her. He did not know at the time that it was a prophecy, but he asked her if she 'wanted the nation of Mozambique'. Through tears, she screamed 'Yes!'

The prophecy itself was secondary to the power and presence of God that Heidi felt at that time. Randy and Heidi both later agreed that without the presence of God, Heidi would not have been able to persevere through the trials that followed. But the 'spirit-filled' style of ritual being led by Randy (calling people to the front for prophecy, anointing etc.) invites participation in powerful and empowering direct experience of God in a way that simply listening to a conventional sermon does not. This active participation introduces an element of unpredictability that gives such rituals a free-flowing form when compared with the 'high ritual' of other traditions (for example Catholic mass). At the time Randy gave this prophecy, Heidi had been 'thinking theologically' and did not believe that the miracles of which he spoke were possible, or that God would ever ask her if she 'wanted' Mozambique or any other nation. This was not consistent with her understanding of God. But at the moment in the empowered interaction with Randy, she felt a 'fire from Heaven that just burned through me and I felt like I was going to die'.

Heidi found herself 'stuck to the floor for days' (i.e. under the power of the Holy Spirit) and returned to Mozambique completely 'undone'. Then after a year of praying for the blind, Heidi reported that they began to see – consistent with Randy's prophetic message. A year later, Heidi went back to Toronto to preach at the same conference as Randy. God had told Randy to 'preach and release the

---

[9]   The account that follows was adapted from several sources, including our interview with Heidi, Disc 5 of the Deluxe Edition of the documentary *Finger of God*, and our interview with Randy Clarke (another important figure in the NAR). For more details, see Lee, Poloma and Post (2013).

apostolic anointing'. Even though she was 'moving in power' at that point in her life – meaning that she was experiencing God's miracles and helping others to have similar experiences – she was sceptical of the word 'apostolic' and saw it as arrogant. In the next instant, she found herself standing on her head in front of thousands of people (and she stated that she is unable to stand on her head). According to Heidi, 'The power of God is pulsating through me … God said to me that apostolic is upside down, it is the lowest place. I'm turning you upside down.' Heidi said she was 'totally humbled' by the experience and developed a clear understanding that the apostle is a servant of others, not a leader bent on consolidating power or being worshiped by followers. She would later report experiencing a divine healing of a debilitating physical illness.

If this account taxes the reader's credulity, we would hasten to add that regardless of whether it is based on facts or fictions it exemplifies the cultural grid through which people in the NAR like Heidi and Randy make sense of their prophetic experiences.[10] Heidi describes her prophetic interactions with God, Randy and other people as a kind of divine inner (or emotional/spiritual) healing, which she claims saved her from burnout and was an integral part of her benevolent ministry, which continues to have a dramatic impact on countless thousands of people. Like many of the people we studied, Heidi is empowered by her prophetic experiences to see beyond her material circumstances – which may appear quite grim at times – to locate her life in God's larger plan for transforming the world through self-giving love.

References

Beverley, J.A. 1995. *Holy Laughter and the Toronto Blessing. An Investigative Report*. Grand Rapids, MI: Zondervan.

Bickle, M. 2008. *Growing in the Prophetic*. Lake Mary, FL: Charisma House.

Enlow, J. 2008. *The Seven Mountain Prophecy*. Lake Mary, FL: Creation House.

Jackson, B. 1999. *The Quest for the Radical Middle: A History of the Vineyard*. Cape Town: Vineyard International.

Johnson, B. 2006. *Dreaming with God: Co-Laboring with God for Cultural Transformation*. Shippensburg, PA: Destiny Image.

Joyner, R. 1997. *The Prophetic Ministry*. Fort Mill, SC: MorningStar.

Kay, W.K. 2007. *Apostolic Networks in Great Britain: New Ways of Being Church*. Waynesboro, GA: Paternoster.

Lee, M.T. and Poloma, M.M. 2009. *A Sociological Study of the Great Commandment in Pentecostalism: The Practice of Godly Love as Benevolent Service*. Lewiston, NY: Edwin Mellen.

---

[10]   For more on fact and fiction in this line of research, see Lee and Poloma (2009).

Lee, M.T., Poloma, M.M. and Post, S.G. [in press; 2013]. *The Heart of Religion: Spiritual Empowerment, Benevolence, and the Experience of God's Love*. New York: Oxford University Press.

Lee, M.T. and Yong, A. (eds) 2012. *The Science and Theology of Godly Love*. DeKalb, IL: Northern Illinois University Press.

Poloma, M.M. 1982. *The Charismatic Movement: Is There a New Pentecost?* Boston, MA: Twayne.

———. 1989. *The Assemblies of God at the Crossroads: Charisma and Institutional Dilemmas*. Knoxville, TN: University of Tennessee Press.

———. 2003. *Main Street Mystics: The Toronto Blessing and Reviving Pentecostalism*. Walnut Creek, CA: Alta Mira Press.

Poloma, M.M. and Green, J.C. 2010. *The Assemblies of God: Godly Love and the Revitalization of American Pentecostalism*. New York: New York University Press.

Poloma, M.M. and Hood, R.W. 2008. *Blood and Fire: Godly Love in a Pentecostal Emerging Church*. New York: New York University Press.

Poloma, M.M. and Pendleton, B.F. 1989. Religious Experiences and Institutional Growth within the Assemblies of God. *Journal for the Scientific Study of Religion*, 24, 415–31.

Robeck, C.M. 2002a. The Gift of Prophecy, in *The New International Dictionary of Pentecostal Charismatic Movements*, edited by S.M. Burgess and E.M. Van Der Maas. Grand Rapids, MI: Zondervan, 1000–1010.

———. 2002b. The Azusa Street Revival, in *The New International Dictionary of Pentecostal Charismatic Movements*, edited by S.M. Burgess and E.M. Van Der Maas. Grand Rapids, MI: Zondervan, 344–50.

———. 2006. *The Azusa Street Mission and Revival: The Birth of the Global Pentecostal Movement*. Nashville, TN: Nelson Reference and Electronic.

Silk, D. 2009. *Culture of Honor: Sustaining a Supernatural Environment*. Shippensburg, PA: Destiny Image.

Tyra, G. 2011. *The Holy Spirit in Mission: Prophetic Speech and Action in Christian Witness*. Downers Grove, IL: IVP Academic Press.

Vallotton, K. 2007. *Developing a Supernatural Lifestyle*. Shippensburg, PA: Destiny Image.

Wagner, C.P. 2002. The Third Wave, in *The New International Dictionary of Pentecostal Charismatic Movements*, edited by S.M. Burgess and E.M. Van Der Maas. Grand Rapids, MI: Zondervan, 1141.

———. 2011. *The New Apostolic Reformation: An Update* [Online 18 August 2011]. Available at: http://globalspheres.org [accessed: 3 February 2012].

Wilder, F. 2011. Rick Perry's Army of God. *The Texas Observer*, 12 July 2011.

Witt, S. 2007. *Voices: Understanding and Responding to the Language of Heaven*. Shippensburg, PA: Destiny Image.

Chapter 7

The Mahdi and the End-Times in Islam

Hugh Beattie

The People of my House shall meet misfortune, banishment, and persecution until people will come from the east with black flags. They will ask for charity but will not be given it. Then they will fight and be victorious. Now they will be given what they had asked, yet they will not accept it but will finally hand it (sc. the earth) over to a man of My Family. He will fill it with justice as they had filled it with injustice. Whoever of you will live to witness that, let him go there even though it be by creeping on snow.

(in Madelung 2006: 4)[1]

This chapter begins by exploring the origins of Mahdist beliefs in the first centuries of Islam, going on to look at some of their historical expressions, and then examining some modern interpretations. It draws attention to their variety and discusses some of the reasons for their past and present appeal.

Origins

Muslims believe that, as well as being the final prophecy in the sense of divinely-inspired utterance, the Qur'an contains prophecy in the sense of the foretelling of future events, referring at a number of points to the resurrection, the last judgement and the afterlife. Although it tells us that we cannot know when the end of the world will come (Q. 33:63), it lists a number of things that will happen beforehand. It mentions, for example, the release of the hordes of Yajuj wa Majuj (Gog and Magog) (e.g. Q. 18:92–9),[2] the emergence of a beast (Q. 27:82), the sky bringing forth clouds of smoke (Q. 44:10), and the darkening of the sun and the dimming of the stars (Q. 81); it also contains what has usually been regarded as a reference to Jesus' return (Q. 43:61).[3] However, it does not go into great detail about these

---

[1]   This is in the collection of *hadiths* by Ibn Maja, usually regarded as the weakest of all the six major works of *hadith* literature (see for example Leaman 2006: 231).

[2]   They were penned up behind two ramparts, one of iron, the other of brass, by Dhu al-Qarnayn, the two-horned one, usually identified with Alexander the Great (Arjomand 1998: 244).

[3]   The view that Muhammad himself anticipated that the end of the world would come very soon and believed that God had chosen him to preside over it is found for example in Casanova (1911).

developments. Nor does it refer to several figures and events that feature in the extensive literature dealing with the end-times that developed subsequently in Islamic tradition (Cook 2005: 123). Instead this literature was mainly based on those *hadiths* ('traditions' or 'reports'), 'in which either the Prophet Muhammad or one of his close companions makes a statement about what will happen at the end of the world. These statements varied in length from phrases of several words to simple sentences to passages equivalent to several pages' (Cook 2005: 7). A 'genre of history of the future' (Garcia-Arenal 2006: 15), they are the nearest equivalent in Islam to the literary apocalypses of Judaism and Christianity (Cook 2005: 7).

As regards the term Mahdi itself, it is derived from the Arabic root *h-d-y* which is used in the Qur'an to mean divine guidance, and during the first days of Islam the term was simply an honorific (Madelung 2006: 1). Its meaning began to change because after the death of Mohammad in 632 (all dates CE unless otherwise noted), the question of who should be his successor (caliph) and lead the Muslims began to divide the new community. Following civil war (656–61) and the assassination of the fourth caliph, Mohammad's cousin and son-in-law Ali ibn Abi Talib, in 661, the Umayyad caliphate was established with its capital at Damascus. However, the Umayyads and their successors, the Abbasids, faced considerable opposition at various points, and there were rebellions and further traumatic civil wars (680–92, 744–50, and 809–33). During these the different parties 'looked to prophetic tradition for inspiration, arguments, and rallying cries' (Filiu 2011: 12). As a result many historical details were incorporated into apocalyptic *hadiths* after the event, '(m)any of the main actors of early Islam were transformed into apocalyptic figures' (Arjomand 1998: 254), and the term Mahdi began to acquire messianic connotations. For example, in 683 the Umayyad caliph Yazid (a grandson of Abu Sufyan) sent an army from Damascus to suppress a rising by a rival, Abdallah ibn al-Zubayr, who lived in Medina. Abdallah moved to Mecca, where he was besieged by Yazid's army. A few weeks later however, Yazid died, the siege was lifted and the troops returned to Syria. These events are reflected in an important *hadith* which includes references to an army sent or led by a descendant of Abu Sufyan, referred to as the Sufyani, the people of Mecca swearing allegiance to 'a man of Medina' between the *rukn* (the corner of the Kabah with the Black Stone in it) and the *maqam* (Ibrahim's station of prayer) in the Great Mosque in Mecca, and to the disappearance of an army in the desert (Madelung 2006: 1–2).

Two years later, in 685, Al-Mukhtar ibn Abi Ubayd proclaimed Muhammad ibn al-Hanafiyya (a son of Ali's) the Mahdi in Kufa in Iraq, and rebelled against the Umayyads. Many of Al-Mukhtar's followers were already familiar with messianic ideas, among them newly-converted Persians from a Zoroastrian background, led by Kaysan Abu Amrah, and formerly pagan southern Arabians. The rebellion was crushed, and Muhammad ibn al-Hanafiyya died in 700. Kaysan's followers, however, claimed that Muhammad ibn al-Hanafiyya was hidden in the Radwa mountains north of Medina and would reappear as the Mahdi and the Qa'im ('the living one' or 'the one standing permanently') (Arjomand 1998: 250–51).

They appear to have been influenced by the Zoroastrian concept of the *saoshyant*, a future saviour who will come one day to defeat the forces of evil and save humanity. For their part, southern Arabians introduced to the Mahdist scenario the figure of the Qahtani, or 'man from Qahtan', Qahtan being their supposed ancestor (Arjomand 1998: 252–53).

The idea of the Mahdi as an apocalyptic leader diffused into the wider Muslim community, as did the *hadith* (spread in Kufa in support of the Abbasid revolutionary movement in the 740s) about people coming from the east with black flags, which appears at the beginning of this chapter. The wars the Umayyads fought against the Byzantines in this period were also incorporated into the Mahdist scenario, so that a truce with, and betrayal by, the Byzantines became one of the signs of the end, and the conquest of Constantinople came to be regarded as the prelude to the appearance of the Mahdi.

The fact that the Mahdi was not mentioned in the Qur'an meant that some Muslims continued to be doubtful about him. *Hadiths* from the two most authoritative collections, those by Bukhari (d.870) and Muslim (d.875), did not refer to him either, although Muslim quoted a Prophetic *hadith* to the effect that 'There will be a caliph in the last (period) of my community who will freely give handfuls of wealth to the people without counting it', which was often taken to be a reference to the Mahdi (Aghaie 2005: 3). They did, however, mention Jesus' return, and Yajuj and Majuj breaking out from behind their ramparts, as well as some events not referred to directly in the Qur'an itself. Among these were the conquest of Constantinople, the rising of the sun in the west, and the appearance of the Dajjal, the false messiah (*al-masih ad-dajjal*) or Antichrist (Filiu 2011: 13–19).

The Dajjal, or Antichrist, is another key figure in Islamic eschatology. In his *hadith* collection Muslim reports Muhammad as saying that the Dajjal will be 'a young man with twisted, curly hair, and a blind eye ... he will appear somewhere between Syria and Iraq and will spread mischief right and left' (Aghaie 2005: 2). Sometimes it is said he will be Jewish, and will be followed by 70,000 Jews from Isfahan. It is said that it will be hard to resist him because of his charisma and special powers, for example the ability to raise the dead.[4]

During the first few centuries after Muhammad's death in 632 therefore, a full apocalyptic scenario about the events leading up to the last days developed. The basic details have remained more or less unchanged ever since, though there are some significant differences of opinion about the exact order of events and the parts played by the different figures.[5] The events before the last Hour were assigned to two categories, the small or lesser signs, and the major or greater signs. Among the many lesser signs are immorality, conflict and violence (Saritoprak 2006: 198). The major signs include the emergence of the Mahdi, who, descended

---

[4]   He has even been envisaged as riding on a donkey presumably in a parody of Jesus' entry into Jerusalem (Cook 2005: 81).

[5]   Some details were subsequently added by, among others, Al-Qurtubi in the thirteenth century and Ibn Kathir in the fourteenth (Filiu 2011: 34–41).

from Muhammad, will be 'a handsome young man with long dark hair, a broad forehead, and a high and prominent nose' (Aghaie 2005: 3).

Views on where he will appear differ. It may be in Syria, in Medina or in Khurasan, (from where his forces carrying black banners will march west),[6] but he will definitely be living in Medina when the tyrannical Sufyani emerges, and sends an army against him. He will go to Mecca where he will be proclaimed as Mahdi, and the Sufyani's army will disappear in the desert. There will be war between Byzantines and Muslims, and Constantinople will fall. This will trigger the emergence of the Dajjal, also from the east, at the head of an army. He will conquer the whole world except for Mecca and Medina, and he will besiege Jerusalem, where many truly believing Muslims will have gathered (Cook 2005: 195, Filiu 2011: 16, Leaman 2006: 164–5). However, Jesus, who did not die on the cross but was taken up to heaven (see Q. 3:54–5), will return. He will descend at Damascus and with the Mahdi's help he will defeat the Dajjal, pursuing him to Lydda where he will kill him. According to Muslim, Jews who have refused to convert to Islam will be put to death (Filiu 2011: 17). The hordes of Yajuj and Majuj will break out from their prison, but Jesus will defeat them too. He will then reign as caliph, and there will be a time of prosperity and peace when the world will turn to Islam (Anawati 2006: 7). Views differ on whether Jesus' role here is more important than the Mahdi's, or vice versa; some have seen them as actually sharing power (Furnish 2005: 97).

After some years, and there are differences of opinion as to how many, Jesus and the Mahdi will die natural deaths, and there will be signs of the end. For example, there will be landslides, smoke will cover the whole world, and the sun will rise in the West. Then a beast (*dabbah*) will appear. With Moses' staff it will draw a line on the forehead of every believer so that their faces will become bright and luminous. It will seal the noses of the non-believers and their faces will become black. A fire will blaze out from Yemen and drive people to the place of their assembly. The four-winged angel Israfil, standing beneath the throne of God, will sound his trumpet. Men and women will be resurrected, and the day of judgement will follow (Ali 1998: 28, Waines 2003: 130).

Sunni and Shiah

Belief in the Mahdi as a divinely-guided man with a mission to restore Islam became very widespread, but for Sunnis it was never a key article of faith (Madelung 2006: 7). Sometimes in Sunni Islam the Mahdi's role has overlapped with that of the *mujaddid*, who according to an important prophetic tradition will be sent by God at the turn of each century to restore and renew Islam. The *mujaddid*,

---

[6]   Khurasan is a term for a historic region covering eastern Iran, much of Afghanistan and parts of Tajikistan, Uzbekistan and Turkmenistan.

however, does not have an apocalyptic role like that of the Mahdi (Aghaie 2005: 3–4, Waines 2003: 210).

By contrast Mahdist belief came to be central for most Shiites (from *shi 'at Ali* – the partisans of Ali, who believed that he rather than Abu Bakr should have succeeded Muhammad as the first caliph). For them an inspired descendant of the Prophet Muhammad, or at least a member of his family, whom they referred to as the Imam, was the only legitimate ruler and guide of the Muslim community; unlike the Sunni caliph, who in theory was chosen by the community, the Shiite caliph was designated by God. They regarded Ali as having been the first Imam, and the majority Shiite view came to be that the Imamate was passed on to his and Fatima's direct descendants in the male line. Some Shiites, the Twelvers or Imamis, believe that the Twelfth Imam, Muhammad al-Mahdi or Muhammad al-Muntazar (the awaited Imam) disappeared in about 873–4 and has been in concealment (*ghayba*) ever since (Amanat 2009: 49). When he reappears, he, not Jesus, will kill the Dajjal, and Imam Ali and his son, Imam Husain, will return and revive Islam and create a just social order (Sachedina 1981: 160–73). The Ismaili Shiah, who followed a different line of Imams after the sixth Imam, Ja'far al-Sadiq, believed that some of the predictions regarding the Mahdi were realised by the Fatimid caliph al-Mahdi, the founder of the Fatimid dynasty (see below). Their eschatological Imam, still expected for the future, was called the Qa'im (Madelung 2006: 10).

Mahdis in History

Although Sunnis have not necessarily attached as much importance as Shiites to the Mahdi, in both traditions the belief that he will come to restore justice on earth has been used to justify claims to political authority (Filiu 2011: 59). In the Shiite traditions, however, there has been more emphasis on this just social order, a period of peace and plenty, which will precede the end. Whereas the Sunni scenarios usually envisaged a relatively short period between the defeat of Yajuj and Majuj's armies and the resurrection and the Day of Judgement (between seven and 40 years), many Shiite traditions anticipated a much longer period (Sachedina 1981: 176–7).

Shiite Mahdism was expressed in a range of revolutionary movements in the medieval and early modern period. The most important were the Fatimids in tenth-century North Africa and the Safavids in late fifteenth-century Iran. The Fatimid movement emerged in 899 when the fourth head of the Ismaili Shiah announced that he was the awaited Imam and Mahdi. In 909 his followers captured Kairouan in modern-day Tunisia and set up a rival Ismaili state in opposition to the Abbasid caliphate in Baghdad. In 969 they conquered Egypt and founded Cairo which became the capital of the new state, usually referred to as Fatimid because its rulers claimed descent from Fatima and Ali. However, as usually happens with movements basing their appeal on their supposed messianic role, once they had taken power, they renounced the eschatological claims which had helped them to gain it (Halm 2004: 170–74).

The Safavid movement emerged out of the political instability which followed the Mongol invasions of the Middle East that began in the mid thirteenth century. The disturbed conditions allowed millenarian movements to flourish in Iran, Iraq and eastern Anatolia, which were often led by men claiming to be the Imam-Mahdi (Halm 2004: 73). Usually they had strong Sufi connections, and the most successful was that of the Safavids who used the spiritual capital built up in the earlier fourteenth century by their ancestor, a Sufi shaykh named Safi-al-Din (1252–1334), to generate support among the nomadic Turcoman tribes. In 1499 the 12-year-old Ismail became its leader. Claiming to be the Mahdi and a reincarnation of Ali and the 12 Imams, he established himself as ruler of north-western Iran and eastern Anatolia in 1501, and went on to conquer much of the rest of modern Iran and Afghanistan. As the Fatimids had done, Ismail abandoned his Mahdist claims once he had secured his position, in his case in favour of a less esoteric and more legalistic style of Twelver Shiism (though Mahdist ideas remained embedded in it) (Cole 2001: 289–90, Halm 2004: 80).

In the meantime Sunni Mahdism had emerged in north-west Africa and Spain. The most important movement was founded by Ibn Tumart in the early twelfth century. He developed and expounded 'a doctrine of divine oneness (*tawhid*)' and gave his followers the name of al-Muwahiddun (unitarians) (Filiu 2011: 59). Condemning the ruling Almoravids for corruption and immorality, he established himself in the remote mountain village of Tinmallal in the Atlas mountains. His followers proclaimed him Mahdi, and taking up arms against the government, he led an attack on Marrakech in 1130 in which he was killed. He had already designated a successor, Abd al-Mu'min, who finally took Marrakech in 1146 and went on to found a dynasty and establish his authority over Muslim Spain as well as Morocco.

A different expression of Mahdism was the Mahdawi movement which was founded in Jaunpur in Gujarat in western India by Sayyid Muhammad (1443–1505), who in 1495 announced that he was the Mahdi. He belonged to the Chishti Sufi order (*tariqa*), and emphasising spiritual discipline as well as social justice and the proper practice of Islam, he set up communities on the model of Sufi lodges. The movement survived his death and spread south into the Deccan; after some violent clashes with the authorities during the first half of the sixteenth century, it became more peaceful. The failure of its prediction that Jesus would appear in the year 1000 of the Muslim calendar (1591) contributed to its decline in the seventeenth century (Furnish 2005: 39, Hodgson 1974: 70–71, Lapidus 2002: 366–7, MacLean 2000). It should be noted, however, that Mahdist discourse was not confined to opposition movements, but was used by rulers too. The Ottoman Sultan Selim I (reigned 1512–20), for instance, referred to himself as Mahdi of the Last Days, and the rule of his successor Suleiman the Magnificent (1520–66) was even presented as the millennium (Garcia-Arenal 2006: 292).

Sunni Mahdism in Modern Times

Beginning in the later eighteenth century various leaders who were regarded as *mujaddid*s, and sometimes as Mahdis, emerged in Africa. For example Uthman dan Fodio (1754–1817) conducted a jihad in what is now northern Nigeria against those whom he accused of being only nominal Muslims (Heine 2000). A little later Al-Hajj Umar ibn Sa'id, who claimed among other things to be the *wazir* (adviser) of the Mahdi, conquered Futa Toro in northern Senegal in 1852. Moving east, he was killed in 1864, but his followers established a state in part of what is now Mali. The French conquest of Algeria which began in 1830 sparked off a series of millenarian uprisings led by men claiming to be Mahdis (Clancy-Smith, 2000, Lapidus 2002: 420, 424–5, 588).

The most important nineteenth-century African Mahdist movement was that of the Sudanese Mahdi, Shaykh Muhammad Ahmad (1848–85). Much of eastern Sudan had been conquered by Egypt earlier in the nineteenth century, and the movement combined Muslim revival with anti-Egyptian feeling. Following a series of visions Muhammad Ahmad, an initiate of the Sammaniyyah Sufi order, revealed himself as Mahdi in 1881. He established himself in the Jabal Qadir mountains in Kordofan, south-west of Khartoum, and introduced a puritanical Islamist regime. In 1885 he took Khartoum, but died in the same year; his successor was defeated by the British at Omdurman in 1898 (Lapidus 2002: 762–4). Mahdist expectation also resurfaced in Nigeria when 'revolutionary' Mahdism swept through the western emirates of the Sokoto caliphate during the years of the colonial conquest (1897–1903)' (Lovejoy and Hogendorn 1990: 217). Mahdist literature and ideas continued to circulate in West Africa. For example, in Senegal, some of the followers of the Tijani Sufi leader, Ibrahim Niass (1900–1975), regarded him as the *mujaddid* and even Mahdi (Falola 1998: 233, Lapidus 2002: 747). A very different approach was that of Mirza Ghulam Ahmed al-Qadiani, who claimed to be the Mahdi and a prophet, and founded a peaceful revivalist movement in northern India in 1889, the Ahmadiyya (Amanat 2009: 60–61).

In other parts of the Muslim-majority world during the twentieth century Mahdist ideas remained popular, although they rarely expressed themselves in political movements. There were a few exceptions, for example there was a brief Mahdist outburst in December 1930 in western Turkey (Bozarslan 2000). The century's most dramatic expression of Mahdism, however, occurred in November 1979. On 1 Muharram 1400 AH (20 November 1979) Juhaymun al-Utaybi, a former member of the Saudi National Guard, Muhammad al-Qahtani, his brother-in-law, and some 300 followers seized control of the Great Mosque in Mecca. Al-Qahtani possessed several of the attributes of the Mahdi according to the *hadiths*; his name for instance recalled the apocalyptic figure of the Qahtani. Juhaymun intended to consecrate him as Mahdi between the *rukn* and the *maqam* in the Great Mosque and await the arrival of the army from the north as predicted by the traditions. In the event troops surrounded the mosque, al-Qahtani was killed after a few days and by early December it was all over (Hegghammer and Lacroix 2007: 112–13).

During the anti-Soviet jihad in Afghanistan in the 1980s messianic ideas were taken up by some of those involved, among them the Palestinian religious scholar, Abdallah Azzam, who identified Afghanistan as the new Khurasan, the centre of a movement to re-establish a caliphate to rule over the Muslim-majority world. Azzam had links with Osama bin Laden, but the Al Qaeda leaders themselves rarely made apocalyptic references (Cook 2005: 174, 179). In fact in the message he released in 2003 Osama bin Laden condemned Mahdist beliefs because, he said, they encouraged passivity and quietism (Furnish 2005: 153–4).

There is no evidence that contemporary militants have been influenced by the work of writers belonging to 'the radical school of apocalypticism', who since the late 1980s have used classical Muslim material to create new apocalyptic scenarios in much the same way that evangelical Christian writers have used biblical material (Cook 2005: 15). One of the most influential examples is *Al-Masih al-Dajjal* (*The Antichrist*), published in 1987 by an Egyptian journalist, Sa'id Ayyub. This purports to be a scholarly work, but focuses mainly on the supposedly nefarious role of the Jewish antichrist throughout history, ending in his defeat by Islam in the final apocalyptic battle (Filiu 2011: 83–84). Among the writers influenced by Ayyub is Muhammad Isa Dawud, who has written a number of books on apocalyptic themes. Rather like *The Late Great Planet Earth* (1970), written by the American dispensationalist and Christian Zionist Hal Lindsey, Dawud's *Al-Mahdi al-muntazar 'ala al-abwab* (*The Awaited Mahdi at the Doors*) (1997), for example, is a history of the end-times (Cook 2005: 145). It describes the appearance of the Mahdi in Mecca during the Hajj, and the long series of wars that follow, ending with the complete defeat of the West and its supporters in the Muslim-majority world, such as Turkey. The Jews are either wiped out or turn to Islam, America is humiliated, the Catholic Church is destroyed, many Europeans accept Islam, and the Mahdi is ready to create his messianic kingdom (Cook 2005: 129–45).

Other writers who have followed in Ayyub's footsteps include Amin Muhammad Gamaleddin, whose *Harmajaddun* (*Armageddon*) (2001) was published soon after 9/11. The war in Afghanistan was, he suggested, the prelude to a wider global conflict in which Israel would be destroyed, and the Mahdi would conquer the world (Filiu 2011: 110–12). One feature of this genre is its anti-Semitism, into which Western anti-Semitic conspiracy theory has been assimilated (Cook 2005: 18–19). Another is the way that writers in this genre often look for signs of the Hour in contemporary political events and try to identify contemporary personalities with figures from the early scenarios. References to figures and events in the Christian Bible, and evangelical Christian interpretations of them also occur (Cook 2005: 35, Furnish 2005: 98–99). Ayyub, for instance, draws on Revelations and applies the description of the rider on the white horse in 19:11–13 (usually understood as referring to Jesus) to the Mahdi (Cook 2005: 39). Another writer in this genre,

Bashir Abdallah, suggests in *Zilzal al-ard al-'azim* (*The Great Earthquake*) (1994) that the Mahdi is the child born in Revelations 12:5 (Cook 2005: 198).

Beyond the Arabic-speaking world, the Turkish writer Adnan Oktar (pen name Harun Yahya) is a well-known contemporary proponent of the Mahdist scenario (Filiu 2011: 171–3). In his writing Oktar often refers to the work of the founder of the influential Nurchuluk movement in Turkey, Said Nursi (1877–1960). Said Nursi tended to naturalise or demythologise the Mahdi, envisaging him as an ordinary human being, 'part of a movement, school, or community, whose activities are spread over a considerable period of time' (Saritoprak n.d.: 6, Leaman 2011: 3–4). Nursi also saw Jesus' defeat of the Antichrist as symbolic rather than literal, expressing the idea that Muslims and Christians would cooperate to 'kill' materialism (Saritoprak 2003: 297–8). Towards the end of the twentieth century the Naqshbandi-Haqqani Sufi order developed an inclusive but more traditional end-times scenario (Filiu 2011: 169). According to this 'the Dajjal and the Mahdi are both alive now, apocalyptic global conflict is imminent, and the fate of the world is sealed'. The Mahdi is waiting in a cave in the Empty Quarter in Saudi Arabia and has commanded Shaykh Nazim to prepare his helpers – 'the Muslims and non-Muslims who will rally behind the "rightly-guided one" when he declares his redemptive mission' (Damrel 2006: 122).

Modern Shiism

In modern times Imamis also began to come up with new understandings of the end-times and the Mahdi himself. In the later eighteenth century the Shaykhi school, founded by Shaykh Ahmad Ahsa'i (d.1826), anticipated Nursi in arguing that the Imam-Mahdi should be seen as an ordinary human being, not a superhuman one with extraordinary powers. It saw the millennial restoration of truth and justice as being achieved only by human effort and sacrifice (Amanat 2009: 53).[7] Ideas of this kind were to be important in the later twentieth century. The radical Iranian scholar Ali Shari'ati (1933–77), for example, turned Shiite messianic expectations into a revolutionary ideology (Amanat 2009: 63). Ayatollah Murtaza Mutahhari (1920–79), who had studied with Ayatollah Khomeini, interpreted the coming of the Mahdi not 'as a sudden and cataclysmic event outside the pale of history, but as the final stage in an ideologically driven revolution to establish Islam's "ideal society"' (Amanat 2009: 64). For him and others who shared this approach, the establishment of a 'just state' would help to bring about the Mahdist revolution. Mahdist ideas played a role in the Islamic Revolution in 1978–79; indeed, although he made no such claim himself, Ayatollah Khomeini was sometimes seen by his supporters as the deputy of the Twelfth Imam or even the Imam himself (Amanat 2009: 65–7).

---

[7]   The Baha'i religion derived from a nineteenth-century Iranian messianic movement inspired by Shaykhi ideas.

In the 1990s conservative figures in Iran launched a propaganda campaign to undermine parliament and the reformers by promoting the Mahdi as an alternative source of authority. Groups within the Islamic Republic began to publish journals, for example the magazine *Mouood* (Ma'ud, the 'promised one'), and set up a range of websites dealing with the Mahdi, not just in Persian, but in a range of other languages too. They started to organise conferences, seminars, youth camps, night vigils and mourning ceremonies, study groups and lavish commemorations of the Mahdi's birthday. Mahdist anticipation increased with the US-led invasion of Iraq, with its considerable Shiite population and its key Shiite shrines, in 2003 (Amanat 2009: 225–27, 236). In 1977 the Iraqi Ayatollah Muhammad Baqir al-Sadr had published a booklet in which he argued that although the Mahdi's reappearance could not be predicted, the present times were propitious for it. A relative, Muqtada al-Sadr, explicitly invoked the eschatological heritage by calling the militia he founded in 2003 the Me(a)hdi Army, which in 2004 clashed with US forces in the holy city of Najaf, where Ali is buried (Cockburn 2008: 172–202, Filiu 2011: 142, 147, Furnish 2005: 161). Another Iraqi Shiite who drew on messianic themes at this time was Ahmad al-Hasan, an engineer from Basra, who claimed to be the representative of the Hidden Imam. He founded a movement called Ansar al-Mahdi (Supporters of the Mahdi), which was involved in fighting against government forces in 2007 and 2008 (Filiu 2011: 160–63).

The current Iranian President, Mahmoud Ahmadinejad, often refers to the Mahdi, and maintains that the 'Advent of the Saviour' will be the 'prelude to peace, social justice, prosperity, and happiness for all humanity' (Amanat 2009: 242).[8] Groups within the Iranian government continue to promote Mahdist discourse. In 2007, for instance, a summary of a series of 12 previously broadcast radio programmes on the Mahdi was posted on its website (Filiu 2011: 152). The life of Al-Mukhtar, who as we have seen led what was probably the first Shiite revolt in 685, has been dramatised in an Iranian TV series, *Mukhtarnameh* (*Tehran Times*, 24 June 2009). In 2011 the Iranian government distributed three million copies of a CD entitled *The Coming is Upon Us* in which recent events are taken as signs of the Twelfth Imam's imminent return.[9] In this the current Supreme Guide, Ayatollah Khamenei is identified with the Khurasani, the Mahdi's standard-bearer, President Ahmadinejad with the Khurasani's lieutenant, Shoaib bin Saleh, and Sayyid Hassan Nasrullah, the head of the Hizbullah militia in Lebanon with the Yemeni (an ally of the Mahdi's in the traditional Shiite scenario) (Filiu 2011: 27, Yaluh 2011: 14). Shiites outside Iran have also endorsed Mahdism. *Al-Mahdi al-mukhaliss* (*Mahdi the Savior*), for example, was published in 2007 by the Hizbullah deputy secretary-general, Shaykh Naim Qassim. Although this

---

[8]	Reportedly his views on the end-times are 'closer than one might imagine' to those of some Christian evangelicals (Majd 2008: 84).

[9]	Yaluh suggests that this CD was produced by Ahmedinejad's supporters as part of a struggle between him and the Supreme Guide, Ayatollah Khamenei to control this discourse (Yaluh 2011: 14).

associates the black banners of Khurasan with contemporary Iran and its leaders, it refers to Hizbullah's struggle as part of 'the movement of the appearance' (Filiu 2011: 157).

Revived interest in the Mahdi can be seen, for example, in the growing popularity of what had previously been a very minor pilgrimage site. This is at Jamkaran a few miles west of Qom, where in 974 a local man had had a vision of the Twelfth Imam and built a small mosque. Since the 1990s Jamkaran has been transformed into a major pilgrimage centre, with five enclosures, 12 minarets and vast interior courtyards and facilities for hundreds of thousands of visitors. Attracting many pilgrims, its midnight congregational prayers for deliverance have become especially popular. There is also a dried-up well through which it is believed one can communicate with the Imam; pilgrims request his help by writing notes to him and dropping them in it, and tying small strings to the metal grills covering it. An online library offers books and treatises dealing mainly with the Jamkaran vision and other sightings of the Mahdi; wallpaper for cell phones and computer screensavers with 'images of Jamkaran and calligraphy with Mahdistic images' can also be downloaded (Amanat 2009: 227–32, Majd 2008: 84).

The Appeal of Mahdism

Mahdism has been a recurrent theme in Islamic history partly because it could be used for political purposes, and one way of trying to understand Mahdist movements is to see them as expressing popular resentment of political, social and economic inequality (Amanat 2009: 34–35). This may help us to understand features of some of the early Mahdist movements like that of Mukhtar in the late seventh century. However, deprivation and oppression and Mahdism are not always related, because, as we have seen, governments have used eschatological narratives too (Amanat 2009: x–xi, Bowie 1997: 13). Moreover Mahdist beliefs and faith in a future golden age can act as a kind of theodicy; human suffering can be interpreted as 'a providential design to expedite the millennial relief' (Amanat 2009: 29). Armed resistance was not the only response to colonial intrusion in late nineteenth-century West Africa for example. Some people saw this intrusion as a sign of the end and advocated withdrawal rather than confrontation (*hijra*), while others called for 'moral regeneration and religious revival' (Umar 1999: 67). The recent publications about the Mahdi, the destruction of Islam's perceived enemies and the restoration of Muslim power, may express, and help people to come to terms with, the perceived injustices of the contemporary world order.[10] Another approach is to focus on rhetoric (Cole 2001: 283). As Amanat argues, to understand the appeal of Mahdist beliefs better we need to take into account the way exposure to and participation in millenarian discourse can create an interpretive 'community'

---

[10]   Amy Frykholm's study *Rapture Culture: Left Behind in Evangelical America* (2004), particularly chapter 8, looks at the appeal of this kind of writing for many Americans.

and 'a millennial rationale', and engender 'a sense of adherence more compelling for believers than any ulterior motive' (Amanat 2009: 35).[11]

The range and diversity of Mahdism today is striking. Sunnis and Shiites disagree amongst themselves almost as much as they do with each other. This is due partly to the fact that, as we have seen, contemporary Mahdist scenarios do not simply rely on traditional narratives. Indeed we may sometimes see in them signs of creative engagement with contemporary problems and challenges. Thanks partly to the Internet, it is now much easier for individuals to reject the authority of conservative keepers of tradition, and draw on previously untapped resources, particularly biblical material, to rethink and rework these narratives (Amanat 2009: 251, Cook 2005: 215, Filiu 2011: 163).

Conclusion

We saw that some signs of the end are described in the Qur'an, including what is taken to be a reference to Jesus' return, but neither the Mahdi himself nor his adversary, the Dajjal, are mentioned. However, the traumatic impact of the civil wars after Muhammad's death, as well as pre-Islamic influences, contributed to the development of a detailed apocalyptic scenario. The Mahdi would return, and having with Jesus' help defeated the Dajjal, inaugurate a period of peace and prosperity when the whole world would turn to Islam or accept Islamic rule. For Sunnis belief in the Mahdi was never a key article of faith, but Imami Shiites in particular envisaged the awaited Twelfth Imam as the Mahdi. Mahdist beliefs have played an important political role at various points, for example in North Africa and Spain in the twelfth century, in fifteenth-century Iran and in Sudan towards the end of the nineteenth century. In modern times both Sunni and Shiite thinkers and writers have engaged with the concept of the Mahdi, sometimes naturalising and demythologising aspects of it. In the later twentieth century, however, a very different genre of Muslim apocalyptic writing emerged in Egypt, and in Iran there has been a revival of popular messianism. Mahdist movements have sometimes been vehicles through which discontents of various kinds were expressed, but Mahdism has not always been oppositional. Rather than encouraging resistance, the promise of ultimate restitution has sometimes helped people to endure injustice and suffering. Contemporary Mahdist scenarios often incorporate new elements and engage directly with current issues and concerns. A better future for humanity is usually their ultimate outcome, but often only after widespread death and destruction.

---

[11]   See for instance Johnson (1978).

References

Abdallah, B. 1994. *Zilzal al-ard al-'azim*. Cairo: [no publisher].

Aghaie, K. 2005. Messianism: Messianism in the Muslim Tradition, in *Encyclopedia of Religion*, second edition, edited by L. Jones, Vol. 9. Detroit, MI: Macmillan Reference USA, 5979–83 [Online] *Gale Virtual Reference Library* [accessed: 18 April 2011].

Ali, A. 1998–2001. *Major Signs before the Day of Judgement* [Online]. Available at: http://www.inter-islam.org/faith/Majorsigns.html [accessed: 11 April 2011].

Amanat, A. 2009. *Apocalyptic Islam and Iranian Shi'ism*. London and New York: I.B. Tauris.

Anawati, G. 2006. Isa, in *Encyclopaedia of Islam*, second edition, edited by P. Bearman et al. [Online] Brill Online [accessed: 2 December 2011].

Arjomand, S. 1998. Islamic Apocalypticism in the Classic Period, in *Apocalypticism in Western History and Culture*, Vol. 2, edited by B. McGinn. New York: Continuum, 238–83.

Ayyub, S. 1987. *Al-Masil al-Dajjal*. Cairo: Fath lil-Alam al-Arabi.

Bowie, F. 1997. Equilibrium and the End of Time: The Roots of Millenarianism, in *The Coming Deliverer: Millennial Themes in World Religions*, edited by F. Bowie with C. Deacy. Cardiff: University of Wales Press, 1–26.

Bozarslan, H. 2000. Le mahdisme en Turquie: L'incident de Menemen en 1930, in *Mahdisme et millénarisme en Islam*, edited by M. Garcia-Arenal, *Revue des mondes musulmans et de la Méditerranée*, no. 9–94. Aix-en-Provence: Édisud, 297–319.

Casanova, P. 1911. *Mohammed et la fin du monde*. Paris: P. Guethner.

Clancy-Smith, J. 2000. La revolte de Bu Ziyan en Algérie, 1849, in *Mahdisme et millénarisme en Islam*, edited by M. Garcia-Arenal, *Revue des mondes musulmans et de la Méditerranée*, no. 9–94. Aix-en-Provence: Édisud, 181–208.

Cockburn, P. 2008. *Muqtada al-Sadr and the Shia Insurgency in Iraq*. London: Faber and Faber.

Cole, J. 2001. Millennialism in Modern Iranian History, in *Imagining the End: Visions of Apocalypse from Ancient Middle East to Contemporary America*, edited by A. Amanat and M. Bernhardsson. London and New York: I.B. Tauris, 282–311.

Cook, D. 2005. *Contemporary Muslim Apocalyptic Literature*. Syracuse NY: Syracuse University Press.

Damrel, D. 2006. Aspects of the Naqshbandi-Haqqani Order in North America, in *Sufism in the West*, edited by J. Malik and J. Hinnells. Abingdon and New York: Routledge, 115–26.

Dawud, M.I. 1997. *Al-Mahdi al-Muntazar 'ala al-abwab*. Cairo: Dar Randa Amun.

Falola, T. 1998. *Violence in Nigeria: The Crisis of Religion Politics and Secular Ideologies*. Rochester, NY: University of Rochester Press.

Filiu, J-P. 2011. *Apocalypse in Islam*. Berkeley, CA and London: University of California Press, first published as L'*Apocalypse dans l'Islam*, translated by M.B. DeBevoise, 2008.

Frykholm, A. 2004. *Rapture Culture: Left Behind in Evangelical America*. Oxford and New York: Oxford University Press.

Furnish, T. 2005. *Holiest Wars: Islamic Mahdis, Their Jihads, and Osama bin Laden*. Westport, CT: Praeger.

——. 2011. *Iran's New Mahdism Da'wah Video: Letting Slip the Jinns of Jihad?* [Online]. Available at: http://hnn.us/articles/138229.html [accessed: 7 January 2012].

Gamaleddin, A.M. 2001. *Harmajaddun*. Cairo: Maktabat al-Tawfiqiyya.

Garcia-Arenal, M. 2006. *Messianism and Puritanical Reform: Mahdis of the Muslim West*. Leiden and Boston, MA: Brill.

Halm, H. 2004. *Shi'ism*, second edition, translated by J. Watson and M. Hill. Edinburgh: Edinburgh University Press.

Hegghammer, T. and Lacroix, S. 2007. Rejectionist Islam in Saudi Arabia: The Story of Juhayman al-Utaybi Revisited. *International Journal of Middle Eastern Studies*, 39, 103–22.

Heine, P. 2000. I Am Not the Mahdi, but …, in *Apocalyptic Time*, edited by A. Baumgarten. Leiden, Boston, MA and Köln: Brill, 69–78.

Hodgson, M. 1974. *The Venture of Islam: Conscience and History in a World Civilization. Volume 3: The Gunpowder Empires and Modern Times*. Chicago, IL and London: University of Chicago Press.

Johnson, N. 1978. Religious Paradigms of the Sudanese Mahdiyah. *Ethnohistory*, 25(2), 159–78.

Lapidus, I. 2002. *A History of Islamic Societies*, second edition. Cambridge: Cambridge University Press.

Leaman, O. ed. 2006. *The Qur'an: An Encyclopedia*. Abingdon and New York: Routledge.

——. 2011. *The Mahdi as a Source of Doctrinal Differentiation in Islam* [Online]. Available at: http://www.mahdaviat-conference.com/prtht-nwd23nq.102.html [accessed: 11 November 2011].

Lindsey, H. 1970. *The Late Great Planet Earth*. Grand Rapids, MI: Zondervan.

Lovejoy, P. and Hogendorn, J. 1990. Revolutionary Mahdism and Resistance to Colonial Rule in the Sokoto Caliphate, 1905–6, *Journal of African History*, 31, 217–44.

MacLean, D. 2000. La sociologie de l'engagement politique: le Mahdawîya indien et l'État, in *Mahdisme et millénarisme en Islam*, edited by M. Garcia-Arenal, *Revue des mondes musulmans et de la Méditerranée*, no. 9-94. Aix-en-Provence: Édisud, 239–56.

Madelung, W. 2006. al-Mahdi, in *Encyclopaedia of Islam*, second edition, edited by P. Bearman et al. [Online] Brill Online [accessed: 7 April 2011].

Majd, H. 2008. *The Ayatollah Begs to Differ: The Paradox of Modern Iran*. London: Penguin.

Qassim, N. 2007. *Al-Mahdi al-mukhaliss (Mahdi the Saviour)*. Beirut: Dar al-Hadi.

Sachedina, A. 1981. *Islamic Messianism: The Idea of the Mahdi in Twelver Shi'ism*. Albany, NY: State University of New York Press.

Saritoprak, Z. 2003. The Legend of al-Dajjal (Antichrist): The Personification of Evil in the Islamic Tradition. *Muslim World*, 93(2), 291–308.

——. 2006. Eschatology, in *The Qur'an: An Encyclopedia*, edited by O. Leaman. Abingdon and New York. Routledge, 198.

——. [no date]. *The Mahdi Question According to Bediuzzaman Said Nursi* [Online]. Available at: http://www.nursistudies.com/teblig.php?tno=324 [accessed: 4 December 2011].

Tehran Times. 2009. 'Mukhtarnameh' Shooting Completed [Online 24 June 2009]. Available at: http://old.tehrantimes.com/NCms/2007.asp?code=197557 [accessed: 3 April 2012].

Umar, M. 1999. Muslims' Eschatological Discourses on Colonialism in Northern Nigeria. *Journal of the American Academy of Religion*, 67(1), 59–84.

Waines, D. 2003. *An Introduction to Islam*, second edition. Cambridge: Cambridge University Press.

Yaluh, R. 2011. Mahdism in Contemporary Iran: Ahmadinejad and the Occult Imam. *Arab Center for Research and Policy Studies Research Papers* [Online]. Available at: www.dohainstitute.org [accessed: 7 December 2011].

Chapter 8

The Coming Golden Age:
On Prophecy in Hinduism

Luis González-Reimann

In traditional Hinduism, the theory that comes closest to prophecy, understood as the prediction of the future of the world and of humanity in a way that impacts believers, is the belief in the succession of four declining world ages called *yugas*. The *yugas* characterise society and its adherence to – or distance from – accepted social conduct and proper religious or spiritual practices. There is no generalised belief in a terminal moment in human history and a final judgement when only the chosen will be saved from some form of eternal damnation.[1] In this chapter, we will look at the origins of the *yuga* theory and its defining role in the way in which traditional Hinduism has explained the past, present and future of human society. We shall see how the image of a rescuer emerged under specific historical circumstances and was later reinterpreted to predict the coming of a future saviour who will inaugurate an era of global spirituality and brotherhood. We will also look at how the arrival of Islam and Christianity in South Asia influenced some movements which combined traditional Hindu ideas about the *yugas* with notions of a day of judgement and redemption.

The Vedic Seers

The dating of texts is notoriously difficult for early literature, but the Vedic period is generally agreed to have lasted from c.1500 or 1200 BCE up to c.400 BCE. Hinduism finds its place as a post-Vedic tradition that emerges at the end of the Vedic period, approximately at the same time as Buddhism and Jainism became established. However, in sharp contrast to these two religious traditions, late Vedic

---

[1]   In a text from the seventh–sixth centuries BCE, the *Śatapatha Brāhmaṇa*, there is mention of a great flood from which Manu, humanity's ancestor, is rescued by a supernatural fish. In Puranic literature of later centuries, this myth was reinterpreted and assigned to the god Viṣṇu, who at the time of periodic deluges rescues 'all living beings' (*bhūtān sarvān*, *Matysa Purāṇa* 2.18) along with gods and religious teachings. The flood story is not about saving the 'chosen', and it does not inform the expectations of believers concerning the future. It is linked to a cosmic cycle called the *manvantara*. For the Indian flood story see González-Reimann (2006).

and post-Vedic Brahmanical Hinduism considers the Vedic texts, the Vedas, as revealed and not human, *apauruṣeya*.

The *Ṛg Veda* is the oldest and most important of the Vedas. It is a collection of hymns composed by different poets that address the gods asking for good health, long life, sons, wealth and a safe journey after death. The Rgvedic poets, the *kavis* or *ṛṣis*, also ask for inspiration when composing their hymns, and when they reach inspired states they claim to see the gods in their minds, and to witness their great deeds. They proclaim to bear witness to past events, especially the moment when the world – and the Vedic ritual sacrifice – were originally created. The composer of hymn 10.130.6 declares that he can witness with his mind's eye the time of the creation of the sacrifice, which is coeval with the creation of the world. This interest in the beginning of the world, however, has no counterpart in an interest in its end. The end of the world and/or of Vedic society was not a matter for concern for the Rgvedic poets. Their interest lay more in understanding the mythological origins of the world and of the Vedic ritual, and in glorifying the gods in order to secure their help.

Non-Believers and Foreign Invaders

By the end of the Vedic period, Brahman priests, the keepers of the tradition, began to feel threatened by the rise of movements that rejected the authority of the Vedas. These movements were labelled by the Brahmans as non-believers, *nāstikas*, and/or as heretics, *pāṣaṇḍas*. There were several such movements, but two were to become long-lasting and influential: Buddhism and Jainism. It became crucial for the Brahman priests, as well as for Buddhist and Jain leaders, to procure the patronage of rulers. In the third century BCE, King Aśoka – the most powerful ruler of the Mauryan Empire – proclaimed that he would follow the Buddhist *dharma*, the Buddhist teachings. The Brahmans, or at least an influential sector among them, perceived this as a threat to their survival as the leading religious community. Many modern scholars now believe that the extant *Mahābhārata*, one of the two great Sanskrit epics composed around the beginning of the Common Era, was in large part a Brahmanical response to the challenges posed by Aśoka's embracing of Buddhism (Fitzgerald 2004: 100–142, and 2010). Although Aśoka did not persecute Brahmans, he certainly did not privilege the Vedic tradition.

In addition to the challenges presented by the rise of Buddhism and Jainism, the early centuries before and after the beginning of the Common Era witnessed the intrusion of successive waves of invaders into the north-west of the subcontinent. Peoples like the Śakas (Scythians) established their rule and caused concern among the upholders of the Brahmanical tradition, a concern that is patently reflected in a short text from the first century BCE called the *Yuga Purāṇa*.[2] It is around this time that the figure of a saviour, a rescuer, appears in Brahmanical Sanskrit literature.[3]

Kalki to the Rescue

This deliverer first enters the scene in a late section of the *Mahābhārata*. The sage Mārkaṇḍeya predicts that the saviour will be a Brahman born in a village named Sambhala. His name will be Kalki Viṣṇuyaśas, and despite being born as a Brahman priest he will take up arms. After obliterating the foreigners (*mlecchas*),[4] he will reinstate the Brahmanical social order and return power to the Brahmans and their kings by performing a Vedic horse sacrifice (3.188.89–3.189.2). The horse sacrifice (*aśvamedha* or *vājimedha*) was one of the prominent ritual sacrifices performed by Vedic kings, and in the first half of the first millennium CE it became a symbol of a king's adherence to Brahmanical tradition.

If this passage of the *Mahābhārata* places special emphasis on Kalki's role as destroyer of foreign rulers,[5] another text from the beginning of the CE, the *Vāyu Purāṇa* (c. third–fourth centuries), also focuses on Kalki's role as destroyer of non-believers and heretics. In the words of the Puranic composer, 'Kalki will strike down the foreigners (*mlecchas*) everywhere, and they will all disappear. The same [will happen] with all the heretics (*pāṣaṇḍas*) and those who don't follow *dharma*.'[6] We now have a prediction announcing the appearance of a deliverer

---

[2]   The emphasis of the *Yuga Purāṇa* is on foreign invaders, but it does include a mention of heretics, *pāṣaṇḍas* (5).

[3]   Buddhist communities also reacted negatively to these incursions by foreigners. Some Buddhist traditions from the same historical period predict the future disappearance of the Buddhist *dharma*, and place an important part of the blame on the invasions of Greeks, Śakas and Parthians in the north-west. Thus, both Brahmans and Buddhists reacted to these incursions by voicing concern about the survival of their respective traditions. See Nattier (1991: 127).

[4]   The word *mleccha* was probably originally used for those who speak an incomprehensible or unrefined language. It is applied to foreigners such as the Śakas (Scythians) and the Yāvanas (Indo-Greeks, in this historical period), and to members of non-Brahmanical or lowly groups. It can be translated as foreigner, barbarian or lowly person, depending on the context. For a study of the meaning of *mleccha* see Thapar (1971).

[5]   Like the *Yuga Purāṇa*, the *Mahābhārata* emphasises the role of foreign invaders but also blames the *pāṣaṇḍas* (3.186.43, 3.189.9).

[6]   'kalkinopahatāḥ sarve mlecchā yāsyanti sarvaśaḥ / adharmikāś ca te 'tyarthaṃ pāṣaṇḍāś caiva sarvaśaḥ //' (*Vāyu Purāṇa* 2.37.390). Elsewhere, the Purana is more specific about the identity of the heretics. In 1.58.64, for instance, it mentions the *kaṣāyins* (Buddhists), the *nirgranthas* (Jains) and the *kāpālikas* (Śaiva ascetics who used a human skull as a begging bowl). A late addition to the *Mahābhārata* reinforces Kalki's role as rescuer and mentions the Buddha, although in this case the Buddha is said to be an *avatāra* of Viṣṇu born for the purpose of confusing mankind with a false teaching. Kalki will then

who will rid the land of foreign rulers and non-believers. Kalki represented a way out of what these Brahman authors saw as the end of the world – their social and religious world. The term used for this end of the world is *yugānta*, the end of the *yuga*.[7]

But their world did not end. It was merely transformed, and it took shape as what we know as Hinduism. By the time of the Gupta Empire (fourth to seventh centuries), the Brahman priests had regained favour among the imperial rulers, and the Brahmanical elite no longer felt a need to be rescued from foreign domination. The role of Kalki as a future saviour continued to be described in the Puranas (texts on mythology, ritual, genealogy and other topics), but there was no longer an imminent terrible political threat that had to be confronted. It is important to add that Kalki was early on appropriated by Vaiṣṇavism and recognised as the future incarnation of the god Viṣṇu. Kalki is the last one of Viṣṇu's *avatāras*, his descents to Earth for the purpose of upholding *dharma*. The Vaiṣṇava appropriation of Kalki went hand in hand with its appropriation of the Vedic idea mentioned above of a great flood from which Manu was rescued by a fish.[8] Vaiṣṇavism construed both the fish and Kalki as *avatāras* of Viṣṇu, and placed them respectively at the beginning and the end of its list of *avatāras*.

The Theory of the Yugas

In the *Mahābhārata*, the image of Kalki was combined with an emerging theory of ages of the world called *yugas*. This theory appears in Sanskrit literature for the first time in the *Mahābhārata* itself and in the *Mānava Dharma Śāstra* (the Laws of Manu), as well as in the *Yuga Purāṇa*, all dated to the centuries surrounding the beginning of the Common Era. There are four *yugas*, and they determine the conditions of society as seen through the lens of the Brahmanical tradition. The *yugas* bear similarities to the Greek ages mentioned by Hesiod, which are named after metals. The names of the *yugas*, by contrast, are drawn from the Indian game of dice, which used four names to indicate winning, losing and two intermediate stages between them. The names of the four dice throws – and hence of the *yugas* – are Kṛta, the winning throw, followed by, in descending order, Tretā, Dvāpara and Kali, the losing throw. The *yuga* cycle begins with Kṛta, when society functions properly; and it ends with Kali, when the social order is turned upside down. When Kali elapses, Kṛta returns, and the descending cycle starts anew. This fourfold cycle is called a 'great *yuga*', a *mahāyuga*. It is repeated 1,000 times before the world is destroyed at the end of a larger cycle called a *kalpa*. As soon as the world is recreated, a new round of 1,000 *mahāyugas* begins. The cycle of four

---

rout all the heretics. See *Mahābhārata* Book 12, Appendix 1, No. 31.1–7, 18–21, translated and discussed in González-Reimann (2002: 171).

[7]   For the different uses of *yugānta* in the *Mahābhārata* see González-Reimann (2010).

[8]   See note 1 above.

yugas is defined by *dharma*, proper conduct. In the Kṛta Yuga everyone follows the Brahmanical *dharma*, but as the *yugas* descend from Kṛta to Kali, *dharma* wanes and people are increasingly less able to follow it.

Just like Kalki, the rescuer, the *yuga* theory made its appearance precisely at the time when the traditional Brahmanical establishment was feeling threatened by foreign rulers and heretics. *Pāṣaṇḍas* (heretics) of different persuasions challenged both the validity of the Vedic ritual and the divine origin of the four social classes (*varṇas*) upheld by the Vedic-based Brahmanical orthodoxy. This hierarchical system places the Brahman priests at the top. Their duty, or *dharma*, is to learn and teach the Vedas and the Vedic ritual. They are followed by the warriors and rulers, the *kṣatriyas*; and next come the *vaiśyas*, the productive class, made up of merchants, agricultural workers and others. At the bottom of the structure are the *śūdras*, the servants, whose duty it is to serve the three upper classes. This is the social world that, in the eyes of Brahmanical authors, was being dangerously threatened by foreigners and non-believers. At the end of the Kali Yuga, it was Kalki's role to re-establish proper Brahmanical *dharma* in society.

The *Mahābhārata* passage that describes Kalki's destruction of foreign invaders details the terrible events of the Kali Yuga, especially as it comes to a close. It refers repeatedly to the end of the *yuga*, *yugānta*, which is not only the end of the Kali Yuga, but also the end of the entire descending sequence of four *yugas*, the *mahāyuga*. Many calamities are enumerated in these descriptions of *yugānta*, as morality descends to its lowest level, but in the mind of the author (or authors) one of the worst characteristics of those trying times is the mixing of the social classes and the blurring of the boundaries that separate them. It is the reversal of roles between servants (*śūdras*) and Brahmans that worries the authors the most, because it is seen as an indicator of the complete breakdown of the social system.[9]

The emerging *yuga* theory served to explain this social catastrophe, and it also provided a framework for its future solution. In fact, it is probable that sometime around the beginning of the Common Era there were expectations within some Brahmanical circles that Kalki would appear soon and a new Kṛta Yuga would be established (González-Reimann 2002: 96–9). As time passed, however, and despite the patronage that Brahmans received from the Gupta rulers, it was clear that the Kṛta Yuga had not returned, as society did not reflect the ideal conditions of the best of the *yugas*, in which there is no mixing of social classes, people tell the truth, there is abundant food, sickness does not exist and morality is at its peak. At this point, the Kali Yuga became the main focus of the *yuga* cycle, and calculations about its duration indicated that it would last for hundreds of thousands of years. The birth of Kalki and the arrival of the Kṛta Yuga were now seen as events located in a very distant future, and not as something of immediate relevance.

In accordance with this mythological/historical framework, every negative condition of society was understood as the inevitable result of living in the Kali Yuga. Hinduism then became the tradition – or traditions – that addressed the

---

[9]   The full description is in *Mahābhārata* 3.188–9, translated in van Buitenen (1975).

difficulties of living in the Kali Yuga. A new concept known as *yuga dharma* emerged. According to its formulation, there is an appropriate *dharma* for each one of the four *yugas*, a *dharma* that is best suited to the characteristics of people living in each age. Because the Kali Yuga is the current age, it became common to posit one's religious tradition as the best path for attaining spiritual liberation in this worst of the *yugas*. Followers of the god Śiva, for instance, declared that Śiva was the god best suited for the Kali Yuga. Worship should therefore be directed to him. The followers of Viṣṇu, on the other hand, claimed that is was Viṣṇu – especially in his descents as Kṛṣṇa and Rāma – who should be considered as the foremost god of the Kali Yuga. Repeating his name constantly was said to be the best path to liberation in Kali. Devotees of the Goddess countered by explaining that in this *yuga* she offered the best way to liberation, while tantric texts claimed that they presented the best teachings for the Kali Yuga.[10]

Belief in the *yugas* became so prevalent in South Asia that the theory also forms part of Buddhist cosmogonical and cosmological descriptions, especially its emphasis on the Kali Yuga as the corrupt present age.[11] The theory was also accepted by many different groups, as we shall see.

Cyclical Time and the End of the World

A fundamental aspect of the *yuga* theory, and of Indian perceptions of life and history, is that time moves in recurring cycles. One of the central tenets of Hinduism and other Indian religions is the belief in reincarnation. Physical death is not a final, unique event. One can be reborn in a physical body as many times as necessary in order to finally attain liberation. Indian traditions that accept reincarnation also believe in the recurrent birth, life and death of the world: just as individuals are reborn after death, the world is also recreated after being destroyed. Thus, in Indian traditions salvation/liberation does not depend exclusively on one's present life, but can be achieved in the course of many lifetimes. Likewise, the notion of a final, definitive day of judgment is largely absent from traditional Hinduism, for which there is never a terminal and final end of the world. Yes, the world is destroyed at some point, but then it is recreated; the cycle is endless.

The end is always linked to a new beginning. The dreadful end of the Kali Yuga is at the same time the marker for the arrival of a new Kṛta Yuga, a positive, glorious age. There is no abiding anxiety about the end of the world because the end of the Kali Yuga will ultimately bring a new Kṛta Yuga which is eagerly expected. In historical terms, the problem does not lie in future events. The problem is in the present. We live in the Kali Yuga, and that accounts for all the terrible things that happen to us individually as well as collectively. From that perspective the main

---

[10]   For references and more analysis see González-Reimann (2002: 172–80).

[11]   See Nattier (1991: 280, n. 3).

concern, in any case, is that the Kṛta Yuga is too far into the future in order for it to make a difference in our current lifetimes.

It seems clear that the cycle of birth, death and rebirth of the world is a projection of the cycle of birth, death and rebirth of the individual. Neither one of these two cycles is present in early or middle Vedic literature. Reincarnation makes its appearance in the Upaniṣads (c.600–200 BCE), while the cycle of world creation and destruction – as well as the *yuga* cycle – appears in the literature slightly later than reincarnation. They both then became widespread beliefs. The medieval Hindu devotional (*bhakti*) traditions accept the existence of the *yugas* and our position in the Kali Yuga as a matter of course. This includes important Sant teachers of the North Indian *nirguṇī bhakti* movement like Kabir, Ravidas (both fifteenth to sixteenth centuries CE) and Guru Nanak (fifteenth century), the founder of Sikhism. All three discard many elements of the Brahmanical tradition, such as the system of social classes and much of Puranic mythology, but they accept the *yugas* (Lorenzen 1995: 16–17).

The full classical system of world ages would become a complex combination of different types of cycles. The *yugas* are related to *dharma*, while the cycle of creation and destruction of the world is known as the *kalpa*, also called the day of Brahmā, the creator god of Hinduism. The two cycles are tied together, because, as we have seen, 1,000 rounds of four *yugas* make up one *kalpa*.[12]

The Arrival of Islam

Many centuries after the appearance of the *yuga* theory there was a new set of invasions that made the Brahmanical elite and others feel seriously threatened. This was the arrival of Islam. Starting around the twelfth century, Muslim rule was established in the subcontinent, and the presence of foreign rulers was once again seen as a consequence of the Kali Yuga.[13] Significantly, however, this time Kalki was not the main image invoked to symbolise a warrior that would confront the invaders. Instead, it was Rāma, the hero god of the *Rāmāyaṇa*, that served as the prototype of the upholder of tradition vis-à-vis the foreign rulers. In the *Rāmāyaṇa*, Rāma rids the world of a powerful group of demons known as *rākṣasas*, and now the invading Muslim rulers were themselves portrayed as *rākṣasas*, the *rākṣasas* of the Kali Yuga. Rāma became the symbol of the ideal king for many Hindu rulers, and it was not uncommon for kings to adopt his name and/or to be considered incarnations of him charged with the task of confronting

---

[12]   In addition to the *kalpas* and the *yugas*, the fully developed system of cosmic ages includes the *manvantaras* (mentioned in note 1) and the life of Brahmā. See González-Reimann (2009) for a detailed study of these cycles and their origin.

[13]   See Granoff 1999 for two texts, one Hindu and the other Jain, that invoke the Kali Yuga in an attempt to explain the destruction of temples and images at the hands of Muslim invaders.

these *rākṣasas*.[14] Two eighteenth-century commentators of the *Rāmāyaṇa* bluntly refer to Muslims as '... the *rākṣasas* of the Kali age ...' (cited in Pollock 1993: 287). And early biographers of the Maratha national hero Shivaji (seventeenth century) depict a Muslim general killed by Shivaji as 'a demonic incarnation of the Kali Yuga' (Laine 2003: 23–4, also 40, 42).

This does not mean that the image of Kalki disappeared from the literature, as different Puranas still retold the standard story. In around the eleventh century, a minor Vaiṣṇava text, the *Kalki Purāṇa*, was composed, probably in Bengal, to exalt him as a form of Viṣṇu and to amplify his familiar role of protector of the Brahmanical social order, destroyer of foreigners and non-believers, and establisher of a new Kṛta Yuga. This Purana emphasises Kalki's role as the destroyer of Buddhism, and it describes a mythological battle in which Kalki conquers the Buddhists (*bauddhas*) with his devastating battle skills (2.7–3.1). Ironically, a Buddhist text, the *Kālacakra Tantra* (c. eleventh century), appropriated the Hindu figure of Kalki as destroyer of foreigners and non-believers, and applied it directly to the Muslim invasions. It predicted a future Buddhist holy war against Islam at the end of the *yuga*.[15] The *Kālacakra Tantra* actually describes an unusual alliance of Buddhist and Hindu forces summoned at *yugānta* in order to rout the invading Muslims. It depicts Kalki – now as a Buddhist saviour – fighting alongside the Hindu gods Viṣṇu, Śiva, Skanda and Gaṇeśa in their battle against the foreign invaders.[16]

The myth of Sambhala (also spelled Śambhala), the native village of Kalki in Hindu traditions, was appropriated by Tibetan Buddhism, and Śambhala became the name of a hidden and inaccessible land where sacred teachings were guarded, and as the place from which a new glorious age would emerge in the future. The rulers of this Buddhist Śambhala bear the name Kalki, and the destroyer of the foreign invaders of South Asia will be the twenty-fifth, and last, Buddhist Kalki to emerge from Śambhala (Newman 1995: 286–7).[17]

The arrival of Islam also brought traditions that blended Islamic ideas with Hindu ones. The Nizari Ismailism (Ismailism is a branch of Shia Islam) that developed in north-western India is a case in point. In poetic songs knows as *ginans*, Nizari composers appropriated the *yuga* theory and the image of Kalki, whom they referred to as Nikalank Avatar. To them, Nikalank (or Niṣkalank) was also Mahdi – the Arabic term that Islam uses for its version of a coming

---

[14]   See Pollock (1993) on the ruler Pṛthvīrāja III (twelfth century). For more references see González-Reimann (2002: 190, n. 28).

[15]   See Newman (1998) for an analysis of the portrayal of Islam in the *Kālacakra Tantra*.

[16]   *Kālacakra Tantra* 1.159–64, translated in Newman (1995: 289). The passage is 1.158–63 in the Vira and Chandra Sanskrit edition.

[17]   The Tibetan myth of Śambhala probably influenced James Hilton's imagined ideal land of Shangri-La, popularised in his 1933 novel *Lost Horizons*, and turned into a movie on two occasions.

saviour (for more on the Mahdi see Chapter 7, this volume) – thus attesting to the composite Muslim–Hindu nature of the Nikalank Avatar. At the end of the Kali Yuga, amid great destruction, Nikalank Avatar will establish a time of peace characterised by Hindu–Muslim unity. In a twist reminiscent of the Buddhist–Hindu alliance against Muslims portrayed in the *Kālacakra Tantra*, Nikalank Avatar will fight against Kali (or Kaliṅga), a personification of the Kali Yuga, with an army made up of a combination of Hindu epic heroes and Muslim figures. The Nizari prophecies about Nikalank Avatar and the end of the Kali Yuga include an element that – as noted earlier in this chapter – is not part of Hindu traditions, but is drawn instead from Islamic sources: the idea of punishment and judgment/resurrection at the time of the end.

Similar descriptions to those of the Nizari Ismaili *ginans* are found in the *agam vanis* ('poems of the time to come') associated with the Nizar Panth, and the Biśnoi and the Jasnathi movements, Hindu sectarian traditions from north-western India which were probably influenced by the same Nizari Ismaili beliefs.[18] As late as 1959 a Sikh messianic *sadhu* (wandering ascetic) by the name of Baghel Singh, head of the Lal Kurti movement in North India, proclaimed that he was an *avatāra* and called himself Niṣkalank Avatar, revealing a lingering Nizari influence (Khan 1997: 422). Baghel Singh attempted an armed struggle against the government, a fight that was to be like a second *Mahābhārata* war, but he was shot in a confrontation with police and his followers were arrested (Fuchs 1992: 183–6).

British Rule and the New Kṛta or Satya Yuga[19]

Just as the image of the demon *rākṣasas* and the influence of the Kali Yuga were sometimes applied to the invading Muslim forces, the gradual and steady spread of British power in India was also often seen as a consequence of the Kali Yuga. The East India Company, founded in 1600 and dissolved in 1858 after vastly extending British influence in India, gave way to formal British imperial rule when Queen Victoria assumed the title of Empress of India in 1877. In the nineteenth century there were movements that advocated eradicating British foreign rule and establishing a new era. One such movement, around 1824, was led by a renouncer who saw himself as the Kalki avatar (Khan 1997: 422, citing H.H. Wilson). Likewise, Birsa Munda, who in 1895 became the leader of an uprising of the Munda tribal groups, considered the desired end of British rule as the end of the Kali Yuga. In Munda's narrative, Queen Victoria was indirectly represented by Queen Mandodarī, the wife of Rāvaṇa, who is the king of the evil *rākṣasas* in the *Rāmāyaṇa*. She had to be destroyed, at least symbolically, in order for British rule

---

[18]   These descriptions of Nikalank Avatar are taken from Khan (1997).

[19]   The term *satya*, truth, had by now largely replaced *kṛta* (done, good), as the name of the best *yuga*.

to be stamped out, and for the Satya Yuga to begin (Luker 1998: 60–61).[20] Birsa Munda, who had been influenced by Christianity, spoke of fire raining from the sky, and stated that only those who remained with him would be saved (Fuchs 1992: 35, Luker 1998: 59). He thus combined Christian ideas of a final judgment with Puranic Hindu ideas related to the *yugas*, just like the Nizari-influenced movements took the notion of a final judgment from Islam.

The push for home rule, and later for independence, imbued Indian intellectuals with a hopeful sense of a better future, a new age free from foreign dominance. By the end of the nineteenth and the beginning of the twentieth centuries, such expectations would often use the trope of a new Satya Yuga as a rallying point. The quest for political independence on occasion went hand in hand with spiritual aspirations of a new era. But the vision of a new Satya Yuga as a purely spiritual idea also gained traction, and it is at this time that the image of Kalki became that of a spiritual leader who will establish an age of brotherhood for all. Within this image, the destruction of foreigners is no longer taken literally but is instead seen as a metaphor for the elimination of ignorance and the triumph of noble spiritual truths. In this idea, the emphasis on the Kali Yuga as the oppressive present shifts and gives way to hopeful expectations of a new Satya Yuga of spiritual brotherhood.

In this respect, we must mention important and influential figures such as Vivekananda (1863–1902), who considered his spiritual guru, Ramakrishna, to have inaugurated the new Satya Yuga with his birth in 1836. For Vivekananda, Ramakrishna was born for the purpose of bringing together the civilisations of Ancient India and Europe, and to get rid of corruption in religion. Aurobindo Ghose (1872–1950), who often praised Vivekananda, wrote of 'the return of the *satyayuga* of national greatness' and of the need to institute a practice of yoga that will 'prepare a perfect humanity and help in the restoration of the Satya Yuga'. M. Gandhi (1869–1948), who sought independence for India by means of non-violent resistance, also spoke of the Satya Yuga. In a speech delivered in 1919 he stated: 'What I am seeking is the resurgence of *Satya Yuga* in India.' The Indian Nobel Laureate poet, Rabindranath Tagore (1861–1941), used similar hopeful language. After the First World War, he wrote that 'the door of the new Age has been flung open at the trumpet blast of a great war', and made a comparison

---

[20]   There are other examples of the importance of the *yugas* in the colonial period. For the use of the Kali Yuga to explain British bureaucratic power in Bengal at the end of the nineteenth century, and for mentions of the coming Satya Yuga, see Sarkar (1989, 1997a, 1997b). For the significance of the Kali Yuga in colonial Orissa in the Mahimā Dharma sect, founded in the 1860s by Mahima Swami, and for the belief that the Swami was the *avatāra* who would end the Kali Yuga, see Banerjee-Dube (2001, 2008). The tenets of the sect were spread by the poet Bhima Bhoi (1850?–95), who declared that the Satya Yuga was on hand (Beltz 2008: 90). In a text attributed to Bhima Bhoi, there is an anachronistic prediction about Kalki being born under the name of Gandhi in order to rid India of the British by means of non-violence, Banerjee-Dube (2001: 25).

between those times and the circumstances surrounding the war described in the *Mahābhārata* epic, a war that is traditionally considered to have marked the beginning of the Kali Yuga.[21] This new age would be the Satya Yuga. As recently as 1996, Rama Coomaraswamy, son of the renowned historian of Indian art A.K. Coomaraswamy, wrote of the approaching end of the Kali Yuga (Coomaraswamy 1996: 111, 113).

The Universalisation of the Saviour

The Theosophical Society played an important role in the modern resurgence of the anticipation of the Satya Yuga and Kalki's arrival. Founded in New York in 1875 by Helena Blavatsky (1831–91), the Society would later establish its Indian headquarters in Adyar, South India. Annie Besant (1847–1933), one of Blavatsky's followers, emerged as a prominent member of the Society and became its president in 1907, a few years after Blavatsky's death. Besant, who was born in England, believed that in previous lives she had been born in India, and considered India to be her 'true Motherland' (Wessinger 1988: 213). She turned into an ardent early activist and advocate for Indian home rule, and her activities and ideas were an important influence in the early drive for Indian independence.

Besant was also a strong believer in the imminent arrival of a world saviour, a spiritual figure that would establish the new age. She referred to him as the World Teacher. Blavatsky had also written about a coming spiritual teacher, but she usually used the Buddhist term Maitreya to refer to him, and equated him with the Kalki *avatāra* (Blavatsky 1971, vol. 2: 99, 192).[22] She did not emphasise Kalki's arrival, although at one point she wrote that the Kali Yuga, or a sub-cycle within it, was ending (Blavatsky 1971, vol. 2: 337, and 1960: 174).[23] In contrast, Besant thought the appearance of the new World Teacher was imminent, and together with fellow Theosophist C.W. Leadbeater, became convinced that a young boy from South India was destined to be the awaited World Teacher. After years of grooming by Besant and Leadbeater, Jiddu Krishnamurti (1895–1986) disavowed

---

[21] For the references in this paragraph and further discussion see González-Reimann (2002: 183–5).

[22] Maitreya is Buddhism's version of a coming saviour. He has a long history in Buddhist literature. See Sponberg and Hardacre (1988, especially the chapters by Nattier and Jaini).

[23] In 1971, vol. 3: 154, n. 2, Blavatsky uses standard Puranic calculations and writes that the Kali Yuga will continue for another 427,000 years, but also states that the '"Sixth Sub-Race", – which may begin very soon – will be in its Satya (Golden) Age …'. Elsewhere, she characterises Puranic calculations as 'exoteric', while the true 'esoteric' ones 'have … never been made public' (1971, vol. 3: 80). Theosophists use a complex and idiosyncratic reinterpretation of Indian cycles.

the role and became an independent and influential spiritual teacher known around the world.

There is an important facet of the way in which Theosophists and others at the time viewed the coming rescuer. We might call it the universalisation, or even globalisation of the image of the expected teacher. It involves the conflation of saviours from different religions in order to create the character of a single spiritual teacher who will be all of them at once. We have seen how the Nizari movement combined the Hindu Kalki with the Mahdi from Shia Islam, and how Birsa Munda incorporated Christian influence. But this tendency to combine different saviours into one reached its height towards the end of the nineteenth century and the beginning of the twentieth. The new spiritual teacher would simultaneously be Kalki, Mahdi, Maitreya, the second coming of Christ and any other saviour expected by other traditions.

For example, the Bahá'í Faith, born in Iran in the nineteenth century, would soon view its founder, Bahá'u'lláh, in this light. Although Bahá'u'lláh himself didn't directly state that he was Kalki, his son, 'Abdu'l-Bahá,' confirmed it when a follower made the identification (Buck 2004: 157, see also Buck 1986: 158). And in Europe it was common for esoteric movements – often influenced in one way or another by Theosophy – to speak of a new global teacher and the beginning of a new universal age of peace and brotherhood. This conflation of religious traditions regarding the coming New Age was taken further by combining it with the emerging belief in the dawn of the astrological Age of Aquarius, a subject that started appearing significantly in European esoteric literature during the first half of the twentieth century. Ultimately, this blend was to give rise to the New Age movements of the 1960s.

Modern Movements in India

In India, the situation shortly before and after independence from Britain evolved along two main lines. For politicians, the religious figure that was to become central in political discourse was Rāma, the hero of the *Rāmāyaṇa*, whose image had fulfilled the role of representative of a truly Hindu kingdom in previous centuries. Modern nationalistic movements have not only rallied around Rāma, but have also adopted Hanuman, a friend and helper of Rāma in the early *Vālmīki Rāmāyaṇa*, and a god and faithful devotee of Rāma in subsequent retellings of his story. Kalki, on the other hand, had now been fully transformed into a purely spiritual teacher, the destroyer of ignorance and bringer of a universal era of brotherhood: the Satya Yuga.

Modern Indian ideas about Kalki and the Satya Yuga have assumed a universalistic tone. Early texts considered that the *yugas* applied only to India, *bhāratavarṣa*,[24] just as the early appearance of Kalki in Brahmanical literature

---

[24] *Mahābhārata* 6.11.3, also stated in several Puranas.

was specifically tied to the desire of ridding India of foreign invaders and heretics. However, just as different redeemers, messiahs or saviours had now been blended into one unique figure for the whole world, the Indian Satya Yuga and its Kalki became globalised and of universal applicability. The *dharma* that Kalki will implement is no longer restricted to the Brahmanical *dharma*, it is conceived as a universal concept related to spirituality, morality and proper behaviour.

It is along these universalistic lines that many modern Indian religious movements see their founder as Kalki and/or as the establisher of the Satya Yuga (in many cases, it is the founder himself that presents himself as Kalki). Salient examples are Maharishi Mahesh Yogi, founder of the Transcendental Meditation (TM) movement, who stated that 'We are on the threshold of a new age in which enlightenment … is increasingly guiding the destiny of human life … The age of ignorance is receding, and the sunshine of the Age of Enlightenment is on its way to bring fulfilment to the noblest aspirations of mankind' (González-Reimann 2002: 200, n. 121). Other spiritual teachers considered by their disciples to be Kalki, or to have opened the new age, are Meher Baba (1894–1969), Swami Sivananda (1887–1963) and Anandamayi Ma (1896–1982).[25] The same is the case with the popular guru Sathya Sai Baba (1926–2011). The Brahma Kumari movement, founded by Dada Lekhraj (1884–1969), considers that we are in the transition between the Kali and Satya *yugas* (Babb 1986: 113 ff.).[26] Yogi Bhajan (1929–2004), a Sikh from the Punjab who arrived in Los Angeles in 1968 and founded the 3HO (Healthy, Happy, Holy Organization), capitalised on the popularity of the theme of the Age of Aquarius and preached that Guru Nanak, the founder of Sikhism, was the guru for the Aquarian Age (Bhajan in Kaur 1972: 5–6). More recently, a guru in South India adopted the name Kalki Bhagavan (1949/1950–), and is believed by his followers to be Kalki. He claimed to inaugurate the new age in 1995, but it apparently would not become realised until 2012 (Narayanan 2002).

Several of these spiritual teachers have a large following in India, while others have been more successful in other countries. Some, like Sathya Sai Baba, have acquired great popularity both in India and the West. When Sathya Sai Baba passed away in South India in April of 2011, the BBC reported that tens of thousands of mourners visited his ashram, as did many Indian celebrities and politicians, including India's Prime Minister, Manmohan Singh.[27]

---

[25] For references see González-Reimann (2002: 200–201).

[26] Or see the cycle of time, on the Brahma Kumaris' website http://www.brahmakumaris.com/rajayoga-meditation/cycle-of-time.html (accessed: 5 March 2012).

[27] BBC online (2011) http://www.bbc.co.uk/news/world-south-asia-13184124 (accessed: 5 March 2012).

Kali or Satya? Contemporary Yuga Chronology

We know that Puranic literature assigns immense durations to the *yugas*. The Kali Yuga alone is said to last for 432,000 years, and it only began in 3102 BCE. How then, can modern intellectuals, gurus and movements proclaim that the Satya Yuga is dawning? This is accomplished in a number of ways. Vivekananda doesn't even address the issue, and simply asserts that the Satya Yuga started with the birth of Ramakrishna. For Aurobindo, the Puranic duration of the *yugas* should not be taken literally, as traditional descriptions only point to a general descending succession of ages. Swami Yukteswar (1855–1936) – the guru of Paramahansa Yogananda (1893–1952), author of *Autobiography of a Yogi* and founder of the Self-Realization Fellowship in the United States – explained the Puranic duration of the *yugas* from a novel angle. He declared that Puranic calculations are not trustworthy because they were put forth by authors living in the Kali Yuga, when people's minds are confused. In his view, the four *yugas* last for only 12,000 years, and instead of descending from Kṛta to Kali and then jumping back to Kṛta for the start of a new downward sequence, from Kali they ascend again in the reverse order. According to this radical reinterpretation, we are now in an ascending Dvāpara Yuga, and the Kali Yuga has been left behind. A salient characteristic of Yukteswar's system is that it links the *yuga* cycle to the precession of the equinoxes, the astronomical movement that gives rise to the theory of astrological ages.[28] This facilitates combining expectations about the Age of Aquarius with expectations related to the *yugas*, although it does so in a very unique way. Yukteswar's version of the *yugas* has been recently revived by American followers of Yukteswar and Yogananda in a grandiose attempt to explain all of world history (Selbie and Steinmetz 2011).

There is another way of circumventing Puranic tradition and announcing the advent of a new age. It is the conviction that although the Kali Yuga is in full sway, a Golden Age within it has begun. This is the position taken by followers of Bhaktivedanta Swami (1896–1977), who founded the International Society for Krishna Consciousness, ISKCON (the 'Hare Krishna Movement'), in New York in 1966. By means of an imaginative interpretation of a passage from the *Brahmavaivarta Purāṇa* (sixteenth century?), some of Bhaktivedanta's disciples see a prediction that a 10,000-year 'golden age' must emerge 5,000 years after the start of the Kali Yuga. Taking the traditional date of 3102 BCE for the beginning of Kali, the dawn of this 'golden age' falls at the end of the nineteenth century, when Bhaktivedanta Swami was born. This procedure makes it possible to pronounce the arrival of a Golden Age without contradicting Puranic authority, which is essential for the movement (González-Reimann 2002: 185–6, Appendix F).

The expectation of a new Satya Yuga has been popular in different sectors of Indian society for several decades now. However, with the exception of movements influenced by Islam or Christianity, it is not accompanied by a need to prepare

---

[28]   Yukteswar (1963: vii–xxii).

with any sense of urgency in order to be saved. Everybody can ultimately attain liberation, if not in this lifetime, then in a future one. The anticipated Satya Yuga is construed today as a new age of brotherhood, well-being and spiritual attainment for the entire world.

Modern India is undergoing significant changes related to its growing economic development and its rise on the international scene, and this could alter the prophetic landscape in the coming years. However, we can undoubtedly expect future variations of the theme of a new Satya Yuga and the arrival of Kalki, both as a local phenomenon and as part of globalised expectations related to a coming saviour and a new age. The interconnected nature of the modern world guarantees that even predictions based on a particular tradition will gain a wide audience, as in the case of speculations surrounding the year 2012 and the Mayan calendar. We should expect new local and global variations on the theme in the future, variations that will continue to reinterpret earlier traditions and cast them in contemporary terms, often using new scientific discoveries and current historical events in an attempt to bolster their claims.

References

Babb, L.A. 1986. *Redemptive Encounters: Three Modern Styles in the Hindu Tradition*. Berkeley, CA: University of California Press.

Banerjee-Dube, I. 2001. Kali y sus contemporáneos: percepciones populares del tiempo en la India oriental colonial. *Estudios de Asia y Africa*, 36, 1(114), 11–32.

———. 2008. Changing Contours of Mahimā Dharma: Bhima Bhoi and Biswanath Baba, in *Popular Religion and Ascetic Practices: New Studies on Mahimā Dharma*, edited by I. Banerjee-Dube and J. Beltz. New Delhi: Manohar, 189–209.

BBC online. 2011. Sai Baba Death: Mourners Flock to Indian Guru's Ashram [Online]. Available at: http://www.bbc.co.uk/news/world-south-asia-13184124 [accessed: 13 December 2011].

Beltz, J. 2008. Apocalyptic Predictions, Prophecies, and a New Beginning: Mahimā Dharma and the Arrival of the Satyayuga, in *Popular Religion and Ascetic Practices: New Studies on Mahimā Dharma*, edited by I. Banerjee-Dube and J. Beltz. New Delhi: Manohar, 79–101.

Bhajan, Y. 1972. Introduction, in *Guru for the Aquarian Age: The Life and Teachings of Guru Nanak*. SAT NAM Series, 1, by S.P. Kaur. San Rafael, CA: Spiritual Community.

Blavatsky, H.P. 1960. *Collected Writings: 1887*, Vol. 8, compiled by Boris de Zirkoff. Adyar: Theosophical Publishing House.

———. 1971. *The Secret Doctrine*. Reprint of the 1962 fifth Adyar edition. 6 vols. Adyar: Theosophical Publishing House.

Buck, C. 1986. A Unique Eschatological Interface: Bahá'u'lláh and Cross-cultural Messianism, in *Studies in Bábí and Bahá'í History*, edited by P. Smith. Los Angeles, CA: Kalimát Press, 157–79.

———. 2004. The Eschatology of Globalization: The Multiple-Messiahship of Bahā'u'llāh Revisited, in *Studies in Modern Religions, Religious Movements and the Bābī-Bahā'ī Faiths*, edited by M. Sharon. Leiden and Boston, MA: Brill, 143–78. [Online]. Available at: http://bahai-library.com/buck_eschatological_interface_messianism [accessed: 23 April 2012].

van Buitenen, J.A.B. (trans. and ed.) 1975. *The Mahābhārata: 2, The Book of the Assembly Hall; 3, The Book of the Forest*, Vol. 2. Chicago, IL: University of Chicago Press.

Coomaraswamy, R. 1996. Cyclical and Linear Time, Progress and Evolution, in *Concepts of Time, Ancient and Modern*, edited by K. Vatsyayan. New Delhi: Indira Gandhi National Centre for the Arts in association with Sterling Publishers, 100–114.

Fitzgerald, J.L. (trans. and ed.) 2004. *The Mahābhārata: 11, The Book of the Women; 12, The Book of Peace, Part One*, Vol. 7. Chicago, IL: University of Chicago Press.

———. 2010. No Contest between Memory and Invention: The Invention of the Pāṇḍava Heroes of the *Mahābhārata*, in *Epic and History*, edited by D. Konstan and K.A. Raaflaub. Chichester, West Sussex and Malden, MA: Wiley-Blackwell, 103–21.

Fuchs, S. 1992. *Godmen on the Warpath: A Study of Messianic Movements in India*. New Delhi: Munshiram Manoharlal.

González-Reimann, L. 2002. *The Mahābhārata and the Yugas: India's Great Epic Poem and the Hindu System of World Ages*. New York: Peter Lang. Indian reprint, Delhi: Motilal Banarsidass, 2010.

———. 2006. Viṣṇu as a Fish: The Growth of a Story from the Brāhmaṇas to the Purāṇas. *Journal of Vaiṣṇava Studies*, 15(1), 221–37.

———. 2009. Cosmic Cycles, Cosmology and Cosmography, in *Brill's Encyclopedia of Hinduism, 1*, edited by K.A. Jacobsen. Leiden: Brill, 411–28.

———. 2010. Time in the *Mahābhārata* and the Time of the *Mahābhārata*, in *Epic and Argument in Sanskrit Literary History: Essays in Honor of Robert P. Goldman*, edited by S. Pollock. New Delhi: Manohar, 61–73.

Granoff, P. 1991. Tales of Broken Limbs and Bleeding Wounds: Responses to Muslim Iconoclasm in Medieval India. *East and West*, 41(1/4), 189–203.

Kaur, S.P. 1972. *Guru for the Aquarian Age: The Life and Teachings of Guru Nanak*. SAT NAM Series, 1. San Rafael, CA: Spiritual Community.

Khan, D.S. 1997. The Coming of Nikalank Avatar: A Messianic Theme in Some Sectarian Traditions of North-Western India. *Journal of Indian Philosophy*, 25(4), 401–26.

Laine, J.W. 2003. *Shivaji: Hindu King in Islamic India*. New York: Oxford University Press.

Lorenzen, D.N. (ed.) 1995. *Bhakti Religion in North India: Community Identity and Political Action*. Albany, NY: State University of New York Press.

Luker, V. 1998. Millenarianism in India: The Movement of Birsa Munda, in *Religious Traditions in South Asia: Interaction and Change*, edited by G.A. Oddie. Richmond, Surrey: Curzon Press, 51–64.

Matsyamahāpurāṇam. 1984. New Delhi: Meharchand Lachhmandas.

Mitchiner, J.E. 2002. *The Yuga Purāṇa: Critically Edited, With an English Translation and a Detailed Introduction*, second edition. Calcutta: The Asiatic Society.

Narayanan, V. 2002. A 'White Paper' on Kalki Bhagavan [Online]. Available at: http://www.montclair.edu/RISA/d-kalki.html [accessed: 12 December 2011].

Nattier, J. 1991. *Once Upon a Future Time: Studies in a Buddhist Prophecy of Decline*. Berkeley, CA: Asian Humanities Press.

Newman, J. 1995. Eschatology in the Wheel of Time Tantra, in *Buddhism in Practice*, edited by D.S. Lopez Jr. Princeton Readings in Religions. Princeton, NJ: Princeton University Press, 284–9.

——. 1998. Islam in the Kālacakra Tantra. *Journal of the International Association of Buddhist Studies*, 21(2), 311–71.

Pollock, S.I. 1993. *Rāmāyaṇa* and Political Imagination in India. *Journal of Asian Studies*, 52(2), 261–97.

Sarkar, S. 1989. The Kalki-Avatar of Bikrampur: A Village Scandal in Early Twentieth Century Bengal, in *Subaltern Studies VI: Writings on South Asian History and Society*, edited by R. Guha. Delhi: Oxford University Press, 1–53.

——. 1997a. Kaliyuga, Chakri and Bhakti: Ramakrishna and His Times, in *Writing Social History*. Delhi: Oxford University Press, 282–357.

——. 1997b. Renaissance and Kaliyuga: Time, Myth and History in Colonial Bengal, in *Writing Social History*. Delhi: Oxford University Press, 186–215.

Selbie, J. and Steimetz, D. 2010. *The Yugas: Keys to Understanding Our Hidden Past, Emerging Energy Age, and Enlightened Future. From the Teachings of Sri Yukteswar and Paramhansa Yogananda*. Nevada City, CA: Crystal Clarity.

Sponberg, A. and Hardacre, H. (eds) 1988. *Maitreya, the Future Buddha*. New York: Cambridge University Press.

Sukthankar, V.S., Belvalkar S.K. et al. (eds) 1933–59. *The Mahābhārata: For the First Time Critically Edited*. 19 vols. Poona: Bhandarkar Oriental Research Institute.

Thapar, R. 1971. The Image of the Barbarian in Early India. *Comparative Studies in Society and History*, 13(4), 408–36.

The Kalkipurāṇam. 1986. Delhi: Nag.

The Vāyumahāpurāṇam. 1983. Delhi: Nag.

Vira, R. and Chandra, L. 1966. *Kālacakra-tantra and Other Texts*. Part 1. New Delhi: International Academy of Indian Culture.

Wessinger, C.L. 1988. *Annie Besant and Progressive Messianism (1847–1933)*. Lewiston, NY: Edwin Mellen.

Yukteswar, Swami Sri. 1963. *Kaivalya Darsanam: The Holy Science*, sixth edition. Ranchi: Yogoda Satsanga Society of India.

Chapter 9

Divination, Prophecy and Oracles in Tibetan Buddhism

Christopher Bell

Tibetan history was written by prophecy. In the Tibetan Buddhist imaginaire, the Buddha himself foretold that when his teachings declined, the Bodhisattva of compassion, Avalokiteśvara, would use the Buddha's doctrine to unite the denizens of the snowy land north of India (Kapstein 1992: 86, Sørensen 1994: 98). Likewise, practitioners of the Tibetan Bön religion – who assert that theirs is the indigenous religion of Tibet – believe that its founder, Shenrap Miwo, prophesied the advent of his teachings in Tibet 'when the time was ripe' (Karmay 1998: 109). In both traditions, the Tibetan landscape itself is pregnant with hidden texts and holy objects waiting to be discovered; many of them already have been by means of prophetic revelations. These items are called 'treasures' (Tib. *gter*), in reference to the precious teachings that they provide. Furthermore, many important religious leaders, famous monasteries and teaching lineages have been validated by prophecies proclaiming their inevitable appearance.

Prophecy is still an important practice in Tibetan communities today. Tibetans make use of divination manuals, consult records of prophecies espoused by important religious masters, and adhere to the clairvoyant advice of oracles possessed by protective divinities. The act can be as simple as an elderly layman counting rosary beads for a sign, or as complex as a large-scale performance by the state oracle going into trance for the Tibetan Government-in-Exile. From individuals to institutions, there is no denying the impact that prophecy has held and continues to hold in Tibetan culture.

According to tradition, Buddhism was first introduced into Tibet in the seventh century under the auspices of King Songtsen Gampo, who, after consolidating the Tibetan empire, had converted to Buddhism at the behest of his Nepalese and Chinese wives. Songtsen Gampo is considered Tibet's first Buddhist king, but the new religion did not extend beyond the courts until over a century later, when Tibet's second Buddhist king, Trisong Detsen, took to the throne and promoted Buddhism further by building monasteries, patronising textual translations and promoting practices among the populace. It was at this time that the Vajrayāna or Tantric form of Buddhism began to take hold in Tibet. After a period of stagnation in the ninth to tenth centuries, Tibetan Buddhism flourished, resulting in an efflorescence of diverse schools of thought and teaching lineages. The history of these schools and lineages is complex, but most of them eventually coagulated into large sectarian institutions. Today, four major sects are recognised, each with their own distinct monastic curriculum, religious practices and liturgical programmes. These sects are called Geluk, Sakya, Kagyü and Nyingma. The Geluk sect, which is the youngest, is perhaps the most famous for being the sect to which the Dalai Lama belongs.

Prior to the arrival of Buddhism and in tandem with its propagation from the seventh century onward, Tibetans had a loose assortment of religious practices that included worshipping local deities, venerating kings and exorcising pernicious spirits. Traditionally, these pre-Buddhist, indigenous practices have been labelled under the broad and diffuse rubric of 'Bön', though there is much scholarly disagreement as to what first comprised the Bön religion, or if it even existed prior to the eleventh century when it began to take on a stronger institutional form. This brief overview of Tibetan religion is a necessary backdrop for understanding how prophecy developed in Tibet.

In the following, I will provide a brief overview of the common Tibetan methods for and sources of prophetic advice, specifically in Tibetan Buddhism, though with occasional reference to Tibetan Bön examples. My goal over the next few pages is not to authenticate or debunk the Tibetan tradition of prophecy, but rather to explain its mechanisms and attempt to understand its social functions.

Divination

As a means of foretelling the future, divination practices (Tib. *mo*) constitute a proactive approach to prophecy. Such practices range from basic acts to complex ceremonies, and can either be done by oneself or by a hired diviner, depending on the circumstances. Lama Chime Radha Rinpoche gives the most cogent explanation for divination's spectrum of utility:

> Recourse to divination might be had about any of the important events and decisions of life: the arranging of marriages, the birth of children, the undertaking of journeys and affairs of business, the choice of site for building a house, the treatment of sickness and disease, the outcome of legal disputes, the recovery of lost articles and animals, social relationships, plans and ambitions of all kinds, and indeed any matter about which a person felt sufficiently anxious to wish to have some reassurance or forewarning in advance of the actual outcome of events (Lama Chime Radha Rinpoche 1981: 4–5).

The means of foretelling such concerns are just as varied. The easiest method is rosary divination (Tib. *'phreng mo*), which can be done without a specialist. A random length of beads is held in one's hand, counted off in threes, and the remaining number is counted and interpreted favourably (if it is an odd number) or unfavourably (if it is an even number) (Ekvall 1963: 34–5). Other methods include using dice, pebbles, butter lamps, songs, arrows or divination cards. Bird divination is also popular, in which the behaviour and specific sounds of ravens and crows are interpreted as certain types of omens. Even scapulimancy has been observed among Tibetan communities; this is where a sheep's shoulder blade is placed in a fire until it cracks, then the cracks are read for signs (Nebesky-Wojkowitz [1956] 1998: 455–6). For a number of these methods, a divination manual (Tib. *mo dpe*) is required to interpret properly the results of the forecast, since it lists all possible results and their meanings. Dreams can also act as powerful portents, especially around significant times of the year or during important life junctures. Astrology is often used alongside these various types of divination in order to determine auspicious or inauspicious days for certain activities. All of these methods provide a means for recognising certain omens in order to come to an informed decision.

Another popular form of prediction is mirror divination (Tib. *pra mo*). This can be performed either with a hand-held mirror or with any reflective surface, including the surface of a lake. This was once one of the primary forms of prophesying the next rebirth of the Dalai Lama. The regent and other officials would go specifically to Lhamo Lhatso Lake, southeast of Lhasa, and see a vision in the lake's reflection that showed the site of the Dalai Lama's rebirth. This lake is believed to be the soul lake of the enlightened goddess Penden Lhamo, who, along with the Nechung deity, is a main protector of the Dalai Lama lineage (Diemberger 2005: 133–6, Lama Chime Radha Rinpoche 1981: 10). This same principle is applied to hand-held mirrors; diviners see visions reflected in a mirror in response to queries they recite out loud. This is usually preceded by panegyrics to a specific deity, like Gesar or Dorjé Yudrönma, who is believed to provide the vision (Nebesky-Wojkowitz [1956] 1998: 462–3).

Divination is just as often used to discover something concealed in the past as it is to reveal the future. For instance, a Tibetan colleague of mine explained that in 2008, a large cyst had begun to grow on his neck just below his chin. Medical aid was of no use, so his mother contacted a *mantric* specialist (Tib. *sngags pa*). The specialist used divination to determine the cause, which was that my colleague had eaten some impure meat. Thinking back, he recalled accidently eating frog meat while he was in Beijing and he thought this must have been the cause. He met the specialist, who reconfirmed the cause through rosary divination, and began a lengthy treatment regimen that ultimately cured the cyst. Many Tibetan oracles also use divination to aid their patrons in determining the causes of illness and misfortune, and to establish the proper course of curative action.

Regardless of the popularity and ubiquity of divination in Tibetan communities, many monks today tend to look down on the practice as superstitious. This may in part be due to the indigenous and pre-Buddhist nature of many of these methods. Though they are often called upon to perform these services for laymen and women, monks sometimes chide devotees for not putting greater faith in the Buddhas and enlightened masters, or for not fully understanding the consequences of their own *karma*.[1] While monks themselves do rely on divination for mundane

---

[1]   Mikmar Tsering, personal communication, 20 November 2011.

matters, despite their discontents with the practice, they nonetheless have access to other sources of prophecy when their activities are oriented toward more transcendental Buddhist goals. The most trusted of these sources is the expansive corpus of Buddhist texts.

The Prophetic Record

Monastics and secular academics alike put great stock in the teachings of Buddhas and other realised masters (Tib. *grub thob*; Skt. *siddha*). The words of the historical Buddha, Śākyamuni, were recorded in the first of three grand collections known as the Three Baskets (Tib. *sde snod gsum*; Skt. *tripiṭaka*). This vast body of scripture – called *sūtra* in Sanskrit – and its larger body of commentaries, was translated into Tibetan and organised into what is now known as the Tibetan Buddhist canon. The canon itself is divided into two main collections. The first is the 'Translated Word [of the Buddha]' (Tib. *bka' 'gyur*), consisting of the Buddha's recorded teachings in over 100 volumes; the second is the 'Translated Treatises' (Tib. *bstan 'gyur*), the Indian commentaries on the Buddha's teachings in over 200 volumes. Many of these works contain prophecies, and some even concern them exclusively. It is to this body of literature that monks and high lamas turn in order to find predictions about a religious master's legitimacy, a monastery's founding or a king's ascension.

Perhaps one of the most well-known examples of such a prediction concerns Lord Tsongkhapa's coming. Tsongkhapa Lozang Drakpa (Tib. *Tsong kha pa Blo bzang grags pa*; 1357–1419) is the famous Tibetan Buddhist master who founded the Geluk sect to which the Dalai and Paṇchen Lamas belong. Many versions of his biography begin with the following prophecy from the *King of Bestowing Advice Sūtra* (Tib: *Mdo sde gdams ngag 'bogs pa'i rgyal po*; see Roerich [1949] 1996: 158 and Warner 2011: 11):

> In the future, in the time of the degenerate age,
> On the outskirts of the land endowed with female yaks,
> A monastery called 'Gé' will be built [by]
> A [man who] will come forth named 'Lozang'.[2]

The biography goes on to interpret explicitly this prophecy as referring to Tsongkhapa. The monastery called 'Gé' (Tib. *dge*) refers to Genden Monastery (Tib. *dge ldan*; a variant spelling of the more common *dga' ldan*), and is also understood by the author of this biography to refer to the Geluk sect (Tib. *dge lugs*). 'Lozang' is interpreted to refer to [Tsongkhapa] Lozang Drakpa (Yeshé Gyeltsen 198?: 417). In this one prophecy, we see not only an important individual being foretold, but also an important monastery and even a Buddhist sect.

---

2   '/ma 'ongs snyigs ma'i dus su ni/ /'bri dang ldan gyi sa mtshams su/ /dge zhes bya ba'i dgon pa 'debs/ /blo bzang zhes bya'i ming can 'byung/' (Yeshé Gyeltsen 198?: 416).

The extensive Buddhist canon is not the only recognised source of prophetic authority, however. Another equally vast and significant corpus of texts consists of 'treasures',[3] briefly mentioned in the introduction. These texts are most often found among the Nyingma Buddhist sect, as well as in the Bön religion; however, there are some treasure texts that are recognised by all the major sects. For Buddhists, most of these texts are believed to have been composed by the great eighth-century Indian tantric exorcist Padmasambhava, who was invited to Tibet by King Trisong Detsen in order to help secure the establishment of Tantric Buddhism there. These texts are believed to have been hidden throughout Tibet, as well as in the mind streams of Padmasambhava's disciples, in order to be recovered later by their future incarnations. Such individuals, called 'treasure revealers' (Tib. *gter ston*), were prophesied by Padmasambhava to reveal these texts when the time was ripe for their teachings. These treasures have continued to be revealed for nearly a millennium, and though the practice has been severely diminished over the last half-century, it is still on-going (Germano 1998).

Many of the legends at the foundation of the treasure tradition intersect with Bön narratives, which include Padmasambhava's own disciples. For instance, the famous translator Vairocana, who was among Padmasambhava's 25 primary students, aided Bön practitioners in concealing important Bön texts so that they could be revealed in the future. As Vairocana was about to conceal an important cycle of texts called the *Golden Stick* (Tib. *gSer thur*) in Bhutan, the Bön master Drenpa Namkha (Tib. *Dran pa nam mkha'*) appeared to him in a vision and prophesied: 'in the future there will be one called Bon-zhig who is your own emanation and who will take out the *gSer thur* from its hidden place' (Karmay 2007: 217). It is important to note that this prophecy was delivered by a master in a vision, another source of divination, and concerns the future revelation of a series of treasure texts.

Like the canon, many Buddhist treasure texts themselves also contain prophesies about future events (Gyatso 1993: 100). In the *Testament of Ba* (Tib. *Dba' bzhed*), one of the most famous accounts of the royal period (seventh to ninth century), Trisong Detsen's father, Tridé Tsuktsen recovers a testament composed by his ancestor, King Songtsen Gampo. This account contains the following prophecy:

> In the time of my descendants, in the time of a king named 'De' (*Lde*), the authentic divine doctrine will emerge, and many renunciates following the Tathāgata, shaven headed and barefoot, wearing the royal banner of ochre on their bodies, will come forth as the objects of worship of gods and men ... (Kapstein 2000: 26).

---

[3]   It must be noted that such 'treasures' can actually refer to holy objects other than scripture, such as *vajras*, statues of holy beings and special stones. For the purposes of this chapter, however, we will focus exclusively on the texts of this complex tradition.

Given the mention of the name 'De', Tri*dé* Tsuktsen presumes that the prophecy concerns him and proceeds to seek out Buddhist teachings. His endeavours are not very successful, but he vows that his son will be even more religious than he. This ultimately proves true when Trisong *De*tsen comes to his majority in 755.

This case exemplifies a rare instance where a treasure text was composed by someone other than Padmasambhava. Other famous (and extant) treasure texts attributed to King Songtsen Gampo include the *Pillar Testament* (Tib. *Bka' chems ka khol ma*), which was revealed by the great reformer Atīśa (982–1054), and the *Maṇi Kambum* (Tib. *Ma Ni bka' 'bum*), rediscovered by several treasure revealers during the twelfth and thirteenth centuries. Since the latter text states that Songtsen Gampo is an emanation of the Bodhisattva Avalokiteśvara, such prophecies and testaments authenticate the king's ultimately enlightened nature (Kapstein 1992). Given these examples, whether Buddhist or Bön, treasure texts are enveloped in a deep narrative of prophesy and revelation, from their initial concealment to their rediscovery, and even in their content.

It merits mentioning that while the treasure tradition is very much a Tibetan tradition, it has its roots in Indian Mahāyāna Buddhist concepts of apocrypha. The second-to-third-century founder of the Mādhyamaka school of thought, Nāgārjuna, has long been held to have retrieved the *Prajñāpāramitā Sūtra* from serpentine spirits. Likewise, the Yogācāra system was believed to have been revealed to the fourth-century Asaṅga by the Future Buddha Maitreya (Davidson 2005: 212).

Some prophecies are not found in the Buddhist canon or in any of the revealed treasure literature, but rather stem from Tibet's strong oral tradition. The translator Vairocana, who was prone to visions like many realised masters, had another one concerning the future establishment of an important monastery:

> During the lifetime of the Tibetan King Trisong Detsen's son, Muné Tsenpo, Samyé [Monastery] was considered the great abode, and [so] this [other] place was called the 'Small Abode' (Nechung; Tib. *Gnas chung*). When the translator Vairocana went to this [latter] place, he saw various miracles manifest from a birch tree, so he told master Padmasambhava about it. The master prophesied, 'In the future, a monastery will appear at this place. That birch tree is [the deity] Pehar's soul tree, and that nearby pond is Pehar's soul pond.'[4]

Here the prophecy is not delivered in a vision, but in response to one. Padmasambhava, being an enlightened being, offers his disciple an interpretation of the latter's visionary experience, explaining the future significance of the place

---

[4]   'bod rje khri srong lde'u btsan gyi sras mu ne btsan po'i dus su bsam yas gnas chen du brtsis pa'i 'dir gnas chung zhes thogs pa yin zhing / lo tsA ba bai ro tsa na sa der phebs pa na gro sdong gcig nas cho 'phrul bstan pa'i skor slob dpon padma 'byung gnas kyi snyan du gsol bas slob dpon gyis ma 'ongs pa na der dgon po zhig chags yong / shing gro sdong de pe har gyi bla shing yin/ de'i 'gram gyi mtshe'u de pe har gyi bla mtsho yin zhes gsungs pa …' (Tibetan Academy of Social Sciences 2009: 439).

in which he had it. This is a popular oral narrative concerning the pedigree of Nechung Monastery's origins. This monastery is significant for having housed the most important state oracle of Tibet, the Nechung Oracle, who has provided prophetic advice to the Dalai Lamas since the sixteenth century. This oracle, who is still active in exile today, becomes possessed by an emanation of the deity Pehar. Prophecies such as these, though not validated by a textual lineage, are nonetheless treated by many monastic and lay Tibetans as authentic due to the involvement of such important figures as Padmasambhava and Vairocana.

Perhaps the oldest of all prophecies is the one that is rooted in India and universally recognised by all Buddhist traditions: that there are four major ages and we are currently in the last and most degenerate one (see Luis González-Reimann, Chapter 8). In this age, the Buddhist teachings are flagging and will soon be extinguished (Nattier 1991). During times of war, inter-sectarian strife and religious persecution, Tibetans reference this prophecy to declare that their own age is the one in which Buddhism will meet its end. In many cases, Tibetans interpret troubled times as a sign that the age of decline has already arrived. For instance, the high lama Pakpa Rinpoche, who became Kublai Khan's imperial preceptor in the thirteenth century, had begun to dress in Mongolian attire rather than religious robes soon after his appointment. This troubled some of his contemporaries, who exclaimed, 'In this degenerate era, ascetics adopt the fashions of worldly leaders' (Shakabpa 2010: 223). Other signs of this dark eon include individuals misunderstanding or warping the meaning of the Buddha's teachings, possessing little merit because of the evil deeds they had accrued, and sowing discord throughout the world. However, there is a happy ending (or beginning) to this scheme of religious decay. As soon as the Buddhist teachings are completely extinguished, it is prophesied that the next Buddha, Maitreya, will come into the world to spread the full glory of the Dharma once again.

The above examples illustrate how all forms of prophecy, whether recorded, recovered or remembered, are influenced by Indian Buddhist traditions, yet have become wholly Tibetan in orientation and significance. These declarations of Buddhas, Bodhisattvas and realised masters have acted as sources of legitimation for kings, religious individuals and important institutions in Tibet for over a millennium. For Tibetan Buddhists today – and especially for monks who rely on these prophecies to secure the place of their masters and monasteries in Buddhist history – these records and testaments are essential for understanding their traditions.

Oracular Prophecy

Divination may be performed by monks and lamas in many instances, but the contempt that religious specialists sometimes show for its practice suggests that they supply these services primarily because of the demands of the laity. Conversely, though the laity are familiar with recorded prophecies, especially those maintained by oral traditions, it is the monastic community that relies on them most to legitimate their lineages, institutions and the spiritual masters who founded them. If we consider the above practices on a spectrum, with divination leaning toward the laity on one side, and recorded prophecies leaning toward monastics on the other, then oracles span the length in between.

An oracle is a human medium who periodically and ritually becomes possessed by a Tibetan protector deity in order to provide clairvoyant advice on anything from personal matters of health and well-being to state matters of national security. Studies on Tibetan oracles show the tradition to be quite diverse and heterogeneous. The origins of the oracular tradition are unknown, though it is generally accepted to have been a pre-Buddhist practice that was later incorporated into the Buddhist cosmological structure. An oracle is commonly renowned for being the vessel of a specific deity, yet most oracles can channel multiple deities in a single trance session, with each deity providing further insight into a communal crisis or prophetic declaration (Havnevik 2002: 276–7, Nebesky-Wojkowitz [1956] 1998: 433–7).

When a deity descends into an oracle, the latter enters into a trance state. This state of possession shows a marked contrast in the behaviour of the oracle. As the deity begins to take over the oracle's body, he or she will shake and tremble, breathe faster and with heavy breaths, and even puff out air or wag their tongue. The oracle's complexion also changes, with his or her face turning red or yellow, depending on the disposition of the deity. The deity's disposition is important, as oracles can channel wrathful or peaceful deities. An oracle possessed by a wrathful deity will grow red-faced and become very violent in their movements; a passive deity will cause an oracle to act more subdued. The oracle will also start to exhibit the specific attributes of the particular deity possessing them, such as walking with a limp or keeping one eye closed. Hanna Havnevik describes a scenario in which the female oracle Lobsang Tsedrön channelled a male hero spirit and accordingly dressed, walked and drank beer like a man; she never drank beer in any other circumstance. Patrons claim that, once out of the trance, nobody could smell beer on her breath (Havnevik 2002: 271).

Supernatural qualities are a significant attribute of the trance state and help to authenticate the sacred activity that surrounds the oracle tradition. These supernatural abilities include twisting swords into knots and exhibiting super strength, such as being able to bear the heavy crown associated with the position of the oracle – this crown is said to be so heavy that two or three men are needed to hoist it onto the oracle's head. The twisted sword, called the 'knotted thunderbolt' (Tib. *rdo rje mdud pa*), is a prized possession among Tibetans, and those honoured enough to obtain one hang it above doorways to ward off demonic influences. Other feats of supernatural ability gained under trance include reports of vomiting coins and thrusting a sword into one's chest until its end comes out the back, and then removing it to show no sign of injury (Nebesky-Wojkowitz [1956] 1998: 440–41, Rock 1935: 477). Such miraculous exhibitions accompany the central powers of clairvoyance and prophecy that are the impetus for these trances.

The goal of oracle trances is to provide a service to the community on multiple social levels. This service involves eliciting the knowledge of the deity, as expressed through the oracle, which provides prophetic advice concerning the future of the community. An oracle can be consulted by individual patrons regarding personal crises such as family problems, wealth and love issues, or for communal concerns such as unsolved crimes and legal matters (Diemberger 2005: 115–16, 139). With village oracles the concern is more local, while state oracles offer advice on a greater political scale.

State oracles are called as such because they act primarily in service to the Tibetan government. For instance, state oracles like those at Nechung and Samyé traditionally prophesied the rebirths of the Dalai Lamas (Nebesky-Wojkowitz [1956] 1998: 453). In particular, the Dalai Lamas usually recorded a prophecy indicating the location of their next rebirth. The state oracles would then be approached to augment the prophecy with more details. Sometimes other methods of divination would be further employed by state officials to ensure an accurate interpretation, since all of these forms of prophecy are prone to ambiguous meanings. In this way, the various prophetic modes inform and support one another in certain contexts. Since the sixteenth century, state oracles like Nechung have served as advisors to the Dalai Lamas and provided counsel on important decisions, especially those that concerned national security or religious expansion (Elverskog 2003: 143–5, 151).

Furthermore, oracles – specifically on the local level – act as healers, using their powers of divination to assess an individual's illness and respond with appropriate advice as to its remedy. Hildegard Diemberger states that the success of an oracle is in his or her ability to mediate at times of personal and public crisis; an oracle's reputation is dependent on their efficacy (Diemberger 2005: 138–40). Oracles have been known to tarnish their reputation by offering bad or incorrect advice; on a political level, this can be especially hazardous. René de Nebesky-Wojkowitz explains an incident where the Nechung Oracle in 1904 predicted a Tibetan victory against the British Expeditionary Force. This did not occur, however, and so the oracle fled with the Thirteenth Dalai Lama to Mongolia when the British reached Lhasa. Upon their return, the Nechung Oracle was dismissed from his office (Nebesky-Wojkowitz [1956] 1998: 451). In many instances, such failure on the part of the oracle is blamed on demon possession. It is believed that sometimes an oracle can let their guard down and become possessed by a pernicious spirit pretending to be the intended deity. In these instances, the oracles provide faulty prophecies and advice, only recognised as such after the fact. If this occurs too often, the oracle will be dismissed from their office (Ricca 1999: 24).

Punishment meted out to oracles for their inadequacy or insubordination has been known to come from the possessing deity as well. Such wrath is usually retaliation for the oracle's disobedience to the deity. In one instance, recounted by Joseph Rock, an oracle was requested by his possessing deity not to marry, yet did so anyway. In response, the deity, during a fit of trance, caused the oracle to disembowel himself and hang his entrails on the statues in his private chapel (Rock 1935: 478).

Even when an oracle has a successful trance session and offers prophecy, advice or both, the meaning can be ambiguous or obscure. Oracles often speak in a strained voice using archaic or poetic language, and their proclamations are usually delivered in rasping whispers into the ears of accompanying secretaries. It is then up to these secretaries to record the oracle's statements and provide some kind of interpretation. With so much mediation, it is understandable that some prophecies fall short. In some instances interpretation takes time, and is only arrived at after much reflection. Anthropologist Urmila Nair, who has studied the Nechung liturgies in exile for nearly a decade, describes her experience when attempting to ask the Nechung Oracle if it was suitable or not to study these rituals:

> It was the trance of the winter solstice, requested annually by the exile-government. Once the Nechung Oracle had responded to the exile-government's questions, and to those of several dignitaries and lamas, the Disciplinarian was supposed to hand [him] the question about my research, printed out on a sheet of paper, together with a pen. The Oracle was then supposed to circle either 'good' or 'not good' (legs sam mi legs) these words being bolded and printed separately within the rest of the text of the Solicitation regarding my research. As things turned out, the Disciplinarian ... forgot about the pen, and the Oracle, in his usual manner, merely prescribed the performance of rituals (the chanting of the sutra and of the mantra), which would generate karmic merit, which would in turn facilitate the possibility of success in my research. On the evening of December 15th, 2005, several monks read the Oracle's Pronouncement on my research and expressed doubts about what it meant. Some of them averred that it was unclear whether I had the Oracle's permission and the rest desisted from expressing any opinion. ... Yet, despite these vicissitudes recounted above, by December, 2007, when my fieldwork was at an end, all the monks to whom I spoke were citing the Pronouncement of December 15th, 2005 ... to me, to each other, and even to outsiders, as proof positive of the Oracle's permission to conduct this research on the Nechung *kang-so* [rituals] (Nair 2010: 285–7).

As this anecdote shows, an oracle's pronouncements can be very ambiguous, yet are reinterpreted later depending on how circumstances play out. This incident illustrates another important aspect of oracular prophecy: advice. In many ways, an oracle dispenses advice more than anything else; however, this is advice tailored by a clairvoyant understanding of the future. The possessed oracle is believed to know what the consequences of both action and inaction will be, and so offers advice accordingly. Oracles often prescribe certain Buddhist rituals, warning that if they are not performed then negative effects will follow. There is also a Buddhist karmic explanation for instances when the prophecy fails to actualise even if the prescribed action is performed. Other unknown conditions may have to be met for the desired results to be achieved. If all of the conditions fail to come about, then even acting on the oracle's advice may not be enough to bring about the intended outcome (Nair 2010: 371, n. 44).

Oracular practices solidify the connection between the lay and monastic community; they reinforce Buddhist cosmology and engage deities through rituals in order to apply their services to local and national concerns. Oracles allow protector deities, as ahistorical mythic figures, to interact with the history of a community and influence social direction. On a smaller scale, oracles provide protection, cures and advice to individuals. When individuals request the services of an oracle, there is also an expected fee or donation to the monastery with which the oracle is affiliated (Havnevik 2002: 261, Nebesky-Wojkowitz [1956] 1998: 432). These same oracles, particularly those associated with monastic institutions, are also used by monasteries to resolve inter-institutional strife. Havnevik explains that the one female state oracle came into existence due to disputes between the monks at the two Geluk monasteries of Sera and Drepung. This oracle tradition pacified the disputes through the advice of the deity given through the oracle (Havnevik 2002: 267). The goal of the deity's presence within the oracle is to provide pragmatic, apotropaic and clairvoyant assistance to individuals, to the community and to the state at large.

Conclusion

One day in January 2011, a monk friend of mine who resides at a monastery in Lhasa, Tibet asked me if I believed the prophecy about the world ending in 2012. This surprised me, since I did not expect a monk in Tibet to know or really care about this Mayan prophecy. He said he had mainly heard about it from the movie *2012*, which came out in 2009. When I told him no, that I did not believe the prophecy or its popular interpretation, I asked him the same question in return. In a sober tone he said yes, then he laughed and declared that he was just joking. There was something in his response, though, that suggested to me that he was not entirely kidding. Whenever I tried to bring up the topic again later in the year, he would either be much more playful about it and refer to the movie or change the subject.

Due to Hollywood movies and globalisation, even something seemingly obscure like the 2012 Mayan prophesy can be found today in Tibet. Conversely, Western New Age practitioners have attempted to find correlations between the Mayan prophecy and the rich tantric system of the *Kālacakra*, which has been popular in Tibet since the eleventh century (Weidner and Bridges 2000: 173). However, whether or not the validity of the 2012 prophecy is accepted by other cultures is another matter. It appears that while Tibetans, at least in Lhasa, may be aware of the prophecy, they do not take it very seriously. This is not surprising since they have their own rich tradition of divination, prophecy and oracular advice to supply them with predictions about the future. Whether it concerns the health of a family member, the welfare of the state or ultimately the degeneration of

Buddhism, each of these approaches to vaticination make up an important element of Buddhist practice in Tibetan communities. Whatever the method, it is clear that Tibetan Buddhism contains not only prophecies about history, but a rich history of prophecy.

References

Davidson, R.M. 2005. *Tibetan Renaissance: Tantric Buddhism in the Rebirth of Tibetan Culture*. New York: Columbia University Press.

Diemberger, H. 2005. Female Oracles in Modern Tibet, in *Women in Tibet*, edited by J. Gyatso and H. Havnevik. New York: Columbia University Press, 113–69.

Ekvall, R.B. 1963. Some Aspects of Divination in Tibetan Society. *Ethnology*, 2(1), 31–9.

Elverskog, J. 2003. *The Jewel Translucent Sūtra: Altan Khan and the Mongols in the Sixteenth Century*. Leiden: Brill.

Germano, D. 1998. Re-membering the Dismembered Body of Tibet: Contemporary Tibetan Visionary Movements in the People's Republic of China, in *Buddhism in Contemporary Tibet: Religious Revival and Cultural Identity*, edited by M.C. Goldstein and M.T. Kapstein. Berkeley, CA: University of California Press, 53–94.

Gyatso, J. 1993. Logic and Legitimation in the Tibetan Treasure Tradition. *History of Religions*, 33(2), 97–134.

Havnevik, H. 2002. A Tibetan Female State Oracle. *Religion and Secular Culture in Tibet; Tibetan Studies: Proceedings of the Ninth Seminar of the International Association for Tibetan Studies, Leiden 2000*, edited by H. Blezer. Leiden: Brill, 259–87.

Kapstein, M. 1992. Remarks on the *Maṇi bKa'-'bum* and the Cult of Avalokiteśvara in Tibet, in *Tibetan Buddhism: Reason and Revelation*, edited by S.D. Goodman and R.M. Davidson. Albany, NY: State University of New York Press, 79–93.

———. 2000. *The Tibetan Assimilation of Buddhism: Conversion, Contestation, and Memory*. Oxford: Oxford University Press.

Karmay, S.G. 1998. A General Introduction to the History and Doctrines of Bon, in *The Arrow and the Spindle: Studies in History, Myths, Rituals and Beliefs in Tibet*, Vol. 1. Kathmandu: Mandala Book Point, 104–56.

———. 2007. *The Great Perfection (rDzogs chen): A Philosophical and Meditative Teaching of Tibetan Buddhism*, second edition. Leiden: Brill.

Lama Chime Radha Rinpoche. 1981. Tibet, in *Oracles and Divination*, edited by M. Loewe and C. Blacker. Boulder, CO: Shambhala, 3–37.

Nair, U. 2010. When the Sun's Rays Are as Shadows: The Nechung Rituals and the Politics of Spectacle in Tibetan Exile. Unpublished doctoral dissertation, University of Chicago, Chicago, IL.

Nattier, J. 1991. *Once Upon a Future Time: Studies in a Buddhist Prophecy of Decline*. Berkeley, CA: Asian Humanities Press.

Nebesky-Wojkowitz, R. [1956] 1998. *Oracles and Demons of Tibet: The Cult and Iconography of the Tibetan Protective Deities*. New Delhi: Paljor.

Ricca, F. 1999. *Il Tempio Oracolare di gNas-chuṅ: Gli Dei del Tibet più Magico e Segreto*. Alessandria: Edizioni dell'Orso.

Rock, J.F. 1935. Sungmas, the Living Oracles of the Tibetan Church. *National Geographic Magazine*, 68, 475–86.

Roerich, G.N. [1949] 1996. *The Blue Annals: Parts I and II* (Bound in one). Delhi: Motilal Banarsidass.

Shakabpa, T.W.D. 2010. *One Hundred Thousand Moons: An Advanced Political History of Tibet*, translated by Derek F. Maher. 2 vols. Leiden: Brill.

Sørensen, P.K. 1994. *Tibetan Buddhist Historiography: The Mirror Illuminating the Royal Genealogies: An Annotated Translation of the XIVth Century Tibetan Chronicle: rGyal-rabs gsal-ba'i me-long*. Wiesbaden: Harrassowitz.

Tibetan Academy of Social Sciences. (ed.) 2009. *Dpal ldan 'bras spungs dgon gyi dkar chag dri med dwangs gsal shel gyi me long*. Beijing: China Tibetology Publishing House.

Warner, C.D. 2011. Re/Crowning the Jowo Śākyamuni: Texts, Photographs, and Memories. *History of Religions*, 51(1), 1–30.

Weidner, J. and Bridges, V. 2000. *A Monument to the End of Time: Alchemy, Fulcanelli and the Great Cross*. Mount Gilead: Aethyrea Books. Cited online at: http://www.cogwriter.com/end-mayan-calendar-2012.htm [accessed: 30 November 2011].

Yeshé Gyeltsen (Ye shes rgyal mtshan; 1713–93). 198?. *Rgyal ba tsong kha pa'i rnam thar*. In *Lam rim bla ma brgyud pa'i rnam thar*, vol. 1. 'Bar khams: Rnga khul bod yig rtsom sgyur cus, 415–522.

Chapter 10
Chasing the Horizon:
Prophecy in Secular Contexts

Wendy M. Grossman

Prediction is difficult – especially about the future.

Niels Bohr

The future is already here. It's just not very evenly distributed.

William Gibson

Life is what happens to you while you're busy making other plans.

John Lennon

Remember when The World As We Know It ended? It wasn't that long ago. Over the course of 1999, as financial years began turning over to 2000 and the computers failed, banks crashed, stocks plunged in value, there were food riots, power outages and transportation failures. Water treatment plants were crippled and then, finally, as the clock ticked over to midnight on 1 January 2000, 4 million (or 4 billion, depending who's counting) computer chips went 'phut'. In the five to ten years of anarchy that followed, four-fifths of the world's population died. Only our careful planning allowed us to be among the lucky survivors …

This was a sample of the predictions posted in all seriousness in 1998 to the Usenet newsgroup *comp.software.year-2000*,[1] set up originally to discuss how to fix the Year 2000 computer problem. The group quickly attracted survivalists and discussion about how to build, where to site and how to protect bunkers, what kinds of food and fuel to hoard, and how many guns it was advisable to stockpile.

The problem of Y2K was first discovered by programmer Bob Bemer as early as the 1950s, when he began work on a genealogical project for IBM. He realised that the programmer's habit of saving memory space by using a two-digit representation for the year was going to be a problem. The genealogical project required him to skip back to dates in previous centuries; to the computer, a six-digit date (two for month, two for day, two for year) in the eighteenth century was indistinguishable from the same date in the twentieth. Reasoning that what was a problem for the past would be a problem in the future, he published his

---

[1]   Time Table for Disaster? June 1998: http://groups.google.com/group/comp.software.year-2000/browse_thread/thread/b0a118e8f2b6d5c3/15833cd11f0df2cb?q=cities+burn+april++group:comp.software.year-2000#15833cd11f0df2cb (accessed: 31 January 2012).

concerns in 1971. In a 1999 interview, Bemer indicated that shortly afterwards he tried to interest President Nixon in the problem, with no success (Williamson 1999). But it was not until 1993 that the problem began to reach the trade press, from where it progressively escalated into public consciousness throughout the rest of the decade.

Among mainstream pundits predicting complete disaster, probably the best-known, most apparently credible doom-sayer was Ed Yardeni, an economist then working for Deutsche Bank. Most computer scientists were worried but pragmatic: they projected that some things would fail, some would be replaced and much would be remediated. After many man-centuries of work, that's what happened, though unfortunately a number of (non-technical) reporters, disappointed when planes didn't fall out of the sky on the night of 31 December 1999, erroneously jumped to the conclusion that the whole Y2K problem had been made up by a rapacious computer industry seeking to shore up business.[2]

Given my background as a technology writer, I was not sceptical about the reality of the Y2K problem: I understood enough about programming to know it was a real issue. But I was highly resistant to the claim that it would cause the collapse of civilisation. For one thing, I remembered the stories I was told in the Republic of Ireland about the banking strike of the 1970s, which went on for many months. During that time, although no one could cash or deposit a pay cheque, the country went on surprisingly close to normalcy: people paid for goods and services in IOUs, which were themselves traded back and forth. At the end of the strike, everyone settled up. Granted, Ireland is a small, somewhat clubby place, but this, I reasoned, is the great thing about humans: people adapt to circumstances. Even in a country the size of the USA, people would find a way.

Scepticism about The End of the World As We Know It (abbreviated on the Net to TEOTWAWKI) was not particularly welcome in *comp.software.year-2000*, however. When I wrote in *Scientific American* (Grossman 1998) that the problem was genuine but that the most likely outcome of the remediation efforts was that civilisation would survive because most people wanted it to, the newsgroup began an email campaign to the editor demanding that he fire 'this dizzy broad'. (In 2008, when a bunch of us checked back into the newsgroup to see what had happened to everyone in the years since, they were graciously apologetic.)

As Damian Thompson, then the recently departed religious correspondent for the *Daily Telegraph*, told me in an interview, the curiously lip-smacking, detailed relish of these projections is typical of end-time beliefs throughout human history. What Y2K helpfully provided, he said, was the *mechanism* by which the apocalypse would happen. Given the mechanism, survivalists, paranoids and attention seekers

---

[2]   On 4 January 2000, computer scientist Peter de Jager defended to CNN his many warnings about the dangers of Y2K, making the points that people had worked hard to remediate a serious issue and that many known problems had surfaced: http://articles. cnn.com/2000-01-04/tech/dejager.y2k.idg_1_y2k-problem-cards-business-people?_ s=PM:TECH (accessed: 31 January 2012).

were free to imagine any disaster they liked, and anyone who wished to could co-opt that mechanism in the service of their existing beliefs.

A similar, though less extreme, pattern was apparent in the debates about RFID (Radio Frequency Identification) that began in around 2005. Cheap enough to be used as tags on all manner of goods, RFID chips allow goods (and prospectively the people carrying them) to be tracked as they move through the supply chain – or anywhere else. The leading campaigner against RFID, Katherine Albrecht,[3] has done respected investigative work exposing the dark side of how these chips may be used, following on from her campaigns on loyalty cards. Albrecht is not alone in her concerns; many other security experts and privacy advocates are concerned about the deployment of RFID. Used in passports and credit card key fobs, RFID may open new avenues of crime. Deployed in clothing and other consumer goods, RFID may create an entirely new avenue for spying on our private lives. But Albrecht's motivation, as you learn when you read the separately released Christian version of her 2006 book, *Spy Chips*,[4] is the promise her grandmother extracted from her: never to 'take a mark'. RFID chips and other types of numbering, including precursors such as Social Security numbers and barcodes, are, for her, signs of the end times (Baard 2006).

Much of the future Albrecht predicts in her book is indeed possible; as she writes, business interests are eager for as much data as they can get about us and our spending and purchasing habits. That side of RFID is an entirely separate issue from whether she is right to believe that RFID and other numbering systems are signs of the impending apocalypse. Her Christian beliefs do not invalidate her research, but they are another example of the way technology may provide a mechanism for an existing religious belief.

Y2K was unusual among secular prophecies in that:

1. The cause – shortcuts taken by programmers from the 1950s to 1980s who did not believe their software would still be in use in 1999 – was known and understood.
2. How to fix it was also known and understood, although the scope and scale of what had to be fixed had to be assessed. Basically, where hardware and software couldn't simply be replaced with more up-to-date systems, programmers had to dive into the code, find all the fields where the date had been limited to six digits, and either enlarge the field to accept eight digits (that is, four-digit years) or alter the underlying assumed window so that 51–99 might mean 1951 to 1999 while 00–50 meant 2000 to 2050.
3. Fixing it was in everyone's interests.

---

[3] Who has a website at www.spychips.com (accessed: 31 January 2012).

[4] The only difference between the Christian and mass market versions of Albrecht's book is a single chapter that tells the story of her relationship with her grandmother and the promise she made.

4. The relatively short time scale – although the first warnings were sounded in the 1970s the issue did not begin reaching mainstream consciousness until 1994, with escalating publicity until January 2000 – meant the results were known fairly quickly.
5. Even before that, it was possible to create simulations covering all the known variables – one date change – and run valid tests.

Compare that to something like climate change, where the threat to humanity is considerably worse and the apocalyptic predictions are coming predominantly from scientists:

1. The general cause – human activity generating rising levels of greenhouse gases that are raising global temperatures – is known but the exact causal relationship and consequences are less clear.
2. How to fix it is complex and disputed.
3. Fixing it is a source of conflict between competing interests.
4. The time scale is longer than a human life, and there's no agreed timetable.
5. We can monitor intermediate progress, but not run valid tests, since there is no complete computer model of the planet.

Y2K could be easily tested; climate change projections cannot. The same goes for other contemporary technology futures such as human-level artificial intelligence (the Singularity), radical life extension and molecular nanotechnology. I think of these as 'chasing the horizon' technologies because they reflect dreams that are probably as old as the human race: who doesn't want to live forever in youthful health with an intelligent companion that anticipates your every wish? They are 'chasing the horizon' in a second sense: the problems that need to be solved are sufficiently hard that although clear progress has been made, achieving the ultimate goal never seems to get any closer. Yet as predictions they have value, in that they inspire smart people to do work that produces useful results, even if those are not exactly the results they were hoping for.

For example, molecular nanotechnology, sometimes called molecular manufacturing, began as a projection first made by the Nobel Laureate physicist Richard Feynman, that it ought eventually to be possible, given small enough 'hands', to manipulate matter at the atomic level (Feynman 1959).

1. The general principle leading to this conclusion – miniaturisation – is understood, though the changes that occur as you get to the quantum level are challenging; there is nothing in Feynman's outline that violates the laws of physics.
2. How to do it is sufficiently complex that progress has been slow and what progress has been made may turn out to be irrelevant. The latest progress as I write this (in 2012) is a 1 nanometer molecular electric motor, announced in September 2011 by scientists at Boston's Tufts University (Fellet 2011).

3. No one is seriously opposed to creating molecular nanotechnology, but doing so requires a lot of expensive research that can be difficult to fund. The scathing scepticism met by the American engineer Eric Drexler when he began promoting the idea in the 1970s led many researchers who call their work 'nanotechnology' to clearly distance themselves from any suggestion that they might be working on molecular manufacturing.
4. The time scale so far is approaching the length of a human life.
5. There is no way to test the hypothesis; we can only monitor progress – but see number two, above.

Can we prove that molecular nanotechnology is impossible? No. Feynman, a distinguished scientist surveying his own field of expertise, made a point of noting that he was working within the known and accepted laws of physics, not violating them by, for example, inventing anti-gravity. Someone who predicts a future in which homes are furnished with a molecular factory that can stamp out anything they want – furniture for special occasions, books, pharmaceuticals – is making a radical guess. But what will derail that projected future is more likely to be social and economic factors than scientific impossibility.

This is a basic principle that ought to be very well known to anyone who invests in the stock market: predicting what will – or may – happen is vastly easier than predicting *when* it will happen. Prediction is hard; timing is near-impossible – and experts may underestimate the difficulty. The artificial intelligence pioneer John McCarthy, for example, told me in 2006 that when he convened the original 1956 conference in Dartmouth he thought the assembled talent would have AI wrapped up in six months. Similarly, Feynman thought of offering a couple of prizes (one to high school students) to kick-start work in this field and said he did not imagine them going unclaimed for long. More than 50 years and many generations of miniaturisation later, we are still not close to molecular nanotechnology, although we do indeed have machines many orders of magnitude smaller than those of Feynman's day. So, when we assess the prediction that molecular manufacturing will be possible in the future, we still cannot say for sure whether it will happen. We can only say with confidence that although it could be possible, as far as we know, it has not happened *yet*.

In his 1991 book *Futurehype*, sociologist Max Dublin argued that many (technology) prophecies are propaganda, containing both advice and warning: 'Predictions do not simply describe the world, they *act* upon it', he wrote (1991: 4). As the pace of technological change has quickened over the last two centuries, secular prophecy, whether in the form of science fiction, futurology or marketing material ('buy my product or service and your life will improve'), provides a way of imagining, understanding and controlling both the future and anxiety about the future.

Dublin had three main complaints. First, that obsessing about the future meant being inattentive to the present. Second, that prophecy that is not grounded in some form of morality is always false. Third, that he did not much like the future that was being pushed at him:

> Feigenbaum, Wolkomir, and many other modern prophets who belong to what might be called the 'techno-romantic' school of futurology seem to be enamoured not merely of the technical fix, the technical solution to a human problem, but of a very particular type of technical fix, one which places individual autonomy and control above social interaction. The point about the celebrated future with machines that they describe above is not only that these devices will be hypothetically accessible to all, but that they will entail a sort of automated enshrinement of their owners' egos; in this way they will, in a sense, fulfil certain individual needs, but always in a banal sort of way. The issue that seems to be of paramount importance to these futurologists is how to achieve individual mastery of personal, isolated environments, and how to put the individual who owns the machine at the commanding center of the environment in which he lives. The type of mastery which they advocate, the only type, it would appear, that seems feasible to their minds, is a sort of petty mastery, like personalized stereo carried to ever greater degrees (1991: 64).

The future Dublin was describing when he wrote that in 1991 was a particular kind of future that was being invented in a particular kind of place: the technology centres of the USA; Silicon Valley and Boston. He cites, for example, Stewart Brand's account of the research in progress at MIT, particularly at its Media Lab, then under the direction of Nicholas Negroponte. When I visited the same lab in 1994, 1995 and 1997, my reaction was similar to Dublin's: sceptical and resentful. How, I wondered, would a future in which everyone's T-shirt could communicate a desired temperature directly to the thermostat in the auditorium play out when no two of those T-shirts agreed on a comfort zone? Did the future really have to be everyone in their own little virtual world ignoring everyone in their immediate vicinity?[5]

Yet the seeds to derail the isolationist, egocentric future Dublin was fretting about had already been sown, though it is not surprising Dublin did not know it. Until 1995, the reshaping power of a technology growing rapidly elsewhere in the forest was missed by many in a position to know better – Microsoft's Bill Gates, for example, as well as the Media Lab. Vice-president Al Gore, however, got it, and in campaigning for funding for the 'information superhighway' he became a hero to many of the early pioneers.[6] Yes: the Internet, particularly the Web, and,

---

[5]   My visits in 1994 and 1995 were written up for *The Guardian* and in 1997 for the *Daily Telegraph*.

[6]   Declan McCullagh, the original source of the 'Gore invented the Internet' meme has made it plain that Gore never made that claim; Gore merely claimed to have 'taken the lead in creating the Internet' and many Net pioneers have defended him: http://www.politechbot.com/p-01428.html (accessed: 31 January 2012).

only a short time later, mobile phones. Taken together, these technologies have remade computers into social devices, not isolationist ones. Today's social Web is the ultimate collaborative medium; computers enable us to share everything from music playlists and geolocations to software development to financial investments in start-up companies.

Dublin's complaint was reasonable given when he wrote and the state of his knowledge; he feared that the hyperbolic predictions being made by technologists[7] would drive that future into being. But as his example shows, unanticipated change can blindside you from a wholly new direction. A religious prophecy becomes laughable when the named date comes and goes and, as in Y2K, the world does not end. A secular prophecy can become laughable even if it is partially or mostly right because intermediate technological changes or apparently unrelated scientific advances have radically altered the cultural field of play. When that happens, the supposedly radical prophecy suddenly looks as dated as the many twentieth-century thrillers whose plots could be short-circuited after only a minute or two if the characters just had mobile phones.

One of the main reasons futurists get blindsided is that they are typically expert on a relatively narrow range of fields. This is where they differ from science fiction authors. Science fiction is often thought to be prediction or prophecy, but it is not; it is (hopefully entertaining) stories woven around the possible consequences of (hopefully sound) extrapolated science. Isaac Asimov's famed Three Laws of Robotics are a good example of this: as Asimov himself said, the Laws were not intended to be taken literally. Rather, when Asimov began writing, as he explains in his autobiography, the cultural cliché was the killer robot: Frankenstein and its descendants. In order to get away from that cultural context, Asimov felt he needed a storytelling device that would allow him to explore what life with socially adapted robots might be like. His fiction and that of his successors has, however, inspired generations of robotics and artificial intelligence researchers to try to build robots that are socially useful and helpful rather than solely military weapons.

A futurologist, on the other hand, is more typically trying to anticipate trends and how they will affect a particular business or industry. British Telecom, for example, had first Peter Cochrane and then Ian Pearson filling this sort of role. Cochrane, who also ran BT's research lab, became notorious in the British press for some of the apparently wild experiments he conducted – building an ant farm as a way of studying collaboration and networking, for example. Yet viewed 15 years later, Cochrane was indeed prescient in doing that, as understanding the changes in social structures due to new communications technologies is essential to BT's business in the twenty-first century. Similarly, the series of 'You will' commercials AT&T ran in 1993 outlining such predictions as ecommerce, video

---

[7]   Of course, the hype around the Internet was even more hyperbolic. See for example any issue of *Wired* magazine c.1990 to 1993.

conferencing, RFID road toll payments and in-car GPS was nearly 100 per cent accurate.[8]

Occasionally, there is someone who can both tell good stories and make interesting predictions about the future, such as the science fiction writers Arthur C. Clarke and Charles Stross.

Clarke helpfully provided a bedrock set of principles for those working on the edges of science. Those working on far-out but still science-based technologies such as molecular nanotechnology (or molecular manufacturing), superhuman artificial intelligence and radical life extension quote them often.

His three laws go like this:

1. When a distinguished but elderly scientist states that something is possible, he is almost certainly right. When he states that something is impossible, he is very probably wrong.
2. The only way of discovering the limits of the possible is to venture a little way past them into the impossible.
3. Any sufficiently advanced technology is indistinguishable from magic.

The first of these expresses a social reality that even the highly expert may resist or fail to understand new developments beyond their personal comfort zones. The second inspires scientists to push the limits and tackle hard problems and/ or justifies the pursuit (and expense) of blue-sky research that may never produce usable results. The third, the most widely quoted and best known, expresses human psychology when confronted with something unfamiliar and poorly understood.

In 1945, for example, the scientist Vannevar Bush published an essay in *The Atlantic* titled 'As We May Think'. Here's what he imagined: a desktop system with screens which can store and display a vast, ever-growing electronic library of research material made up of both personal memories and published material; additions could be made by hand writing a note or dropping in a document to be scanned. The material would be immediately searchable and would include not only text but pictures and sound, and would be internally linked into what Bush called 'associative trails' which individuals could create and share with each other. He called it the 'Memex'. Well, now, doesn't that sound a lot like the World Wide Web?

But Bush was writing in the analogue era. His library was stored on microfilm, the documents were photographed rather than digitally scanned and the pictures were stills. Well, of course: technologies like digital computers and video recording had not been invented yet, and audio recording was still too expensive to be in widespread use outside the broadcasting industry. Yet Bush, who was a leading engineer and who had imagination, confidence in human inventiveness and some inside knowledge of the work researchers were doing, could extrapolate from the

---

[8]   On YouTube: http://www.youtube.com/watch?v=4PJcABbtvtA (accessed: 31 January 2012).

technology he already knew to envision walnut-sized, head-mounted cameras, dry photography, the possibility of being able to make millions of identical, very cheap copies, speech recognition, giant, high-speed electronic calculators and even direct man–machine electrical symbiosis.

Like generations of inventors before and since, Bush was outlining an answer to a personal frustration: the amount of knowledge in his field was growing past what a person could reasonably keep in his head and a manageable library of books. His idea of the Memex inspired later researchers, such as Doug Engelbart (who invented the first graphical computer interface), Ted Nelson (who has spent decades labouring to build a hypertext system) and Tim Berners-Lee (the inventor of the World Wide Web) to explore the possibilities of hypertext. He imagined it; they built it. But what made building it possible was a profound change in technology that Bush did not foresee: the switch from analogue to digital.

The same year as Bush's Memex article, 1945, Arthur C. Clarke made his most famous accurate prediction, that geostationary satellites in low orbits would be used for earthbound communications. Many more of his predictions were less successful, such as his 2001 prognostications for *Reader's Digest* that the last coal mine would close in 2006 and that the first human clone would be developed in 2004. In that essay, Clarke noted the difficulty of timing that's already been mentioned; new inventions or events, he wrote, '… can render predictions absurd after only a few years'.[9]

We have seen examples of technological predictions becoming absurd already in the case of the Internet and Max Dublin. But greater than that is the far less foreseeable impact of social change, which is much more like the unforeseeable 'black swan' that Nicholas Nassim Taleb writes about in his book by that title (2007). In 1950, for example, the magazine *Modern Mechanix* got some, though not many of the technological possibilities right in imagining the suburban American home of the year 2000: solar-powered, built from light sheet metal and plastic, supplied with converged television, radio and telephone, and furnished with biologically produced plastics. The author, Waldemar Kaempffert, the science editor of the *New York Times*, was right when he said we would be shopping via picture phone (though his vision was more like the TV shopping channel QVC than ecommerce), and also close enough when he predicted no one would cook any more except a few quaintly old-fashioned senior citizens because prepared, flash-frozen meals would be delivered to the home ready for heating. He was wildly optimistic about energy and plastics prices, imagining that the home would cost a mere $5,000. On the other hand, a lot of people might like his idea of a home whose furnishings can be gathered together every morning and quickly hosed down and dried. He based the details of this prospective future on ongoing research with which he was familiar, and thought all that could prevent it would be vested interests such as labour unions.

---

[9]   Sir Arthur C. Clarke's Predictions: http://www.arthurcclarke.net/?scifi=3 (accessed: 31 January 2012).

But there is a common key element that makes both Kaempffert's and Vannevar Bush's visions hilariously off-base to the modern eye. Bush: 'One of [the giant computers of the future] will take instructions and data from a whole roomful of girls armed with simple key board punches, and will deliver sheets of computed results every few minutes.' Kaempffert: 'When Jane Dobson cleans house ....' Yes. These guys were very smart, and they were up on all the latest research in their field. But they had no clue about women or how women's roles would change. The first female-controlled contraception, the birth control pill, did not hit until 1960, and when it did it helped usher in nearly two decades of profound social change.

This type of blind spot is an extreme example of the fact that most secular prophets base their visions on what they know about what's happening at the time. We see this every day in the speculation about stock prices that passes for financial news. A stock has been going up all year – it's going to keep going up, or it's hit a 'top' and is going to plateau, or it's going to drop as people 'take profits'. What you don't see, or rarely, is pundits predicting that the top brass at Enron will be exposed as crooks and the stock will collapse. Afterwards, of course, everyone can explain how obvious it was if you just looked at the numbers.

And so back to the futures of our day. Y2K was a bust – fortunately. What about the optimistic futures that we hear about now: the Singularity and AI, molecular nanotechnology, radical life extension and immortality? The chasing-the-horizon stuff: what about that?

The first two of those rely on the massive growth of computing power since 1950, which in turn depends on the incorrectly named Moore's Law. In 1965, Intel co-founder Gordon Moore, observed that the number of transistors that could be cheaply fitted onto a single integrated chip doubles approximately every two years. If it holds up, the thinking goes, at some point our cheap computational power will match the processing capacity of the human brain ... and then keep going to produce superhuman intelligence. The transition point was dubbed 'the Singularity' by science fiction writer and physicist Vernor Vinge in 1993 after discontinuous phenomena in astrophysics such as black holes.[10] Because it is a discontinuity, no valid predictions can be made about what might happen after the Singularity, he argued.

Vinge said he would be surprised if the Singularity occurred before 2005 or after 2030. Other proponents of this idea, such as the futurist and inventor Ray Kurzweil, keep track of increases in computing power as a way of testing the prediction. Kurzweil, who for many years has annually updated a set of charts covering various indicators, believes his charts show that computational power is accelerating right on schedule.[11]

---

[10]   What Is the Singularity? by Vernor Vinge. At http://mindstalk.net/vinge/vinge-sing. html (accessed: 31 January 2012).

[11]   Wikipedia tracks the various predictions Kurzweil has published: https://en.wikipedia. org/wiki/Predictions_made_by_Ray_Kurzweil#The_Age_of_Spiritual_Machines (accessed: 31 January 2012).

The really big question is not whether they are right given their assumptions, or not exactly. If you assume that the amount of available, cheap computing power will continue to accelerate exponentially and that computing power is sufficient to create artificial intelligence, then the Singularity is a logical, if not inevitable consequence. The really big question is whether those assumptions are right.

The small objection is that improvements in software engineering have by no means kept pace with the increase in computing power. The Chief Technology Officer of Intel, Justin Rattner, tends to believe the Singularity will happen, and yet, when pressed in a 2008 interview, he had to admit to misgivings:

> I once asked our speech recognition team if there was any direct relationship between machine computing speed and recognition accuracy and after a long pause, they said – because they knew I was not going to be happy with the answer – no. He [Rattner] asked why: 'Our recognition performance is limited by our algorithmic understanding, not by our instruction speed. We can give you the wrong answer much faster, but we can't give you the right answer much faster' (Grossman 2008).

The big question, however, is that outlined in a 2007 talk by Charles Stross: are these pundits looking in the right direction? Moore's Law is not a law in the same sense as the laws of thermodynamics. It is merely an observation that could cease to be true – and indeed, researchers in technical fields have put considerable effort into estimating when Moore's Law might run out.

Stross's main point is that the paradigm by which we project the future may change entirely. It has, he argues, happened before: 'Around 1950, everyone tended to look at what the future held in terms of improvements in transportation speed', he writes, going on to outline the impressive acceleration of travel technologies from the 1800s to the 1950s. Certainly, the science fiction of the first half of the twentieth century imagined space exploration and colonisation, faster-than-light travel to distant stars, and interactions with multiple extraterrestrial species. Contemporary science fiction's dominant themes are computers, artificial intelligence, and virtual and augmented reality; the space that is being explored by writers from William Gibson to Neal Stephenson (and Stross) is cyberspace. If you are old enough to remember the moon landings, modern science fiction is as profound a disappointment as the sadness expressed by a computer scientist who was 10 when Neil Armstrong set foot on the moon: 'I knew', he told me on the fortieth anniversary in 2009, 'that my future was going to be lived in space.' Instead, the moon landings, like the supersonic Concorde, were a dead end. Meanwhile, the social consequences of the transport decades took more decades to make themselves plain: suburban sprawl, air pollution, climate change and millions of old people separated from their distant families.

By 1970, Stross continues, progress was seen in terms of computational power:

> The cultural picture in computing today therefore looks much as it did in transportation technology in the 1930s – everything tomorrow is going to be wildly faster than it is today, let alone yesterday. And this progress has been running for long enough that it's seeped into the public consciousness. In the 1920s, boys often wanted to grow up to be steam locomotive engineers; politicians and publicists in the 1930s talked about 'air-mindedness' as the key to future prosperity. In the 1990s it was software engineers and in the current decade it's the politics of Internet governance.

> All of this is irrelevant. Because computers and microprocessors aren't the future. They're yesterday's future, and tomorrow will be about something else (Stross 2007).

Stross goes on to make a guess about the nature of that 'something else': the social impact of today's new technologies that will only fully reveal itself decades hence, when everyone logs their entire lives, getting lost is impossible, nothing is forgotten, everything is public, self-driving cars are the norm and many, many laws will have to be redefined.

This is not, he told his audience of engineers, the future they thought they were building. It's not – and it's not the future today's consumers thought they were signing up for when they bought their first computer.

But if there is one mistake that secular prophecies commonly make, it is to assume that change happens evenly and universally and, as we have seen, to focus only on a narrow field. Manhattan and other dense urban areas are full of people who do not drive cars – and not only is urbanisation growing but for today's urban teens mobile phones provide the independence that used to be associated with a car. The scarcity of energy and water may derail everything. The potential for personal genomics and bioinformatics may draw off the next generation of talented researchers who might have gone into AI. Fifty years from now, we may well still be chasing the same horizons we are now, just like my space-deprived computer scientist.

It has been widely observed that historical Hollywood dramas can be easily dated by their costumes and set decoration, which inevitably reflect the obsessions of their time. In the 1950s, peasants were clean and well-dressed; by the 1990s they were filthy and tattered. The future shown in many science fiction films is like that: homes are sparsely furnished and everyone is identically dressed. It looks inhuman and it jars, because most humans do not throw out everything on a given date when 'the future' arrives. In movies like *Brazil* and *Twelve Monkeys* the filmmaker Terry Gilliam gets this right: his interiors are filled with a jumble of old and new, more junkyard than pristine reinvention. The future is always with us. The prophecies we make about it reflect the preoccupations of the time in which they are made. We laugh at them – and then go on and make the same mistake. Because: human nature does not change, or not that much.

References

Albrecht, K. and McIntyre, L. 2006. *Spychips: How Major Corporations and Government Plan to Track Your Every Purchase and Watch Your Every Move.* New York: Plume.

Baard, M. 2006. RFID: Sign of the (End) Times? *Wired News*, 6 June 2006 [Online]. Available at: http://www.wired.com/science/discoveries/news/2006/06/70308 [accessed: 30 April 2012].

Bush, V. 1945. As We May Think. *The Atlantic*, July 1945 [Online]. Available at: http://www.theatlantic.com/magazine/archive/1945/07/as-we-may-think/3881/ [accessed: 30 April 2012].

Dublin, M. 1991. *Futurehype: The Tyranny of Prophecy*. New York: Dutton.

Fellet, M. 2011. Single Molecule Is Tiniest Electric Motor Ever. *New Scientist*, 10 September 2011.

Feynman, R.P. 1959. There Is Plenty of Room at the Bottom. Lecture given at the annual meeting of the American Physical Society, 29 December 1959 [Online]. Available at: http://www.zyvex.com/nanotech/feynman.html [accessed: 30 April 2012].

Grossman, W.M. 1998. The End of the World as We Know It? *Scientific American*, October 1998.

——. 2008. Intel's Rattner Says Machines Will Get Us in the End. *The Inquirer*, 12 November 2008 [Online]. Available at: http://www.theinquirer.net/inquirer/news/393/1049393/justin-rattner-intel-winker [accessed: 30 April 2012].

Stross, C. 2007. Shaping the Future. Talk given to a technology open day for TNG Technology Consulting, 13 May 2007 [Online]. Available at: http://www.antipope.org/charlie/blog-static/2007/05/shaping_the_future.html [accessed: 5 December 2011].

Taleb, N.N. 2007. *The Black Swan: The Impact of the Highly Improbable*. New York: Random House.

Vinge, V. 1993. What Is the Singularity? Talk for the VISION-21 Symposium, 1993. [Online]. Available at: http://mindstalk.net/vinge/vinge-sing.html [accessed: 30 April 2012].

Williamson, D. 1999. Y2K: Computer Glitch Came as No Surprise. *The Abilene News*, 25 June 1999 [Online]. Available at: http://www.bobbemer.com/SCRIPPS.HTM [accessed: 6 December 2011].

PART III
Contemporary Case Studies

Part III consists of five chapters which focus on prophecy in contemporary minority religious movements and milieus, from the diffuse 'conspiracy milieu' to more bounded new religious movements: The Family International, the Church of Jesus Christ of Latter Day Saints, the Unification Church and the Branch Davidians. This section differs from the preceding sections in that not all of the papers are written by academics: member and former-member perspectives are also represented here. Whilst the academic, outsider perspective provides important overview and analysis, an empathetic understanding of those whose lives are lived through, or directly affected by, prophecy is essential for grasping why prophecy persists.

The first chapter of this section is written by Abi Freeman May, who joined The Family International (TFI), a group with an End-Time focus as a young adult, living in communities until 2007. She offers a personal reflection of her experiences of living with an expectation that Christ would return within her lifetime. May outlines how despite changes in TFI's structure, beliefs and practices over time, belief in the imminent return of Jesus was consistently one of the defining aspects of the movement. She believes that it was primarily the practical implications of this belief on the member's day-to-day living which distinguished TFI from other Christian groups with similar eschatological views. May outlines some of the positive and negative consequences of this belief, with a focus on three particular areas. First, she argues that a positive consequence was an awareness of world events as members looked to the news for signs of the coming End Times. However, a negative consequence of this was that particular world events were singled out by founder David Berg as more important than others so that sometimes members had a greater knowledge of what was happening in another part of the world than in their own neighbourhoods. Second, members valued every minute of life but this was combined with the negative consequence of feeling under constant pressure, with the belief that you could impede the return of Jesus by not reaching enough people with the Gospel. Finally, members invested in personal talents, including the creative arts and a healthy lifestyle, in order to further God's work. But this was coupled with the negative consequence of a lack of preparation for the future, particularly manifested in lack of thought regarding pensions and older age, limited outside employment experiences and lack of formally accredited education for many of the children born into the group. May contends that these are on-going problems arising from TFI's End-Time beliefs, although she also acknowledges that the movement's current leadership has attempted to address these concerns.

Chapter 12 returns to an academic format with sociologists Gordon and Gary Shepherd providing a 'Theory of Prophecy in the Development of New Religious Movements', illustrated with case studies of The Family International (TFI) and the Mormons (the Church of Jesus Christ of Latter Day Saints [LDS]). These movements are selected as examples of 'prophetic religions' – religions which originate in the founder's prophetic claims. These are not claims of a predictive or cataclysmic nature, but rather proclaim a moral vision based on divine guidance, transcendent authority and supernatural powers. The Shepherds propose that an understanding of the emergence and institutional development of these prophetic religions can be gained through an analysis of various factors that include the form of prophecy construction and its transformation over time.

They propose a theoretical model in which 'prophetic modality' (that is whether prophecy is 'oracular' [i.e. the divine word given through an oracle] or 'inspirational' [i.e. inspired and sanctioned by God but not claiming to be a verbatim message]) interplays with 'prophetic channel' (i.e. whether prophecy is received by a designated individual or a group of collaborators). The interaction between modality and channel variables gives rise to four 'ideal types'. The Shepherds go on to describe a process in which prophecy in TFI moved from inspirational/ designated individual (in the person of founder David Berg) to oracular/group of collaborators (at least until the 'Reboot' in 2010). In contrast, prophecy in the development of Mormonism moved from oracular/designated individual (in the person of founder Joseph Smith) to inspirational/group of collaborators. In both cases, prophecy was 'routinised' as it moved from the domain of the individual to the group, but prophetic modality moved in opposite directions in the two groups. The Shepherds propose that oracular prophecy is more marginalising than inspirational prophecy, as it is more declarative, taken as the literal word of God or other divine entity, and is thus associated more with 'strong charisma'. They suggest that this could be a contributory factor to TFI's marginal social position as compared to that of the LDS Church. The Shepherds end their chapter by recognising the need for further comparative studies of prophetic religions in order to test their model.

Chapter 13 is written by Hani Zaccarelli who was born and raised in the Unification Church (UC) as a 'blessed child' (a child born of parents who had been matched and blessed by Rev Moon and who consequently were considered to have a 'pure' blood line and the potential to form the foundation for the Kingdom of Heaven on Earth). Zaccarelli's childhood experience was of living in the 'last days' and with understandings that not only were UC members set apart from wider society but that blessed children were sometimes also set apart from non-blessed. Throughout the narrative of his up-bringing, Zaccarelli reflects on the prophetic beliefs that informed the very foundation of the movement: that the Divine Principle should be read as explaining why Rev Moon was 'the fulfilment of ancient prophecy' and how he and his followers would usher in Heaven on Earth. His conclusion implies that partially due to what he came to perceive as 'untruths' of his childhood, his faith weakened, and he eventually abandoned the faith of his parents.

Chapter 14 is written by Livingstone Fagan, a survivor of a dramatic and tragic standoff at Waco, Texas in 1993 between a communal religious group, the Branch Davidians, led by David Koresh, and a branch of the American Federal Government. Fagan first met David Koresh while completing a post-graduate degree at a theology seminary near London in 1988 and he visited the Mount Carmel community on several occasions prior to 1993. He and his family were at the community during the 51-day stand-off between government forces and the Branch Davidian community; Fagan was asked to leave the community during the siege to act as a theological spokesperson for the group. The majority of members, including Fagan's wife and mother, died in the fire of 19 April 1993. A year later Fagan was among a small number of survivors detained and tried in what he claims was an 'obvious political trial'. Fagan explains that although he and his fellow Branch Davidians were acquitted of the charges brought against them, they were nevertheless given 40-year prison terms. After serving almost 15 years in US Federal Prisons, the US Supreme Court overturned the prison sentences and Fagan was returned to England in the summer of 2007. Despite the injustice, Fagan claims, it remains an honour and privilege to be part of this historic and prophetic event. In this chapter, he outlines the importance of Biblical prophecy to the community at Waco and his continuing belief both that the Waco event was prophesised in Scripture as was Christ's return to Earth in the figure of David Koresh. Fagan explains that the tragic events at Waco have served to strengthen the survivors' faith in the coming Kingdom of Heaven on Earth.

In the final chapter of this section (Chapter 15), David G. Robertson investigates prophecies within the contemporary 'conspiracy milieu', focusing on a case study of American radio presenter and film-maker, Alex Jones. Robertson's paper is important in tracing the rise of prophecy and millennial thinking in this academically-neglected milieu, as well as in introducing a theory of 'rolling prophecy' to indicate the ways in which prophetic utterances are constantly revised and reinterpreted so that they never appear to fail. Through this mechanism, illustrated with examples of two of Alex Jones' prophecies, the 2008 financial collapse and 9/11, cognitive dissonance is avoided and prophecy is better able to fulfil the function of social critique. Millennial thinking within this milieu focuses on the subordination of the masses by a controlling force, frequently labelled the Illuminati or New World Order, with individual prophets such as Alex Jones, David Icke and David Wilcock working to expose this force to allow for the emancipation of the people and a coming transformed age. Robertson argues that within Jones' 'rolling prophecy' we are always on the brink of this transformation. Thus Robertson elucidates how prophecy is as equally about the present as it is the future: arguing that for Jones' sympathisers, his prophecy is a theodicy which allows for social critique, and endurance of an unjust situation in the expectation that things are always about to get better.

Chapter 11

Living in the Time of the End:
A Personal Commentary from
My Experiences with the Children of God
and the Family International

Abi Freeman May

In this chapter I will explore the practical implications of living in a milieu where there is a deeply held belief that it is the 'Time of the End', and that Jesus Christ will return to earth within our lifetime. My observations are drawn from approximately 30 years of living in communities of the 'Children of God' (COG), later 'The Family International' (TFI). The following is a personal reflection. I am not seeking to represent the position of the movement's leadership or current membership, in fact, I am fairly certain many would not agree with elements of my analysis. The controversial history and practices of TFI have been well documented in a number of scholarly volumes, including *The Endtime Family* by William Sims Bainbridge (2002). This paper will focus solely on one aspect of TFI belief and lifestyle: the End Time.

The Significance of the End Time for the Children of God and
The Family International

The COG started around 1968 amongst the hippies of southern California, under the guidance of its founder, David Berg. Fundamentally Christian, but with some fringe beliefs and interpretations, the movement experienced rapid growth in its formative years, and then levelled off to about 7–10,000 members by around 1974. Despite its American origins, members evangelised with zeal and quickly spread around the globe, first arriving in the United Kingdom around 1970, which is just a few years before I encountered the movement and its message.

The structure, leadership and practices of The Family International of today bear scant resemblance to the COG of the hippy years, yet some of its basic doctrines have remained constant. The End Time is one of these. Beliefs about the Time of the End have not only been an intrinsic part of the theology of TFI, but have also had a profound impact on the daily lives of members. The current leadership attempted to mitigate some of the repercussions of these beliefs through the movement's major restructuring in 2010 (see Shepherd and Shepherd, Chapter 12, this volume).

My initial education about the End Time consisted of sitting in a living room with around 20 other people, also residents of the COG community that I had joined in the 1970s, spending hours studying the Bible books of Daniel, Ezekiel and Revelation, along with a focus on prophetic passages in the Gospels and Epistles.

To a great extent, these studies were neither unique nor unusual within Christian theology. The expectation that Jesus Christ would visibly return to earth, resurrecting the dead and establishing the Kingdom of God on Earth, is part of the Christian tradition: in the New Testament, one verse in 25 deals with Christ's return, and the Christian church has lived in 'blessed hope of His appearing' since its earliest days. Jesus is quoted in Matthew 24 as predicting:

> Then shall appear the sign of the Son of Man in heaven: and then shall all the tribes of the earth mourn, and they shall see the Son of Man coming in the clouds of heaven with power and great glory. And he shall send his angels with a great sound of a trumpet, and they shall gather together his elect from the four winds, from one end of the earth to the other.[1]

The Apostle Paul uttered a similar prophecy:

> For the Lord himself shall descend from heaven with a shout, with the voice of the archangel, and with the trump of God; and the dead in Christ shall rise first; then we which are alive and remain shall be caught up together with him in the clouds to meet the Lord in the air; and so shall we ever be with the Lord.[2]

The Nicene Creed, familiar to both Anglicans and Catholics, proclaims:

> He will come again in glory
> to judge the living and the dead,
> and his kingdom will have no end.[3]

Thus, for TFI members, the totality of the End Time is not a gloomy expectation of the complete end of the world, but rather a joyful anticipation of a coming change to the world as we know it, with the visible return of Jesus Christ to resurrect the 'dead in Christ', and then to rule and reign on the earth. TFI members eagerly await his arrival, believing it will usher in an era of peace, plenty and justice, along with the balanced restoration of the natural earth. They believe that salvation and eternal life in heaven are, in the first instance, for those who accept Jesus'

---

[1]   Matthew 24:30–31 (KJV).

[2]   1 Thessalonians 4:16–17 (KJV).

[3]   http://www.creeds.net/ancient/nicene.htm (accessed: 24 May 2012).

sacrifice on the cross for their sins. Yet in their view, God's love is for all people, no matter their religion or lack thereof. This is a universal event – good news for *all* humankind.

The End Time Thread

The End Time has been a constant thread throughout both TFI's teachings for members and evangelical literature, and is still evident on its international website.[4] One of the major themes has been an expectation that the return of Jesus will be preceded by the rise of a world government, as implied by the Book of Revelation. The government will appear benign, at least at the start, but will be led by an anti-God leader, usually referred to as the 'Antichrist'. This administration will restrict personal and religious freedom, turning viciously on devout followers of all religions, particularly the monotheistic faiths of Christianity, Judaism and Islam. Jesus will return after a time of trouble, understood to be three and a half years.

Much emphasis was placed on interpreting the 'signs' of when this would happen, as suggested by Jesus in Matthew 24. TFI teachers interpreted Biblical and other prophecies, along with the signs, to suggest that Jesus would likely return within the lifetime of the generation who started the movement. Except for a prophecy by David Berg about 1993,[5] which he later re-interpreted, no precise dates were set. However, there was a general understanding that the generation who sees the signs fulfilled would be alive to witness the return of Jesus.

One of the favourite publications amongst TFI members and friends was the *Endtime News Digest* which was a collection of news clippings with commentary and prophetic messages, suggesting how current events fit in with End Time expectations. Recurring topics included whether microchip technology could be leading towards the 'mark of the beast', as mentioned in Revelations 13, and thus part of the arsenal of the coming world government; whether the recurrent financial crises would lead to the collapse of the global economy and then give rise to the one world government; and so on. Earthquakes and natural disasters were often interpreted as fulfilling the prophecies of Jesus: before his return, there would be 'earthquakes in diverse places'.[6] The *Digest* was published monthly from 1998 to 2008.[7]

---

[4]   http://www.thefamilyinternational.org/en/viewpoints/future/63/ (accessed: 10 May 2012).

[5]   David Berg. *The 70 Years Prophecy of the End*, Letter no. 156, March 1972.

[6]   See Matthew 24:7.

[7]   This is an example of the type of content that could be found in the *Endtime News Digest*: http://www.countdown.org/end/ (accessed: 10 May 2012).

Such interpretations and discussions are not unique to TFI: examples abound of other Christian movements holding similar conversations.[8] However, what has arguably set TFI apart from more traditional forms of Christian eschatology is the manner in which these beliefs about the End Time were embraced and incorporated into daily life. In particular, it has been the expectation of the imminent return of Jesus that has had profound implications for members.

From my perspective, there were both positive and undesirable consequences of this belief, which I will now analyse.

An Awareness of World Events, But from a Narrow Perspective

The majority of TFI members followed (and presumably still follow) the 'signs of the end' eagerly, and consequently felt a responsibility to stay aware of world events. Listening to the news on the radio was encouraged right from the beginning of the movement; in the 1970s, David Berg recommended that members should have a shortwave radio in order to access BBC World Service.[9] As world news became more readily available on cable television, watching CNN was often part of the regular routine in TFI communities. Later, the availability of news on the Internet became a useful resource.

This was supplemented with commentary by David Berg in his general 'letters' to members, in which he described and analysed world events. His views carried a lot of weight; however, his opinions reflected his personal outlook and interests. As a result, TFI members may have had more detailed knowledge of an event happening across the globe than they knew about their own country, much less neighbourhood. As an example from my own experience, in 1973–74, I was acutely aware of developments in the Middle East, but despite the fact I was living in the UK at the time, I have no memory of the major industrial unrest and strikes taking place during the same period.[10]

Whilst TFI members were not cloistered, nor unaware of significant world events, the focus throughout the decades was on looking at those events through the prism of the End Time. For instance, the 'coming economic crash' was a constant theme in TFI teachings. David Berg wrote his letter *The Crash*[11] in 1973; it was always expected as a 'sign of the times'. Jesus had warned of 'famines' before his return,[12] and there was an expectation that the Antichrist's 'One World Government' would probably take power through peaceful means, picking up

---

8   See http://www.prophecyupdate.com/ for an example of a non-TFI website with a focus on signs of the End Time (accessed: 10 May 2012).

9   David Berg. *Gotcher Flee Bag?*, Letter no. 386:13, 14 January 1976.

10   http://www.nationalarchives.gov.uk/releases/2005/nyo/politics.htm (accessed: 10 May 2012).

11   David Berg. *The Crash*, Letter No. 284, 16 December 1974, World Services.

12   See Matthew 24:7.

the pieces after a global economic meltdown. The Black Monday Crash of 1987 was interpreted as an intermediate fulfilment of these prophecies. A recent (2012) headline, 'Crash Alert: The Stock Market is Falling like a Stone'[13] would come as no surprise to TFI members; what is happening in the global economy now is what has been expected for four decades.

There was a degree of awareness of the impact of these 'signs' on the lives of ordinary people. In fact, this concern was behind the launch of humanitarian ministries to support and encourage the needy, as Berg described in his letter, *Consider the Poor*, in 1991, referring to the economic crises of the times:

> People are hard up in the U.S. right now! So to our people who have gone back to North America – that formerly proud, high-falutin', luxury-loving area of the World which used to be rich, but now is becoming poor – the Lord is saying, 'Search out the needy, the lonely, the lost & the helpless & the homeless, the lowest of the low & those that nobody else wants – & give them Jesus – just like you did when you first started!'[14]

However, this link with charitable work was an exception; the End Time focus was primarily about discerning signs and giving warnings. On occasion Berg and other members took this further by turning their attention to what might be going on behind the scenes to usher in a world government. There are probably some TFI individuals even today who are quite fixated on these matters, and perhaps would be labelled by outsiders as 'conspiracy theorists'.

The End Time was not only an internal focus; a lot of effort was also put into creating and distributing literature, music, videos and electronic media with the goal of warning the people of the world about coming events, such as warnings not to take the 'mark of the beast'.[15] Perhaps there should have been more emphasis on the here and now; more 'pleading the cause of the poor and needy'[16] would have been a better balance, especially considering that ordinary people rarely have much power to influence world events.

Valuing the Minutes, but Feeling Everything Is Urgent

> We must work even harder and faster now, for the Lord has shown us that the time is even shorter and it's later than you think![17]

---

[13]   http://www.globalresearch.ca/index.php?context=va&aid=31027 (accessed: 24 May 2012).

[14]   David Berg. *Consider the Poor! – Psalm 41:1*. Letter no. 2755, December 1991.

[15]   See Revelation 13:16–17.

[16]   Psalm 109:22 (KJV).

[17]   David Berg. *To Our Worldwide Family*, Letter no. 307A, July 1974.

Living in the Time of the End, in TFI context, meant making the most of your time, valuing the minutes. 'Our days are identical suitcases, all the same size, but some people can pack more into them than others' is a contemporary quotation that does not originate with TFI, but variations on this theme are quoted by TFI members, and it certainly reflects the ethos: getting things done, rather than procrastinating; facing a challenge rather than delaying; fitting more into your day, not wasting time. Efficiency and time management were important topics in TFI, and, as usual, were supported by Scripture: 'redeeming the time, because the days are evil.'[18]

However, making the most of one's time also meant feeling that everything was urgent and living somewhat under pressure. Several of David Berg's letters had the phrase 'time is short' in the title,[19] but this was the tip of the iceberg: there were many references throughout his letters to the shortness of time before Jesus would return.

The zealous efforts of TFI members to evangelise the world were driven primarily by a sincere desire to share the good news of the Gospel, but they were also partly driven by the belief that failure to do so would impede the return of Jesus. In Matthew 24:14, Jesus predicts, 'this gospel of the kingdom shall be preached in all the world for a witness unto all nations; and then shall the end come.' This particular prophecy was a serious concern. TFI members understood this to mean that Jesus would not come back if the Gospel was not first preached globally; therefore if they failed to preach the Gospel effectively, they could be responsible for delaying that wonderful event.

That is a heavy weight to carry. Perhaps the stress of this responsibility, coupled with frequent reminders of being on the brink of the rise of the Antichrist, along with the feeling of never being able to do enough, contributed to problems of burnout, particularly amongst some of the leadership. It can indeed be quite emotionally and mentally exhausting to be living on the edge of the apocalypse.

Making the Most of Your Life and Talents in Order to 'Love God, Help Others', but not Preparing for Life Ahead

> The whole idea is: we haven't got much longer to go, it's later than you think! It won't be long now![20]

It was a general understanding amongst TFI members that we were responsible to invest our lives and talents in God's work: to love Him and help others.[21] The fact that we were 'living in the End Time' only added urgency to these priorities.

---

[18]   Ephesians 5:16 (KJV).

[19]   David Berg. *Time Is Short*, Letter no. 1347, December 1982; *Now It's Speed! – Not Perfection! – Time is Short!*, Letter no. 1636, October 1983.

[20]   David Berg. *It Won't Be Long Now*, Letter no. 1474, 29 January 1983.

[21]   See Matthew 22:37–40.

This had some excellent personal outcomes. Members developed their own creative talents, as well as encouraging them in the children and teenagers growing up in the movement. Art and music; song-writing and performing; creative writing and the development of excellent teaching materials are all part of the legacy.

There were also health benefits. Members saw their bodies as the temples of God, to be cared for.[22] Staying healthy was, in essence, a religious duty. This involved eating a well-balanced diet, avoiding junk food, keeping at a good weight, having daily exercise in the fresh air, keeping clean and getting enough rest. There was no smoking or drugs, and only limited consumption of alcohol. Regular medical, optical and dental check-ups were recommended.

Staying healthy in the present was also seen as an investment in the future. We needed to be fit enough to 'flee the armies of the Antichrist during the Great Tribulation'. However, the expectation of this happening within 20 or 30 years meant that very little other preparation was made for the future. For instance, when I joined the movement, I did not expect to see my fortieth birthday; Jesus would be back before then. Another example is how Berg had encouraged those living in Hong Kong under British rule not to worry about the handover to China in 1997, as Jesus would be back ….[23] And so on.

I believe there are several serious consequences from these shortened life expectancies. Some of these problems have been addressed to an extent through TFI's major restructuring in May 2010, with a move away from dogmatic interpretations, encouragement to pursue employment and education, and a lifting of the bureaucratic requirements for membership. This went alongside the specific acknowledgement by Peter Amsterdam, the movement's co-leader, of the impact of End Time beliefs on members over the years.[24] Although members have now been encouraged 'to be prepared for the possibility that the Lord won't decide to return at the time we hope or think He should return',[25] the repercussions of what went before remain for both current and former members.

First, while the Bible does teach 'take no thought for the morrow', we are also told to make adequate preparations.[26] This was not evident amongst most TFI members, who rarely made any meaningful preparation for later life. There was no serious consideration given to how we would manage during advanced old age or retirement, no saving towards pensions, rarely any investment such as buying a house, preferring instead to rent our living accommodation.

Most members who are now in their fifties and sixties find it is too late to arrange a good pension. In much of Europe there is an adequate social security net, at least for the present, preventing too dire consequences, but for Americans and those from the developing world, this can be a real problem. The current TFI

---

[22]   See 1 Corinthians 3:16–17.

[23]   David Berg. *More on No Blank TRFs!*, Letter no. 1732:20, January 1984.

[24]   Peter Amsterdam. *Backtracking through TFI History*, May 2010.

[25]   Peter Amsterdam. *The Change Journey*, Letter no. 3737, 2009.

[26]   See Matthew 6:34, Proverbs 24:27.

leadership is trying to help the oldest members, and is setting up a token pension scheme for those born before 1955, yet this is an enduring problem for many of the first generation members who have lived in community for up to 40 years.

Second, there was little planning for conventional employment, nor forethought about how one would manage should TFI communities be dissolved. This did happen to a large extent with the restructuring of May 2010, which meant that communal living was no longer a requirement for core membership, nor was secular employment discouraged.

This was a major change of direction. For the vast majority of TFI's history, full-time, core members lived communally, with few opportunities or allowances for outside employment. Although members may have developed great skills, they could be excellent secretaries or handymen, musicians or teachers, they rarely obtained formal qualifications. On top of this, most members spent many years as missionaries outside their home countries, often with few remaining ties with old friends, nor sometimes even with their families.

For a middle-aged person to find a job in the present (2012) economic climate can be difficult enough, with limited employment possibilities for those over 50; but when that person has little conventional working history, no 'normal' job references or qualifications, it can be very difficult indeed, even with the life skills and adaptability that came from being a missionary. It is not impossible, and some have adjusted without too much difficulty, but others struggle.

There are also emotional consequences; members who had lived communally for decades may be surprised at the relative isolation of a more conventional lifestyle. Living communally meant being surrounded by friends, always having someone with whom to share the joys and sorrows of the day, as well as the responsibilities for managing the household and paying the bills. By contrast, living alone, or even as a couple, can be unexpectedly quiet and lonely.

A third major consequence of living with the End Time vision involves those born and raised in TFI communities: the second and third generations. There was a naïve assumption that the young people would grow up to become missionaries, but whatever the case, if we, the first generation, did not expect to see our older age, how much less likely for those born later.

The impact of this upon the young people has many dimensions which are beyond the scope and space of this chapter, and is a topic that warrants further research. One aspect I will mention briefly regards preparation for life through education.

Most TFI members – at least core membership – taught their children through home schooling. Although the pre-school, primary and early secondary levels of education were generally very good, the emphasis after that was almost entirely skills and vocationally based. For the most part, young people did gain excellent transferable skills such as languages, literacy, computer literacy, and soft skills such as time management, working with people, initiative, good work ethics etc. However, the lack of formal qualifications and competitive experience present some challenges when they enter the conventional job market. It does seem that after an initial transition, the majority make the adjustment, and are able to go on to further education and/or successful careers, with the possibility of achieving their true potential. This is not the case for every young person who was born in TFI, who, as individuals, respond differently according to their personalities, aptitudes and experiences.

Conclusion

There is a quotation attributed to Martin Luther, 'Even if I knew that tomorrow the world would go to pieces, I would still plant my apple tree.' In my opinion, this is quite far removed from the attitude in the TFI over the past four decades, who, whilst expecting Jesus to come back in their lifetime, simply did not take much stock in preparing for the future.

In attempting to analyse the impact of End Time beliefs on TFI members, I have identified some positive and negative outcomes. This leaves some important questions unanswered. Were the negative aspects simply unfortunate, unforeseen consequences? Was this part of the natural evolution of a new religious movement that started out with more zeal than wisdom, and hopefully has learnt from earlier mistakes?

It has been five years since my husband and I moved out of TFI communal living – although we still have some involvement with the movement at a distance – and these are the type of questions we have often discussed.

This brings me to my conclusion, on a personal note: not so long ago, I attended a Christmas Eve service at a Catholic church. A colleague from the college where I have been teaching was playing the organ; the carols were wonderfully familiar and I enjoyed every song. Then the priest gave the sermon. He spoke about advent – not about the first advent of Christ – but of the wait for the second advent. 'Jesus will come again' was the message he imparted, echoing the words in John chapter 14:

> There is plenty of room for you in my Father's home. If that weren't so, would I have told you that I'm on my way to get a room ready for you? And if I'm on my way to get your room ready, I'll come back and get you so you can live where I live.[27]

'I'll come back and get you.' That is a promise. Perhaps it is presumptuous to claim to know when it will happen; it is in God's hands, not ours. Personally I believe there is a much higher possibility that I will go to see Jesus than he will return before my earthly end. Nevertheless, the promise remains. Whether he comes back, or we go to him, either way, we will see him face to face; that is the Christian hope, and the hope I hold.

---

[27] John 14:2–3 (The Message).

References

Bainbridge, W.S. 2002. *The Endtime Family: Children of God*. Albany, NY: State University of New York Press.

Whitney, M. 2012. *CRASH ALERT: The Stock Market Is Falling Like a Stone* [Online]. Available at: http://www.globalresearch.ca/index.php?context=va&aid=31027 [accessed: 24 May 2012].

Chapter 12

Mormonism and The Family International: Toward a Theory of Prophecy in the Development of New Religious Movements

Gordon Shepherd and Gary Shepherd

In this chapter we are concerned with understanding the emergence and institutional development of prophetic religions – that is, new religions that originate in peoples' acceptance of and adherence to prophetic claims made by religious founders. In particular, our focus is on what Max Weber (1978: 339–634) classified as ethical prophecy in occidental, monotheistic religions rather than the exemplary prophecy tradition of oriental religions.[1] Wherever we refer to prophets or prophecy we are talking about the former rather than the latter mode of prophetic expression. By prophetic claims we mean more than simply forecasting future events, cataclysmic or otherwise. Prophecy and the individuals deemed to be prophets by their followers characteristically proclaim a moral vision through divine guidance. This is in contrast to the justification of a particular moral order based on tradition or rationally reasoned arguments. Prophetic figures in the Western tradition claim a transcendent source of authority and typically invoke access to supernatural powers.

Our assessment of the development of prophetic new religions includes consideration of the following topics: prophecy and social action in religious economies; prophecy and commitment in new religions; oracular and inspirational modes of prophecy construction; and the marginalisation/integration of prophetic religions. Our comparative case-study religions for discussing these topics are 'Mormonism' and The Family International (originally known as the Children of God), for which we sketch brief synopses in the first section of our paper. 'Mormon', 'Mormons' and 'Mormonism' are, of course, popular nicknames used

---

[1]   The ethical prophet in Weber's conceptualisation is one who presents himself as an emissary commissioned through revelation by a transcendent creator God to communicate laws with which people are commanded to comply as a moral duty (for example, Moses, Muhammad, Joseph Smith). In contrast, the 'exemplary prophet' is not 'sent' and does not proclaim a revelatory moral mandate to change a corrupt world. Rather, through personal insight and example, the exemplary prophet points others to the correct path of salvation and fulfilment in harmony with the intrinsic order of the universe (for example, Buddha, Lao Tzu, Prabhupada).

in reference to the doctrines and members of the Church of Jesus Christ of Latter-day Saints (or LDS Church). Throughout our analysis we find it convenient to employ interchangeably 'Mormon' and various Latter-day Saint designations as synonymous. Likewise, we conveniently use the abbreviation TFI when referencing The Family International.

Our primary justification for selecting TFI and the LDS Church for purposes of comparison is pragmatic: they are both 'heretical' Christian religions that believe in contemporary prophetic guidance, which we have studied separately and at some length in previous works (Shepherd and Shepherd 1984, 1998, 2005, 2006a, 2006b, 2007, 2009, 2010a, 2011). By heretical, of course, we don't mean intrinsically wrong or wicked. We simply mean doctrines and corresponding practices that are at variance with the authority of established orthodoxies in both the predominant Catholic and Protestant constellations of creedal Christianity. It is precisely belief in contemporary prophetic revelation and their insistence that they have obtained oracular directives and scriptures, supplemental to the Bible, which are central to both LDS and Family International heresies. It is these supplemental scriptures that justify the doctrines and practices in both groups that deviate most sharply from standard Christian orthodoxies. While there are considerable differences in the organisational ages of our two comparison groups, as well as the historical contexts in which they developed, we adopt the basic sociological assumption that both groups' revelatory claims and doctrinal outcomes that guide members' lives are 'socially constructed', i.e. conceived, formed and changed through a complex set of meaningful human interactions over time. (See Berger and Luckmann 1967 for the classic theoretical exposition of this assumption as it applies to all social institutions, including religious institutions.) One may also assume that there are differences as well as similarities in the ways that prophetic revelations are constructed in these two groups.

Synopsis of LDS and TFI Prophetic Origins and Development

Though different in many of their particulars, both the contemporary LDS Church and Family International are prophecy-based religions whose histories originated in the charismatic claims of their founders, Joseph Smith (1805–44) and David Berg (1917–94), respectively. Of the two, the formally untutored Smith was more clearly a religious prodigy and innovator, who in 1830 at 24 years of age published a 531-page book (*The Book of Mormon*), which he claimed was an ancient scriptural text obtained and translated through divine revelation (Givens 2002, Vogel and Metcalfe 2002). In that same year he founded what he and his followers proclaimed to be the restored church of Jesus Christ. In contrast, Berg was a middle-aged evangelical preacher with ties to Pentecostal, evangelical Christianity. In 1968 Berg commenced a self-appointed ministry to win souls for Jesus among 'hippies' and other youthful dropouts from the counterculture in Southern California. Subsequently, Berg's enthusiastic young 'revolutionaries for Jesus' proselytised throughout the United States and Canada and eventually spread their missionary efforts to over 90 countries throughout the world (Bainbridge 2002, Chancellor 2000, Shepherd and Shepherd 2010a). Both Smith and Berg enacted prophetic leadership roles as religious founders by claiming divine authorisation in issuing frequent doctrinal and organisational instruction to their followers. Both early Mormon converts and Children of God recruits were millenarians who believed through their founders' revelations that they had been chosen to aid in the realisation of God's apocalyptic designs for the last days. Thus, Mormons designated themselves as 'Latter-day Saints', while the Children of God considered themselves to be God's 'End-Time Disciples'.

Smith's early revelations were recorded by scribes and partially printed in 1833 as the *Book of Commandments*. Subsequently, these revelations were reorganised by a committee, edited, updated, and published as the *Doctrine and Covenants* in 1835. Subsequent revelations by Smith were included in later editions of the *Doctrine and Covenants*. Long after his death, additional prophetic writings by Smith were canonised in 1880 by vote of a general conference of the LDS Church in a volume entitled the *Pearl of Great Price*. Along with the King James Bible, Latter-day Saints regard *The Book of Mormon*, *Doctrine and Covenants* and *Pearl of Great Price* as the their 'standard works', or canonical scriptures (Cook 1985).

Smith's leadership did not merely consist in dictating religious revelations attributed to God: he was in every sense an active leader, not only planning but actively participating in political, business, educational, missionary and even military affairs as the growing Mormon community of Latter-day Saints migrated from rural upstate New York to Ohio, Missouri and Illinois. Berg, however, after only a few years of personal presence among his growing flock of followers, sequestered himself from active involvement in the daily lives of these youthful converts, who dispersed themselves in communal missionary homes worldwide for the purpose of Christian evangelising. Berg maintained leadership control through regular epistles (called *MO Letters*) in which he provided a steady stream of doctrinal and organisational instruction as well as spiritual admonishment and practical advice on a wide range of mundane topics. The *MO Letters* were printed, distributed to every communal home and regarded reverentially by Family members as God's contemporary word to his End-Time Disciples. Today, Berg's *MO Letters* enjoy a quasi-scriptural status within TFI and are regularly referenced by current leaders in the exposition of new policies or programmes.

The prophetic doctrines and corresponding practices advocated by both Joseph Smith and David Berg were (and are) regarded as heretical by other Christian denominations, especially with regard to marriage and sexual norms. Thus, Smith taught the doctrine of plural marriage (officially abandoned as a practice by the LDS Church in 1890), and Berg promulgated 'flirty fishing' as a proselyting strategy (abandoned in 1987) and the principle of sexual sharing among consenting adults, which is still an optional practice for TFI members. Due to these controversies (and many others) both groups experienced substantial legal and extra-legal opposition in their early histories. At the same time, through accommodating adjustments, both groups have produced religious cultures that continue to be anchored by belief in divine guidance through contemporary prophecy and revelation.

In the Mormon's case, following Smith's assassination by a mob in Carthage, Illinois, a majority of Latter-day Saints were led in 1847 by Smith's successor, Brigham Young, to religious sanctuary in the desolate mountains and valleys of the Great Salt Lake (Arrington 1986). There, the once despised sect built its headquarters, solidified the loyalty of its lay priesthood organisation to Young's leadership, and eventually flourished through its persistent worldwide missionary efforts. Young assumed the mantle of God's 'prophet, seer, and revelator', a title that has devolved on every succeeding president of the LDS Church, a position whose occupant is believed to be God's designated spokesman. Succession to the status of Prophet occurs through seniority in the Council of the Twelve Apostles which, aside from the President and his chosen counsellors in the First Presidency, is the highest echelon in the ecclesiastical organisation of the LDS Church (Quinn 1994). While very few official revelations promulgated by an incumbent President have been included in the LDS scriptural canon since Joseph Smith's assassination in 1844,[2] twenty-first-century Latter-day Saints maintain their fundamental faith in contemporary prophecy and continue to believe that interpretations of existing scripture and official proclamations or policies authorised by the current Prophet and his counsellors in the First Presidency are tantamount to the revealed will of God (LeCheminant 2007).

In the TFI case, as Berg aged, a small coterie of devoted attendants evolved into an effective staff organisation (subsequently called World Services) that undertook the task of producing and publishing the group's religious periodical literature. After Berg died in 1994, he was succeeded by his wife, Karen Zerby (known as Maria within TFI), a disciple convert who was much younger than Berg. Maria subsequently married Stephen Kelly (known as Peter Amsterdam within TFI), another early disciple who had for years been one of Berg's select entourage and a leader in World Services. Today, Maria and Peter are the co-leaders of The Family International. One of the most remarkable things about TFI history from David Berg's death until 2009 was a dramatically *increased* rather than diminished emphasis placed on the need for on-going revelation to guide the unfolding mission of Berg's organised following in the twenty-first century. This increase in the published announcement of prophetic revelations not only refers to the frequency of such announcements but, even more surprisingly, to the large number of individuals in the organisation who helped 'channel' official revelations. These messages are typically attributed to Jesus Christ, but they may also be channelled from Father David's spirit or any other number of departed souls or spirit entities.

---

[2]   Since the death of Joseph Smith, only five statements under the imprimatur of succeeding church presidents have been added as official texts to the *Doctrine and Covenants* of the LDS Church. These are dated as being issued in 1844, 1847, 1890, 1918 and 1978.

In both TFI and the LDS Church, the formulation of official prophecies or revelations has shifted from the pronouncements of singular prophetic figures to a group process. In TFI, from around 1995 until late 2009, Maria routinely assigned members of her staff to pray for and channel God's word in response to numerous topic problems and questions. The response messages which staff members 'channelled' from designated spirit entities typically were written down and saved as word files. These initial messages were forwarded to other staffers who, in effect, edited them through their own channelled revelations, which served to confirm, qualify, clarify and specify God's will. Before publication, final drafts were sent to Maria for approbation through her prophetic 'gift of discernment', after which they finally were issued as official policies and doctrinal statements.

Similarly, according to an informed source, the way in which most contemporary LDS policies, official programmes or doctrinal pronouncements are promulgated is 'not so different from the usual committee process that occurs in various complex organisations, especially voluntary ones, including religious denominations. In actual practice a lot of participation occurs, not only up and down the LDS hierarchy, but up and down the professional bureaucracy that advises the hierarchy' (Shepherd and Shepherd 2009: 743). Thus, need for a new policy, programme or even scripture might be identified by the executive leadership of the LDS Church, consisting of the First Presidency (the current Prophet and his two personally selected counsellors) and the Quorum of Twelve Apostles (individually selected and appointed for life, from member ranks, by the First Presidency and the Quorum of the Twelve). The next church echelons –

> the Seventy or perhaps Presiding Bishopric or General Relief Society [other organisational divisions in the LDS hierarchy] – will be asked to take the matter under advisement, and they typically will delegate to their paid professional staffs (and/or ad hoc committees recruited through the professional staffs) the responsibility for conducting the research and preparing the proposals that will be sent up the leadership chain, where some of them will eventuate in 'inspired utterances' from top priesthood leaders. These utterances can take the form of letters from the First Presidency or from the Twelve, or (in rare cases) the addition of sections to the *Doctrine and Covenants* (Shepherd and Shepherd 2009: 743).

All such statements are considered to have been received through revelation and carry the imprimatur of the President of the Church, who is regarded as a living prophet.

The most remarkable product of group prophecy for TFI has been the relatively recent, dramatic dismantling of long-established organisational structures and group norms, such as communal living, non-employment of members in secular jobs, home schooling of children, regular reporting and monitoring of compliance with numerous regulations, sexual sharing expectations among consenting adult members and more. (See Chancellor 2000 and Melton 2004 for more detailed discussions of prior TFI lifestyles, practices, and methods of organisational control.) At the 2009 Center for Study of New Religions (CESNUR) Conference, co-leaders Maria and Peter announced that Family International leadership was going to implement prophetically derived major policy changes that would relax membership and communal living requirements, as well as readjust the millennial timetable for the expected second coming of Jesus for an unspecified but significantly extended period of time (Zerby and Kelly 2009). Among many other effects, these changes allow, if not encourage, secular education of children (even the pursuit of higher education and professional training for older youth), along with the elevation of nuclear family homes as an appropriate model of family living for members in good standing. Also, Family members may now seek salaried positions or self-employment rather than depend on 'provisioning' of donations for their material needs. Centralised regulation and monitoring of compliance with specified rules have virtually been abandoned. World Services (TFI's headquarters unit) and all other organisational layers of planning and control have been effectively dissolved; individual members have become responsible for establishing their own level of missionary commitment and spiritual development.

It is too early to tell how these fundamental transformations of TFI governance and lifestyle will play out in practical terms over the long run. But for our purposes here, what is notable is the degree to which these drastic changes were brought about through the corporate prophecy mode described above and elaborated below.

For devout members of both The Family International and the LDS Church, the policies and doctrinal interpretations of their ecclesiastical leaders seem perfectly plausible and convincing – their plausibility sustained by cardinal belief in contemporary revelation of God's will through authorised prophetic leadership. For many outsiders, religious requirements, practices and changes based on such beliefs may seem highly implausible or, in some cases, even nonsensical or absurd. What accounts for the emergence and sustainability of new religions like Mormonism and The Family International that are based on belief in contemporary prophecy?

Prophecy and Social Action in Religious Economies

Weberian scholar Edward Shils (1965) argued that most people most of the time value order over uncertainty, and that those individuals who are able creatively to dispel human confusion and uncertainty through their art, science, philosophy or leadership in economic, political, military or religious affairs are accorded the highest respect by their peers. 'Whatever embodies, expresses, or symbolizes the essence of an ordered cosmos or any significant sector thereof awakens the disposition of awe and reverence, the charismatic disposition' (Shils 1965: 203). According to Shils, the 'charismatic disposition' – the propensity to attribute extraordinary (sometimes supernatural) authority to innovators and supremely confident leaders – is intrinsic to the human condition in all societies and historical epochs.

It is in the context of religious issues concerning ultimate value and meaning – especially in times of uncertainty, stress and upsetting social changes – that 'charisma' is often attributed to the founders of new faiths that arise to challenge the cosmological and moral foundations of precursor faiths. Prototypical prophets, such as Moses, Jesus and Mohammad issue authority claims that stand outside the normative structures of tradition or law and, in fact, typically call into question the legitimacy of existing institutional authority. Likewise, both Latter-day Saints and TFI members esteem the proclaimed revelations of their founders, Joseph Smith and David Berg, respectively, as spiritually authoritative. The words and moral vision of the prophet are attributed to a transcendent source and, through claims of divine guidance, command compliance in the name of God as being wholly superior to any worldly authority or human power. Not all would-be prophets, of course, succeed in winning converts to their transcendent claims. The only empirical test of prophetic charismatic authority is whether a sufficient number of followers willingly acknowledge the prophet's claims and render loyal obedience to his or her moral mandates in order to sustain a new religious community (Weber 1978: 1114–15). If and when such communities form, regardless of whether outside observers approve or disapprove, we may speak of charisma and its social correlates.

Acknowledgement and obedience cannot simply be manufactured out of nothing. There must be a receptive audience to the prophet's visionary message and commanding guidance. A successful prophet's message clarifies peoples' doubts in social situations of uncertainty and dissatisfaction, while resonating with their ultimate aspirations for meaning, order and justice. Stated in market terms, in order for prophetic new religions to expand and flourish they must effectively appeal to the religious aspirations of some segment of what Stark and Bainbridge (1985, 1987) call a 'religious economy' (see also Finke and Stark 1992, Iannaccone 1992, Sherkat and Wilson 1995, Young 1997). An active religious economy exists most openly when religious freedom, and therefore religious choice, is countenanced by the political institutions of the state. To the extent that religious choice is possible, and competition among different denominations for adherents is allowed by political authorities, we may speak of a religious market.

As in other market economies, action in a religious economy is shaped by both supply and demand (Cragun and Lawson 2010). For prophetic new religions to attract converts in a religious economy they must have a certain amount of market appeal – they must appeal to those religious consumers who already are predisposed to mystical belief in divine revelation and supernatural powers, but are dissatisfied with what currently is offered by established religious traditions. If religious consumers are satisfied with already available religious options – if there is no contemporary demand for new religious products – enduring new religions cannot take root or develop. This is particularly true of prophecy-based religions legitimated through belief in contemporary revelation.

Joseph Smith's earliest converts were religious seekers – Christian 'primitivists' who were alienated from the sectarian, creedal religions of their day and longed for a restoration of the primitive apostolic church and its charismatic claim to spiritual gifts, especially the gift of prophecy and revelation from the living God (Bushman 1997, Hill 1968, Rust 2004, Vogel, 1988). In a different historical era, Berg's young disciples were erstwhile idealists and counter-culturalists who, in a time of civil rights struggles and the Vietnam War, had become disillusioned with all forms of institutional authority, including the stifling strictures of their parents' organised religious traditions (Melton 2004). In both cases there were already concentrations of individuals with whom Smith and Berg could connect – individuals who were dissatisfied with conventional religion and in the market for a new, revitalising faith that would transform their aimlessness into a collective sense of transcendent mission.

One important inference derived from the social dynamics of a religious economy is that prophetic religions that emerge and gain institutional traction in a particular time and place can never be adequately understood as the product of a single religious prodigy or prophetic oracle. Successful new religions are always the product of an interactive social process in which numerous receptive and likeminded individuals converge to mutually construct new modes of thought and action. It is a socially creative process. In this process some individuals typically contribute substantially more than others to the development of new doctrines and religious norms and to the organisational means for implementing them. But even in charismatic, prophet-centred religions like Mormonism and TFI, the prophet is necessarily influenced by and depends on loyal lieutenants to help propagate a new faith. 'Prophecy' itself may be understood as an interactive process in which transcendent religious claims are socially constructed in response to the shared problems and concerns of some number of people in a religious economy.

Joseph Smith, for example, was aided immensely in his initial revelatory project through the appearance of country schoolteacher, Oliver Cowdery, a literate scribe who shared the Smith Family's visionary restorationist beliefs and provided the young prophet with a stimulating dialogic partner while taking dictation for what became the *Book of Mormon* (Bushman 2005). Other Mormon converts – most of whom were already religiously opinionated and better educated than Joseph Smith – also played influential roles in sparking his religious imagination and shaping his theological innovations in ways that were consistent with the supernatural literalism and emerging community needs of his Latter-day Saint followers. In the case of TFI, David Berg had to respond to the rapid formation of a transient community of socially and occupationally unencumbered young people eager to commit themselves to winning souls for Jesus in preparation for Armageddon. While expert at quoting the Bible and a prolific writer, Berg was not an apt manager and relied first on his adult children to assume organisational leadership roles, and later became dependent on his World Services staff to oversee the development of TFI rules for communal living and missionary operations.

Although very different in their contemporary life styles and modes of worship, both Mormons and Family disciples believe that prophecy and revelation are gifts democratically available to all worthy members for guidance in their personal lives. At the same time, both also maintain that official revelations of God's word for the religious community as a whole must come through official channels. It is through the contemporary official channels in both religions, as previously described, that we see most clearly the social construction of religious prophecy.

Prophecy and Commitment in New Religions

In addition to stalwart lieutenants, successful new religions require the formation of institutional practices that effectively stabilise the authority of the religious community and reinforce members' faith and commitment, particularly when confronted with the concerted disapproval of powerful religious and secular opponents from outside the faith (Wilson 1992). Such practices are what Rosabeth Kanter (1972) called group commitment mechanisms and they are essential to the enduring prospects of any new religion. Group commitment mechanisms unite people while reinforcing shared beliefs and values that justify the expenditure of their resources in compliance with group requirements in the pursuit of group goals. Shared commitments are, of course, precisely what make human communities strong and resilient. To the degree that shared commitments weaken, communities lose their unity and resilience.

Based on a combination of prescriptive and proscriptive rules, commitment practices in socially unconventional communities, according to Kanter, typically involve group sanctioned forms of self-denial such as dietary restrictions, austerity norms, sexual abstinence or, conversely, in many new religions (including both nineteenth-century Mormonism and the contemporary Family International) development of unconventional sexual, marital and family relationships that shift individuals' priority commitments from monogamous units to the larger community. Community commitment in socially unconventional new groups is also often enhanced by constructing both physical and psychic boundaries through withdrawal or separation of group members from routine contact with outsiders. Boundaries are maintained by emphasising in-group self-sufficiency and upholding distinctive customs, speech patterns, modes of dress or any other social markers and lifestyle requirements that set group members apart from people outside their community. Simultaneously, a distinctive way of life is strengthened by frequent in-group contacts through regularly scheduled meetings, community work projects, sharing of material resources and other normative activities that routinely require the active cooperation of group members, generating a shared sense of mutual purpose and identification. In our own application of Kanter's commitment categories to analysing Mormon historical development, we have shown that religious worship services in particular – through ritual, song, prayer, the symbolisation of transcendent authority, and the exposition of core beliefs and aspirations – reinforce people's shared convictions, justifying their oft times sacrificial commitments to the community and reassuring them of ultimate compensation (Shepherd and Shepherd 1984: chapters 5 and 6, Shepherd and Shepherd 2010b).

Communities most likely to be successful at retaining their members' affiliation, generating group solidarity, and exercising normative control over adherents' beliefs and practices are groups that strike the right balance between community demands and community rewards. The community demands of personal sacrifice, renunciation of dependency on outsiders and self-mortification in submission to the authority of the group must be adequately compensated by the anticipated rewards of material and spiritual investment returns, mutual caring and communion with like-minded others, and the cognitive-emotional transcendence of belief in ultimate meanings and purpose. It is this latter belief-criterion that is critical to understanding the resilience of prophetic religions.

How do religious communities like Mormonism and TFI actually secure members' commitment? How do they achieve and maintain a compensatory balance between sacrificial demands and ultimate rewards? Belief in prophecy and revelation are an essential aspect of the commitment process in these religions. For religious believers, transcendent claims of divine instruction and moral sanction channelled through purported revelations from God provide the strongest kind of justification for compliance with religious behavioural requirements of sacrifice, renunciation of outsiders and personal submission to group authority (Shepherd and Shepherd 1984: 141–3). At the same time, devout commitment to new religious faiths anchored by shared belief in prophetic revelation generates group practices that often are perceived by outsiders and nonbelievers to be exploitative, abusive and fanatical. Nineteenth-century Mormonism was widely represented by religious officials, politicians and the mass media in precisely these terms (Flake 2004, Mason 2011). Likewise, TFI has weathered numerous legal challenges, highly negative media portrayals, and continues to maintain a combative stance toward establishment secular and religious institutions (Shepherd and Shepherd 2011).

Continued belief in and submission to contemporary prophetic guidance – even when vigorously denounced and prosecuted by external authorities – is closely connected to what Gary Wills (2007) calls 'ultra-supernaturalism'. Ultra-supernatural beliefs characterise religious cultures that do not merely posit the existence of supernatural entities and a spirit world that transcend mundane human existence. Rather, ultra-supernaturalism promotes a miraculous rather than a naturalistic worldview by emphasising the *permeability* of the boundary separating the spirit world from the natural world. In this worldview various 'spirit' entities are believed to routinely transgress this boundary, speaking to or appearing before human actors in dramatic displays of their super-human powers. Conversely, human actors' reports of being transported in time and space to experience contact with and/or receive empowerment from transcendent entities are given reverential credence. Ultra-supernatural beliefs serve to explain virtually every aspect of daily life and human history as the result of supernatural intervention in human affairs.

The struggle between good and evil is literalised as a ferocious spiritual clash between the evil forces of the Devil and the Godly forces of Heaven. Through the lens of ultra-supernatural belief, human conflicts are interpreted as the dramatic unfolding of this cosmic clash by anthropomorphising specific spirit entities, both good and evil, who relentlessly labour to achieve their conflicting ends by deploying miraculous powers and recruiting human agents into the struggle. Ultra-supernaturalism characterised the religious worldview of the New England Puritans (cultural ancestors of many of Mormonism's early leaders, including Joseph Smith and Brigham Young) and was an essential ingredient in the first and second 'Great Awakenings' that fuelled the rise of American evangelical Christianity in the nineteenth century (Ahlstrom 1972, Goodbeer 1992, Hall 1990, Kidd 2009, McLoughlin 1980, Miller 1983). Today, similar ultra-supernatural beliefs continue to be strongly emphasised by many contemporary evangelical Christians and Pentecostals, who are cultural ancestors to the contemporary Family International (Shepherd and Shepherd 2010a).

In what follows we compare and contrast the modes of prophetic revelation practised historically in Mormonism and TFI. Based on these case study comparisons, we make a general argument that different modes of prophecy are likely to have different consequences for marginalising or integrating contemporary religious movements within the social dynamics of the larger religious economies in which they operate (see also Shepherd and Shepherd 2009).

The Strong Charisma of Oracular Prophecy

The divisive, polarising character of religious movements is especially true of new religions like Mormonism or TFI that proclaim the charismatic authority of divine revelation and prophetic guidance in connection with their origins and subsequent development. In particular, it is those prophetic religions that attract followers on the basis of *oracular* prophecy that are most likely to be polarising religions that attract hostile opposition from both established religious and secular groups. Oracles are perceived by believers to be spiritual intermediaries through whom ultimate truths are directly transmitted that transcend the range of ordinary human knowledge or understanding. As a form of communication, oracular prophecy is typically declarative, highly personalised and often epigrammatic; it aims to have a stimulating and motivational affect on people's thought and action by announcing a divine message. More specifically, oracular prophecies consist of revelatory pronouncements formulated as the literal voice of God, channelled through selected prophetic oracles, for instructing, admonishing and rewarding human actors in exchange for their obedience. Obedience in this context means compliance with what are construed as God's laws, commandments and divine principles that typically set adherents apart from non-believers. When formalised in writing and officially certified by the recognised authorities of a particular religious tradition, such pronouncements attain the status of holy writ or scripture for guiding and judging adherents of the faith.

Oracular prophecy can be contrasted along a conceptual continuum with *inspirational* prophecy. Like oracular prophecy, inspirational prophecy may also be canonised in scripture, but its style of communication typically is didactic, expository and less personal. It too aims to stimulate and inspire followers to action in God's name but claims only God's sanction and approval. Inspirational prophecy is less radical than oracular prophecy, less strong and demanding; it does not profess to dictate directly God's verbatim words to the people. For example, *ex cathedra* pronouncements contained in Papal Encyclicals issued by the Catholic Church are considered by Catholics to be revelations of God's will to his vicar on earth but are scarcely expressed in the language of oracular prophecy. In contrast to what might be called the 'strong charisma' of oracular prophecy, the 'milder charisma' of inspirational prophecy tends to be less polarising.

Oracular claims make stronger demands on peoples' obedience and are more likely to provide divine justification for those who already are prepared to make a break from the conventional religious order. Joseph Smith is exemplary in this regard. While historical analysis shows that official oracular prophecies proclaimed by Joseph Smith declined in number as he matured in his prophetic role over time (Brodie 1995, Bushman 2005), his publication of the *Book of Mormon* and initial founding prophecies published in the *Doctrine and Covenants* were overwhelmingly oracular. Likewise, early in his ministry as founder of the Children of God/The Family International, David Berg occasionally offered oracular prophecies to his religiously untutored flock, but such statements soon were greatly outnumbered by the prolific volume of his inspirational writings published over the years in the *MO Letters*. Berg was opinionated and emphatic in character; he spoke confidently and, occasionally, even oracularly. But he relied more often on his own words than on reciting verbatim messages from Jesus or other spirit beings when composing homilies, Bible interpretations, advice and instructions published for his followers. And the language Berg used in his voluminous writings was chatty, vernacular – often earthy and even vulgar – but seldom poetic or magisterial as though registering the voice of God.

Thus we may speak of two types of prophets: what we have previously called the inspirational prophet and the oracular prophet (Shepherd and Shepherd 2009). These prophetic types are not mutually exclusive. Oracular prophets typically are also inspirational and those prophets who primarily are inspirational may, on occasion, also impart prophetic statements in an oracular mode. The difference between oracular and inspirational prophets is ultimately one of degree. Their proper classification depends on which modality of prophetic expression is most characteristic of their promulgated teachings and their modus operandi as prophetic leaders over the course of their religious careers. In our typology, based on his published revelations and the documented status accorded him by his followers, Joseph Smith closely approximates the prototypical oracular prophet. In contrast, David Berg, based on examination of his voluminous published writings and the limited nature of his personal interactions with followers, more closely resembles the inspirational prophet.

In addition to the different modalities by which religious instruction is articulated in prophetic religions, we assume that, to a greater or lesser degree, prophecy is always shaped through a process of social interaction. In this regard we may speak of the prophetic *channel* or *channels* through which either inspiration or God's literal words are delivered, the two major possibilities being: 1) a designated individual or 2) a group of collaborators. Most prophetic religions begin the story of their histories with reference to a designated prophetic figure, whether oracular or inspirational, who is given credit as God's agent for expelling the mists of moral ambiguity and doctrinal confusion from which people suffer and clearing a new pathway to righteousness and salvation. But even creative religious geniuses, whether oracular or merely inspirational, are not immune from social influence; far from it. To have a significant impact on people's lives, any religious innovations must resonate with the real concerns and needs of some segment of a religious economy.

Typically, prophetic religions once established tend to move away from primary dependence on a particular individual for God's direction to the collective guidance of a group of institutional officials who form a collaborative hierarchy. Both TFI and the LDS Church are exemplary in this regard. Even though a titular head of the hierarchy may be invested with ultimate authority, planning and decision-making routinely are constructed through group discussion and a negotiated consensus. This is just another way of stating Max Weber's (1978: 246–71, 1111–58) hypothesis concerning the routinisation of charisma in prophetic religions. Typically the doctrinal and policy statements issued by groups of official religious collaborators in this manner are viewed and accepted by the religious communities they lead as inspired rather than oracular. Here again we propose that inspirational prophetic leadership expressed through a group of collaborators typically is less controversial or polarising than oracular leadership provided by either designated individuals or a collaborative hierarchy.

In contrast to the LDS Church, what arguably is of greatest sociological interest about TFI is that it persisted expanding oracular prophecy for so long a time (approximately 15 years) in the successor regime developed by Maria and Peter before finally beginning to show signs of conforming to the dominant pattern of prophetic institutionalisation posited by Weber, in which organisational controls are developed to limit the proliferation of official oracular statements (in, for example, Christianity, Islam, Seventh Day Adventism and many hundreds more, including the LDS Church). Until very recently, TFI employed numerous prophetic channels and socially constructed God's official will through an interactive editing process. Thus – like official statements issued under the imprimatur of the LDS First Presidency – TFI prophecies up until at least 2009 were attributable to a group of collaborators. Unlike LDS First Presidency statements, however, TFI prophecies typically were expressed in an oracular rather than inspirational mode.

That is, they were declaratively stated (and believed) to be the verbatim words of divine beings, channelled and blended through a multiplicity of oracles.

One might argue fairly that it is simply too early in TFI history to conclude that the oracular mode of prophecy that prevailed until (what is now termed) the 2010 'Reboot' will permanently shift to a less radical form of inspirational prophecy – as eventually was the case in the significantly older LDS Church. But it would be ironic indeed if oracular prophecy in TFI were to give way again to inspirational prophecy in compliance with a series of oracular prophecies to do so.

In any event, by combining our two prophecy variables – prophetic modality (inspirational or oracular) and prophetic channel (designated individual or group of collaborators) – we derive four theoretical types of prophecy, which we simply identify as Type I through Type IV (see Table 12.1). Type I prophecies consist of inspirational expositions or statements articulated by a designated individual; Type II prophecies are inspirational expositions or statements constructed by a group of collaborators; Type III prophecies consist of oracular declarations or statements articulated by a designated individual; and Type IV prophecies are oracular declarations or statements constructed by a group of collaborators.

From our case study materials, we conclude that the majority of David Berg's writings best illustrate Type I prophecy. Statements issued under the imprimatur of the President and First Presidency of the contemporary LDS Church best exemplify Type II prophecy. Joseph Smith's proclaimed translations and doctrinal revelations in the *Doctrine and Covenants* typify Type III prophecy. And finally, The Family's published World Services prophecies from 1995 through 2009 typify Type IV prophecy. Applying this typology historically we see the LDS Church moving from Type III prophecy to Type II – that is, from primary reliance on oracular prophecy through Joseph Smith, to inspirational prophecy through a group of collaborators, namely the First Presidency and the Quorum of the Twelve Apostles. In contrast, TFI moved historically from primary reliance on Type I prophecy to Type IV – that is, from primary reliance on inspirational prophecy through David Berg to oracular prophecy through a group of collaborators, namely Peter, Maria and a multitude of World Services staff and field members who channelled and edited prophecies for TFI publications from 1995 through 2009.[3]

---

[3]   Since late 2009, there has been a dearth of oracular prophetic material issued as official verbatim declarations from Jesus or other supernatural entities in the former manner of TFI publications from World Services. Indeed, given the present dissolution of World Services, it seems unlikely that any such prophecies will be forthcoming in the near future. However, Maria and Peter have not disavowed the principle of prophecy nor the prophetic gifts and responsibilities they believe they possess as leaders of TFI. They appear to have abandoned the corporate mode by which oracular prophecies were generated for the prior 15 years. But there is no reason to believe they will not, if perceived necessary at some later time, resort once again to employment of oracular prophecy as the basis for undertaking new TFI initiatives, policies or interpretations of their circumstances and evangelical obligations.

Table 12.1   LDS versus TFI prophecy patterns

	Prophetic Channel	
Prophetic Modality	**Designated Individual**	**Group of Collaborators**
Inspirational	*Type I Prophecy*	*Type II Prophecy*
	David Berg	Contemporary LDS
Oracular	*Type III Prophecy*	*Type IV Prophecy*
	Joseph Smith	Contemporary TFI

Other historical patterns are also theoretically possible. Thus, for example, prophecy might move from an inspirational founder (Type I) to an inspirational group of collaborators (Type II). This pattern, we suspect, has been fairly common in many religious traditions, particularly in Protestant Christianity. Likewise, prophecy might shift from an oracular founder (Type III) to an oracular group of collaborators (Type IV), although this pattern seems less likely to occur. It is even possible for a new religious tradition to *begin* with a group of prophetic collaborators, whether inspirational or oracular, and subsequently produce a particularly gifted individual whose prophetic voice subsequently becomes dominant within the group. Which types of prophecy are most likely to undergo transformations in which directions, under what conditions, are questions that can only be answered by more systematic comparative research of a larger range of prophetic religious traditions.

The Marginalisation and Integration of Prophetic Religions

A comparison of The Family International and the LDS Church demonstrates certain similarities as well as important differences in their prophetic traditions and practices. Most importantly, the history and current functioning of neither group can be comprehended apart from a shared belief in the extra-biblical guidance of their respective religious communities through contemporary revelation and prophecy. Both groups were founded by prophetic figures, and both groups subsequently have institutionalised what they believe to be authentic, revelatory processes for obtaining God's word. At a more specific level of comparison, however, one of the most notable differences between the Family and LDS cases is the contrasting way in which their prophetic traditions have unfolded: the LDS Church has moved from reliance on an oracular, prophet-founder to an executive body of collaborators whose collective judgment and policies are considered by believers to be inspired expressions of God's will. In contrast, The Family International moved from an inspirational, prophet-founder to an executive body of collaborators whose publications, until 2010, were considered by believers to be the oracular will of God expressed through melded, channelled messages from a multitude of spiritual beings (including, besides Jesus, the departed spirit of David Berg, various angels and a multitude of named 'spirit helpers').

An even more obvious institutional difference is that the LDS Church has become an influential international religion with over 14 million members and still growing, while TFI – though scattered in scores of countries throughout the world – is a small sect of fewer than 5,000 core members facing an uncertain future. The LDS Church is well integrated in both the structure of American politics and the global religious economy. TFI, by contrast, is perched precariously on the social and religious margins of the modern world. This institutional disparity can be explained by, among other things, the organisational age differences between the two religions and especially the fact that the LDS Church has aggressively emphasised growth through missionary recruitment (Shepherd and Shepherd 1998), while TFI has concentrated on 'witnessing' to the unsaved more so than mobilising resources in recruiting new members who are explicitly committed to TFI and a life of fulltime missionary service. Unlike Mormons, most TFI members are only now, after a history of 40 years, beginning to explore active engagement in worldly occupations. Individuals have thus not acquired private wealth, property or retirement security, and TFI as an organisation has only meagre financial resources to fund its basic operations. They are not politically integrated in any society, and, in contrast to the politically powerful and very wealthy modern LDS Church, exercise approximately zero influence on secular institutions outside their own religious community.

What difference, if any, has the persistence of oracular prophecy in TFI made to its developmental career in contrast to the LDS Church? Our analysis of these two religions leads to the following propositions: (1) Prophetic religions like the LDS Church which, through a body of collaborators impose constraints on oracular prophecy, are more likely to achieve accommodation with other religions and greater integration with secular institutions. (2) Prophetic religions like The Family International, which continue to encourage rather than constrain oracular prophecy, are less likely to achieve either accommodation or integration. Such religions are less likely to survive, expand their numbers or have a significant historical impact on society than prophetic religions that move from oracular to inspirational guidance.

Our primary conclusion is that modality of religious revelation is correlated with a religious group's relationship to the larger society. When oracular prophecy is the principal mode of guidance employed by religious organisations, they are more likely to be viewed as heretical by other religions and, reciprocally, more likely to form boundaries between themselves and other groups, both religious and secular, in the societies in which they operate. Alternatively, when inspirational prophecy is the principal modality of instruction and guidance, religious organisations are less likely to be viewed as heretical and more likely to become accommodated and integrated in the societies in which they operate. This is not to say, of course, that oracular claims alone 'cause' religions like nineteenth-century Mormonism or twenty-first-century TFI to become socially marginalised.

Most marginalised religious groups ultimately are spurned for their unorthodox practices and not merely for their heretical beliefs. At the same time, indubitable belief in the supernatural authenticity of religious revelation stimulates, guides and justifies defiant commitment to unorthodox practices. This is especially likely to be true when justifying beliefs are founded in emphatic, oracular-style revelations.

The Family's 2009 prophetically proclaimed 'Change Journey' (which eventuated in what is now called the 'Reboot') seems to be moving TFI along an accommodating path similar to the one travelled by the LDS Church – from the margins of society and the international religious economy to greater integration with established cultural institutions. Thus, for the foreseeable future, we are likely to see a corresponding shift from oracular to inspirational prophecy as The Family International's primary mode of religious guidance. The Family's future organisational development should provide empirical tests of several of our hypotheses concerning the construction and correlated social functions of oracular and inspirational prophecy, attributed either to designated individuals or groups of collaborators. Indeed, systematic comparative study of a much larger range of prophetic religious traditions needs to be done in order to test these hypotheses adequately.

References

Ahlstrom, S. 1972. *A Religious History of the American People*. New Haven, CT: Yale University Press.

Arrington, L.J. 1986. *Brigham Young: American Moses*. Urbana and Chicago, IL: University of Illinois Press.

Bainbridge, W.S. 2002. *The Endtime Family: Children of God*. Albany, NY: State University of New York Press.

Berger, P. and Luckmann, T. 1967. *The Social Construction of Reality: A Treatise in the Sociology of Knowledge*. New York: Anchor.

Brodie, F. 1995. *No Man Knows My History: The Life of Joseph Smith*. New York: Vintage Books.

Bushman, R.L. 1997. The Visionary World of Joseph Smith. *BYU Studies*, 37, 183–204.

———. 2005. *Joseph Smith: Rough Stone Rolling*. New York: Alfred A. Knopf.

Chancellor, J.D. 2000. *Life in The Family: An Oral History of the Children of God*. Syracuse, NY: Syracuse University Press.

Cook, L. 1985. *The Revelations of the Prophet Joseph Smith: A Historical and Biographical Commentary of the Doctrine and Covenants*. Salt Lake City, UT: Deseret Book.

Cragun, R.T. and Lawson, R. 2010. The Secular Transition: The Worldwide Growth of Mormons, Jehovah's Witnesses, and Seventh Day Adventists. *Sociology of Religion: A Quarterly Review*, 71(3), 349–73.

Finke, R. and Stark, R. 1992. *The Churching of America: Winners and Losers in Our Religious Economy*. New Brunswick, NJ: Rutgers University Press.

Flake, K. 2004. *The Politics of Religious Identity: The Seating of Senator Reed Smoot, Mormon Apostle*. Chapel Hill, NC: University of North Carolina Press.

Givens, T.L. 2002. *By the Hand of Mormon: The American Scripture that Launched a New World Religion*. New York: Oxford University Press.

Goodbeer, R. 1992. *The Devil's Domain: Magic and Religion in Early New England*. New York: Cambridge University Press.

Hall, D.D. 1990. *Worlds of Wonder, Days of Judgment: Popular Religious Belief in Early New England*. Cambridge, MA: Harvard University Press.

Hill, M.S. 1968. The Role of Christian Primitivism in the Origin and Development of the Mormon Kingdom, 1830–1844. Ph.D. dissertation, University of Chicago, Chicago, IL.

Iannaccone, L. 1992. Religious Markets and the Economics of Religion. *Social Compass*, 39, 123–31.

Kanter, R. 1972. *Commitment and Community*. Cambridge, MA: Harvard University Press.

Kidd, T. 2009. *The Great Awakening: The Roots of Evangelical Christianity in Colonial America*. New Haven, CT: Yale University Press.

LeCheminant, D. 2007. Foreword, in *Statements of the LDS First Presidency: A Topical Compendium*, compiled by G.J. Bergera. Salt Lake City, UT: Signature Books.

Mason, P.Q. 2011. *The Mormon Menace: Violence and Anti-Mormonism in the Postbellum South*. New York: Oxford University Press.

McLoughlin, W.G. 1980. *Revivals, Awakenings, and Reform*. Chicago, IL: University of Chicago Press.

Melton, J.G. 2004. *The Children of God: The Family*. Salt Lake City, UT: Signature Press.

Miller, P. 1983. *The New England Mind: From Colony to Province*. Cambridge, MA: Harvard University Press.

Quinn, M.D. 1994. *The Mormon Hierarchy: Origins of Power*. Salt Lake City, UT: Signature Books.

Rust, V.D. 2004. *Radical Origins: Early Mormon Converts and Their Colonial Ancestors*. Urbana, IL: University of Illinois Press.

Shepherd, Gary and Shepherd, Gordon. 1998. *Mormon Passage: A Missionary Chronicle*. Champaign, IL: University of Illinois Press.

——. 2005. Accommodation and Reformation in the Family/Children of God. *Nova Religio*, 9(1), 67–92.

——. 2006a. The Family International: A Case Study in the Management of Change in New Religious Movements. *Religion Compass*, 1(1), 1–16.

——. 2007. Grassroots Prophecy in The Family International. *Nova Religio*, 10(1), 38–71.

——. 2011. Learning the Wrong Lessons: A Comparison of FLDS, Family International, and Branch Davidian Child-Protection Interventions, in *Modern Polygamy in the United States: Historical, Cultural, and Legal Issues*, edited by C.K. Jacobson and L. Burton. New York: Oxford University Press, 237–58.

Shepherd, Gordon, and Shepherd, Gary. 1984. *A Kingdom Transformed: Themes in the Development of Mormonism*. Salt Lake City, UT: University of Utah Press.

——. 2006b. The Social Construction of Prophecy in The Family International. *Nova Religio*, 10(2), 29–56.

——. 2009. Prophecy Channels and Prophetic Modalities: A Comparison of Revelation in The Family International and the LDS Church. *Journal for the Scientific Study of Religion*, 48(4), 734–55.

——. 2010a. *Talking with the Children of God: Prophecy and Transformation in a Radical Religious Group*. Champaign, IL: University of Illinois Press.

——. 2010b. New Religions and Community. *Nova Religio*, 13(3), 5–13.

Sherkat, D.E. and Wilson, J. 1995. Preferences, Constraints, and Choices in Religious Markets: An Examination of Religious Switching and Apostasy. *Social Forces*, 73, 993–1026.

Shils, E. 1965. Charisma, Order, and Status. *American Sociological Review*, 30(2), 199–213.

Stark, R. and Bainbridge, W. 1985. *The Future of Religion: Secularization, Revival, and Cult Formation*. Berkeley, CA: University of California Press.

——. 1987. *A Theory of Religion*. New York: Peter Lang.

Vogel, D. 1988. *Religious Seekers and the Advent of Mormonism*. Salt Lake City, UT: Signature Books.

Vogel, D. and Metcalfe, B.L. (eds) 2002. *American Apocrypha: Essays on the Book of Mormon*. Salt Lake City, UT: Signature Books.

Weber, M. 1978. *Economy and Society: An Outline of Interpretive Sociology*, edited by G. Ross and C. Wittich. Berkeley, CA: University of California Press.

Wills, G. 2007. *Head and Heart: American Christianities*. New York: Penguin.

Wilson, B.R. 1992. *The Social Dimensions of Sectarianism: Sects and New Religious Movements in Contemporary Society*. New York: Oxford University Press.

Young, L.A. 1997. *Rational Choice Theory and Religion*. Oxford: Routledge.

Zerby, K. and Kelly, S. 2009. The Future of The Family International: Establishing a Culture of Innovation and Progress. Paper presented at the annual CENSUR Conference, Salt Lake City, Utah.

Chapter 13

The Dispensation of Providence: Growing Up as a Blessed Child in the Unification Church

Hani Zaccarelli

There was nothing strange about it. We knew that the great big outside world of fallen people was infinitely more populous than our community consisting of very tiny groups of awakened people, but being in the minority made it feel especially normal. There were enough of us at least to obviate all but the briefest occasional interaction with outsiders, and the invisible taint of original sin that came off on our hands whenever we encountered them could be cleansed with a pinch of the sacred salt above the cupboard next to the icing sugar. Two pinches if you had a lot of shopping.

If anything, it was those content to live in the fallen world that were weird. They lived and breathed and ate and carried on making little fallen people, the whole time tolerating the dominance of satanic law and wilfully believing what the media told them about us, that we were 'brainwashed'. It was predictable that they would persecute us, we were trying to save them and saviours are always persecuted.

'Just as in the time of Noah, people laugh and mock, satisfied to wander aimless in the darkness underground.' Our songs reminded us why we should remain strong, and what was beautiful about our lives. We had all the answers, but those outside the family didn't even know what the question was. They might not ever get it but their children would, and if they didn't then their children would – the truth was inescapable. Eventually they would all have their spiritual experience and one by one all would recognise Father. Their reluctance to see the truth of what we were saying could only last so long and it was just a matter of time before they would beg us to let them into the ark of 'The Blessing'.

The 'Restored World' was by now all but inevitable, there was little question about that. There was some disagreement among the teachers about exactly when it would happen, as Father had never really been pinned down on that one point. So, naturally, the question of the timing of the arrival of the Kingdom of Heaven on Earth was the most relevant and important question a child could ask. We asked it not only of every teacher, but also of every other member that would occasionally pass through our school. This went on until it began to seem as if all of their guesses, always so carefully considered and then emphatically delivered, weren't actually informed by anything other than a gut feeling. Happily the one thing all their answers had in common was that it would be during our lifetime, definitely, depending on how long we lived, obviously.

The details of what the 'Restored World' would be like weren't ever explicitly defined in social or economic terms, like those lessons from the National Curriculum about what life had been like in Roman Britain. The specifics of how things would be different didn't actually need to be spelled out, it just went without saying that they'd be perfect. If the whole world were to recognise Father as the messiah then effectively everyone would be in the church, and as happy as us.

Joining the church would be the start, but perfection could only be reached by those conceived from parents who had received the blessing. The spiritual ethnicity of Satan could be seen clearly in those among us who weren't blessed children. Their eyes didn't shine as brightly and their behaviour was more uncouth. We, the blessed children, could be distinguished by our radiantly pure auras. We seldom disobeyed the teachers and any misbehaviour was usually due to the other children leading us astray. We were suitably segregated from the others in a small number of important ways. We shared the same eating and sleeping arrangements, but our bodies and clothes were washed separately. Whilst everyone would chant the Korean pledge of pious dedication every Sunday, we would then make an additional pledge while the non-blessed children were silent. We would also periodically be invited to exclusive workshops where we'd study the Divine Principle away from the others.

Not all workshops were exclusively for blessed children, and the ones that weren't would often have some new faces. These workshops were always a special time, a break from our normal lives where we could concentrate on our spiritual development. We'd study the Divine Principle together, all 13 chapters that explained why Father was the fulfilment of ancient prophecy.

We'd compete to be attentive and obedient when the teachers were around and we'd compete to be naughty when they weren't. Unless it was an exclusive blessed children workshop, in which case there was no break in the slow collective crescendo of zeal.

The non-blessed kids didn't have a special name, and weren't ever referred to explicitly although they were referred to indirectly on a regular basis to exclude them from things that were just for blessed children. They had an uncanny ability to talk to fallen children that blessed children didn't have. Once, when we arrived a few hours early for a workshop, some of the non-blessed children struck up a conversation with some local fallen kids who they met on the street and found out that a new season of 'The A-Team' would be on soon. How the fallen kids got hold of such information was a source of great mystery, and filled the rest of us with awe. Very slowly, some of the blessed children realised that they could talk to the fallen kids too without anything bad happening. We had never been explicitly told we couldn't, we had just been led to fear ever doing it.

Occasionally at the weekend the teachers would let us run around in a public playground and bit by bit we began to talk to the other kids we met there. The teachers would mix it up so we wouldn't go to the same playground more than once every few months and we never formed anything like a lasting acquaintance, but somehow even still, we slowly gained a loose familiarity with the kids in that tiny playground that was just a mile up the road. When we were seen having any kind of prolonged discussion with local urchins this sort of thing was broken up quite quickly and we didn't go back there, but as we continued to get older it became harder and harder to avoid verbal contact with children our own age.

Inevitably, we soon encountered a group of kids almost exactly like ourselves at the large playground in Trowbridge. This was the biggest and best playground for 20 miles as far as we knew. It was home to the biggest slide and the newest roundabouts, and as we found out completely by mistake one day, also the stomping ground of a handful of kids our age whose parents were members of the church of Mormon. How exactly we happened to find this out wasn't clear, and was lost in a babble of an enthusiastically friendly discussion between the adults, who loudly agreed that we should definitely all meet for a chat at our school.

A week later there was a very important meeting at our school, where the adults witnessed to each other and the kids were left alone to watch some agreeable television. It was interesting to both groups of kids to hear and talk about the TV shows the others weren't allowed to watch. When the grownups had finished talking, our teachers were briefly out of earshot while the Mormon teachers came in to help their kids put their coats on, and they gleefully celebrated their success in front of us. With excited grins they said, 'They're really coming around to our way of thinking.' Five minutes later, while waving goodbye to our guests, our teachers were saying the same exact words to each other with the same ecstatic self-congratulating certainty. We had understood that there were other small churches purporting to have all the answers, like our own in every respect except that they in fact preached falsehood. In theory this made sense. But in practice, seeing the uncanny similarities in the way the two groups of teachers approached and perceived their respective attempt to convert each other left a strong impression on our young, inquisitive minds.

Another thing that left its mark in our understanding of society was what happened when we established a club for pooling our pocket money. Our weekly allowance of 25 pence each would buy enough confectionery to last a self-disciplined child about an hour, but the non-blessed children had the idea of collecting everyone's pocket money and buying in bulk. We all eagerly participated in the scheme because we were persuaded we were joining some kind of an elite clique, but we were disappointed when the rations of fruit pastilles and fractions of mars bars that were distributed by the club leaders came to less than what we could have bought independently. Our teachers didn't like the way we had organised ourselves outside of their control and it came as quite a relief when they made it 'against the rules' to be in a club.

Once a year the school inspector would come and there would be at least a month of preparation. We were instructed not to discuss church teaching with the inspector and to 'act normal'. Having the inspector observe us was very tense, we couldn't be sure which inadvertent action would betray us. It was hard to act normal when we had no frame of reference. We had been taught about gravity in the context of the duality of God's essence, so for us everything was intertwined with the Divine Principle. Year after year the inspectors came, and probably thanks to all the prayer conditions we made for this to go smoothly, somehow each time we succeeded in satisfying the fallen officials, rendering unto Caesar what was Caesar's.

Our teaching could not be easily separated from the teaching of the fallen world because it all made a lot of sense. It was actually hard to see why the whole world hadn't already accepted it. The first dozen chapters of the Divine Principle told a tantalising story. For the most part they were a decoding of the cryptic Old Testament stories, retold as a clear battle between God and Satan for the soul of mankind, where the trivial actions of key players (such as giving one's brother some food) led to spiritual consequences of cataclysmic importance.

God, we were taught, knows everything except what man will do next. Satan is pretty smart too, and there were spiritual laws that they both understood which determined which of them was the father of mankind. The adventures of Abraham's dynasty were the most crucial piece of history in bringing mankind back to God, by preparing the way for the second Adam (Jesus Christ). A similar uncharted and completely unknown story described the way an obscure Korean lineage had been carefully managed for the third Adam (True Father). There was one uncharacteristically literate church member who pointed out that the manipulation of blood lines by God resembled that which Frank Herbert described as the artificially bred lineage that led to the 'Kwisatz Haderach', the messianic protagonist of the *Dune* novels. This science fiction character shared other qualities with the third Adam that were never pointed out, such as claiming the highest standard of education the local empire had to offer and being more in love with his concubine than his wife.

We were taught how the Bible was largely intended by God to be a combination of symbolism and literal fact. The biggest and most important internal symbolism was the representation of coitus as the fruit of the tree of knowledge of good and evil. There were also lots of metaphors in the ramblings of the prophets, and of course Jesus. Fascinatingly there was inverse biblical symbology too, where the real world actually symbolised the Bible. From God's point of view, Korea was the Adam country. England had been given the chance to be Eve but of all the stupid mistakes, her Majesty Queen Elizabeth II had turned down the opportunity to marry Father, and so now America was the Eve country. It would later emerge that there was some confusion between the Americans and Japanese on this point. Quite a few of the Japanese blessed children were under the impression that Japan was the Eve country.

The internal split between God and Satan that plagued all humans was manifested at the national level too, and from God's point of view the clearest place this could be seen was in Korea. To some extent, though, the same political struggle between left and right had its manifestation in every country. God's plan for mankind could only be realised when the authority to rule the world was commanded by God directly, so our mission to restore mankind meant the funding and active support of all the anti-communist parties worldwide. Seeing from God's point of view wasn't just advantageous for those who wanted to back the winning team. Failing to see things the way God saw them was the thin end of the wedge of all sin. Our very thoughts had to be the right ones.

In 1984 we learned how someone called Orwell had predicted a world under communist rule, and that his frightening future would materialise if we failed in our mission. The free will that God had given mankind meant there were two possibilities for the future. Which would manifest into reality hadn't yet been absolutely determined, but at this stage in the game it was much less likely to be Ingsoc in Oceana than the Kingdom of Heaven on Earth. Earlier prophecies, like the biblical ones were obviously very confusing to the Christians in the fallen world and their enigmatically tangled contradictions had probably been why the Jews hadn't recognised Jesus. Isaiah had foretold that the second Adam would be 'king of kings', and the lack of pomp with which Jesus had arrived had totally thrown the Jews off the scent. If the Romans had wanted their empire to span the globe they should have been the vehicle for his gospel and elevated him within their imperial structure to 'Wonderful, Counsellor, Mighty God, Everlasting Father, Prince of Peace'. The fall of their empire was the price for allowing Jesus to follow the 'despised and rejected' path divergent from God's providence. For their betrayal, the elect people that God had spent so long preparing to accept him would be punished most cruelly, most unflinchingly.

What we were now seeing in 1984 was, in stark contrast to Orwell's nightmare, in fact the imminent success of Father in the West. The momentum toward the salvation of all of humanity was already at escape velocity, if we could only keep it going. We could take comfort in the growing wealth and influence of the second coming of Christ, well on his way to being 'seated on a throne, high and exalted'. In fact, Father often appeared on a throne at various ceremonies, most notably at the massive weddings. This was what a messiah should look like, nothing at all like the pathetic failure of Jesus. Miracles were obviously no use whatsoever. Jesus had tried that, and look where that got him! This time God had instead instructed the anointed one to acquire practical worldly power, although, of course, Father obviously could perform miracles if he wanted to.

Persuading the world to accept Father could be easy if he advertised who he was, but that wasn't how God wanted to play it. Father didn't actually claim to be the messiah when giving a speech to outsiders; that was a fact they would find out if they accepted the invitation to spend a weekend at a theological retreat. Of course, when among very close disciples, he had often told the story of how Jesus had approached him in 1935 to ask him to continue the first failed mission, and how he had begrudgingly accepted, but at no point did he come right out and publicise his status of saviour to the uninitiated. Part of the bargain between God and Satan was that the fallen world had to figure it out for themselves.

And figure it out they all did, after attending the two-day, seven-day and then 21-day workshops. By the middle of the seven-day workshop, aspiring members could see where this was going and those without a taste for it would never come back. Those who knew which side their bread was buttered on had to wait for the conclusion of the 21-day workshop for the explosive truth. This truth was that logically, only a country that had been persecuted for 40 years could give rise to the messiah, filtered further to be one with a clear dividing line between God and Satan. Anyone cynical enough to find it problematic that these dependencies prevented there being a messiah from Korea until at least 1945 would have been weeded out by one of the earlier workshops. There was also the compelling argument that Korea, which to be sure had dabbled in its fair share of paganism over the eons, had at least always done so in a monotheistic way. God regarded this sort of qualification as an important factor when choosing a nation that everyone should unite under in the last days.

But Korea was in the Orient, and the line at the 38th parallel which separated the Communist North from the 'free' South Korea was a remote, almost fictional boundary in the eyes of the average European. The Berlin Wall was a great focal point for the Western world in recognising the cosmic ultimatum. Everyone in the West had heard the compelling stories about Germans overcoming the obstacles to their escape from the satanic realm. When our church organised a rally in Berlin in 1987, the success of the event was overwhelming. Many of our brothers and sisters were physically attacked by the same kind of communists with punk hairstyles that had assaulted the members whose mission had been to campaign for Jean-Marie Le Pen in France. Such skirmishes were not enough to disrupt the rally and this time Satan had failed to invade. Things would change quickly now that the Messiah had said the words 'Die Mauer muss weg' (The Wall must go). The Wall would come down like it did in Jericho, perhaps a bit more slowly.

For many of the same reasons Father was the messiah, God had chosen Korean as his favourite language and there was a programme in place to ensure we all learnt it. When those of us who were born pure of original sin came of age, we followed our destiny to Korea to join our peers in studying God's chosen language. Not everyone who arrived in Seoul had the same spiritual preparedness, and some of us had advanced further through the growth stage (or into formation and almost completion) than others. Some of the less promising students didn't even know yet how to read the Korean phonetic alphabet and needed to be taught in the classroom. Those of us who could read the pledge in 'hangul' on Sunday mornings were well on the way to being as good as those of us who had memorised it.

By 1988 the providence was in full swing. The Olympics were now central to the world's attention. All eyes had turned to South Korea. At this time the blind servants of Satan were in the streets of Seoul revolting against the forces of goodness. Corrupted students were attacking their brothers and sisters in the riot police who were the stalwart defenders of the peace and freedom. For at least a year the itch of tear gas was always kept fresh at street level throughout the whole city. We'd go to the mountains to think clearly, and breathe clearly. We went there so often that eventually the teachers realised they needed to step in and organise these trips. We had played Dungeons and Dragons there in handfuls after school, built forts and drank soda in pairs or in threes on Saturdays, but now we went there altogether as a big group to pray first thing in the morning. After the group prayer we were told we could stay there on our own if we liked, but for some reason the mountain no longer had the same appeal.

Whenever there was a sporadic evolution of social gatherings initiated by the students the teachers would step in to make it 'centred on God'. After a couple of successive Friday nights on which we started listening to pop music and dancing downstairs in the evening, this became a regular officially scheduled 'rock-out', sanctioned by the teachers. What had been an informal shaking of rumps and throwing of shapes was now a school disco that started and ended with a group prayer.

Every now and then one of the students would interrupt dinner by standing up and channelling the spirit of Father's deceased son Heung Jin Nim. It always began with words to the effect of 'My dear brothers and sisters I love you all so much' and ended with the medium regaining control over their body and everyone whispering in awe to each other. One year this happened so frequently and intensely to so many students that we received a commandment from the church's central office to stop receiving the revelations. After this the inter-realm communication petered out until there were just two girls the same age who would take turns receiving revelations from one day to the next, each time outdoing the other's inspiring and uplifting message from the day before.

One evening we found out somehow that there was to be an impromptu gathering in the central Seoul church headquarters where we could receive a very important message to the whole world from Heung Jin Nim. While brothers and sisters were still arriving from all over Seoul, and people were still taking their pews in the unusual setting of church at night, an audience member stood up at the back and proclaimed that they had received a revelation that this gathering had actually been forbidden by Heung Jin Nim. Without further ado everyone promptly went home.

It was around then that the revelation to trump all the other revelations came to pass. A brother from Zimbabwe had somehow managed to become completely and, it seemed, permanently possessed by Heung Jin Nim. Father spent three days talking to him before he acknowledged that yes, this was indeed his son. The news of this miracle spread like wild-fire. Some of the students in Korea had known Heung Jin Nim while he was alive and an emissary was dispatched to Seoul with the news. We received an admonition that no-one must show any familiarity whatsoever to the returned spirit. If he heard what he thought might be a reference to an event that had occurred during his first life, we were warned, Heung Jin Nim would fly into a rage. Even if it had been meant in a friendly way the old acquaintance would be physically beaten for testing him and testing God, so even with the best of intentions we were to be very careful to avoid that.

After his verification by Father, Heung Jin Nim immediately embarked on a world tour where he compelled all church members to confess to their sins, and introduced a new form of indemnifying the guilty, by inviting members to beat each other with a stick. Husbands and wives were told that if they really cared for each other they'd clobber each other as hard as they could and everyone was amazed at how dearly some husbands loved their spouses. Heung Jin Nim watched these ceremonies of indemnity closely, and with a broad smile. Never before had Satan been so easy to punish.

There was obviously a lot of confusion and uncertainty at this time. Heung Jin Nim took great delight in publicly humiliating the Korean leaders, and beat several of them on stage, hospitalising Father's primary translator at one point. But Father had sanctioned the legitimacy of this second incarnation and we could not deny that a dramatic wave was sweeping over the whole movement. Heung Jin Nim's encouragement led to countless childless church couples being given or promised babies by surrogacy at this time and we were clearly seeing the fruition of the prediction that Father had made when Heung Jin Nim's first body had died. That sacrifice had been declared a 'Victory of Love' that would accelerate God's providence. If we hadn't known before what such acceleration would look like, we knew now.

About two years later, at a workshop in New York, the same emissary who had informed us of the apparently permanent possession once again flew in to deliver another urgent message to the blessed children about Heung Jin Nim's adventures in body-hopping. What he came to inform us all about this time was that Heung Jin Nim's spirit had at some unspecified point left the second body and been replaced by some evil entity. The emissary could not say exactly when this had happened, but he was sure it was some time after he had followed Heung Jin Nim's second body back to Zimbabwe along with 11 other members. He told us that Heung Jin Nim, without noticeably changing his demeanour or preaching style, had one day started to claim that his body was no longer just hosting the spirit of Heung Jin Nim but he had in fact vaguely become …the new messiah. The emissary told us that when he heard this claim, something about it had seemed somehow suspicious. Acting on instinct he made his escape, leaving the other members in the jungle.

So ended the entire episode of Heung Jin Nim, and there were no more revelations from him after that. The picture of him that had been placed next to all pictures of the True Parents wherever members prayed was removed. Asking teachers and parents to explain the details of how all the spirits and bodies had been switched on multiple occasions like peas under cups received a completely random answer depending on who was asked. A few said they didn't know the answers to such things, but a surprisingly large number claimed to have always suspected he was a fraud. These members argued that whether or not he truly was Heung Jin Nim was a secondary question to 'was his ministry a good thing for the church', to which everyone agreed the answer must undeniably be given in the resounding affirmative. He might have been fake but even so he had fulfilled his mission from God who moves in mysterious ways.

Every year Father gave the whole church a mission at special New Year's ceremonies, and for several successive iterations of these in the years on either side of 1990 our goal was declared to be the unification of North and South Korea. We expected this unification to bear fruit at any moment. There were signs, rumours of signs and a great deal of chatter, but nothing tangible. When the Berlin Wall came down in 1989, for those who followed the spiritual news, this event was obviously thanks to Father and the members who had been figuratively blowing the Jericho trumpets in Berlin just two years before. It signalled that both ethereally and practically, things were really moving for the world now. We expected North Korea to implode imminently, but this was apparently a much harder nut to crack.

And there was no recognition of Father from the fallen world. Communism for the most part had been utterly destroyed by us and our allies in the spiritual world, and yet everywhere man was bound by Satan's chains. From Father's speeches the reason for the tenacity of Satan's power on a post-communist planet earth seemed to be primarily that mankind remained promiscuous. The fornicators amongst us had to be stamped out and AIDS would help do this. We were told we should all make a point of exposing those who had been punished with that illness, forcing them to wear T-shirts with a giant 'A' on them. Father's speeches became increasingly graphic and specifically about the biological apparatus for physical love. Around this time he gave fewer speeches and stepped away from direct involvement in matching members for marriage, which was something he now delegated to local leaders.

Over the next few years most of those of us who had been in Korea together were matched to each other and started families that led to third generation children being born. But those that went along with the blessing were just as likely to lose their faith as those that avoided it, and few of these marriages lasted. Sometimes the marriage lasted but the couples lost their faith together. We mostly all stayed in touch with each other and remained close to a few of those we had genuinely liked. Despite some predictable whining from those of us that had enjoyed the least difficult lives growing up in the church, few of the blessed children made much of an attempt to voice regret about the circumstances of our childhood. It may have been a crazy childhood but everyone seemed to agree there are worse ways to grow up. If anything, we would find it a peculiar advantage to have been injected at a young age with such a weak form of untruth.

Chapter 14
Waco: Living Prophecy

Livingstone Fagan

> And when he had opened the fifth seal, I saw under the
> altar the souls of them that were slain for the word of
> God, and for the testimony which they held: And they
> cried with a loud voice, saying, How long, O Lord, holy
> and true, dost thou not judge and avenge our blood on
> them that dwell on the earth? And white robes were
> given unto every one of them; and it was said unto them,
> that they should rest yet for a little season, until their
> fellow servants also and their brethren, that should be killed
> as they [were,] should be fulfilled

Rev. 6:9–11[1]

About the turn of the seventh century BCE, at a time of great geo-political change, the prophet Isaiah received a vision of which he wrote,

> And it shall come to pass in the last days, that the mountain of the Lord's house shall be established in the top of the mountains, and shall be exalted above the hills; and all nations shall flow unto it. And many people shall go and say, come ye, and let us go up to the mountain of the Lord, to the house of the God of Jacob: and he will teach us of his ways, and we will walk in his paths: for out of Zion shall go for the law, and the world of the Lord from Jerusalem. And he shall judge among the nations, and shall rebuke many people: and they shall beat their swords into plowshares and their spears into pruning hooks: nation shall not lift up sword against nation, neither shall they learn war any more.[2]

This was God's vision of the future for mankind. It has been repeated and expanded on throughout the prophetic texts of scripture. In a veiled reference Christ made mention of it in the Gospels by saying, '… a city set on a hill cannot be hid'.[3]

The saving virtue of faith is that we might believe before the thing hoped for becomes fact. We are then drawn into the event as it is realised, becoming one

---

[1]   Unless otherwise stated, all textual references are from the KJV. This is of importance for the richness and unity of the textual comparison.

[2]   Isa. 2:2–4 (25:6–9; 60; 62; cf. Micah 4:1–3; Ezek. 36; 40–48; Dan. 2:34, 35, 44, 45; Zech. 14; Ps. 48).

[3]   Mt. 5:14.

with it. The act of believing is much like casting a vote. But instead of temporal concerns we are dealing with the eternal matters of the spirit. Prophecy plays an important part in this. It tells us about these matters before they come to pass. Our faith is then informed, which helps us recognise the event for what it is when it occurs. Without prior knowledge it would otherwise come as a surprise and a potential cause of fear, resulting in our rejecting it.

The idea that there exists an intelligence not confined to time and space should come as no surprise. This is how prophecy is made possible. In the biblical sense we would be talking about God. Here it is deemed a testament to the power of God to see the end from the beginning. He reveals this through the medium of prophecy, also referred to as direct revelation. Prophecy also then becomes one of the means by which the existence of God can be affirmed. Comparing this with science, I am informed it was the philosopher Karl Popper who defined science as a discipline that creates hypotheses which predict phenomena (usually new ones) that can be tested. This idea is not new, neither is it unique to science. It is a variation on the workings of prophecy in its dealings with the spiritual. A prophecy is deemed true as the thing it speaks of comes to pass. This was the test established back in the days of Moses.[4] Modern science adapts and applies this principle to the physical world. It then surreptitiously challenges the religionist for authority over what is Truth. But is this about ego or can this save us? Does the salvation of man come of the physical or the spiritual?

Well, as with the physical, there are also laws of the spirit. These are fundamental to life itself and are affected by the decisions and choices we make. Through prophecy God appeals to our intelligence in the hope we might make the right ones. But this is not guaranteed. We saw a demonstration of this with Adam and Eve in the Garden of Eden.[5] Where prophecy fails the only other recourse is mercy born of love. Here God acts on our behalf in spite of ourselves but this requires of us faith in order for it to be ratified. It would otherwise be an infringement of our free will. Ultimately, the salvation of mankind results as an act of God, through faith, rather than the works of man. The dynamics of this is tied to what the scriptures refer to as the 'Mystery of God'.[6] There is a link here to new religious movements. Bear in mind that what appears outwardly as a religious movement is in fact a movement of the spirit initially experienced at the level of consciousness.[7]

In terms of the relationship between prophecy and new religious movements, the Christ event of 2,000 years ago provides us a perfect example. This was a new religious/spiritual movement firmly rooted in prophecy. You will recall it was stated by Christ, 'Think not that I am come to destroy the law, or the prophets:

---

[4]   Deut. 18:15–22.

[5]   Gen. 2:16, 17; 3:1–24.

[6]   Rev. 10:7.

[7]   Mt. 3:16, 17; Luke 4:1, 14–18 (Isa. 61).

I am not come to destroy, but to fulfill.'[8] The Old Testament prophets were given visions of the advent of Christ long before his appearance on earth 2,000 years ago. Of particular note was the prophet Isaiah.[9] It was this information, not merely the historical circumstances of his birth and life, which provided the *context* by which he was to be understood. The significance of this relates to how he would be received.[10]

This also contrasts with the rituals of religion or just obeying a set of rules concerned with dos and don'ts. By themselves these cannot save us. They are a *means*, not an end. We were to mature beyond them. Life is not lived to follow rituals and obey rules. It is about finding *true happiness*. This involves a *certain spirit* and *state of being*. Without this, what significance is there in our having life? Certainly not to live it merely to cater to the needs of the body that eventually dies. Living to die is not the ideal of life either. The truth of the Spirit which we identify as the true source of prophecy is a higher principle. It takes us beyond the law of commandments to the *divine ideal of Life* which these laws were intended to reflect. From this position it is seen that the law is broader than it is often defined and applied by men, according to their limited reasoning born of sensory perception. You will recall Christ's many conflicts with the religious leaders of his day concerning this. We have the example of the Sabbath and also adultery.[11] How Christ dealt with these showed that the spirit behind the law reflected that of a helpful guide to Life not as a stern instrument of death and condemnation. The misuse of law to promote hidden agendas rather than true justice lessens regard for it. But where do we go from there if we are to avoid descending into complete lawlessness. Well, despite opposition, the Christ event later became what is now referred to as Christianity, a new religious movement that for better or worst became an established religion. Its legitimacy rested in recognition of who Christ was in relation to God and by following his lead and teachings. But has this always been the case?

Further on, the protestant movement associated with Martin Luther in the 1500s, the Millerites (USA) and the birth of the Seventh-day Adventists in the mid-1800s were all new religious/spiritual movements rooted in prophecy. Their purpose was to restore and bring to light further understanding of truth and God. Significantly, and as was the case with us at Waco, these movements also met opposition from the established order. The belief that advancement in the knowledge and truth of God comes only through the established religious organs and governance is here shown not to be so. The need for new religious movements often arises because the established order has gone off track. It has stopped following on to know the truth. This was true in the case of the Jews at the advent of Christ 2,000 years ago as it is today with Christianity.

---

[8] Mt. 5:17.
[9] Isa. 7:14; 49:1–7; 53.
[10] 1 Cor. 2:4–10.
[11] Mt. 12:1–21; John 8:1–11.

This is partly why our community at Waco came into being. We were raised up by God as were the prophets in times past to deliver a message. I don't say this lightly, the prophecies also confirm this.

At our Mt Carmel community, prophecy played a major role. Not only did it shape how we understood ourselves and the way we saw reality, but also how we acted. This is linked to the book Sealed with Seven Seals shown in Revelation 5. It opened to our view new vistas of consciousness and understanding about God and Salvation. This included further insights into prophecy. By addressing the issue of how we are defined and who defines us, it brought added assurance and hope, strengthening our faith and commitment for what we would face. It is against this backdrop that we are also properly understood.

There have been questions raised about some of our practices, mainly our having guns and David having multiple wives. I understand how this might appear to an outsider with no knowledge of the underlying theology. But assuredly there is a legitimate explanation and purpose behind all this. Needless to say, God is not bound by the traditions and conceptions of men.[12] In any case, these were secondary to the matter concerning David Koresh himself. Before he was killed on 19 April 1993, a day earlier he made this statement to one FBI negotiator, 'Look, you denounce the fact that I have a God that communicates with me. That's the first mistake …' (quoted in Wessinger 2000: 108). The most important question of Waco is not about guns or the fire. It is about whether or not David truly had these communications with God. How this is answered clarifies everything else.

Believe it or not, and I make no apology by saying this, David Koresh was anointed of God to do the things he did. He took on the mantle of Christ. But unlike 2,000 years ago, on this occasion he came as a sinner. One born from among men in the same way all men are born on earth, through both male and female seed. This allowed him to take on both our sinful body and our *fallen human nature*. He would himself then take hold of the same grace he ratified 2,000 years ago. To restore him back to the righteousness that is by faith. This sets the standard and proof of its effectiveness. It worked, as evinced by David's ability to reveal the meaning of the book Sealed with Seven Seals shown in the right hand of God in Revelation 5. This is in connection with the long awaited Judgment of the World which was to occur at the end of time. Those of us who were there bear witness of this. At the opening of the sixth seal the world is to know the truth of this for itself.

That Christ would appear on earth again prior to his long awaited return in glory was surprisingly well documented in the prophetic scriptures. Apparently veiled from our understanding until the time it would be fulfilled. But truthfully, like the Jews at his advent 2,000 years ago, we were not really looking for it. There is a belief among Christians that the birth, life and ministry of Christ, along with his death, resurrection, ascension and promised return in glory constitute the sum of the matters concerning Christ. This perception blinds the mind to seeing

---

[12]   Isa. 20:2; Hosea 1:2; 3:1; Ps. 18:24–6.

anything else. But there remained yet more to be revealed of the work of Christ here on earth prior to his glorious return.

Speaking to his disciples shortly before his crucifixion Christ stated, 'I have yet many things to say unto you, but you cannot bear them now. Howbeit when he the spirit of truth is come, he will guide you into all truth …'.[13] The Gospels do not contain all the truth concerning Christ. They largely serve to confirm the historical fact of his advent 2,000 years ago. In Luke 24:44, he directed them to the Law of Moses, to the Prophets and to the Psalms as the real depository of truth concerning himself. These were the focus of study at our Mt Carmel community. Through the aid of the Spirit we came into the knowledge of these additional matters concerning Christ. David was privileged to learn them by an even more direct route, arising from an experience he had while on a trip to Jerusalem in 1985. This was given specific mention by the prophets.[14]

There is a lot of detail here. It helps to have a working knowledge of the language and nuances of the prophetic text. But focusing on some of the main points takes us to the book of Genesis. In chapter 49, before his death the patriarch Jacob foretells of what would become of his sons. In verse 10, he speaks of Judah, stating, 'The scepter shall not depart from Judah until Shiloh come; unto him shall the gathering of the people be.' It is now understood that the Christ event 2,000 years ago was what he referred to. There are of course other references which confirm this.[15] In addition to Judah, Jacob also foretold of one who would come through the lineage of Joseph, referred to in verse 24 as, '… the shepherd, the stone of Israel'. Bearing in mind the separation of the 12 tribes after the reign of Solomon, this indicated he would come of the northern tribe of Israel rather than of Judah. Again there are other references which support this.[16]

With regard to the Waco event itself, like the Christ event 2,000 years ago, this too was prophesied in the scriptures. We're taken to the prophecies in the book of Daniel. Notice the reference to Michael the prince in Chapters 10:21 and 12:1. This was the name of Christ in heaven before he came to earth. He is the one spoken of as Messiah the prince in Chapter 9: 25–7. This particular reference relates to his coming 2,000 years ago. It is further noted in Dan. 11:18 and 22, in connection with the prophecies about the king of the North.

Centuries later, down to the present time we pick up the story again in verses 31–5. Here it speaks of *another* event relating to Christ. This is in connection with a matter referred to as the '*daily*' being *taken away* – verse 31.[17] Uncovering the meaning of this takes us to the system of sacrifices God gave to Israel under Moses. Among these were TWO lambs that were to be offered *daily*, the one in the morning

---

[13]   John 16:12ff.

[14]   Isa. 41:25; Zech. 2:1–5; Rev. 10.

[15]   See note 3, Ps. 16:10; 22 (Mk. 15:34); 40; 118:18, etc.

[16]   Eccl. 12:11; Jer. 49:19; 50:44; Ezek. 34:23, 24; Isa. 55:3, 4; Hosea 3:5, etc.

[17]   Note also Dan. 8:9–12.

and the other at evening.[18] Similarly on the Day of Atonement there were TWO goats offered, one inside the camp and the other – the scapegoat – was released to the wilderness.[19] These were of symbolic significance to our understanding of the plan of salvation and the matters concerning Christ. The *taking away* of the *daily* noted here in Daniel links to verse 33, which states, 'And they that understand among the people shall instruct many; yet they shall fall by the sword, and by flame, by captivity, and by spoil many days.' This describes what happened to our community at Waco. It even notes the fire that killed scores of our members on 19 April 1993. This was also referred to by the prophet Isaiah where he laments, 'The righteous perish, and no man layeth it to heart: and merciful men are TAKEN AWAY, non considering that the righteous is taken away from the evil to come. HE shall enter into peace: THEY shall rest in their beds, each one walking in his uprightness.'[20] There are other references. Christ made mention of it by stating, 'For wheresoever the carcase is, there will the eagles be gathered together.'[21]

I noted that this event was in connection with the Judgment of the world that was to occur at the end of time. The Judgment takes place in heaven first before being revealed here on earth. It precedes the coming of the kingdom of God. The apostle John was taken to heaven to see this. He wrote about it in the Book of Revelation.[22] At the centre of it is a *book* shown in the right hand of God *sealed with seven seals* and the simple question, '*Who is worthy to open it?*' The revealing of the meaning of the seals sets the Judgment here on earth. It provides the means by which God would judge the world. This was the burden of faith placed upon David and our Mt Carmel community. The Waco event became the form it took because of how we were received. How men responded to it would result in them unwittingly pronouncing judgment upon them themselves. This is similar in its workings to the plot devised by Solomon in his judgment of the two harlots recorded in 1 Kings 3:16–28. The prophet Isaiah also gave prior warning of this.[23] It continues today as a witness before the world and reaches its climax at the opening of the sixth seal. Then the truth of this becomes unmistakably clear.

Alongside the prophecies relating to the Judgment and this second revelation of Christ there were also those prophecies dealing with the Messianic Kingdom. Given that the first two of these events have taken place the way is now paved for the coming of the Kingdom. This will be a monumental event in the history and

---

[18]   Ex. 29:38–42; Num. 28:3–10.

[19]   Lev. 16:5–34.

[20]   Isa. 57:1.

[21]   Mt. 24:28.

[22]   Rev. 4–8ff.

[23]   Isa. 28:16, 17, particularly verse 17. These verses speak of two distinct events occurring at different times. We know the first referred to the Christ event 2,000 years ago. But what about the second, verse 17? The world saw this fulfilled in the matters concerning David Koresh and what happened at Waco in 1993. This event also marked the countdown leading to the end of the present world order.

future of mankind. Sadly, and despite the wealth of information contained in the prophecies, very few have a clear grasp of it. At his advent 2,000 years ago Christ sought to keep the matter of the Kingdom before his hearers. It was a constant theme throughout his ministry. In the prayer he taught his disciples and which has been on the lips of believers down through the ages he stated, 'Our father which art in heaven, hallowed be thy name. *Thy Kingdom come. Thy will be done in earth, as it is in heaven* …'.[24] In the same discourse he proceeded further,

> Therefore take no thought, saying, what shall we eat? or, what shall we drink? or, wherewithal shall we be clothed? … for your heavenly father knoweth that you have need of these things. But *seek ye first the kingdom of God*, and his righteousness; and all these things shall be added unto you ….[25]

Earlier in mystical note he stated, '… A *city* that is *set on a hill* cannot be hid.'[26]

Whilst under inspiration the apostle John records being shown the future descent of the Kingdom from heaven to the earth, 'And he carried me away in the spirit to *a great and high mountain* and shewed me the great city, the holy Jerusalem, descending out of heaven from God.'[27]

The realities concerning the Kingdom remain as much a mystery in the minds of men today as they were 2,000 years ago. This was among the main focus of study at our Mt Carmel community and a core tenet of our message to the world.

The bulk of the prophecies regarding the Kingdom were already given in the Old Testament. Much of what these prophets wrote was for the end times and centred around the Judgment and the Kingdom of God. In the beginning of this chapter I referred to one of the many prophecies of Isaiah regarding this (Isa. 2:2–4). Isaiah further sought to depict the spirit and life of the Kingdom when he wrote,

> The wolf also shall dwell with the lamb, and the leopard shall lie down with the kid; and the calf and the young lion and the fatling together; and a little child shall lead them. And the cow and the bear shall feed; their young ones shall lie down together: and the lion shall eat straw like the ox. And the suckling child shall play on the hole of the asp, and the weaned child shall put his hand on the cockatrice' den. *They shall not hurt or destroy in my holy mountain*: for the earth shall be full of the knowledge of the LORD, as the waters covered the sea.[28]

Literally! This quote, along with Isa. 2:2–4, Ezek. 47 and others, highlights the extent and impact the coming Kingdom will have on the contemporary world.

---

[24]   Mt. 6:10.

[25]   Mt. 6:31–3.

[26]   Mt. 5:14 (last part).

[27]   Rev. 21:10 (note further verses 11–27 and Rev. 22:1–5).

[28]   Isa. 11: 6–9.

Not only will war among nations cease, it will also bring harmony to the animal kingdom and the reordering and cleansing of the earth itself (land, air and sea). A new consciousness emerges that reflects our shared humanity and connectedness to nature and the universe. This is depicted still further in the following quote from Isaiah,

> And *in this mountain* shall the LORD of host make unto all people a feast of fat things, a feast of wines on the lees, of fat things full of marrow, of wines on the lees well refined. And he will destroy the face of the covering cast over all people, and the veil that is spread over all nations. He will swallow up death in victory; and the Lord God will wipe away tears from off all faces; and the rebuke of his people shall he take away from off all the earth: for the LORD hath spoken it. And it shall be said in that day, lo, this is our God; we have waited for him, and he will save us: this is the LORD; we have waited for him, we will be glad and rejoice in his salvation.[29]

Given that the coming of the Kingdom is a supernatural (not man-made) event, this will invariably bring a reaction from among men. These prophecies help inform our understanding so as to prevent an adverse reaction. This is about saving mankind not destroying it. Noting the response of the rulers of the world at the arrival of the Kingdom the Psalmist exclaims (emphasis added),

> GREAT is the LORD, and greatly to be praised in the city of our God, *in the mountain of his holiness.* Beautiful for situation, the joy of the whole earth, is *mount Zion*, on the sides of the north, the city of the great king … *For, lo, the kings were assembled, they passed by together. They saw it, and so they marveled; they were troubled, and hasted away. Fear took hold of them there, and pain, as a woman in travail* … As we have heard, so have we seen in the city of the LORD of hosts, in *the city* of our God: God will establish it for ever. Selah.[30]

Having been shown the vision of the future, the prophet Daniel, writing c.2,500 years ago, further expands on this theme.[31]

The location where the Kingdom appears and the physical events surrounding its appearance are also detailed in the prophecies. Bringing together the two themes of the coming of Christ and the Kingdom the prophet Zechariah wrote,

> And his feet shall stand in that day upon the *mount of Olives*, which is *before Jerusalem* on the east, and the mount of Olives shall cleave [split] in the midst

---

[29]   Isa. 25:6–9.

[30]   Ps. 48:1, 2, 4–6, 8.

[31]   Dan. 2:34 (entire chapter noting particularly verses 34, 35, 44, 45; note also Dan. 7:9–14, 23–7).

thereof towards the east and toward the west, and there shall be *a very great valley*, and half the mountain shall remove toward the north, and half of it toward the south. *And ye shall flee to the valley of the mountains* … and the Lord my God shall come … And it shall come to pass in that day, that the light shall not be clear, nor dark … but it shall come to pass, that at evening time it shall be light. And the LORD shall be king over all the earth: in that day shall there be one LORD, and his name one. All the land shall be turned as a plain … and *it shall be lifted up* … And men shall dwell in it, and there shall be no more utter destruction; but Jerusalem shall be safely inhabited.[32]

The prophet Ezekiel adds extensively to this detail. He even describes the scene surrounding the coming of God.[33]

I noted it was part of our message to inform the world of these events before they occur. It is important to grasp the detail in the text as I sought to demonstrate here. This allows our faith to be grounded in the plain statements of scripture, perceiving its hidden meanings even as we become one with its spirit.

These truths concerning the Kingdom are more relevant to us today than ever. We are living in the time of its realisation. The Kingdom comes at a specific location here on earth (the Mount of Olives east of Jerusalem) and will supersede this present order and state of the world which cannot continue by reason of corruption. It then lasts a thousand years before giving way to a new heaven and a new earth where death and hell will have been destroyed.[34] During the thousand years the saved among men will have grown up to the full stature of Being, allowing this further cosmic transformation to take place. The temporal gives way to the eternal as the veil that now separates heaven and earth is removed.

In the almost two decades since Waco (1993) the world has seen some momentous events, natural and man-made. These have been gathering momentum as each year passes with no seeming end in sight. An apt description is that of the birth pangs of a woman during childbirth. With these occurrences comes what can best be described as an awakening of human consciousness. The question arises what does this all mean? It is as though mankind is being prepared for an event not yet realised. This event is of such magnitude that, although it is yet in the future, its effects are presently felt. For the surviving members of our community these events, tragic though they are, have served to affirm and strengthen our faith. In the aftermath of Waco we expected the continued unfolding of prophecy. In particular there were those prophecies dealing with the temporal affairs of men, i.e. the matters concerning the king of the North spoken of by the prophet Daniel.[35]

---

[32] Zech. 14 (entire chapter).

[33] Ezek. 40:2; 43:2 (chapters 40–48 describe the coming of God and the Kingdom in great detail). This event is noted with much fanfare in Ps. 18; 50. Consider also Isa. 60; 62; 65:8–24; Ezek. 36; Micah 4:1–3; Zech. 8:1–5, 20–22; Ps. 72.

[34] Rev. 20; 21:1–8.

[35] Dan. 7 (note particularly verses 19–27); 8:9–12, 23–5; 11:36–45; 12:1–3.

Simultaneously there were the matters of the spiritual dealing with the sealing of those who are to be saved.[36] These events take place in the run up to what the scriptures described as 'The Time of Trouble' (The Great Tribulation) that the world goes through prior to the birthing of the Kingdom.[37] It is in light of this that the prophecies were given. They afford an important source of guidance, support and encouragement helping us through this difficult time of great change and uncertainty.

In conclusion, the plan of Salvation encompasses far more than is generally understood. After the fall of man, the idea of God becoming man in order to save mankind stunned Lucifer. The profound self-sacrificing principle this revealed left him speechless and all of heaven in astonishment. Lucifer had argued that the creation of man was a mistake. Despite being the cause he pointed to the fall of Adam and Eve as proof, claiming that man could not be trusted to keep the law jeopardising the peace of the universe. His charge implied God was wrong and concealed a plot to unseat God using man as ammunition.[38] When Christ came to earth 2,000 years ago he proved otherwise. He took our sinful flesh with its centuries of corruption yet he lived a *sinless life*. Lucifer then went on to argue that fallen man could not now be salvaged. In these matters we've been discussing concerning David Koresh, this charge is now also laid to rest. In spite of our *sinful flesh* and *fallen human nature* no one needs to be lost. The struggle of our lives has been a choice whether to be a pawn in Lucifer's plot or to accept salvation. This comes at the expense of Christ yielding up his *equality* with God. It is the *life* of Christ that saves us not his death.[39] His *life*, as GOD, is more than sufficient an exchange for the entire human race, the infinite for the finite. It allows our fallen human nature to be replaced with the divine nature restoring us as Sons of God. We are saved as Sons of God, not as servants of sin. This takes effect in us by faith and is experienced here and now as a certain spirit and consciousness with its peculiar understanding. It is to also animate what will be our glorified bodies. Without this the human race, by reason of the fact it is not inherently self-existent, must otherwise perish. Having yielded up his state of equality with God, Christ too will bear this new humanity. He dwells among us as the first among equals, himself sustained by the Life he gave up. As the very life within us how much closer can God come to mankind? For me this is no abstract theory, it is a living reality. Something I am very much personally involved in.

---

[36]   Rev. 7:1–8, 9–17.

[37]   Dan. 12:1–3; Mt. 24:15–22; Rev. 3:10–12 (7:13–17); 6:12–17.

[38]   Gen. 3:1–5; Job 1:6–12; 2:1–7; Isa. 14:5–17; Ezek. 1–19; Zech. 3:1–5; Mt. 4:1–11; Rev. 12; 20:1–3, 7–10.

[39]   Mt. 20:28; John 5:24; 6:63; Rom. 5:10.

References

Wessinger, C. 2000. *How the Millennium Comes Violently: From Jonestown to Heaven's Gate*. New York and London: Seven Bridges Press.

Chapter 15

(Always) Living in the End-Times: The 'Rolling Prophecy' of the Conspiracy Milieu

David G. Robertson

Introduction

> In the near future, Earth is dominated by a powerful world government. Once free nations are slaves to the will of a tiny elite. The dawn of a new dark age is upon mankind. Countries are a thing of the past; every form of independence is under attack, with the family and even the individual itself nearing extinction. Close to 80% of the world's population has been eliminated. The remnants of a once-free humanity are forced to live within highly controlled, compact, prison-like cities. Travel is highly restricted. Super-highways connect the mega-cities and keep the population from entering into unauthorised zones. No human activity is private. AI super-computers chronicle and categorise every action. A Prison Planet dominated by a ruthless gang of control-freaks, whose power can never be challenged. This is the vision of the global elite, their goal: a program of total dehumanisation, where the science of tyranny is law. A worldwide control grid, designed to ensure the overlords' monopoly of power for ever. Our species will be condemned to this nightmare future, unless the masses are awakened to the new world order master plan and mobilised to defeat it (Jones 2007).

In the introduction to his film *Endgame: Blueprint for Global Enslavement*, from which the above is taken, Texas-based broadcaster Alex Jones lays out his vision for the future of the US and the world. Although exact figures are difficult to ascertain, *Endgame* has received millions of online views, despite never receiving a cinematic release. His radio show – broadcast for three hours every weekday, and two hours on Sundays – is broadcast on 63 FM and AM channels in the Southern US, where talk radio has a broad appeal amongst a largely rural population who are dependent on the automobile (Zaitchik 2011). However, Jones reaches larger audiences through his websites, principally infowars.com, which consistently ranks as around the 500th most popular website in the US, and 1,700th worldwide, with an audience of primarily middle-aged single males with some college education.[1] Jones is arguably the most popular and influential conspiracist in the world today, although he himself prefers to describe his milieu as the 'alternative media'. Such is his popular appeal that many believe that much of the material in Glenn Beck's hugely popular broadcasts on the mainstream FOX News channel is taken from Alex Jones' output (Zaitchik 2011). A considerable part of that appeal stems from the perception that Jones is a successful prophet.

Prophecy and millennialism are widespread in conspiracy milieu, although this has received little academic attention. These narratives have typically been predictions of the imminent enslavement of society by one or other hidden, all-powerful group, such as the Illuminati,[2] communists or Zionists. Due to a cross-fertilisation with certain New Age narratives during the 1990s, however, conspiracist prophecy has also increasingly included declarations of an imminent 'global awakening', when the mass of humanity will realise their enslavement and overcome their oppressors.

This chapter attempts to show how millennialist prophecy operates in this diffuse milieu of popular conspiracism, with Jones as a case-study. By examining some of Jones' allegedly successful prophecies, I demonstrate how they employ what I will call 'rolling prophecy', an on-going process of interpretation. I suggest that rolling prophecy provides a mechanism by which the cognitive dissonance produced by failed date-specific prophecies can be avoided, enabling conspiracist prophecy to function primarily as a form of social critique, reflecting on the present more than predicting the future. As such, it functions as a popular theodicy which attempts to account for the perceived inequalities of contemporary Western society, while offering a Utopian alternative.

Conspiracism

Conspiracy can be defined simply enough: it is 'an agreement between two or more persons to do something criminal, illegal, or reprehensible' (*Oxford English Dictionary* 1989). However, a *conspiracy theory* does not mean simply a theory which posits a conspiracy. Both the official and conspiracist explanations of the events of 11 September 2001, involve conspiracies, yet the Al Qaeda theory, as presented by the 9-11 Commission Report, is never referred to as a conspiracy

---

[1]   http://www.alexa.com/siteinfo/infowars.com# (accessed: 4 April 2012). By way of comparison, facebook.com ranks 2nd and nationalgeographic.com 452nd in the US on the same date.

[2]   The concept of the Illuminati comes from *Proofs of a Conspiracy against All the Religions and Governments of Europe* (1797) by John Robison, Professor of Natural Philosophy at the University of Edinburgh. He claimed that the short-lived Order of the Illuminati, founded by Bavarian intellectual Adam Weishaupt to promote Enlightenment thought, had in fact continued covertly, seeking world domination, a theme that has remained popular in conspiracist narratives ever since (Partridge 2005: 273).

theory (Coady 2007a: 132). A theory which involves a conspiracy, in other words, does not a 'conspiracy theory' make.

The implication of this is that the approach taken by most scholars, most influentially in Richard Hofstadter's 'The Paranoid Style in American Politics' (1964) – that conspiracy theories should be taken as evidence of mental ill-health, paranoia or irrationality – cannot be correct (Pigden 2007: 222). Such an approach assumes a fundamental difference between unproven *conspiracy theories* (for example, those claiming the moon landings were faked) and proven *conspiracies* (such as US President Nixon's complicity in covering-up the break-in at the Watergate hotel). In fact, Watergate is only one of many now-accepted historical events which have at one point been regarded as conspiracy theories (Bartlett and Miller 2010: 16). We cannot, therefore, define a conspiracy theory by its contents.

Rather, the term 'conspiracy theory' has a rhetorical function (Coady 2007b). As employed in political discourses, a conspiracy theory is understood to be 'an explanation that conflicts with the account advanced by the relevant epistemic authorities', and therefore the term's application is ultimately concerned with power (Levy 2007: 181). In short, by labelling an account a conspiracy theory, epistemic authorities including governments and scientific institutions seek to marginalise that account by portraying it as inherently irrational.

To avoid epistemic judgements, I have therefore adopted Barkun's term *conspiracy belief*, denoting a discreet unit of belief that 'an organisation made up of individuals or groups has or is acting covertly to achieve some malevolent end' (2003: 3). These malevolent ends, of course, are culturally determined and therefore open to interpretation; the promotion of policies concerning centralised world government or gun control may be viewed as benevolent by left-leaning groups, at the same time as forming the malevolent agenda of the conspirators in right-wing groups.

Knight places the beginning of today's popular conspiracist culture with the establishment of the CIA and the commencement of the Cold War in the late 1940s (2000: 28–31). During the Cold War, conspiracy beliefs were largely restricted to the cultural margins, but during the 1990s, these narratives began to enter the mainstream, with publications such as *The New World Order* (1991) by Pat Robertson, an influential televangelist, becoming best-sellers. Events such as the 1993 siege of the Branch Davidian compound by the Bureau of Alcohol, Tobacco and Firearms at Waco, Texas, and the 1995 bombing of the Alfred P. Murrah building in Oklahoma City were broadcast in real-time on the new 24-hour TV news channels. Conspiracist explanations of the events were adopted by the US militia movement and disseminated enthusiastically on the Internet and on independent and public access radio stations (Goodrick-Clarke 2002: 281). The attacks on the World Trade Center and the Pentagon on 11 September 2001, brought conspiracist narratives to an even broader public already primed with an atmosphere of fear; whereas for those already in the conspiracist milieu, it provided only confirmation of the existence of the conspiracy (Goodrick-Clarke 2002: 168–9). It is worth mentioning at this point that the conspiracist milieu is not typically made up of tight-knit groups with social interactions which reify their belief systems, but rather with a diffuse milieu, disseminated through books, the Internet and local radio stations, in which particular writers and broadcasters act as focal points rather than de facto leaders. One of those who became a conspiracist focal point in the post 9-11 period was Alex Jones.

Prophecy and Millennialism in the Conspiracist Milieu

Conspiracism tends to be eschatological, i.e. concerned with the end of time (*eschaton*). Conspiracists, in uncovering a 'hidden history', are led necessarily to extrapolate where the conspirators' plan is heading. Broadly speaking, eschatological narratives take two forms: the *apocalyptic* and the *millennial*. By apocalyptic, I refer to eschatological systems in which the outcome of the end time is total and destructive, for example, the righteous being taken up to heaven and the remaining world consumed by flames. In millennial eschatologies, however, the world is not destroyed but rather transformed, and a better world instigated, as in the Christian belief of the return and thousand-year reign of Christ as recounted in Revelation.[3]

Conspiracist eschatological narratives have typically been of the apocalyptic type, positing the ultimate victory of the globalist conspirators, as in the quote from Alex Jones at the top of the chapter. Humanity is crushed, even wiped out, through the machinations of the New World Order. Boyer charts how the post-war development of international governance bodies and financial agencies led Christian millenarian writers in the US to be increasingly concerned with global conspiracy, focusing on the United Nations and the Trilateral Commission (1992: 263–72). A hidden evil force can also help to explain away the failure of the end times to arrive (Barkun 2003: 3).

During the 1990s, a number of right-wing conspiracist narratives began to appear in the New Age milieu (Goodrick-Clarke 2002: 299). The influence seems to have been mutual, however, as conspiracist prophecy has increasingly included predictions of an imminent 'global awakening' (Ward and Voas 2011: 112). In these narratives, the apocalyptic eschatology is replaced by a millennial eschatology in which the world is remade, rather than destroyed. These narratives see the growth of millennial conspiracism as indicative that the masses are beginning to 'wake up' to their enslavement, and predict the imminent deposition of the conspirators, adding a more hopeful, even Utopian, narrative to popular conspiracism.

---

[3]   This terminological distinction is my own. Cohn counts 'apocalypticism' as a form of 'millenarianism' (1970: 19–21), whereas Landes differentiates between 'millenarian' (transformative) and 'eschatological' (destructive), with 'apocalyptic' taken to refer to imminentist expressions (2006: 6–13). Neither of these schemas is universally employed however, and my own distinction, I feel, is simpler and closer to common-sense.

This idea of an imminent 'global awakening' has, in the work of David Icke,[4] David Wilcock[5] and others, allowed for a hybrid of conspiracist millennialism and New Age to develop (Barkun 2003: 173–4).

Alex Jones' output lies somewhere between these two polarities: alongside the dire apocalyptic predictions of *Endgame*, he makes frequent exhortations as to how humanity is 'waking up' and will ultimately overcome their oppression. Both types of prophecy are central to his popular appeal.

Alex Jones

Jones was born in 1974 in Rockwall, a well-to-do suburb of Dallas, Texas. While he was at high school, Jones claims to have seen local police dealing cannabis to some of the pupils. Not long afterwards, he was stopped while driving, and accused the officer of corruption, which, perhaps unsurprisingly, elicited an angry response. The family moved to Austin to avoid further trouble; the Rockwall Sheriff was indicted on organised crime charges two months later (Zaitchik 2011).

Around this time, Jones read *None Dare Call It Conspiracy* (1971) by Gary Allen, which outlined the New World Order conspiracist narrative (Zaitchik 2011). Allen was a representative of the John Birch Society, a well-known, though secretive, conservative activist group. They were founded in 1958 by Robert Welch, a businessman and sometime politician, with the intention of organising and mobilising conservative opinion (Schoenwald 2001: 62). By 1960, they had between 20,000 and 100,000 members (Schoenwald 2001: 64). Their small government and anti-federalist rhetoric was remarkable only for its elaboration into a fully-developed conspiracist narrative which saw communists attempting to undermine the American libertarian project (Wilcox 1988: 432). In Welch's view, the only explanation for what he saw as the decline of the US was that the federal government, and in particular President Eisenhower, were active communist agents acting against the interests of the US citizens, attempting to establish a centralised global New World Order (NWO) (Schoenwald 2001: 71–3). NWO conspiracism can be understood as an amplification of nineteenth-century Illuminati narratives, where the conspirators do not merely influence the state, but actively create it.

The book's themes seem to have resonated with Jones' suspicion of widespread corruption and abuses of power by representatives of the state. These suspicions were confirmed to him in the spring of 1993 when the BATF siege of the Branch Davidian compound began in Waco, two hour's drive from Jones' home.

---

[4]   In an interview during Jones' 27-hour 'moneybomb' broadcast on the 3rd November 2011, David Icke described the Occupy movement as evidence of this 'global awakening'. http://rss.infowars.com/20111103_Thu_Alex2.mp3 (accessed: 16 December 2011).

[5]   http://divinecosmos.com/start-here/davids-blog/1035-divineintervention1 (accessed: 26 April 2012).

'I remember ... seeing that famous footage of the [B]ATF loading their video cameras before going in ... They were going to lose their funding. This was [a] PR stunt' (Kay 2011: 16). According to Kay, the impact on Jones was such that by the time of the Oklahoma City bombing in 1995, he was already presenting and producing his own public access television programme, moving into radio a year later (Kay 2011: 16).

Although the John Birch Society are considered right-wing (Stone 1974: 184), Jones' political position is somewhat more complex. Rejecting the terms conservative and Republican, he instead refers to himself as a Libertarian or 'paleoconservative', in other words identifying with the ideology of the founders of the constitution, rather than the more neo-conservative agenda of the present Republican Party. He considers both Republican and Democratic parties to be equally working for the agenda of the globalists: 'Ignore the right or left wing, study the brain of the bird' (Zaitchik 2011). Jones' overarching theme is that a 'global elite' is covertly attempting to consolidate power in their hands to form a World Government, the New World Order. Gun control legislation, the fluoridation of drinking water, measures to curb global warming, the 9-11 attacks and the stock market collapse of 2008 are all taken as evidence of this centralisation of power. The elite – identified as the Bilderberg Group, the Trilateral Commission, the Council for Foreign Relations and others – intend to seize the wealth of every country in the world, and instigate a eugenics programme aimed at decimating the world's population.

These themes are most succinctly delineated in Jones' parallel career as a film-maker. His early films, such as *America: Destroyed by Design* (1998) were concerned with the imminent takeover of the US by NATO and FEMA (Federal Emergency Management Authority), and its subsequent absorption into a global socialist super-state. One mechanism allegedly used to achieve this are what Jones' terms *false-flag* operations – attacks which, although apparently by the enemy, are in fact by the home power. Two films responding to the attacks of 11 September 2001, his own *9-11: The Road to Tyranny* (2002), and Dylan Avery's *Loose Change: Final Cut* (2007), which he co-produced, argued that the attacks were false-flag actions carried out in order to pass the Patriot Act to give the president (and therefore the NWO) the power to act without the approval of the Senate or House, and for citizens to be held indefinitely without charge. Indeed, his on-air accusations of Bush's complicity in the 9-11 attacks, made on the day, led to him losing syndication on a number of radio stations (Zaitchik 2011).

Jones became more widely known in the conspiracist milieu after he and an assistant covertly entered Bohemian Grove, a 2,700-acre private camping ground in California belonging to an exclusive club made up of some of the world's most powerful politicians and businessmen. His footage of the opening ceremony, known as 'The Cremation of Care', which he claimed shows a Satanic ritual including a mock human sacrifice before an enormous owl statue representing Moloch, was widely disseminated on the Internet (Ronson 2001: 301–37). His rise was further helped by his relentless courting of celebrities, with country singer

Willie Nelson, rapper KRS-1 and former wrestler and Governor of Minnesota Jesse Ventura having appeared on his radio show or in his movies. Given that he had previously called him a 'con-man' (Ronson 2001: 86), the frequency with which Icke appears on his show may also be considered as taking advantage of his notoriety. Most recently, Charlie Sheen's public breakdown, which led to his being fired from the popular CBS show *Two and a Half Men*, began during his interview on the Alex Jones Show broadcast on 24 February 2011 (Pilkington 2011).

Alex Jones' Use of Prophecy

Jones' tone is that of a southern preacher, capable of rising to a fever-pitched, impassioned rant. At other times, he evokes the embattled messiah of Matthew's Gospel; 'People laughed at us, and now it's all coming true. Even though I'm sick of doing this, I do it anyway. Somebody's got to do this' (Kay 2011: 18). He played a preacher in two Richard Linklater films, *Waking Life* (2001) and his adaptation of Philip K. Dick's *A Scanner Darkly* (2006), in which he rants into a bullhorn before being bundled into an unmarked car.

Jones is at the more lucid end of the conspiracist spectrum, eschewing discussions of UFOs, crop circles or paranormal phenomena, and the use of channelled sources *à la* Icke and others. His claims are generally referenced with mainstream media sources, albeit filtered through his particular world-view. In the typology presented by Barkun in this volume (Chapter 2), Jones would be a prophet of the second type who discovers 'signs of the times' in the events of the day. But in order to be seen as a successful prophet, Jones' predictions are re-interpreted and re-prioritised on an on-going basis. I will demonstrate this by examining two of his apparently successful prophecies; the 9-11 attacks on the World Trade Center and Pentagon, and the present (2008 onwards) financial collapse.

The claim is frequently made by Jones and his followers that he 'predicted 9-11' (Kay 2011: 17). Like many of Jones' interpretations, this is not *strictly* accurate. The following transcript is from the broadcast in question, on 25 July 2001:

> America is the shining jewel the globalists want to bring down, and they will use terrorism as the pretext to get it done … Call the White House, tell them we know the government's planning terrorism, we know Oklahoma City and the Trade Center were terrorism, we know the Joint Chiefs of Staff wanted to blow up airliners … If you do it, we're going to blame you, 'cos we know who's up to it. Or if you let some terrorist group do it, like the World Trade Center, we'll know who to blame.[6]

---

6   http://www.youtube.com/watch?v=R_foQofbDnQ (accessed: 19 December 2011).

Jones' prediction, then, is of an imminent (though not date-specific) false-flag attack on the US, possibly involving the blowing up of US planes, and likely blamed on Osama Bin Laden. His references to the World Trade Center, however, are to the 1993 bombing as an example of a previously occurring false-flag attack, not the nature of the predicted attack. An attack did happen that autumn, for which Bin Laden was blamed; that much is true, but nothing else can be taken as correct, however, unless one accepts *a priori* that the attacks were a false-flag operation. To those who believe that Bin Laden was indeed responsible for the attack, Jones' prophecy was a failure. Therefore, to suggest that the prophecy is evidence that 9-11 was a false-flag attack, as Jones does, is a logical fallacy. Nevertheless, this example demonstrates that Jones is prepared to re-interpret his own words in order to be seen as having prophesied the attacks.

Another example of Jones' re-interpretation is to be found in the prophecies made in his 2009 film, *Fall of the Republic, Vol. 1: The Presidency of Barack H. Obama*. In late 2011, prisonplanet.com included a news story intended to remind readers of how

> the crucial issues covered in it – the bankrupting of the U.S. economy by offshore banksters and the unswerving implementation of a scientific dictatorship – are now coming to pass as Jones predicted in 2009.[7]

The film argues that Obama is the agent of a globalist elite whose aim is to 'destroy national sovereignty and individual independence' (Jones 2009). He outlines the Obama administration's close links to Wall Street, and argues that despite a campaign predicated on the slogan 'Change', Obama has continued or even amplified the policies of his Republican predecessor, George W. Bush, including extending the Patriot Act and continuing the incarceration without charge of the inmates at Guantanamo Bay. Obama's intention, Jones argues, is to continue the transfer of US power and wealth into the hands of off-shore international banks, owned by the global elite. The second half of the film outlines this in some detail, particularly in regards to the North American Free Trade Agreement (NAFTA) and global warming, which Jones believes is a myth created in order to implement new forms of taxation. Ultimately, he predicts that the present economic crash will 'make way for a global currency and a new bank of the world' (2009).

Again, the success of Jones' prophecies depend largely on whether you agree with him to start with. The US economy has not, to date (2012), been declared bankrupt or had its credit rating downgraded, nor has a global currency been put in place. The success claims of his prediction of a 'scientific dictatorship' can only be considered in any way accurate with reference to events in Europe, specifically the installation of unelected 'technocrat' leaders in Spain and Italy (Campbell 2011).

---

[7]   http://www.prisonplanet.com/watch-alex-jones-landmark-documentary-fall-of-the-republic-in-hq-free-online.html (accessed: 14 December 2011).

Again, we see that Jones is willing to exaggerate his prophetic 'successes' and de-emphasise his inaccuracies in order to portray himself as a successful prophet.

Jones' prophecy is strongly resilient to time; indeed, he's been making generally the same predictions since his career began in 1995. His broadcasts tell his audience on a daily basis that today is the worst things have been, and the New World Order takeover is kicking into a higher gear; for example, at the end of 2011, Jones' website declared that now 'the mega-banking elite switches into overdrive to implement their world government totalitarian system'.[8] Yet he made essentially the same claim in his first film, *America: Destroyed by Design* in 1998. Despite the fact that the only prophetic successes he can claim are relatively minor and, as we have seen, tenuous, his prophecy rolls on.

For many, Jones' vision of the imminent enslavement of the many by the few will seem pessimistic in the extreme. It is tempered, however, by a more hopeful narrative concerning a developing 'global awakening'. Jones interprets his growing audience, the increasing prominence of conspiracist narratives in mainstream media and recent events (2011–12) including the Arab Spring and the worldwide Occupy movement, as signs of an acceleration in the numbers of those 'waking up' to the globalist conspiracy:

> We'd like to present an overview of issues demonstrating that all is not lost. Just the opposite, in fact. The powers-that-be have admitted that they are scrambling for purchase amid humanity's global awakening. This new knowledge has led to an increasing number of people being exposed to alternative information that questions the official version of events, and the underlying secret mechanisms of control. This worldwide wake-up call has led to a great many conspiracy theories becoming conspiracy facts.[9]

Introducing David Icke on his radio show in late 2011, he said: 'David Icke, ladies and gentlemen, on how we're winning, how we're going to win, how the false reality is being lifted, the curtain is being lifted, and we are going to win. Resistance is victory.'[10]

It seems that, for Jones, we are always living in the end times, where it is simultaneously the critical moment for both the conspirators' plans and the cusp of the 'global awakening'. As such, his work consists of what I call *rolling prophecy*, in which his prophecies are being updated, reinterpreted and replaced on a daily basis. Rolling prophecy allows Jones to emphasise apparently successful

---

8 http://www.prisonplanet.com/alexs-final-thoughts-on-this-christmas-weekend.html (accessed: 29 December 2011).

9 http://www.prisonplanet.com/a-21-truth-salute-to-activists-and-the-alternative-media-the-journey-from-conspiracy-theory-to-conspiracy-fact.html, 3 August 2011 (accessed: 22 December 2011).

10 http://www.davidicke.com/headlines/52232-twenty-minutes-with-david-icke-the-alex-jones-show-humanity-rise-like-lions (accessed: 2 January 2012).

prophecies while de-emphasising the unsuccessful, and thus appear as a successful prophet. The apparent success of his prophecies about 9-11 and Obama lead his audience to give credence to his larger predictions about a coming totalitarian global super-state, despite their logical failings. Jones' prophetic failures, however, such as the prediction of imminent attack on Iran in *Endgame*, are quickly and quietly dropped. Jones' rolling prophecy thus remains in a liminal state, neither proven nor disproven. The upshot of this is that the cognitive dissonance produced when date-specific prophecies fail is avoided.

What Is the Appeal of Jones' Prophecy?

While prophecy is a prominent narrative in southern states, and Texas particularly (Boyer 1992: 13), it would be a mistake to lay responsibility for Jones' prophetic persona entirely on his Baptist upbringing. There is a practical point to his prophesying; when he claims that he predicted 9-11, or that Obama would win the election, he is establishing his authority in the conspiracist milieu. The perceived success of prophecies discussed above brought him to the attention of a broader audience. Jones promotes himself as a man who is so 'in the know' that he knows what's coming, therefore validating his overarching conspiracist worldview. If Jones can convince the audience that he is always right, and knows what's going on, he increases his authority and therefore his market share. While I do not suggest that Jones is deliberately using prophecy to raise advertising revenue, it is undeniable that Jones is a canny self-promoter, as demonstrated by his above-noted courting of celebrities. His website Infowars.com has several employees and premises including a TV studio, and Jones is estimated to be personally worth $5 million.[11]

The value of Jones' prophecy for his audience, however, seems less obvious. What do people gain from believing in eschatological conspiracy theories? After all, most of Alex Jones' listeners haven't retreated to cabins in the mountains and become fully-fledged survivalists.[12] Damian Thompson has argued that such high personal investment in inherently risky date-specific prophecies is, for most people, simply not cost-effective (2005: 26–7). He suggests this is the reason why date-specific 'predictive' millennialism has been largely supplanted by 'explanatory' millennialism, in which millennial narratives are used to analyse the events of the present day (2005: 26–7). Explanatory millennialism requires considerably

---

[11]   http://www.therichest.org/celebnetworth/celeb/radio-personality/alex-jones-net-worth/ (accessed: 14 April 2012).

[12]   Intriguingly, several media outlets have recently carried pieces on the growth of a class of urban and middle-class survivalists, calling themselves 'preppers'. Although their motivations are the same – to survive the collapse of civilisation – their activities tend to involve buying long-term storable food and water purification systems, rather than stockpiling weaponry and building armoured bunkers (Bennett 2009).

less investment, as its interpretations of events is constantly shifting and therefore avoids the threat of the failure of a date-specific prophecy (2005: 31). Importantly, explanatory millennialism is intended 'not to provoke action but to make sense of the present moment in terms of an overarching scheme of history' (2005: 27). It is therefore a form of social critique.

Jones' conspiracist narrative, then, is a secular form of explanatory millennialism, offering 'a strikingly comprehensive critique of contemporary mass society as dehumanising and dangerously centralized' (Boyer 1992: 254). His prophecies of a 'nightmare future' can be seen as a *reductio ad absurdum*, describing what the present situation would result in if allowed to continue unchecked. For his audience, this allows for the expression of a critique of the impersonal and unassailable structures of modern global capitalist society from which they may feel disenfranchised (Goodrick-Clarke 2002: 299).

Jones' conspiracism is a detailed description of why life for his audience and himself is not fair or deserved – specifically, because a small elite are secretly oppressing the masses. To put it simply, the appeal of conspiracist prophecy is that it presents a popular theodicy which addresses the perceived inequalities of contemporary society. A theodicy, simply defined, is an explanation of the existence of evil in the world and its uneven distribution, and is generally agreed to be one of the primary benefits of religions (Thompson 2005: 15). Colin Campbell summarised the function of a theodicy thus: 'they should tell people what to think and feel about the world and about themselves, on what basis their own experience of life – and indeed existence in general – is "fair" or "deserved", and if predominantly undesirable, can be, or will be, "compensated for" in due course' (2001: 76).

Jones' more millenarian prophecies of 'global awakening' suggest how this unfairness will be compensated for: through the overthrowing of the global elite and the re-enfranchisement of the individual. Thus the conspiracist prophecy of Jones and others can be understood, at least in part, as an expression of Utopian ideals of how a more equal world might look (Fenster 1999: 225). Indeed, many of Jones' audience may see his actions as a form of resistance, helping to eventually avert these catastrophic visions of the future by changing the present.

Conclusion

From an examination of two of Jones' prophecies, I have demonstrated how prophecy operates in the conspiracist milieu. Rolling prophecy is used to create and sustain the impression of successful prophecy, while avoiding the cognitive dissonance of failed prophecy. Jones' rolling prophecy allows his prophecy to function primarily as a critique of the present day. Thus millenarian conspiracism functions primarily as a popular theodicy, explaining perceived social inequalities, and placing the blame for the suffering of its subscribers with the conspirators of the NWO.

Scholars generally think of prophecy as the currency of small, tightly-knit religious groups, but this chapter has shown that it also operates in larger, more diffuse and secular contexts. With several conspiracist motifs presently at the forefront of popular political debate in the US and worldwide, Alex Jones and other millenarian conspiracists may already have influenced political discourse, and so understanding their appeal is of considerable importance. We are always living in the end times, but these prophecies of the future have much to tell us about our own times.

References

Allen, G. and Abraham, L. 1971. *None Dare Call It Conspiracy*. Rossmore, CA: Concord Press.

Avery, D. (dir.) 2007. *Loose Change: Final Cut*.

Barkun, M. 2003. *A Culture of Conspiracy: Apocalyptic Visions in Contemporary America*. Berkeley and Los Angeles, CA and London: University of California Press.

Bartlett, J. and Miller, C. 2010. *The Power of Unreason: Conspiracy Theories, Extremism and Counter-Terrorism*. London: DEMOS.

Bennett, J. 2009. Survivalism Lite. *Newsweek*, 27 December [Online]. Available at: http://www.thedailybeast.com/newsweek/2009/12/27/survivalism-lite.html [accessed: 2 January 2012].

Boyer, P.S. 1992. *When Time Shall Be No More: Prophecy Belief in Modern American Culture*. Cambridge, MA: Belknap Press of Harvard University Press.

Campbell, C. 2001. A New Age Theodicy for a New Age, in *Peter Berger and the Study of Religion*, edited by L. Woodhead with P. Heelas and D. Martin. London and New York: Routledge, 73–85.

Campbell, M. 2011. Unelected Technocrat Saviours Face First Test. *The Sunday Times*, 20 November [Online]. Available at: http://www.thesundaytimes.co.uk/sto/news/world_news/Europe/article825476.ece [accessed: 22 December 2011].

Coady, D. 2007a. Introduction: Conspiracy Theories. *Episteme: A Journal of Social Epistemology*, 4, 131–4.

———. 2007b. Are Conspiracy Theorists Irrational? *Episteme: A Journal of Social Epistemology*, 4, 193–204.

Cohn, N. 1970. *The Pursuit of the Millennium: Revolutionary Millenarians and Mystical Anarchists of the Middle Ages*. New York: Oxford University Press.

Fenster, M. 1999. *Conspiracy Theories: Secrecy and Power in American Culture*. Minneapolis, MN and London: University of Minnesota Press.

Goodrick-Clarke, N. 2002. *Black Sun: Aryan Cults, Esoteric Nazism and the Politics of Identity*. New York and London: New York University Press.

Hofstadter, R. 1964. The Paranoid Style in American Politics. *Harper's Magazine*, November, 77–86.

Jones, A. (dir.) 1998. *America: Destroyed by Design*.

——. (dir.) 2002. *9-11: The Road to Tyranny*.

——. (dir.) 2007. *Endgame*.

——. (dir.) 2009. *Fall of the Republic, Vol. 1: The Presidency of Barack H. Obama*.

Kay, J. 2011. *Among the Truthers: A Journey through America's Growing Conspiracist Underground*. New York: HarperCollins.

Knight, P. 2000. *Conspiracy Culture: From Kennedy to The X-Files*. London and New York: Routledge.

Landes, R. 2006. Millenarianism and the Dynamics of Apocalyptic Time, in *Expecting the End: Millennialism in Social and Historical Context*, edited by K.G.C. Newport and C. Gribben. Waco, TX: Baylor University Press.

Levy, N. 2007. Radically Socialized Knowledge and Conspiracy Theories. *Episteme: A Journal of Social Epistemology*, 4, 181–92.

Linklater, R. (dir.) 2001. *Waking Life*.

——. (dir.) 2006. *A Scanner Darkly*.

Palmer, S. 2004. *Aliens Adored: Raël's UFO Religion*. New Brunswick, NJ and London: Rutgers University Press.

Partridge, C. 2005. *The Re-Enchantment of the West*, Vol. 2. London: T&T Clark.

Pigden, C. 2007. Conspiracy Theories and the Conventional Wisdom. *Episteme: A Journal of Social Epistemology*, 4(2), 219–32.

Pilkington, E. 2011. Two and a Half Men Axed after Rant Leaves Sheen Looking a Proper Charlie. *The Guardian*, 25 February [Online]. Available at: http://www.guardian.co.uk/culture/2011/feb/25/two-and-a-half-men-sheen-charlie [accessed: 2 February 2012].

Robertson, P. 1991. *The New World Order*. Dallas, TX: Word Publications.

Ronson, J. 2001. *THEM: Adventures with Extremists*. London: Picador.

Schoenwald, J. 2001. *A Time for Choosing: The Rise of Modern American Conservatism*. New York: Oxford University Press.

Stone, B.S. 1974. The John Birch Society: A Profile. *Journal of Politics*, 36(1), 184–97.

Thompson, D. 2005. *Waiting for Antichrist: Charisma and Apocalypse in a Pentecostal Church*. New York and Oxford: Oxford University Press.

Ward, C. and Voas, D. 2011. The Emergence of Conspirituality. *Journal of Contemporary Religion*, 26, 103–21.

Weber, T.P. 1979. *Living in the Shadow of the Second Coming: American Premillennialism 1875–1925*. New York and Oxford: Oxford University Press.

Wilcox, C. 1988. Sources of Support for the Old Right: A Comparison of the John Birch Society and the Christian Anti-Communism Crusade. *Social Science History*, 12(4) (Winter), 429–49.

Zaitchik, A. 2011. Meet Alex Jones. *Rolling Stone*, 17 March [Online]. Available at: http://www.rollingstone.com/politics/news/talk-radios-alex-jones-the-most-paranoid-man-in-america-20110302 [accessed: 12 December 2011].

PART IV
2012 Prophecies

The final section of this book is comprised of four chapters which focus on a recent and relatively pervasive milieu of prophecies: those interpretations of the Mayan calendar which suggest that 'something big' is going to happen on 21 December 2012[1] whether this be the end of the world, a natural or planetary event, or a spiritual transformation/elevation of consciousness. Interest in this group of prophecies ranges from individuals (who may or may not be part of a wider group) who are invested in the belief and are making preparations for it, to individuals who explore the ideas online but otherwise make no changes in behaviour, to its use in popular media forms such as books, television documentaries, Hollywood movies and advertising campaigns.[2]

Andrew Fergus Wilson opens this section with an analysis of both the origins of the 2012 prophecies (providing invaluable descriptions of the work of the two key authors in the 2012 field, Terence McKenna and José Argüelles) and their pervasiveness in contemporary popular culture. He argues that the '2012 industry' which has moved into mainstream culture is a good illustration of continued popular fascination with end time prophecies, which provide a discursive space for the exploration of popular utopian and dystopian hopes and fears. Such hopes and fears transcend a religious/secular dichotomy he argues, although 'secular'/

---

[1]   Other dates have been suggested as marking the end of the Mayan calendar including 23 December 2012 (to take into account an adjustment for GMT) and 28 October 2011. The latter date is that given by the Swedish Mayan enthusiast Carl Johan Calleman, website at http://www.calleman.com/ (accessed: 25 June 2012), who argues that the universe is now in a state of 'unity consciousness', and the Arab Spring, the collapse of the financial institutions and the 'Occupy Movement' are all taken as evidence.

[2]   Examples from the world of advertising include Lynx deodorant (an advert for Lynx 2012: The Final Edition, screened in 2011, shows a man building a wooden ark and The Lynx Effect website includes an overview of 2012 prophecies – see http://www.lynxeffect.com/uk/blog/2011/12/09/2012-the-facts/ [accessed: 25 June 2012]) and General Motor's advert for the Chevy Silverado truck shown surviving the 2012 apocalypse, screened at the American Super Bowl in February 2012. According to media articles, the Super Bowl provides American TV's most valuable advertising time with an audience of around 100 million people and at a cost to advertisers of $3.5 million for a 30-second advert. See http://www.reuters.com/article/2012/02/06/us-superbowl-advertising-idUSTRE8150SO20120206 (accessed: 25 June 2012).

scientific prophecies tend to focus on dystopia whilst religious/spiritual prophecies tend to focus on the utopian outcome, for believers at least. 2012 prophecies, he notes, emerge from what has been termed the 'New Age', which itself is an amalgam of ideas from the 'cultic milieu', from both religious and secular sources, and yet they also transcend the 'New Age'. 2012 prophecies must thus be placed in the wider context of an existing field of apocalyptic prophetic activity.

In Chapter 17, astrophysicist Kristine Larsen, provides seven reasons why the world won't end in December 2012. From mid 2007 an email purporting to give seven reasons why the world would end in December 2012 began circulating widely as one person after another 'forwarded' it to many of the individuals in their address book. Larsen first traces the origins of this 'viral email' to a specific post on an Internet 'forum' dating from May 2007. Larsen traces some of the justifications for the end of the world in 2012 listed in this document – from the Mayan calendar to the Book of Revelation, to ideas drawn from science such as sunspots and magnetic pole reversal – before debunking each reason as part of her mission to dampen not only what she terms the '2012 apocalypse hysteria' but also the proliferation of 'bad science' in society in general, a mission which is furthered in her participation in the 2012hoax.org website. Larsen, in her analysis of forum-posts in response to the email, is concerned not only by those who accept the email but also by those who attempt to debunk it whilst themselves using 'bad science'. She argues that 'science illiteracy', fuelled by reliance on the Internet as a source of scientific information, is the wider problem of which the '2012 apocalypse hoax' is an example.

Chapter 18 provides a voice from the opposite end of the spectrum written as it is by a 2012 'believer'. Suzanne Rough is the UK-based founder of an astrology school called the DK Foundation. Her work has grown out of the Theosophical writings of Alice Bailey, astrology, and from contact with Ascended Masters (which she understands as a level and quality of awareness) including Djwal Khul. Rough's beliefs are not derived from an interpretation of the Mayan calendar; it is from the Master Kuthumi that Rough received information about the planetary transformation which she believed would take place on 17–18 December 2012. This information is published as the 'Red Letters' on the DK Foundation's website (www.dkfoundation.co.uk). In a footnote, Rough explains that this transformation will involve an immersion of the planet in water, likened to a baptism. The focus of the chapter, however, is not on the specifics of the event but on the wider beliefs underpinning it. Rough explains her understanding of the 'hylozoic Universe', the idea that the Universe is comprised of seven different but interconnected worlds, each with their own consciousness, destiny and energy levels transmitted to the worlds above and below. She explains that the events in December 2012 will be a necessary transmission of energy from mankind (world six) to our planet in the fifth world, on to world four, the world of the sun. This is necessary she argues as, to put it crudely, mankind has not been pulling its weight by only using our lower *chakras*, and so is in an energy debt. December 2012, she argues, is not about mankind but is about the planet, which has to off-load a weight of unproductive humanity in order to become energy efficient. From mid-December 2012, Rough was describing on her website the focus on specific catastrophic events in 2012 as 'a myth for our time' and emphases that '[Myths] give us our goals, supply the map, and give us the strength to undertake the journey.' In January 2013, Rough was still promoting the veracity of all courses of action the ascended masters advised.

The section closes with Jean-François Mayer's chapter about 2012 prophecies which draws on ethnographic fieldwork conducted in Switzerland in 2011. Mayer, like Wilson, provides descriptive information about the origins of 2012 in the 'cultic milieu', covering the work of Argüelles and McKenna, but unlike Wilson, he focuses on 2012 as a re-emergence of a millennial theme in the 'New Age'. Mayer argues that an analysis of 2012 prophecies must situate them within the wider cultic milieu and also that the prophecies are a good illustration of the way that beliefs circulate in alternative spirituality networks. He argues not only that the core audience for 2012 beliefs are already familiar with the themes of the cultic milieu but also that 'Authors and speakers incorporate the 2012 theme into an already existing, more general discourse, with a cumulative effect' (page 267). Furthermore, he suggests, many authors and groups emphasise the non-apocalyptic side of 2012, the belief that it is but one significant date in a much wider transformatory period. He thus argues that 2012 beliefs are adopted in a flexible way; they can be incorporated into a variety of pre-existing messages and can be used to help to launch new players on the alternative religious scene. But for the majority of authors and groups, 2012 prophecies are just one additional element rather than a key component of their belief system. This could be a contributory factor to limiting the impact of prophetic failure, he suggests.

The issue of prophetic failure, and more especially, the issue of why prophecies will persist, is taken up again in the concluding chapter written by J. Gordon Melton.

Chapter 16

From Mushrooms to the Stars: 2012 and the Apocalyptic Milieu

Andrew Fergus Wilson

2012 and the Beginnings of the End Date?

The '2012 industry' continues apace and variations on the 2012 theme proliferate but they do so within the context of an existing field of prophetic activity. Despite a number of core texts which, in general terms, shape the scope of 2012 apocalyptic prophecy it is notable that a selection of narratival effects associated with earlier apocalyptic discourse formation are present within 2012 apocalyptic prophecy. This chapter, then, is an attempt to demonstrate the embeddedness of 2012 discourse within existing currents of apocalyptic prophecy and also argues the case for an 'apocalyptic milieu' which intersects a variety of North American and European Christian beliefs, popular culture and emerging religious formations.

In 1971, still enraptured with the hippie ideals of 1960s California, Terence McKenna, his brother Dennis and a small band of fellow travellers, embarked on a journey into fresh fields of physical and mental space. Travelling to La Chorerra in Amazonian Columbia in search of new psychedelic experiences they, 'were involved, [Terence McKenna] imagined, in a deep jungle search for … plants containing the orally active drug di-methyltryptamine (or DMT) and the psychedelic brew ayahuasca … the patterns of their use, which were unique to the Amazon jungles, had not been fully studied' (McKenna 1993: 2–3). With a desire to produce a visionary anthropology which McKenna termed 'ethnobotany', they sought innovative perspectives on the relationship between humans, consciousness, worship and psychoactive natural substances. In the midst of this journey, they experienced a series of revelations which they believed afforded them new understandings of history and its progress.

After their return, Terence revealed his theory of the zero time wave (McKenna and McKenna 1975), a cyclical conception of history which described the presence of 'novelty' in the world; 'Time is seen as the ebb and flow of two opposed qualities: novelty versus habit, or density of connectedness versus disorder' (McKenna and McKenna 1993: 171). Upon returning to California he became transported by a series of revelatory theories based on his jungle experiences, his brother Dennis' mathematical knowledge and contemplation of the *I Ching*. McKenna describes a conception of history in which progress is spurred by successive, regular waves of 'novelty'; 'These waves are discrete periods of change … I came to realize that the internal logic of the timewaves strongly implied a termination of normal time and an end to ordinary history' (1993: 161). He suggested that at a number of rare but predictable points in history a heightened intensification of the flow of novelty would produce a dramatic alteration of human consciousness. This would usher in a new phase in human history, new forms of thought would emerge and humanity would be transformed; writing in the second half of the twentieth century he understood human history to be involved in, 'a long cascade into greater and greater novelty that reaches its culmination early in the twenty-first century' (1993: 161).

These revelations of the time wave concept are at the heart of one strand of the 2012 phenomenon and McKenna also provided inspiration to the author of the other central strand, José Argüelles' interpretation of the Mayan calendar: 'My meeting with Terence McKenna ... contributed greatly to this understanding of the Mayan factor ... So it was that I threw myself with renewed abandon into the Mayan Factor' (Argüelles 1996: 39). Although initially McKenna did not identify a clear date beyond the vague allusion to a point 'early in the twenty-first century', according to the second edition of *The Invisible Landscape*, and also in popular belief, Friday 21 December 2012 is one of those points and humanity is rushing towards a dramatic transformation. In its most basic structure this account fits a recognisable pattern of millenarian prophecy: a visionary or seer returns from a spiritualised space (whether it be a 'holy place' or mental construct) with a message of a soon-to-come moment in which humanity will experience profound and irreversible change in material and mental life. This transformative journey and redemptive promise is a familiar refrain and one which is used to offer hope to disparate communities of believers from across the spectrum of faiths, from the mainstream and diverse splinters and schisms of the world religions to small-scale groups of believers awaiting a variety of hidden masters, redeemers and/or paradisiacal living.[1] Although associated with religious belief it should be noted that secular beliefs can also be understood within this apocalyptic framework. For instance, the inherent promise of Marxism is founded upon a teleology that has a strong whiff of the eschatological about it: a paradise on Earth (the dictatorship of the proletariat) will follow a period of cataclysmic change (revolution) brought about by selected 'messengers' (the vanguard party). So, for example, Hall (2009), Zimdars-Swartz and Zimdars-Swartz (2000) and Baumgartner (1999) consider the millenarian aspects of Marx whilst other writers also look at the manner in which, say, environmentalism can be understood as an apocalyptic belief (Lee 1995) or the widespread fear of nuclear war during the 1970s and 1980s (Beres 1980, Wojcik 1997). With the exception of Marxist utopian hopes, secular apocalyptic

---

[1]   Continuum's three-volume set *The Encyclopedia of Apocalypticism* gives some indication of the global range and diversity of apocalyptic beliefs whilst also demonstrating the continuities and discontinuities between apocalyptic narratives over the course of the last three millennia (Collins 2000, McGinn 2000, Stein 2000).

prophecy tends to be dystopian whereas faith-based prophecies of the end tend to have utopian outcomes for 'the faithful'.

2012 prophecy is rooted within ideas, attitudes and beliefs that tend to be associated with New Age belief and tends towards a utopian outcome with human consciousness having evolved and with this providing the basis for a coming golden age. The two primary sources of 2012 prophecy – Terence McKenna's time wave zero date and José Argüelles' reading of the Mayan calendar – are rooted in New Age tendencies and beliefs. Both suggest the kind of radical transformation that is implicit in what Paul Heelas (1996) describes as the spiritually purist and the counter-cultural tendencies within New Age belief. Being primarily syncretic in nature the New Age absorbs elements of faith traditions and secular beliefs and knowledge.

In general terms, the threads which form the weft and weave of the New Age can be characterised as 'stigmatised knowledge', to use Michael Barkun's formulation (Barkun 2003), that is to say beliefs and insights that are seen to have been suppressed, ignored or rejected by conventional wisdom. Whilst Barkun developed this idea to build upon Colin Campbell's (1972) earlier concept of the 'cultic milieu' it should be considered that the cultic milieu still has relevance to emergent forms of non-traditional religiosity in general and to 2012 prophecy in particular (see also Jean-François Mayer, Chapter 19, this volume). The cultic milieu describes the sharing and spread of new, or re-discovered, forms of stigmatised knowledge amongst an ever-shifting body of 'spiritual seekers' who consume, syncretise and constantly renew and disseminate the ideas they encounter. Whilst their origins can be traced to the cultic milieu, it is argued here that the 2012 prophecies are not wholly distinct from apocalyptic prophecy as a whole.

2012 in the Soil of American Apocalyptic Millennialism

The Western world has seen its history shaped, to a large extent, by Judeo-Christian beliefs and values. Until relatively recently the expectation of the fulfilment of biblical prophecy was a prevailing motif within culture and belief across Europe and beyond. Norman Cohn (1957) inspired academic work looking at populist apocalyptic belief with his detailed study of millennial prophecy and chiliastic uprisings in Europe during the Middle Ages. Such beliefs were not limited to the dispossessed of the European Middle Ages; amidst the early stirrings of modernity and towards the end of the Middle Ages, the New World was encountered by European explorers partially inspired by the hope of discovering allies with whom to defeat an Ottoman empire that was identified with the Antichrist of Revelation (Baumgartner 1999). Christopher Columbus was a collector of millennial prophecies and believed he was engaged in God's work, fulfilling prophecy as, 'the messenger of the new heaven and the new earth of which [God] spoke in the Apocalypse of St. John ... and he showed me the spot where to find it' (Baumgartner 1999: 120).

A century and a half later, Puritan settlers fleeing persecution in England brought radical millennial visions to the northern territories of the American continent. In seeking to escape the perceived tyranny of a Europe which they condemned for its intolerance towards their beliefs, their faith-based exile provided the inspiration from which a strong, geographically rooted, millennial desire could be drawn. Following an initial wave of apocalyptic preachers such as the Mather family and Samuel Danforth in New England, millennial discourse expanded along the Atlantic coast of North America during the eighteenth century and has ebbed and flowed within and across the US thereafter (see, for instance, Boyer 1992, Wojcik 1997).

With a post-aboriginal origin myth into which millennial prophecy is woven, the US has shown itself to be particularly prone to a continued susceptibility to belief in the impending immanentisation of the Christian eschaton. Although the recent doomsday prophet Harold Camping provides an example of the way in which Christian prophecy has, to some extent, fallen onto a less than fully accepting public ear it should be remembered that relatively recent US presidents such as John F. Kennedy and Ronald Reagan have drawn upon the symbolism of John Winthrop's 1630 'City on the Hill' speech. In each instance the America described is one to which other nations look for example just as the New Jerusalem of Revelation 21 is illuminated by God's light and leads the world: 'the nations of them which are saved shall walk in the light of it' (Revelation 21:24). Indeed, it has been argued by Philip Jenkins that the American religious mainstream, 'remains what it has been since colonial times: a fundamentalist evangelicism with powerful millenarian strands' (Jenkins 2000: 5).

Just as Kennedy's Catholicism was not immune to the millenarian pull at the heart of American spiritual life, it is possible to see the extent to which an apocalyptic outlook has shaded numerous cultural expressions within the US. Whilst there is a very strong tradition of writing the apocalypse and the millennium into overtly Christian literature, film and other cultural forms it is also the case that secular popular culture has adopted apocalyptic tropes which proceed from and transform the Christian millennial tradition whilst retaining much of the imagery and structure of apocalyptic prophecy. This is a commonplace stance within much academic literature and rightly so for the fictional depiction of a wide variety of utopian and dystopian pre-, post- and mid-apocalyptic scenarios has been the basis of many popular culture texts (Forbes and Kilde 2004, Gribben 2009). The flow of ideas is not straightforwardly unidirectional and secular themes can feed back into religious visions of the end just as secular texts may produce worldly variations on religious end time stories.

Conrad Ostwalt (1998) makes a strong case for the extent to which popular culture reflects an ongoing fascination with apocalyptic narratives but in a form that is more suited to a culture in which secularisation plays an increasingly powerful role, '[S]ecularization has not done away with the apocalyptic consciousness.

Rather it has assisted in creating a new apocalyptic myth, one that is more palatable to contemporary, popular culture' (Oswalt 1998: §19). Secular and religious fictions both spin around the apocalyptic centrifugal centre, their paths crossing endlessly. The receptivity to apocalyptic prophecy in, and of, the US is one of the currents in which 2012 prophecy emerges. Both genuinely held beliefs regarding a fast approaching end times and works of the imagination constitute an 'apocalyptic milieu' which permeates American cultural and spiritual life. The apocalyptic milieu is one that is well established and provides the intertextual framework in which the 2012 prophecies are rendered meaningful.

The New Age Milieu, 'Occulture' and the Spread of 2012 Themes

Christian prophecy is an on-going feature of American culture in general but there has also been a flourishing of prophecies which have emerged from the so-called New Age or 'cultic milieu' which has prospered in post-Second World War America, Europe and as the twentieth century closed, amongst cosmopolitan populations worldwide. Although indebted to nineteenth-century precedents such as Theosophy and currents of Victorian esotericism, the New Age flourished during the latter half of the twentieth century. It is deeply syncretic in nature and borrows from and blends a range of religious and spiritual beliefs. This constant absorption of diverse beliefs means that it is peculiarly open to new developments but it also remains, in essence, concerned with the development of a deep inner spirituality although, as Heelas suggests, this is manifest across a broad spectrum from world rejecting to world affirming (Heelas 1996, see also Sutcliffe 2003 on the limitations of the term 'New Age'). Whilst the 2012 prophecies are generally recognised to have their basis in the writing of Terrence McKenna and José Argüelles, their substance has undergone numerous reinventions as they have been embraced and re-situated in a variety of spiritual frameworks within the broad, loose church of the New Age.

The manner in which Dorothy Martin's failed prophecies of the 1950s and her subsequent spiritual journey have been incorporated into several New Age understandings of the 2012 prophecies is typical of the manner in which ideas dormant within the cultic milieu can be re-invented and re-absorbed into dominant currents within the milieu. Over half a century prior to the current predictions of global cataclysm, Dorothy Martin (later Sister Thedra of the Association of Sananda and Samat Kumara) found fame of sorts as the source of a failed prophecy of the world's end on 21 December 1954. The prophecy was received in a series of psychic contacts between enlightened beings ('the Guardians') from the planet Clarion and Dorothy Martin during August 1954. It was claimed the world would be 'purified' by flooding before the formation of new land masses and the re-emergence of the lost continent of Mu. Humans who accepted and were responsive to the Clarion call would be saved by Guardians in UFOs. Two years later, in *When Prophecy Fails*, Leon Festinger, Henry Riecken and

Stanley Schachter renamed Dorothy Martin as Marian Keech and recounted the development of Martin's prophecy and the moment of its failure (Festinger et al. [1956] 2008). Framing the experience of Martin and her small group of followers in Festinger's idea of 'cognitive dissonance' they provided an influential study of apocalyptic belief and, importantly here, the circulatory discursive currents of the milieus from which those beliefs emerged. With a background that included involvement or interest in Dianetics, the I AM movement, post-Adamski UFO contact groups, psychic abilities and Theosophy, Dorothy Martin typifies many members of what was to become the New Age movement.

Whilst New Age syncretic tendencies are apparent in the mix of beliefs that formed the fertile ground from which her own grew, it is interesting to note that Dorothy Martin's principle contact amongst the Clarion Guardians, Sananda, was understood to be an ascended form of Jesus. Whilst this view of Jesus as an initiate of esoteric knowledge is present in Theosophy (Blavatsky [1938] 1952), the figure of Jesus-Sananda grew increasingly key to Martin as her channelling of messages from him developed; after her initial failed prophecy she published a pamphlet of messages from him which underlined not only her dedication to him but also Jesus-Sananda and the Guardians' continued concern for humanity (Martin 1962). The syncretic nature of the cultic milieu is apparent in the varied sources which contributed to Martin's beliefs and this is further underlined by the subsequent use of the messages that she channelled from Jesus-Sananda.

In turn Martin's messages resonated with others in this milieu; her messages are featured in Mark Amaru Pinkham's (2002) *The Truth Behind the Christ Myth: The Redemption of the Peacock Angel* as support for his thesis that the figure known as Jesus Christ (and Jesus-Sananda) is, in fact, Sanat Kumara, a Venusian master, and central figure in Theosophy and related spiritual movements. This link between Jesus-Sananda and Sanat Kumara is frequently cited as evidence of spiritually enlightened benign aliens with a protective and interventionist interest in humanity with a number of sources referring to Martin's claim that Jesus-Sananda introduced himself to her with the following words, 'My name is Esu Sananda Kumara.'[2] Amongst them is Alexandriah Stahr's, *Star Essenia – 2012 and Beyond* which claims to represent Ashtar Command Healing Division and to be 'sponsored by the Collective Christ: Lord Sananda, Commander Ashtar, The Ashtar – Solar Star Command (formerly known as The Ashtar Command, The Galactic Command and The Intergalactic Command), The Ascended Masters of Light and The Angels of Light' (Stahr 2009). Sananda is central here and it is Martin's version of Sananda that shapes the vision of work which is dedicated to 'preparation for Return of the Christ Vibration on Earth and the 2012 Planetary

---

[2]   For instance, the Wolf Lodge – Golden Braid native American ministry (http://www.wolflodge.org/), 'Joseph Almighty's Site – Firstborn Son of Almighty God' (http://josephalmighty.multiply.com/journal/item/642) and 'Amethyst's Garden's blog [sic]' (http://www.myspace.com/amethystsgarden/blog/308231975) (all accessed: 22 February 2012).

Ascension, now known as 13.13.13 Solar New Earth Reality Timeline' (Stahr 2009) and is authored by Rev. Alexandriah Stahr of the Star-Essence Temple. This short journey from Dorothy Martin's prophecy for 21 December 1954 to the set of prophecies converging on 21 December 2012 is illustrative of the circuitous, shared narratives of the cultic milieu and the tendency for this milieu to self-hybridise to such an extent that seminal texts can rapidly become secondary to emergent themes. This tendency is as true of the central works in 2012 prophecy as it is of other, less well known texts.

The link between the cultic milieu and the counterculture is strong. Both Partridge (2004) and Tramacchi (2000) describe the popularity of McKenna's shamanic anthropology with psychedelically spiritual ravers during the 1990s. With his roots in the psychedelic awakening of the 1960s but an active interest in ideas prevalent amongst later echoes of this moment, McKenna's appeal was cross-generational. He had a resonance with both the first wave of baby boomer 'spiritual seekers' (see, for example, Roof 1993) and to their children, both literal and spiritual. His idea of 'time wave zero' and the significance of 21 December 2012 found a twofold audience within the New Age milieu and what Christopher Partridge (2004) terms 'occulture', the complex tapestry woven by the warp and weft of occult themes through the serried texts of popular culture. As has been mentioned, McKenna's idea of time wave zero emerged from a period of intense experimentation with psilocybin mushrooms in the upper reaches of the Amazon rainforest and this has given his work a counter-cultural audience of the type described by Partridge.

Like McKenna, José Argüelles has significant connections to the late 1960s counterculture. A professor of art history at University of California, Davis in the early 1970s, Argüelles was a key figure behind the Whole Earth Festival and engaged in and drew inspiration from the same milieu as McKenna. The evidence that Argüelles draws on borrows from similar strands of 'stigmatised knowledge' to those employed by McKenna: the *I Ching* and UFO lore, in addition to the Book of Revelation and the source for which he is best known: the Mayan calendar (Argüelles 1987). The syncretic weave of Argüelles' text typifies a New Age approach to spiritual enlightenment and demonstrates the textual richness of the so-called Mayan prophecies. 'So-called' because although the Mayan Long Count calendar reaches the end of a significant cycle on the 21 December 2012 and although Argüelles has done a great deal to popularise this fact, the range of evidence that Argüelles offers and the range of ways in which the prophecy has been interpreted is too broad for the 2012 prophecy simply to be referred to as a 'Mayan' prophecy.

Certainly, Sitler (2006) is ready to point out that whilst a generalised apocalyptic current is present within a very few traditionalist Mayan communities, on the whole, currently living Mayans are being exposed to the 2012 date more by visiting New Age activists, celebrants, researchers and seekers than via tradition. As an inherited tradition, the current speculation fails to be definitively Mayan. The few academic treatments to consider the 2012 prophecy acknowledge the potential for archaeological evidence to point to the veracity of the 2012 date being the end of the 5,126 year Long Count (Sitler 2006: 25, 35, n. 4) but situate the current fascination with 21 December 2012 not with the Mayans, or even Mayanists such as Argüelles, but with the *I Ching* and hallucinogen-inspired Terence McKenna (Hannegraaff 2010), or with 1970s countercultural psychonauts in general: Hoopes rather dismissively wrote, 'If some assertions about 2012 sound as if they were imagined by people on drugs, it is because they were' (Hoopes 2011: 243). Hoopes also compares adherents of the 2012 prophecy with Creationists and cites a parallel, 'rejection of the "official" narratives ... and with them the rejection of academic authority' (Hoopes 2011: 246). This is certainly so and Hoopes is also right to suggest that, 'the 2012 phenomenon may be far more interesting as a window into our contemporary culture ... than for anything it reveals about the ancient Maya' (Hoopes 2011: 246). Unfortunately, he does not explore the relationship between these two statements and the extent to which the milieu from which 2012 prophetic discourse emerges is typified by rapidly hybridising and interwoven forms of 'stigmatised knowledge.'

Despite the central role in popularising and framing 2012 prophecy played by McKenna's zero timeline and Argüelles' popularisation of the Mayan calendrical cycles, the 2012 prophecies have developed beyond the concerns (if not outcomes) that McKenna and Argüelles describe. To a certain extent this was always an inevitable consequence of the adoption of their work within the New Age milieu. The narratival drift of 2012 prophecies away from the McKenna-Argüelles axis around which the core prophecies orbit is, in some instances quite marked with other prophecies being combined with their work to produce entirely novel combinations. A strong example would be the way in which Zecharia Sitchin's (1976) pseudo-astronomical prediction of the discovery of a lost planet, Nibiru, became combined with messages channelled from the binary star system Zeta Reticula by Nancy Lieder (1996). Sitchin suggested in a series of books that the planet Nibiru orbits the Sun in an elliptical orbit which brings it into the inner Solar System every 3,500 years or so. With it come an advanced race of space beings, the Anunnaki, who visited Earth during the last close pass of their home planet Nibiru and inspired early human civilisation in Sumeria. Nancy Lieder identified Nibiru with Planet X, a planet that Zeta Reticulans ('the Zetas') warned would pass close enough to Earth to bring cataclysm and an end to current civilisations. Lieder initially suggested that this would happen in May 2003 but has subsequently stated that this was a, 'White Lie', designed to, 'fool the establishment' (Lieder 2010). Although Lieder still suggests that the event will occur during the early years of the twenty-first century she distances herself from the 2012 prophecy and sees it as part of an 'establishment' plot; 'When the 2012 craze first began, years ago, this was far into the future and thus considered safe by the establishment, who want first and foremost for their slave classes to tend to their jobs and not rush away from coastal cities' (Lieder 2011). Nonetheless, this has not prevented the Sitchin-Lieder hybrid narrative from being appropriated by believers in a 2012 cataclysm.[3]

The Proliferation of Endings in Apocalyptic Discourse

What is also fascinating is the way in which this astronomical anomaly has been co-opted by traditional faith groups in the US. The Christian-New Age hybrid has been mentioned above in reference to the cultural 'prophetic readiness' of US culture but here we see a reversal of the indebtedness of New Age prophecy to Christian eschatology in the adoption of New Age themes by Christian preachers and churches. For the most part these preachers are dismissive of non-Christian hermeneutical endeavours and seek to warn Christians against false prophets, particularly New Age ones (more of this shortly when would-be Christian prophets warn of a New Age/New World Order Antichrist conspiracy) but, for some, the New Age prophecy provides an opportunity to reveal the potential for the fulfilment of Christian prophecy. Unaffiliated Christian author Tim McHyde projects Revelation's 'Wormwood' onto Planet X/Nibiru and thus is able to develop an eschatological reading of the 2012 prophecy which reinterprets the New Age date as a potential point for the return of Jesus. He is, however, sceptical and in 2008 wrote that he was unconvinced that sufficient signal events had occurred to confirm that the end times were upon us. For instance we are yet to see,

> [T]he coming Middle East nuclear war predicted by an abundance of prophetic chapters, including Psalm 83. This particular event has to happen before Wormwood comes, for reasons I won't go into here. To make a long story short, since this war has not materialized, we can rule out 2012 as a year of any type of prophetic fulfilment (McHyde 2008: 16).

Instead his key dates are set later in the decade with Wormwood/Planet X passing the Earth between Pentecost and early summer of 2019 (McHyde 2009: 90–91). Whilst McHyde is able to incorporate Planet X into Revelation, the prophecy website *The 2012 Warning* is keen to warn its viewers, 'Don't trust the Maya – Trust the Messiah!' The website is clearly intended to appeal to casual 'web seekers' searching for information relating to 2012 prophecy. The title of the site is vague and could be interpreted as being written from any one of the many perspectives that are offered on '2012'; it is certainly not immediately apparent that the site is owned, and presumably authored, by Pastor Dan Kaighen of the Lighthouse Baptist Church. The Christian content of the website's 'warning' is, however, quite apparent to even the most casual browser; the warning is a warning

---

[3]   See, for instance, 'The Church of Critical Thinking' (http://churchofcriticalthinking. org/planetx.html) and 'Your Own World USA' (http://yowusa.com/planetx/) (accessed: 22 February 2012).

not to turn away from Christ: the site pits 'Eternal Bible truths' against 'Mayan myths' and wittily warns, 'Everybody is talking about December 2012. They ought to worry about *Revelation 20:12!*' (Kaighen 2008: 1).

Although *The 2012 Warning* website is clearly using a popular interest in 2012 prophecy to attract potential converts to its prophecy-based beliefs it also contains content that sits closely aligned to the conspiracy theories which have incorporated the 2012 motif into their paranoid worldview. *The 2012 Warning* not only warns against the acceptance of false prophecy but it also warns against the origin of that false prophecy, namely what it refers to as the 'New Age Movement'; this refrain is repeated by *polarshift2012.net* which warns in an article entitled, 'Nibiru 2012 Planet X Barack Obama Evolution' that US President Barack Obama is, 'the next antichrists [sic]' (Jones 2009: 3).[4] And thus the 2012 prophecy is recontextualised within the contemporary nexus between conspiracy theory and millennialism described by Michael Barkun as 'improvisational millennialism' (Barkun 2003). Still further from McKenna and Argüelles but within the field of improvisational millennialism, David Icke (2011) recasts the 2012 prophecy as part of an incursive and nested conspiracy designed to distract the general population from the machinations of the hidden elite. Whilst elsewhere *Grailcode.net* purports to reveal Prince William as the antichrist and 2012 as the year of reckoning for both him and humanity as a whole (Ortiz 2008).

In such dark prophecies, and in other similar uses of 2012, McKenna, Argüelles, the Mayans and *I Ching* are long forgotten, if they were ever considered. In this discursive drift from novelty or ancient calendrical reckoning to antichrists and conspiracy, the field of our contemporary apocalyptic milieu is revealed. The Mayan element is a partial feature of 2012 prophecies; whilst it provides a mobilising element of the most well-known form of 2012 prophecy, it is not a defining feature of all 2012 prophecies. Hybrid prophecies in which Christianised New Age tropes and ancient astronauts constantly combine and recombine to become renewed abound and in this the Ancient Maya provide a jumping off point for fresh interpretations of Revelation, messages from the stars or offer clues of the plots of hidden elites. It is tempting to consider 2012 prophecies as emblematic of a moment in which 'New Age' beliefs have reached the cultural mainstream but to do so would be to overlook the extent to which the uses (and misuses) of 'karma' or 'the power of positive thinking' have passed into popular discourse. No, instead 2012 should be considered as evidence of the surprising vitality of the apocalyptic milieu; of the readiness for significant sections of the Western population to hope for profound, indeed cataclysmic, change. The promise of transformation, of the dawning of a new era and the waning of old influences and tyrannies of evil is deeply embedded in the cultural fabric of the West and whilst the content and detail of prophecies will be constantly renewed and recontextualised the pull of

---

4   This site appears to exist in order to provide links to the home page for *Contact 2012* a self-published 2012 'survival guide' by Christopher Jones.

an impossible promise delivered from beyond the mundane world will always resonate across divided communities and with disconsolate individuals.

References

Argüelles, J. 1987. *The Mayan Factor: Path Beyond Technology*. Rochester, VT: Inner Traditions/Bear & Company.

——. 1989. *Surfers of the Zuvuya: Tales of Interdimensional Travel*. Rochester, VT: Inner Traditions/Bear & Company.

——. 1996. *The Mayan Factor: Path Beyond Technology*, second edition. Rochester, VT: Inner Traditions/Bear & Company.

Barkun, M. 2003. *A Culture of Conspiracy: Apocalyptic Visions in Contemporary America*. Berkeley, CA: University of California Press.

Baumgartner, F.J. 1999. *Longing for the End: A History of Millennialism in Western Civilization*. Basingstoke: Palgrave.

Beres, L.R. 1980. *Apocalypse: Nuclear Catastrophe in World Politics*. Chicago, IL: University of Chicago Press.

Blavatsky, H.P. [1938] 1952. *The Secret Doctrine: Synthesis of Science, Religion and Philosophy* [Adyar Edition]. Wheaton, IL: Theosophical Press.

Boyer, P. 1992. *When Time Shall Be No More: Prophecy Belief in Modern American Culture*. Cambridge, MA: Belknap Press of Harvard University Press.

Campbell, C. 1972. The Cult, the Cultic Milieu and Secularization, in *A Sociological Yearbook of Religion in Britain*, Vol. 5, edited by M. Hill. London: SCM Press, 119–36.

Cohn, N. 1957. *The Pursuit of the Millennium: Revolutionary Millenarians and Mystical Anarchists of the Middle Ages*. London: Secker & Warburg.

Collins J.J. (ed.) 2000. *The Encyclopedia of Apocalypticism Volume 1: The Origins of Apocalypticism in Judaism and Christianity*. London: Continuum.

Festinger, L., Riecken, H. and Schachter, S. [1956] 2008. *When Prophecy Fails*. London: Pinter & Martin.

Forbes, B.D. and Kilde, J.H. (eds) 2004. *Rapture, Revelation and the End Times: Exploring the Left Behind Series*. New York: Palgrave Macmillan.

Gribben, C. 2009. *Writing the Rapture: Prophecy Fiction in Evangelical America*. Oxford: Oxford University Press.

Hall, J.R. 2009. *Apocalypse: From Antiquity to the Empire of Modernity*. Cambridge: Polity Press.

Hanegraaff, W.J. 2010. 'And End History. And Go to the Stars': Terence McKenna and 2012, in *Religion and Retributive Logic: Essays in Honour of Professor Garry W. Trompf*, edited by C.M. Cusack and C. Hartney. Leiden: Brill, 291–312.

Heelas, P. 1996. *The New Age Movement*. Oxford: Blackwell.

Hoopes, J.W. 2011. A Critical History of 2012 Mythology. *'Oxford IX' International Symposium on Archaeoastronomy Proceedings IAU Symposium No. 278*, 240–48.

Icke, D. 2011. David Icke – 2012 Is a Hoax [Online]. Available at: http://www.davidicke.com/headlines/52144-david-icke-2012-is-a-hoax [accessed: 5 November 2011].

Jenkins, P. 2000. *Mystics and Messiahs: Cults and New Religions in American History*. Oxford: Oxford University Press.

Jones, C. 2009. Nibiru 2012 Planet X Barack Obama Evolution. *Polar Shift 2012* [Online]. Available at: http://polarshift2012.net/nibiru-2012-planet-x-barack-obama-evolution.php [accessed: 4 January 2012].

Kaighen, D. 2008. Revelation 20:12. *The 2012 Warning* [Online]. Available at: http://www.the2012warning.com/category/revelation-20-12 [accessed: 27 November 2011].

Lee, M.F. 1995. *Earth First! Environmental Apocalypse*. New York: University of Syracuse Press.

Lieder, N. 1996. Welcome to ZetaTalk [Online]. Available at: http://www.zetatalk6.com/ [accessed via: http://web.archive.org/web/19961203182550/http://www.zetatalk.com/ 17 November 2011].

——. 2010. Pole Shift in 2003 Date [Online]. Available at: http://www.zetatalk6.com/index/psdate.htm [accessed: 5 December 2011].

——. 2011. ZetaTalk Chat Q&A for November 26, 2011 [Online]. Available at: http://www.zetatalk6.com/ning/26no2011.htm [accessed: 5 December 2011].

Martin, D. (as Sister Thedra) 1962. *The Prophecies from Other Planets Concerning Our Earth*. Sedona, AZ: Association of Sananda and Sanat Kumara.

McGinn, B. (ed.) 2000. *The Encyclopedia of Apocalypticism Volume 2: Apocalypticism in Western History and Culture*. London: Continuum.

McHyde, T. 2008. 2012 Doomsday and Bible Codes Prophecy. *Escape All These Things* [Online]. Available at: http://www.escapeallthesethings.com/2012.htm [accessed: 23 November 2011].

——. 2009. *Know the Future: A Bible Prophecy Breakthrough*. Costa Rica: Tim McHyde.

McKenna, T. 1993. *True Hallucinations*. San Francisco, CA: Harper San Francisco.

McKenna, T. and McKenna, D. 1975. *The Invisible Landscape: Mind, Hallucinogens, and the I Ching*. New York: Seabury Press.

——. 1993. *The Invisible Landscape: Mind, Hallucinogens, and the I Ching*, second edition. New York: Seabury Press.

Ortiz, C. 2008. *The Return of the Once and Future King: A Destiny Revealed* [Online]. Available at: http://grailcode.net [accessed: 29 December 2011].

Ostwalt, O. 1998. Visions of the End: Secular Apocalypse in Recent Hollywood Film. *Journal of Religion and Film*, 2(1) [Online]. Available at: http://avalon.unomaha.edu/jrf/OstwaltC.htm [accessed: 15 November 2011].

Partridge, C. 2004. *The Re-Enchantment of the West, Volume 1: Alternative Spiritualities, Sacralization, Popular Culture and Occulture.* London: T&T Clark.

Pinkham, M.A. 2002. *The Truth Behind the Christ Myth: The Redemption of the Peacock Angel.* Kempton, IL: Adventures Unlimited Press.

Roof, W.C. 1993. *A Generation of Seekers: The Spiritual Journeys of the Baby Boom Generation.* New York: HarperCollins.

Sitchin, Z. 1976. *The 12th Planet.* New York: Stein and Day.

Sitler, R.K. 2006. The 2012 Phenomenon: New Age Appropriation of an Ancient Mayan Calendar. *Nova Religio: The Journal of Alternative and Emergent Religions*, 9(3), 24–38.

Stahr, Rev. A. 2009. About Star-Esseenia.org [Online]. Available at: http://www.star-esseenia.org/ [accessed: 23 November 2009].

Stein, S.J. (ed.) 2000. *The Encyclopedia of Apocalypticism, Volume 3: Apocalypticism in the Modern Period and the Contemporary Age.* London: Continuum.

Sutcliffe, S. 2003. *Children of the New Age: A History of Spiritual Practices.* London: Routledge.

Tramacchi, D. 2000. Field Tripping: Psychedelic Communitas and Ritual in the Australian Bush. *Journal of Contemporary Religion*, 15(2), 201–13.

Wojcik, D. 1997. *The End of the World as We Know It: Faith, Fatalism and Apocalypse in America.* New York: New York University Press.

Zimdars-Swartz, S.L. and Zimdars-Swartz, P.F. 2000. Apocalypticism in Modern Western Europe, in *The Encyclopedia of Apocalypticism, Volume 3: Apocalypticism in the Modern Period and the Contemporary Age*, edited by S.J. Stein. London: Continuum, 265–92.

Chapter 17

Viral Email and the 2012 Apocalypse Contagion: Seven Reasons Why the World WON'T End in 2012

Kristine Larsen

Introduction

Beginning in May 2007, a message began spreading across the Internet, finding its way to email inboxes, blogs and discussion boards. Named '7 Reasons Why the World Will End in 2012', the post was a mixture of equal parts bad science and bad logic, and succeeded in further fuelling the 2012 apocalypse hysteria. What was most disconcerting about this text was the preamble, which insisted that 'Scientific experts from around the world are genuinely predicting that five years from now, all life on Earth could well finish' (Phillip 2007). The insinuation that there was a scientific basis behind the 2012 apocalypse hysteria was clearly meant to play on the general public's lack of scientific knowledge. The seven doomsday scenarios were culled both from the 2012 'hypotheses' then common in the pseudoscience community (such as misunderstandings of the Maya calendar, the solar activity cycle and magnetic pole reversals) as well as recent advances in scientific understanding which were as equally misunderstood and thus ripe for manipulation in the public mythos (such as the Large Hadron Collider and discoveries concerning past mass extinctions). What are curiously missing from this list are two of the most commonly hyped 2012 predictions, namely that there will be some sort of alignment with the centre of the galaxy, and that Planet X/Nibiru will collide with Earth. Not coincidentally, these are two of the easiest suggestions to debunk. This chapter will examine this list, both with the purpose to debunk all seven suggestions, and to examine it as a cultural phenomenon which illustrates quite vividly the chasm between the scientific establishment and the general public.

History of the List

A Google search for '7 Reasons Why the World Will End in 2012' conducted on 20 November 2011 yielded 207,000 results. Given the viral nature of this piece of 2012 propaganda, one might presume it would be impossible to uncover the initial source; however, this is not necessarily the case. The first text appears to originate on 17 May 2007, when 'Phillip', a member of the MessengerPlus! Community Forum since January 2006, posted a message entitled '7 reasons the world will end in 2012'. This post consisted of a list of seven scenarios and three unattributed pictures – a Mayan temple, a close up of the active sun and an image of Mt St Helens erupting.[1] The seven reasons given were:

1. Mayan Calendar [supposedly predicts the end of the world]
2. Sun Storms [i.e. solar flares, linked with the solar cycle maximum, will destroy the earth]
3. The Atom Smasher [i.e. the Large Hadron Collider, will create a black hole or other disaster]
4. The Bible Says [that the world will end in 2012]
5. Super Volcano [i.e. the Yellowstone caldera will have a 'supereruption' in 2012]
6. The Physicists [i.e. unnamed Berkeley scientists predict a catastrophic event is overdue]

and the strangely titled

7. Slip-Slop-Slap-BANG! [his term for the reversal of the earth's magnetic field polarity].

Comments to Phillip's post appeared almost immediately, the first being a debunking of the seven reasons by fellow poster 'Cookie Revised'. Initially the post was met with humour and critical analysis, until a series of new posters joined, beginning in January 2008. Many of these new posters were openly hostile to Phillip, not only debunking the 'reasons', but specifically criticising Phillip for invoking fear. Other posts took on a decidedly religious flavour, stating both that the Bible did and did not predict the end of the world in the coming years (depending on one's individual interpretation). As the thread took on a life of its own, Phillip was asked several times to provide a source for his list, which he vaguely named in posts on 18 May 2007 and 1 March 2008 as 'a magazine', although he never produced a citation. Phillip also admitted that he did not believe the 'evidence' he had posted, and that he had only done it because it was 'interesting' (18 May 2007) and posted

---

[1]   A Mayan temple, taken from http://www.themayantraveler.com; a NASA image of the active sun, taken from http://www.apollopony.net; and an image of Mt St Helens erupting, taken from http://www.unmuseum.org.

it 'for a laugh' (1 March 2008). On 16 February 2008, he felt it necessary to edit his original post, adding the following disclaimer: 'Note: This was posted just for a general chit chat. The thread was not meant to scare anyone and I personally believe that the world is *not* going to end in 2012' (emphasis his). However, threats were posted, and members of the forum discussed ways to prevent 'newbies' from finding the thread on Google; on 28 April 2008 the thread was finally locked, after being read a quarter of a million times.

However, the list had already spread to other sites. Members of the MessengerPlus! Community Forum noted in March 2008 that the list was posted word-for-word elsewhere, and Phillip pointed out that he had posted first. As he explained in a 3 March 2008 post, 'I typed mine word for word. I did not say this was my idea, I thought of it first I own you etc.' In fact, the plagiarism had begun almost as soon as Phillip's post had appeared. For example, the owner of factsabout2012.com posted the list on his site on 18 May 2007, only a day after Phillip's original, typos and all. While undoubtedly a number of identical versions of the list appeared before the original thread was locked, the most widely viewed (and commented upon) plagiarism of Phillip's list was posted on 13 August 2008 on the 'Funny Buburuza' blog, a self-described assortment of 'funny stuff' (buburuza.net). To this day the most popular page on the website, Buburuza's post (entitled 'Seven Reasons The World Will End In 2012 – Proven Scientifically') includes the preamble 'Don't know whether its [sic] true or not, but just thout [sic] of sharing it to you', but no other information concerning the original author.[2] Interestingly, the first comment to Buburuza's post (by someone posting under the pseudonym 'Aravind') was identical to the first reply to Phillip's original post, complete with typos, thus making it a plagiarised reply to a plagiarised post. On 28 January 2008, someone using the name Phillip (claiming to be the original author of the list) posted under the Buburuza post 'I wrote this' and included the URL for the original msghelp.net post. Two weeks later, another poster noted the plagiarism, and at some point afterwards a disclaimer was added to the end of the Buburuza list, citing the original post by Phillip. Factsabout2012.com and buburuza.net are certainly not the only sites guilty of lifting the post, the list appears to have been increasingly 'borrowed' in the month after Buburuza's post.[3]

By January 2009, the 2012 apocalypse hysteria, as evidenced by Internet activity and genuinely anxious questions posed to scientists interacting with the general public, had reached such a level that a group of amateur astronomers, engineers and other scientifically-minded people founded 2012hoax.org, a website devoted to collecting and debunking claims made by the 2012 apocalypse community.

---

[2] http://buburuza.net/2008/08/seven-reasons-the-world-will-end-in-2012-proven-scientifically (accessed: 6 March 2012).

[3] For example, it was posted on the perthstreetbikes.com Forum by member 'XSorXpire' on 23 August 2008 on survivalistboards.com by a poster named 'Revilo' on 19 September 2008 and by a writer named 'Universe' on his/her millliondollarblogspot. com on 11 September 2008.

Among the items debunked was the '7 reasons' post (http://www.2012hoax.org/7-reasons). I am a relative latecomer to the website's volunteer staff, and have taken part in the debunking of various 2012 claims, both on that website and in a number of presentations and papers. In that spirit, what follows here is a brief debunking of each of the seven 'reasons' in turn.

Debunking the Claims

The Mayan Calendar

According to Phillip's original post, 'The first mob to predict 2012 as the end of the world were the Mayans, a bloodthirsty race that were good at two things: Building highly accurate astrological equipment out of stone and Sacrificing Virgins.' Here we see the unfortunate racism all-too-often connected with discussions of Mayan history and accomplishments, including placing undue emphasis on the role of blood sacrifice in their culture (Van Stone n.d.). This begs the question, if the Maya were merely a 'bloodthirsty race', why put such stock in their 'astrological equipment?' According to the poster,

> Thousands of years ago they managed to calculate the length of the lunar moon as 329.53020 days, only 34 seconds out. The Mayan calendar predicts that the Earth will end on December 21, 2012. Given that they were pretty close to the mark with the lunar cycle, it's likely they've got the end of the world right as well.

Ignoring the leap of logic in equating the proper prediction of a roughly month-long lunar cycle visible to naked-eye observers with precisely predicting the end of a 4.6 billion year old planet, there are several other problems with this statement.

Firstly, scholars have debunked the idea that the Mayan calendar suggests the end of the world will occur in 2012 (Sitler 2006, Van Stone n.d.). Secondly, the phrase 'length of the lunar moon' is nonsensical. This is probably a typo for 'lunar month'; if so, the poster's statement is still in error, as the synodic period of the moon (the time between successive new moons) is (on average) 29.5306 days, not 329 (apparently another typo), and the period fluctuates up to half a day due to the elliptical shape of the moon's orbit around the earth (Stephenson and Baolin 1991). This, coupled with the fact that the synodic period is not close to a whole number of days, has led to the complexities in various cultural lunar and luni-solar calendars, such as the Muslim, Tibetan and Jewish calendars. The Mayan lunar calendar, like each of these, would have a set of rules for adding extra days every-so-often to realign the calendar with the actual lunar cycle. Thus the Mayan lunar calendar (only one of this culture's calendars) was certainly not an anomaly in terms of its accuracy, and certainly not in the realm of precision claimed by the poster.

Solar Flares and the Solar Cycle

The second reason given in the post is that 'Solar experts from around the world monitoring the sun have made a startling discovery: our sun is in a bit of strife. The energy output of the sun is, like most things in nature, cyclic, and it's supposed to be in the middle of a period of relative stability.' So far, these statements have some (albeit twisted) kernels of truth. As a ball of hot gas, the sun's magnetic field behaves differently than our planet's. For example, the sun rotates faster at the equator and slower at the poles, resulting in its magnetic field lines getting tangled up like a ball of yarn in the paws of an exuberant kitten. The tangled lines are periodically shed into space, causing high energy events called coronal mass ejections (CMEs), and along with energetic outbursts called solar flares, they temporarily intensify the outrush of high energy charged particles from the sun, called the solar wind.

Over time, a fresh new magnetic field is established, one with a reversed polarity – i.e., the positions of the north and south magnetic poles are reversed. Note that the rotation of the sun itself does not change; the rotational poles of our star are unaffected. As the magnetic field lines exit the visible surface of the sun (called the photosphere), energy is transferred from the surface to the outer layers (the chromospheres and corona, usually only visible during a total solar eclipse), resulting in a variety of phenomena including sunspots. The number of sunspots waxes and wanes with the 11-year solar cycle, with times of maximum sunspots roughly corresponding to times of maximum CMEs and solar flares. If the solar cycle is the 'strife' the poster referred to, then the sun is in good company; a 20-year study has shown that a number of sun-like stars also have a decade-long cycle in magnetic activity (Lockwood et al. 2007). Since the sun was sliding into sunspot minimum at the time of Phillip's post, this is possibly what he meant by 'period of relative stability'.

However, Phillip's post then warns that 'recent solar storms have been bombarding the Earth with so much radiation energy, it's been knocking out power grids and destroying satellites. This activity is predicted to get worse, and calculations suggest it'll reach its deadly peak sometime [sic] in 2012.' It is true that if the next solar maximum brings with it high CME and flare activity earth-orbiting satellites and astronauts would be at risk, the former due to their sensitive electronics and the latter from radiation damage to their cells. In addition, power grids across the globe could be subject to overload, resulting in blackouts and perhaps damage to the electrical infrastructure (Chang 2003). However, while early predictions of the upcoming solar maximum did indeed suggest it would be a strong one and would occur in 2012 (Cain 2006), the sun has been slow to rebound from its last, deep minimum, and more recent models suggest that the next solar maximum will not only be the weakest since 1928, but will actually occur in 2013 (Hathaway 2011). While Phillip (or his source) were obviously unaware of these later predictions, the 2012 movement has clearly ignored these more recent scientific predictions, as they continue to merely copy-paste the 2007 list without revision.

The Large Hadron Collider

Item three on the list warns that 'Scientists in Europe have been building the world's largest particle accelerator. Basically its [sic] a 27 km tunnel designed to smash atoms together to find out what makes the Universe tick.' If one substitutes 'subatomic particles' for 'atoms' Phillip's description of CERN's Large Hadron Collider (LHC) is no worse than the normal news report's description. Phillip then correctly notes that 'the mega-gadget has caused serious concern, with some scientists suggesting that it's properly [sic] even a bad idea to turn it on in the first place. They're predicting all manner of deadly results, including mini black holes.'

Fear of particle accelerators entered the public consciousness in March 1999, after the publication of an article in *Scientific American* that explained the scientific expectations for Brookhaven National Laboratory's soon-to-be-commissioned collider named RHIC (Relativistic Heavy Ion Collider). By smashing together protons and atomic nuclei at high velocities, RHIC would attain temperatures and densities not 'seen in the universe for several billion years' (Mukerjee 1999: 60). Using 'processes that mimic the big bang', the experiment had the possibility to create conglomerates of quarks and antiquarks 'and innumerable other hypothetical phenomena' (Mukerjee 1999: 63–4). The experiment could even create phenomena 'as yet unimagined by theorists' (Mukerjee 1999: 67).

A letter to the editor written by Walter Wagner, a lawyer with a BS in Biology with a Minor in Physics, was published in the July 1999 issue, and asked if RHIC could possibly create miniature black holes, such as those proposed in the late 1970s by famed physicist Stephen Hawking. Wagner further posed the possibility that such a black hole could be 'drawn by gravity toward the center of the planet, absorbing matter along the way and devouring the entire planet within minutes' (Wagner 1999: 8). *Scientific American* gave rebuttal space to Princeton physicist (and later Nobel Prize recipient) Frank Wilczek, who had been quoted in the original article. While Wilczek reassured the readers that RHIC could not create black holes, he suggested that strangelets – stable chunks of rare strange quarks – could be produced, and could 'grow by incorporating and transforming the ordinary matter in its surroundings'. Wilczek added that strangelets 'if they exist at all, are not aggressive, and they will start out very, very small. So here again a doomsday scenario is not plausible' (Wilczek 1999: 8).

Despite Wilczek's assurances, the damage had been done. The possibility that dangerous black holes and strangelets might be created in a particle accelerator gained traction in the popular press. To do damage control, the director of Brookhaven convened a commission of four scientists from Yale, MIT and

Princeton, including Wilczek, to craft a safety report that would hopefully allay fears. The report was released on 28 September 1999 and reported that the collisions would not be powerful enough to create black holes, and that the production of strangelets could only occur if they came in doubly unexpected negatively charged and stable configurations (Busza et al. 1999: 4).

Although public concerns over RHIC died down after the release of these documents, the battle was just beginning as far as the LHC was concerned. As Johnson (2009) explained in a lengthy article in *The Tennessee Law Review*, a scientific 'tit-for-tat' began in the scientific community, where physicists and mathematicians began criticising each other's calculations of the probability of the production of these exotic phenomena at the LHC. In response to criticisms from both the public and a minority in the physics community, CERN commissioned two safety reports during the construction of its machine, both of which came to the conclusion that the LHC and its experiments did not pose a threat to the planet (Blaizot et al. 2003, Ellis et al. 2008).

CERN's opponents were not placated, including lawyer Walter Wagner, the author of the letter to *Scientific American* that started the backlash against RHIC in 1999. Wagner's LHCDefense.org is merely one of a number of websites dedicated to mis-informing the general public about the theoretical dangers of the LHC. Despite the fact that Wagner is not an expert on hadron colliders, black holes or particle physics, his alarmist pronouncements are taken as gospel by many on the Internet (as seen by Phillip's list). Not surprisingly, a poll taken by the BBC in 2008 found that 66 per cent of people surveyed believed the LHC was too dangerous to switch on, and 61 per cent of those surveyed in an AOL newspoll agreed with this assessment (Sample 2010: 160). The public fears also resulted in death threats against physicists, who were perceived as mad scientists bent on destroying the planet (Zahn 2008).

While the LHC did not destroy the world when it was first switched on in September 2008, it did suffer a serious accident, when a faulty electrical connection between two of its powerful magnets created a spark and resulted in the damage of several of the magnets, and ripped some of the magnet anchors out of the concrete base. The machine has since come back on-line, is producing scientific results, and Phillip's prediction that 'when this machine is fired up for its first serious experiment in 2012, the world could be crushed into a super-dense blob the size of a basketball' has certainly not come to pass.

The Bible

According to Phillip, 'If having scientists warning us about the end of the world isn't bad enough, religious folks are getting in on the act as well. Interpretations of the Christian Bible reveal that the date for Armageddon, the final battle between Good an [sic] Evil, has been set down for 2012.' While the post does appear to make a cursory division between science and religion, the difference was lost on many of the list's readers. For the sake of completeness, despite the fact that this statement does not fall under the purview of science, it is nonetheless easy to refute, and has been by those more knowledgeable of the Bible than myself. For example, in an article posted on the Christian Broadcasting Network website, a number of well-known pastors and Christian writers (including the co-authors of the famous *Left Behind* series) pointedly reject the notion that the Bible has set 2012 as the moment of Armageddon (Anderson 2011).

Phillip then goes on to argue that 'The I Ching, also known as the Chinese book of Changes, says the same thing, as do various sections of the Hindu teachings.' In actuality, the I Ching is a personal method of divination, not a series of concrete prophecies, and a quick perusal of the Internet will show that various Hindu organisations are already posting the dates of their holy days for 2013 – hardly evidence that their belief system is predicting the end of the world a year earlier.

The Yellowstone Caldera

Phillip once again gets the science only partly correct in the fifth 'reason'. As he notes, 'Yellowstone National Park in the United States is famous for its thermal springs and Old Faithful geyser. The reason for this is simple – it's sitting on top of the world's biggest volcano, and geological experts are beginning to get nervous sweats.' The Yellowstone caldera is certainly considered one of the largest active volcanic structures on the planet – a 'supervolcano'. However, stating that geologists are getting 'nervous sweats' over Yellowstone is a flagrant exaggeration, onto which Phillip piles more inaccuracies by claiming:

> The Yellowstone volcano has a pattern of erupting every 650,000 years or so, and we're many years overdue for an explosion that will fill the atmosphere with ash, blocking the sun and plunging the Earth into a frozen winter that could last up to 15,000 years. The pressure under the Yellowstone is building steadily, and geologists have set 2012 as a likely date for the big bang.

Fortunately, for any given supervolcano, supereruptions are rare, perhaps on the scale (but not cycle) of a few million years. The Yellowstone Caldera's last supereruption was about 640,000 years ago, but there is 'no predictive value in knowing when the last supereruption occurred' for any such structure on earth (Miller and Wark 2008: 14). As depicted in the film *2012*, ash from a Yellowstone supereruption has and may again blanket much of North America (Self and Blake 2008: 42). In addition to creating immediate hazards to aircraft, such volumes of volcanic ash can adversely affect agriculture, collapse roofs and change the amount of sunlight reflected from the earth's surface.

Volcanic gases can also cause deleterious changes to the atmosphere's chemistry, resulting in acid rain and the cooling of the surface by decreasing the amount of sunlight passing through the atmosphere (Self and Blake 2008: 44). This in turn could lead to weather and climate changes that would not last for a dozen millennia (as proposed by Phillip) but rather on the scale of a few years. For example, the 1991 eruption of Mt Pinatubo in the Philippines caused a half degree Celsius drop in global temperatures for two years (Self and Blake 2008: 44). Yellowstone is monitored carefully by geologists because of its past supereruptions. Although it is true that the caldera has recently experienced both small earthquakes and a slight uplifting of parts of the caldera itself (on the order of centimetres), volcanologists do not have a clear picture of the relationship (if any) between such changes and supereruptions (Lowenstern and Hurwitz 2008: 35). So while the general public should respect the destructive potential of Yellowstone, there is no evidence that a supereruption is likely in the next few years, nor could a potential eruption be predicted with reasonable precision five years beforehand.

The Berkeley Physicists

Phillip's sixth piece of 'evidence' is the vaguest and the most elusive for debunkers looking for the source of the misconception. According to the post,

> Physicists at Berkeley Uni have been crunching the numbers. and they've determined that the Earth is well overdue for a major catastrophic event. Even worse, they're claiming their calculations prove, that we're all going to die, very soon – while also saying their prediction comes with a certainty of 99 percent – and 2012 just happens to be the best guess as to when it occurs [all typos original].

Assuming that 'Berekely Uni' is actually the University of California, Berkeley, I was able to trace the source of this 'reason' to a 2005 scientific paper published in the prestigious journal *Nature* by physicist Richard Muller and his graduate student Robert Rohde. The university press release (probably the version read by the original author of the list as opposed to the actual scientific paper) uses phrases such as 'stunning surprise', 'mysterious cycles' and 'science has no satisfactory explanation' to describe the results (Yarris 2005). The paper itself reports the apparent discovery of an apparent 62 +/-3 million year periodicity in the diversity of marine life, with the authors' mathematical analysis claiming a 99 per cent statistical significance. Given that the most recent example was the mass extinction that occurred 65 million years ago and took out the dinosaurs and many other species, the analysis could be interpreted to mean that another event might be in our future. However, since Rohde and Muller (2005: 209) state in their paper that the cycle is 'somewhat less regular and well developed during the last ~150 M yr' and we are still within the three million year error bar for the timing since the last event, the comment that such an event is 'overdue' is false.

Interestingly, among the explanations which Rohde and Muller explore and reject as possible causes of this presumed cycle are several touted by the 2012 apocalypse community as doomsday scenarios, including the solar activity cycle, widespread volcanic eruptions and the impact of a large object from space (a comet or asteroid).[4] It should be noted that Muller himself has raised such possibilities before. In the aftermath of the accumulation of evidence to support Walter Alvarez's now-famous asteroid impact theory for the mass extinction of the dinosaurs, palaeontologists David Raup and John Sepkoski (1984) studied mass extinctions during the last 250 million years of the fossil record, and reported evidence of a possible periodicity in such events, of either 26 million or 33 million years (depending on one's interpretation of the data). Astronomers rushed to come up with models which combined Alvarez's model of mass extinction with Raup and Sepkoski's timeline, and the most widely popularised was the so-called Nemesis or 'Death Star' model. In this model the sun is hypothesised to have a distant, dim companion star or brown dwarf which interacts with the Oort Cloud, a reservoir of billions of comets at the edge of the solar system, every 26 million years (Davis, Hut and Muller 1984). Despite decades of searching with infrared telescopes for 'Nemesis', no concrete evidence for its existence has surfaced. In the end, '2012' is not mentioned in Rohde and Muller's 2005 paper, and there is nothing to suggest that 2012 will suddenly mark a crisis in diversity (other than the ongoing crisis caused by anthropogenic extinctions of endangered species).

A Magnetic Polarity Reversal

Finally, Phillip invokes a common trope in the 2012 apocalypse literature that a change in the polarity of the earth's magnetic poles will bring about the end of life on earth in 2012. As Phillip explains it, 'the magnetic poles we call north and south have a nasty habit of swapping places every 750,000 years or so – and right now we're about 30,000 years overdue.'

While the basic structure of the magnetic field is well known, mysteries remain. For reasons not completely understood, the polarity of the field sometimes switches, an event referred to in the popular press as a magnetic polarity flip. An important point to note (and one that is often ignored by 2012 apocalypse proponents) is that this is completely independent of the rotational poles of our planet (the poles which define geographic north and south). The length of time between magnetic polarity flips does not appear to be periodic, although it is generally on the scale of a few million years. The last reversal occurred approximately 780,000 years ago (Lanza and Meloni 2006: 38). Since there is no cycle, we can hardly be 'overdue' for such a change.

But Phillip argues that 'Scientists have noted that the poles are drifting apart roughly 20–30kms each year, much faster than ever before, which points to a pole-shift being right around the corner.' It is true that the magnetic poles naturally drift, and that the strength of the earth's magnetic field has decreased about 5 per cent per century since the mid 1800s. Scientists have no way to know if this does mark the start of a new polarity swap, but even if a polarity flip has begun, it will

---

[4]   For a thorough debunking of the Planet X/Nibiru 2012 claims, see Morrison (2009) and Plait (2008).

not complete itself by 2012, as geological evidence strongly suggests that such an event takes thousands of years to complete (Merrill, McElhinny and McFadden 1998: 206).

Even if a polarity switch is imminent, Phillip's claims as to what a switch could do to life on earth are again highly exaggerated. He warns that 'While the pole shift is underway, the magnetic field is disrupted and will eventually disappear, sometimes for up to 100 years. The result is enough UV outdoors to crisp your skin in seconds, killing everything it touches.' At present, geologists do not know if the strength of the earth's magnetic field decreases before the polarity begins shifting, or if both events occur nearly simultaneously. It is also not known how dramatically the strength of the magnetic field decreases during the transition. It is true that the planet's magnetic field plays an important role in protecting us from the high energy particles of the solar wind, but even when the earth's magnetic field is nowhere near a polarity switch it is an imperfect defence system at best. Particles from the solar wind interact with the earth's magnetic field, producing aurora (the so-called Northern Lights), disrupting radio communications and in extreme cases overloading electrical transformers (by increasing the current flowing in power lines). These effects are most noticeable close to the magnetic poles, where the magnetic field lines enter the earth, and hence our defence system is weakest. Further damage to the ozone layer (and hence increased exposure to cancer-causing ultraviolet rays) could result. However, this would be a temporary effect, lasting only several years (Chang 2003), and our ecosystems would hardly be fried to a crisp, as they have clearly managed to survive numerous magnetic field reversals in the past (as well as the well-known damage to the ozone layer already caused by human activity).

Comments to the List: Peering into the Minds of the Public

It is clearly easy to debunk all seven 'reasons'; however, the damage has already been done, as the list has spread across the Internet like a virus. However, all is not bad news, as a survey of comments posted to this list allows us not only to peer into the minds of those who are uncritical consumers of these misconceptions and misappropriations of science, but just as importantly to discover the scientific illiteracy of those well-meaning posters who are trying to debunk the list based on their own limited understanding of the underlying science.

The first thing one notices when reading the comments to any copy of the list is that some of the 'reasons' are debunked far more often than others, partly because some of these 'reasons' are easier to debunk scientifically for those with a basic scientific background (such as the Mayan calendar argument). Religious posts are very common, divided between those exhorting people to repent and prepare for the end, those who believe the end is coming but that God will either change His mind or protect us from the catastrophe, and those who argue that no one but God knows the timing of the end. Racism directed toward the Maya is also unfortunately evident, such as a 2 August 2009 comment to the Buburuza thread by a poster named 'Sara': 'So what if a bunch of savages said we're going to die? There's a reason why they were called savages.' Another interesting trend is that some of the periodic surges in popularity of the list can be directly tied to particular events, such as the film *2012* in November 2009 and the well-publicised end-of-the-world prediction of Harold Camping in May 2011 (McKinley 2011).

A close reading demonstrates the various thought processes behind the posts. In a small number of posts, the writer debates the 'scientific' nature of the list. For example, 'Ian', a poster to the Buburuza thread, asked on 19 May 2011 'How is this scientifically "proven"? Each paragraph is missing A. cited references, i.e. hyperlink content providing detailed research by accredited studies and B. logical conclusive evidence.' Other posters point out the difference between science and religion. One such comment was posted to the Buburuza thread by 'Jered Lacks' on 6 January 2011: 'You cannot connect the Bible with science anyhow. They are two different things.' However, more often posters fail to see the difference and either accept or assign blame for the entire list because it is supposedly attributed to scientists. For example, 'Jesseca' wrote on the Buburuza thread on 17 July 2009 'well if it is scientifically true it might actually happen so I wouldn't doubt anything!' 'Trea' argued on the same thread 'Look the world is not going to end its [sic] just a bunch of scientists trying to scare our youth!!!' (18 June 2010). 'Dave' warned 'No one knows when the world will end except God!!! Sooo [sic] all you dumb scientists stop working up your brains out there' (15 October 2009). A final example comes from 'tennis dude's' post a week earlier on the same thread, when he pointed out that scientists can't 'even get the weather right'.

While it is unfortunate that some posters clearly do not understand the difference between science and religion, just as concerning is the number of posters who try to debunk the various claims using what they think is correct science, but which in actuality is misconception or pseudoscience. For example, 'Dave R' tried to debunk all seven 'reasons' on the Buburuza thread on 18 November 2009, but managed to confuse more than enlighten. For example, he claimed that there is 'an atom smasher or collider working in Texas right now, with virtually no black holes'. He is probably referring to the Superconducting Supercollider (SSC), a project that was never completed. Dave continues, 'I'll give you that Yellowstone is a geological hot spot, but 650,000 years ago EVERYTHING was erupting, as the earth was so much more unstable.' Simply put, there is no science to back up this comment. Finally, he offers 'Yes the magnetic pole shifts …. But it always shifts in a circle around true north.' He is apparently confusing the polarity shift of the magnetic poles with the precession of the axis of rotation (true north and south), a 26,000 year wobble of the earth that results in true north sweeping out a circle relative to the stars. A poster named 'Charles' also tried to debunk the entire list on buburuza.net on 4 January 2011, but only succeeded in displaying his own lack of scientific understanding when he claimed that 'the sun is dieing as we know it' and that there is no need to be concerned about Yellowstone because 'no body goes there and its in the middle of the forest' (typos original).

Two of the supposed apocalypse scenarios are sometimes combined, as in the case of a post by 'Sakkhi' on buburuza.net (8 January 2010). Here he/she stated with authority that 'volcanoes are going to happen because of the sun storms'. While a number of posters to the 2012hoax.org's '7 Reasons' debunking page have made the same claim, there is no connection between the two phenomena. Finally, a poster ironically named 'Scientist' wrote on the Buburuza thread 'yes the sun is becoming closer' (20 April 2010). No, it is not, but Scientist's statement and many others found in comments on the various '7 Reasons' sites demonstrate the confidence many people have in their misconceptions concerning science.

Conclusion: Science Illiteracy and 2012

It can be argued that without the Internet, the 2012 apocalypse hoax would have never reached the fever pitch it has. For example, studies have shown that 28 per cent of Americans surveyed rely on the Internet as their primary source of science information, and 54 per cent use the Internet as their source of information on specific scientific issues (National Science Board 2010: 7–10). Even the posters themselves are aware of the problem relying on this new technology has caused. For example, 'WayneMc' noted on Buburuza.net (13 July 2011) that 'this crap's freaking me out. But I believe it's mostly because everyone is using their easy to access information these days via internet, and spreading rumors and hyping it up.' 'Santa' noted 'It's all quite funny – but many children are coming across these stories and getting very frightened because they think it is for real' (Buburuza.net, 4 April 2011). This is corroborated by Cornell University astronomer Ann Martin, who notes that her 'Curious? Ask an Astronomer' website is 'getting e-mails from the 4th graders who are saying they're too young to die' (Stevenson 2009). If history is any indicator, people *are* going to die because of this misinformation and hysteria, just as they did during the 1910 passing of Halley's Comet, and the Heaven's Gate suicide cult in 1997. Buburza.net poster 'Jered' voiced similar concerns on 23 August 2011: 'What is going to sicken me the most are the nut jobs that are going to kill their family's [sic] and then themselves before the date of the alleged Armageddon.'

The '7 Reasons' phenomenon is therefore a microcosm of the 2012 apocalypse hysteria, and is an excellent laboratory to study both the movement and situate it in the context of a much larger issue facing society, namely science illiteracy. Survey data compiled by the National Science Board (2010) has clearly demonstrated that most Americans cannot pass a basic science knowledge test. This science illiteracy is coupled with a widespread acceptance of a variety of pseudosciences, such as astrology, alien abductions and, yes, the 2012 apocalypse. As Happs (1991: 171) noted, these two issues are related, and should be a serious concern to science educators. But it is not only the science educators who should be concerned, but rather all of us who live in an increasingly technological society, where science appears not only in the classroom, but also on our iPads, our laptops and increasingly at the ballot box.

References

Anderson, T. 2011. 2012: Will It Affect You? *Christian Broadcasting Network* [Online 19 February 2011]. Available at: http://www.cbn.com/spirituallife/BibleStudyAndTheology/Perspectives/2012-end-of-the-world-Anderson.aspx [accessed: 20 October 2011].

Blaizot, J.-P. et al. 2003. Study of Potentially Dangerous Events during Heavy-ion Collisions at the LHC. *CERN Scientific Information Service* [Online]. Available at: http://cdsweb.cern.ch/record/613175/files/CERN-2003-001.pdf [accessed: 15 September 2011].

Busza, W. et al. 1999. Review of Speculative 'Disaster Scenarios' at RHIC. *Brookhaven National Laboratory* [Online]. Available at: http://www.bnl.gov/rhic/docs/rhicreport.pdf [accessed: 20 September 2011].

Cain, F. 2006. Next Solar Max Will Be a Big One. *Universe Today* [Online]. Available at: http://www.universetoday.com/2006/03/14/next-solar-max-will-be-a-big-one/ [accessed: 10 October 2011].

Chang, K. 2003. Magnetic Field Is Fading, But No Dire Effects Are Foreseen. *New York Times* [Online 12 December 2003]. Available at: http://www.nytimes.com/2003/12/12/science/12MAGN.html [accessed: 13 September 2011].

Davis, M., Hut, P. and Muller, R.A. 1984. Extinction of Species by Periodic Comet Showers. *Nature*, 308, 715–17.

Ellis, J. et al. 2008. Review of the Safety of LHC Collisions. *CERN Scientific Information Service* [Online]. Available at: http://lsag.web.cern.ch/lsag/LSAG-Report.pdf [accessed: 15 September 2011].

Happs, J.C. 1991. Challenging Pseudoscientific and Paranormal Beliefs Held by Some Pre-Service Primary Teachers. *Research in Science Education*, 21, 171–7.

Hathaway, D. 2011. Solar Cycle Prediction. *Solar Physics* [Online]. Available at: http://solarscience.msfc.nasa.gov/predict.shtml [accessed: 10 November 2011].

Johnson, E.E. 2009. The Black Hole Case: The Injunction against the End of the World. *Tennessee Law Review*, 76, 819–908.

Lanza, R. and Meloni, A. 2006. *The Earth's Magnetism*. Berlin: Springer-Verlag.

Lockwood, G.W. et al. 2007. Patterns of Photometric and Chromospheric Variation among Sun-like Stars: A 20 Year Perspective. *Astrophysical Journal Supplement Series*, 171(1), 260–303.

Lowenstern, J. and Hurwitz, S. 2008. Monitoring a Supervolcano in Repose: Heat and Volatile Flux at the Yellowstone Caldera. *Elements*, 4, 35–40.

McKinley, J. 2011. Despite Careful Calculations, the World Does Not End. *New York Times* [Online, 21 May 2011]. Available at: http://www.nytimes.com/2011/05/22/us/22doomsday.html [accessed: 1 October 2011].

Merrill, R.T., McElhinny, M.W. and McFadden, P.L. 1998. *The Magnetic Field of the Earth*. San Diego, CA: Academic Press.

Miller, C.F. and Wark, D.A. 2008. Supervolcanoes and Their Explosive Supereruptions. *Elements*, 4, 11–16.

Morrison, D. 2009. Doomsday 2012, the Planet Nibiru, and Cosmophobia. *Astronomy Beat*, 32, 1–6 [Online]. Available at: http://www.astrosociety.org/2012/ab2009-32.pdf [accessed: 1 November 2011].

Mukerjee, M. 1999. A Little Big Bang. *Scientific American*, 280(3), 60–67.

National Science Board. 2010. *Science and Engineering Indicators 2010*. Arlington, VA: National Science Foundation [Online]. Available at: http://www.nsf.gov/statistics/seind10/ [accessed: 10 November 2011].

Phillip. 2007. 7 Reasons the World Will End in 2012. *Messenger Plus! Community Forum* [Online 17 May 2007]. Available at: http://www.msghelp.net/showthread.php?tid=74463 [accessed: 12 October 2011].

Plait, P. 2008. The Planet X Saga: Introduction. *Bad Astronomy* [Online]. Available at: http://www.badastronomy.com/bad/misc/planetx/index.html [accessed: 15 November 2011].

Raup, D. and Sepkoski, J. 1984. Periodicity of Extinctions in the Geologic Past. *Proceedings of the National Academy of Sciences*, 81, 801–5.

Rohde, R.A. and Muller, R.A. 2005. Cycles in Fossil Diversity. *Nature*, 434, 208–10.

Sample, I. 2010. *Massive: The Missing Particle That Sparked the Greatest Hunt in Science*. New York: Basic Books.

Self, S. and Blake, S. 2008. Consequences of Explosive Super Eruptions. *Elements*, 4, 41–6.

Sitler, R. 2006. The 2012 Phenomenon: New Age Appropriation of an Ancient Mayan Calendar. *Nova Religio*, 9(3), 24–38.

Stephenson, F.R. and Baolin, L. 1991. On the Length of the Synodic Month. *Observatory*, 111, 21–2.

Stevenson, M. 2009. 2012 Isn't the End of the World, Mayans Insist. *AP Wire Service* [Online 11 October 2011]. Available at: http://www.astro.cornell.edu/~amartin/doc/mayan2012.PDF [accessed: 12 November 2011].

Van Stone, M. [no date]. 2012 FAQ. Foundation for the Advancement of Mesoamerican Studies [Online]. Available at: www.famsi.org/research/vanstone/2012/faq.html [accessed: 19 November 2011].

Wagner, W. 1999. Black Holes at Brookhaven? *Scientific American*, 280(5), 8.

Wilczek, F. 1999. Reply to Black Holes at Brookhaven? *Scientific American*, 280(5), 8.

Yarris, L. 2005. Fossil Records Show Diversity Comes and Goes. *Research News, Berkeley Lab* [Online 11 March 2005]. Available at: http://www.lbl.gov/Science-Articles/Archive/Phys-fossil-biodiversity.html [accessed: 20 November 2011].

Zahn, D. 2008. Fear of Black Hole Machine Triggers Threats to Researchers. *World News Daily* [Online, 6 September 2008]. Available at: http://www.wnd. com/?pageId=74461 [accessed: 10 September 2011].

Chapter 18

Remembering the Future:
2012 as Planetary Transition[1]

Suzanne Rough

At no time since I was invited to speak at the Inform Seminar on New Religions and Prophecy, held at the London School of Economics on 22 November 2008, have I intended to speak in detail about the events that are going to make up '2012'. We have a website (www.dkfoundation.co.uk) where these details can be freely accessed by those who want to know. I will confine myself to talking about their context: how they came into being and why. This way those who do not want to know do not get drawn in. I do not consider that those attending an academic conference on Prophecy have given their consent to hear graphic and unsettling detail about 2012; and I consider that I have a responsibility to avoid the formation of situations in which negative emotion is likely to be generated. We have more than enough negativity pressing down on us. We do not need to generate more.[2]

So who am I to be taking on this responsibility? A generation ago I would have been called an occultist or an esotericist. But as neither of these terms has the right

---

[1]   This paper is based on a talk given at the Inform Seminar, New Religions and Prophecy, held at the London School of Economics, 22 November 2008 and has been supplemented with material taken from a www.dkfoundation.co.uk web-page, 'The Particular: Where We Are Now', written for web site readers June 2011.

[2]   As presented on the DK Foundation website, the 'Red Letters', given to Suzanne Rough by the master 'Kuthumi', reveal that 'The nature of the occurrences of 2012 will be appreciated where there is understanding of the mystery of baptism and, specifically, the purpose of immersion. Immersion in water heals and restores. There are those who view the immersion of an infant at baptism as an act of unkindness because that is the way that human thinking has gone; and there are those who will view the immersion of terra firma in water as a judgement upon mankind. This is not the case. In 2012, to permit it to raise its vibration, the planet will see its most polluted parts immersed. ... On December 17th and 18th 2012, the configuration of planets interacting with stellar influences will pull our planet into a more upright position. The situation may be likened to a bent person straightening up. This motion will change the moon's orbit. Amongst the effects of this will be, that: 1. The moon will be visible from only a relatively small proportion of the Earth's surface 2. The changed angle of Earth's axis in respect of the sun will create a more temperate and more uniform climate on the planet 3. The changed angle of its axis will also mean that new constellation will be identifiable from Earth.' http://www.dkfoundation. co.uk/dkfoundation/RedLettersIntro.htm#_edn6 (accessed: 15 January 2012).

sound for the present time I tend to avoid them; I prefer the term auditor. What I audit is the energetic exchange between our planet and the larger system of which it is a part and to which it must make a suitable contribution.

And I have to tell you that I have never considered myself to be involved in prophecy. I am not saying that I am not, nor that I will not use the term in this paper. But the term creaks with age. And mostly I don't talk about the activity at all: I just get on with the job – because time is short.

Although we can dispense with outmoded terms we cannot dispense with what stands to be a bigger obstacle to understanding, and that is our differing paradigms which give us different ways of constructing reality and understanding causality and underpin every statement and assumption that we make. We have to accept that this is one of the constraints on meaningful exchange in a meeting of this kind where intellectuals, scientists and people from a range of different spiritual traditions are involved. Not only do we not share a common language we do not share a reality. I start this talk knowing that what I am about to say is going to be double Dutch to most here, and it may not even have the merit of being entertaining. What I can promise is that I will not go on for a long time.

The paradigm within which I work is constructed around a hylozoic Universe. This structure with its seven interconnected worlds, each with its own quality of consciousness, each distributing and transforming energy on behalf of the world above and below, each smaller world more dense than the world above, is discernible at the esoteric heart of all the major religions, but it is not a Universe that, as far as I am aware, is known to science.

The term hylozoic may be unfamiliar but the principle it describes is not. The Russian doll embodies a hylozoic principle: a smaller replica fits inside a larger one and the smaller doll is itself the larger doll to the one which fits within it.

Our planet takes its place in the Fifth World. With the other planets of our solar system it has to make a return to World Four, the world of the Sun itself.

Mankind (which with the other forms of organic life on our planet make up World Six) is our planet's only variable. By this it is meant that it is not simply the numbers but the quality of being of those making up the human family which determine the quality of the return that the planet is able to make for the life force which flows down to our planet from that great transmitter, the Sun. The other kingdoms in nature, the animal, the vegetable and the mineral can be only what they are; man alone has the choice to be ergonomically efficient and a planetary contributor depending on how many of the seven major energy centres in our physical vehicle we are using.

As far as I am aware, medical science does not acknowledge in any systemised way the etheric counterpart of the physical body or the energy centres (or *chakras*) contained within it but it does, of course, acknowledge the endocrine system which is a lower correspondent of the *chakra* system. The seven major glands are situated in approximately the same location as the *chakra* to which they correspond so that gives an idea of the structure of the *chakra* system: the major *chakras* are to be found in the trunk and head.

Since time immemorial our spiritual traditions have been concerned with the raising of humanity's vibration by opening the energy centres above the diaphragm in order to improve output for the planet and build an escape tunnel for human consciousness through planetary consciousness. What we are escaping from is the pull from the world below (World Seven). World Seven is where the materials for the construction of the physical world are collected; it resembles a perpetual construction site. Nature services this world, pirating constantly from the human family to give to this lower world. The on-flowing of the life force into ever more forms on lower levels is an aspect of continuity.

The different figureheads, their teachings, messages and practices exist as attempts made at different times in history to interest mankind in its own development and escape. And prophecy has always existed to assist this process by informing man of what a higher world requires. Prophecies are never in advance of what the teaching of the time enables consciousness to access.

When the heart centre is open we feel connected to each other; when the brow centre is open we know we are part of the planet; when the crown centre is open we know we can access the stellar worlds. When only the lower centres are open we breed a lot, die a lot and remain preoccupied with survival.

To Nature mankind is worth more dead than alive, asleep in consciousness rather than awake, because this way we give her what she wants which is the substance which is released when we die. As far as Nature is concerned, this is the lead from our roofs. Using wars, epidemics and disasters, her ruthless but effective means, Nature will collect up all the lead that that she needs from our planet to pass down to the endless construction site that is World Seven.

Until man's head centres are engaged in the process of energy transformation the planet receives nothing back from mankind; it has to give everything it gets from us to the world below because the System is set up that way. Our planet which is a living entity with its own destiny and path to follow is supporting a population of seven billion which is giving it next to nothing back on a level that supports the planet's development because modern living has worked against the opening of the head centres. The seat of the intellect is the throat centre (lower correspondent: the thyroid gland). Of itself the energy of the intellect does not serve the planet but it can be put into the service of the ideas which will encourage the opening of the higher *chakras*.

The events we are calling 2012 will be a massive energy harvest. It was always going to happen because the system requires this down-payment from our planet if it is to take a step up on the solar system.

As regards that harvest, the choice that mankind has always had is to help the planet and to protect that escape tunnel or to get shaken off like an animal shakes off parasites and fall more completely into the service of World Seven.

The Red Letters which are the work into which I have put the prophecies about 2012 are concerned with that choice.

Astrology is one of my tools, but I shall be disappointing those who assume that the prophecies I have made about 2012 have come from astrology. They have not. Astrology is a language, a process of inquiry, which in the modern world we have used to come to a better understanding of man in incarnation. We do not yet know how to use the language in a way that places the planet rather than man at the centre of the inquiry, although we are now ready to take this step. DKF's Koruna project in Lapland is concerned with formulating the language of a new, planet-centred astrology.

The Source of my information about 2012 is an Intelligence in World Five which is dedicated to service to humanity. It is from this level that I was given the detail about 2012 which I have passed on through the Red Letters and other publications via our website.

It is unavoidable, I suppose, that we want to think of the planetary servers of this level as personalities because we like things that we can recognise and which give comfort, but doing this diminishes them somewhat. I recommend that we keep in view the fact that these planetary servers constitute an Intelligence (the *Daimon* of the Ancient Greeks). They are the manifestation of an intention in the mind of this living being, our planet. It is a level of consciousness that we can access when we know we are part of planetary consciousness and service is the intention in our own minds. An intention is more than a desire or a sentimental impulse; an intention is something which shapes our lives. Service is a commitment which takes over our lives. It will take everything but what it does in return is turn around the telescope and offers us the other end to look down. We will realise then that we have been looking at things the wrong way round.

The primary objective of the prophecies with which I have been involved is to offer out something that would help those who are ready and able to take action (and 2012 is *a priori* knowledge to many people alive at this time) to help them organise their expectations and coordinate their activities. It is a muster: a call to action. It is not to alert or to warn the unwary in the best Hollywood disaster movie tradition because it is unlikely that those who are unprepared are going to be able to create a constructive relationship with the events because they will not know whether or not to believe what they are being told. The intellect cannot help. They will simply fret and worry and generate negativity which will worsen mankind's position.

It has ever been this way with prophecy. Prophecies are for those who can be stirred into action through remembrance of the plans for our planet and for their own lives. These plans are stamped through us like the words through Brighton rock. They are encoded in our energetic blue print. The intuition knows these plans; good quality astrology works with them.

Those with remembrance will recognise what they are being told by a process which in the New Age has become known as resonance, which takes over where sensory perception leaves off. This is why I have called this paper 'Remembering the Future'.

We do not need to make our choices about 2012 a matter of public debate because it is not intellect which decides what kind of relationship to make with information of this kind; it is the intuition which recognises what is being said (resonance). Those who do not want to accept or even to listen to the message are entitled to reject it. That is an option, and for very many, the one that will serve the best.

In as much as I have encouraged anything, I have encouraged people to view the right decision as the one that they can make work.

In the past five years a group of us whose relationship with the information given to me by the Intelligence expressed itself through unconditional acceptance of the message, have organised ourselves to move, away to a location which we understand to be safe, in as much as its outside the latitudes which define the danger zone for inundation and pollution. We are calling ourselves the Koruna Project.

At first, we talked principally about the logistics of survival. As time moves on and we have developed a more settled relationship with this information and the place in the scheme of things of this event we are calling 2012, different awareness has come into play.

We understand now that we are on a journey, and an integral part of that journey is tidying up before we leave, which has its material and emotional aspects. Most if not all of us are finding this a slow, tiring and dispiriting process, but we know that we cannot simply walk away. That option is there, of course, but it is not one that any of us could make work because we all perceive that we have commitments of various kinds and responsibilities for our families that do not end because they have rejected the opportunity to join us. The only right decision is the one that is workable for the people we are.

Besides, something has to act as grit in the shell to produce the pearl that is human consciousness. Leisure and comforts, whether material or emotional, do not serve us for long. Why not accept, then, that for us the grit is taking this form and go on with the job with good grace? Increasingly, we are.

We have all come to realise as so many others have before us, that the value of what we are doing is not in the arrival but in the journey. Not all of our group may make it to Lapland, and those of us who do may or may not be adequately prepared.

The truth is we do not know what prepared is in the circumstances we face, because knowing and understanding are not the same thing, and, in terms of human time scales, understanding is often a good way behind knowing; but when we were offered the information and we made a relationship of acceptance with it, we created for ourselves the huge challenge of finding out what our lives are worth to us and how to respect the potential that is within each of us. We are doing the best that we can with the understanding that we have, to co-operate with the process of change, to serve the future, to let go of the past responsibly and to honour opportunity which planetary life is reliant upon.

Our efforts may be inadequate to the point of risible but our intention is sound, and we have affirmed and re-affirmed that intention in the past five years, pushing through material difficulties, confusion, fear and despondency to do so. This is as close to a definition of spiritual activity as we will get. A spiritual activity is one that raises vibration; spirituality is a process of distillation, turning what is gross into something more refined. All spiritual forms, from the prophets to the teachings, the ceremonies to the paraphernalia, the litanies to the affirmations, are simply the means to this end.

As regards 2012 I am offering no words of comfort: I am an auditor. My job is to draw attention to the fact that the human family is not doing a good job of contributing towards the coming energy harvest and so we must expect the consequences of this. The world population has reached seven billion: the Intelligence that we call the planetary servers consider that the planet is now 1,000 times overpopulated, based on the return that is being made to it. The energy generated by this enormous number of inhabitants can be likened to a seven watt lamp bulb. That kind of low out-put does not lend itself to much, and the planet cannot do much with this weight of parasitical humanity except shake it off.

In popular culture mankind's poor performance is being widely explained in terms of our lack of regard for the environment and natural resources, but that is only a part of it. Our lack of regard for ourselves is as big a problem. Why do we choose to use only three cylinders (energy centres) when we have another four to fire up? We live like battery hens when, like eagles, we could have the freedom of the skies and generate a much higher quality energy for the planet as we soar. Religion has been trying to address this problem since the story of man began.

Mankind is relentlessly self-centred; and educated man is relentlessly self centred *and* sure of his own significance and effectiveness. We should be aware of the trap in this because 2012 is not about us; it is about the planet. In this situation Man calls no shots whatsoever – none of us. What we can do is create the kind of relationship with this event that enables us to see ourselves as members of the planet, to cooperate with it and engage positively with the options that are available to us.

The Red Letters and the Koruna Project and indeed everything that the DK Foundation has undertaken in the past 10 years exist for this purpose.

This then is the context for our prophecies. I must leave you to make of it what you will.

Chapter 19

2012 and the Revival of the New Age Movement: The Mayan Calendar and the Cultic Milieu in Switzerland

Jean-François Mayer

During most of 1999, researchers working on millenarian movements received requests from journalists – and even from law-enforcement officers – asking them about Y2K and how likely it was that groups of believers in the end times would undertake something spectacular. Most scholars could only say that few of these groups in the Western world gave much significance to the year 2000 per se. Fears about the turn of the millennium as they could be observed in Switzerland (since this country will be the focus of the present article) were primarily secular beliefs about computers that would no longer work or ATMs that would refuse to issue money to customers.

The media have recently started a similar enquiry, but this time about 21 December 2012. But there is also a major difference to the pre-2000 frenzy: sources for theories around 2012 are located in the alternative, 'New Age' religious subculture. They first flourished in this milieu before reaching wider audiences. The role of Roland Emmerich's movie *2012* (2009) was important in the process of popularising the 2012 theme.

Based on research conducted in Switzerland and a reading of 2012 literature found in Swiss bookshops (in part translated from English or other languages) and on relevant websites, this article will attempt to show how the 2012 phenomenon, beyond its intrinsic interest, can help us to understand the functioning of the alternative spirituality networks and will also analyse the nature of apocalyptic discourses on 2012.[1]

During 2011 I identified meetings and other initiatives focused on expectations for, or discussions on, developments that were supposed to take place in late 2012. Libraries patronised by the alternative religious milieu and gatherings attracting this type of audience were visited. This led to an unexpected observation:

---

[1]   This chapter was completed in March 2012 with December 2012 still in the (near) future. This explains why the chapter deals with expectations about 2012 as if the year had not yet ended.

everybody in the milieu was familiar with 2012; a well-known esoteric bookshop had a shelf exclusively devoted to 2012 literature; but no group seemed to be centred around 2012 and there were only a few meetings or seminars on the topic (with most of these taking place in the German-speaking part of Switzerland).[2] This can be explained by the way in which the 2012 theme is inserted into the tapestry of the milieu.

'Cultic Milieu' and the 'New Age': From Alternative Religiosity to Millennial Hopes

This chapter will use two concepts that need to be briefly clarified before proceeding further. The first one is 'cultic milieu', a term coined by Colin Campbell in a seminal article (1972). In a later encyclopaedia entry, he summarised it as referring

> ... to a society's deviant belief systems and practices and their associated collectivities, institutions, individuals, and media of communication. [It includes] 'the worlds of the occult and the magical, of spiritualism and psychic phenomena, of mysticism and new thought, of alien intelligences and lost civilizations, of faith healing and nature cure' (Campbell 1971: 122), and it can be seen, more generally, to be the point at which deviant science meets deviant religion. What unifies these diverse elements, apart from a consciousness of their deviant status and an ensuing sense of common cause, is an overlapping communication structure of magazines, pamphlets, lectures, and informal meeting, together with the common ideology of *seekership* (Campbell 1998).

The concept of a cultic milieu as defined above remains as valid today as it was 40 years ago. It has also convincingly been applied to political oppositional subcultures in addition to religious ones (Kaplan et al. 2002). The process of questioning ideas perceived as dominant often covers more than one area: once accepted ideas in one field are called into doubt, there is no reason not to challenge others.

The second concept is that of the 'New Age'. This label became widely popular in the 1980s, but it could cover so many different contents that its use appeared problematic: at the very time the label was acquiring wide popularity, many of the leading proponents of messages associated with the New Age were eager to distance themselves from what they saw as its commercialisation. However, New Age thinking has persisted, although researchers have questioned its use, due to its vagueness: '"New Age" is not a distinctive empirical formation but a (now rather stale) codeword for the heterogeneity of alternative spirituality' (Sutcliffe 2003: 11).

---

[2]   By the early spring of 2012, with the date coming closer, a slight increase could be observed, as well as more lectures around the topic in the French-speaking areas of Switzerland, but without altering the situation portrayed here.

Moreover, from this viewpoint, it is stressed that 'emic affiliation with "New Age" is optional, episodic and declining overall' (Sutcliffe 2003: 197).

While conceding that the 'New Age' concept is a poorly defined label, Wouter Hanegraaff considers the New Age movement as one of a secularisation of Western esotericism

> characterized by a criticism of dualistic and reductionistic tendencies in (modern) western culture, as exemplified by (what is emically perceived as) dogmatic Christianity, on the one hand, and rationalistic/scientistic ideologies, on the other. It believes that there is a 'third option' which rejects neither religion and spirituality nor science and rationality, but combines them in a higher synthesis (Hanegraaaf 1996: 517).

From this angle, the New Age movement becomes strongly associated with the cultic milieu and both categories overlapped at a specific time: 'The New Age movement is the cultic milieu having become conscious of itself, in the later 1970s, as constituting a more or less unified movement' (Hanegraaff 1996: 522). Researchers have debated whether they should restrict the label 'New Age' to a narrow category or use it broadly. Whatever one's preferences, the New Age theme significantly contributed to the process of popularising alternative religious beliefs.

For the purpose of this chapter, the emphasis needs to be placed on the key original idea of the New Age, as indicated by its very name, i.e. the expectation that humankind is about to enter a new era – astrologically, the passage from the Age of Pisces (associated with Christianity) to the Age of Aquarius. Apocalyptic views had been embraced by proponents of the New Age idea in the 1950s and 1960s, but then gave way to a message emphasising a less turbulent move to a new era of peace and light, and a new spiritual orientation away from materialism and in harmony with nature. Individuals who were transforming themselves would create a critical mass and contribute to a planetary transformation. In accordance with the evolutionary leanings of modern esotericism, humankind could thus take a giant step upwards.

After the peak of the New Age movement in the late 1980s, several scholars claimed that it had come to an end: the milieu that had developed under the New Age banner continued to prosper, but the great majority of New Age figures had 'abandoned any hope of social transformation' (Melton 2000: 288). In order to escape the 'crisis' caused by the lack of the awaited complete social transformation, the exit strategy was a switch to the 'Next Age', i.e. an emphasis on personal transformation and well-being, but at the same time allowing those who embraced the idea to keep most of the benefits derived from New Age practices (Introvigne 2000: 17). The milieu clung to the ideal of the emergence of a new global culture, but 'with the lack of a timetable' and the perspective of a 'long-term gradual spread of the higher consciousness' (Melton 2007: 94, 95).

While the 'assumed decline of the New Age' was a matter for discussion and the 'Next Age' could be seen rather as 'an increased assimilation of New Age perspectives and practices into mainstream culture' (Hanegraaff 2007: 29, 30), the assessment of a lesser emphasis on millennial dimensions seemed to ring true until a few years ago. However, the emergence of the 2012 narrative has made clear that the aspirations of the New Age to a global transformation are far from gone.

Roots of 2012: Memories of the Harmonic Convergence

At least in the United States, the New Age movement reached a peak that brought its ideas to the mainstream in 1987. This same year, an event linked to the 2012 theme took place: the Harmonic Convergence. On 16–17 August 1987, people around the world gathered at selected sacred sites for collective meditation and to open the doors to 'an era of unprecedented change and preparation for a new evolutionary cycle on Earth' that would culminate in 2012. The gatherings were supposed to fulfil 'prophecies calling for 144,000 awakened sun dancers to dance the new age into being'.[3] The emphasis was non-catastrophic, since the event would, said its main organiser, signal 'the elimination of Armageddon' (quoted in Lucas 1992: 205). 'The event was by all accounts the first large-scale simultaneous multinational meditation in history' (*New York Times*, 2 April 2011).

The mind behind the Harmonic Convergence was José Argüelles (1939–2011). The son of a Mexican father and an American mother, he trained as an art historian and received his doctoral degree in Art History and Aesthetics in 1969 from the University of Chicago, subsequently teaching at various universities in the United States. He was very much a child of his time, going through his 'beatnik years' (South 2009: 63–7), interacting with counterculture and immersing himself in the psychedelic subculture. He had the profile of a spiritual seeker: as an MA student, '[l]ate at night, José studied the writings of many mystics, including Jacob Boehme' (South 2009: 69). As an assistant professor of Art History at Princeton in 1966, 'he began the ardent study of Wilhelm Baynes edition of the *I Ching*, supplemented with studies of Tibetan mysticism, shamanism and aboriginal thought' (South 2009: 94). He turned 'to [Alice] Bailey's [1880–1949] esoteric writings in the fall of 1967' (South 2009: 100). In 1969, in addition to Bailey, he read the work of astrologer Dane Rudhyar (1895–1985) (South 2009: 112); according to Argüelles, Rudhyar told him in 1973 that he considered him to be his successor (South 2009: 150). In 1970 'he was studying *The Secret Teaching of All Ages*, Manly Hall's compendium of esoteric knowledge' (South 2009: 118). In 1971 he resided for some time at a friend's house that had been turned into an ashram of Baba Hari Dass (b. 1923), then freshly arrived in California

---

[3]   'August 16 (Blue Magnetic Eagle) Marks the 24th Anniversary of the Harmonic Convergence, just One Year before Harmonic Convergence 2012 and the Launching of the Rainbow Bridge!' http://www.lawoftime.org/infobooth/hc24.html (accessed: 1 March 2012).

(South 2009: 123). In the same year he met Tibetan master Chögyam Trungpa (1939–87), accepted him as his teacher and started his Vajrayana practices in 1974 (South 2009: 155). He would consider Trungpa as his teacher until Trungpa's death. After recovering from a serious alcoholism problem in the late 1970s, in 1983 Argüelles initiated the Planet Art Network (PAN, http://www. planetartnetwork.info), seeing art as a foundation for global peace (South 2009: 192). Thus Argüelles' life story interacted with alternative spiritualities and the contemporary search for another way of life.

Due to his part-Mexican background, Argüelles had been interested in pre-Columbian civilisations quite early – not only Mayan, but also Aztec: in 1964, he went through a powerful experience linked to the figure of Quetzalcoatl (South 2009: 77–8). In 1972 Tony Shearer (b. 1926) first made him aware of the significance of 1987 and the sacred count of the Maya (South 2009: 142). In the previous year, Shearer had published his book *Lord of the Dawn*; he had come to his belief in 16 August 1987 based on an alleged prophecy of Quetzalcoatl, taking the landing of Cortes and his conquest of Mexico to be a form of Rosetta stone. 'The prophecy was true – for those with the eyes to see it', Shearer later wrote, remembering the Harmonic Convergence: 'the New Age had been born' (Shearer 1995: 11).

In 1986, while he was preparing the Harmonic Convergence, Argüelles started writing his book *The Mayan Factor*, which was published in 1987.

> This book was the opening to the complete understanding of the prophetic date of 2012, the closing of the Mayan Great cycle. At this point, José understood that humanity, living in ignorance of the laws of nature, would have to make a great shift from destructive material civilization to a civilization based on natural cycles of the order of the universe (South 2009: 216).

The idea of the Harmonic Convergence had obviously been influenced by some of Argüelles's previous experiences. Sympathetic to the civil rights movement, he had participated in the March on Washington, led by Martin Luther King, in August 1963 and probably realised there for the first time the impact of a large crowd of people in stimulating energies of change: 'José felt surges of positive energy as he entered the great masses gathered for the cause of social justice and world peace. The feeling of solidarity between more than 200,000 black and white people held an inexplicable power that penetrated his core' (South 2009: 74).

In 1970, while teaching at the University of California at Davis, he had organised the first Whole Earth Festival, with the participation of Eastern gurus (Yogi Bhajan, Swami Satchidananda) and native medicine men (Sun Bear): 'On the last day of the event, Spring Equinox, a global peace meditation was held, synchronized with spiritual and Earth Day groups in India, Australia, Europe, and North America' (South 2009: 116).

Thus the Harmonic Convergence was an expression of New Age aspirations rooted in a specific cultural context. The event was seen as a success and was widely reported in the American media. 'However, attempts to perpetuate the Harmonic Convergence idea within the New Age movement have met with minimal enthusiasm', J. Gordon Melton observed a few years later, attributing this to 'the speculative nature of Argüelles's dating scheme developed from Mayan sources' and to the coincidence of the event with a time at which not a few New Age figures had become sceptical of 'apocalyptic schemes of social transformation' beyond the experience of personal transformation (Melton 1990: 205). It would have been relatively rare to hear people referring to 2012 during the 1990s.

José Argüelles thus played a key role, but he was not the only important figure behind the 2012 idea. Terence McKenna (1946–2000) had arrived at the significance of the 2012 date independently of the Mayan calendar (Hanegraaff 2009; South 2009: 207; see also Chapter 16, this volume). Alleged convergences between information derived from various sources and spiritual traditions have become a major argument in the apologetics of 2012 proponents (Stray 2005).

By the time the 2012 theme reached a wider audience in the last decade, it was to a large extent spreading independently of Argüelles, although the Foundation for the Law of Time (http://www.lawoftime.org), which he founded in 2000, along with associated websites and groups, continues to this day to present his message to the world. But most people who are interested in 2012 have not read Argüelles's books. This is even more obvious in Switzerland and other European countries: *The Mayan Factor* is out of print in German and it was not published in French until 2009, with a modest circulation since.

The 2012 theme has thus been propagated through a variety of authors and speakers, leading to quite varied perspectives about the meaning and consequences of the date. Around a common narrative according to which the Maya Long Count Calendar points to crucial events for our planet in 2012 (on 21 December, according to most interpretations), different views are expressed, encompassing both turbulent and peaceful perspectives on the immediate future. Expectations around 2012 have acquired a dynamic of their own, escaping the control of any authoritative source of interpretation and subject to uses ranging from spiritual messages to sheer commercialisation by the media both playing upon and debunking the 2012 theme.

The 2012 Scene in Switzerland (and Beyond)

A simple look at the books on 2012 found in Swiss bookshops shows that a number of them are works translated into French or German, mostly from English. People interested in the theme in Switzerland share material with people in other Western countries. The high level of Internet penetration in Switzerland reinforces this relative homogeneity. The following observations, gleaned during field research in Switzerland, should therefore be applicable to the 2012 phenomenon in other European countries, with perhaps some local variations.

The core audience interested in 2012 is made of people already familiar with other themes associated with the cultic milieu. While 2012 has gained a much wider audience, the cultic milieu is instrumental in producing discourses articulating the message.

The fact that the 2012 theme has been circulating far beyond the circles interested in alternative worldviews is one more instance of New Age worldviews no longer being fringe, but integrating into popular culture, becoming what has been labelled 'popular spirituality' (Knoblauch 2009, 2010). However, most people would integrate some beliefs selectively without adopting all of them. Similarly, a vague awareness that something might happen in 2012 and that there are discussions on the theme does not mean adhering to more specific expectations of the date marking a transition to a new era.

More elaborate beliefs around 2012 remain the preserve of the cultic milieu. Attending various meetings and lectures on the topic of 2012 in Switzerland during 2011 made clear that most people who attended were already socialised in the cultic milieu. They had read literature and attended lectures related to alternative spiritualities and therapeutic practices. Some of them were full-time authors, therapists or spiritual teachers; others spent a significant part of their free time in such activities. Speaking about channelling or Atlantis would be done in a natural way, without any need to explain such beliefs to an audience that was well acquainted with these concepts. People attending such meetings were therefore speaking the same spiritual language.

Thus 2012 emerges out of the cultic milieu and is not a topic floating around alone: from the start, it is part of a wider body of beliefs, flexible enough to be adjusted to individual inclinations, but still sharing common foundations. These pre-existent sets of beliefs provide plausibility to the 2012 speculations.

Even when a topic such as 2012 reaches wider audiences, the cultic milieu and its 'activists' remain necessary: they produce practices and ideas, some of which will generate a larger echo. Since 'popular spirituality' needs to renew itself and make new products available for public consumption, it is dependent upon the committed core (the cultic milieu) for creating such products.

Authors and speakers incorporate the 2012 theme into an already existing, more general discourse, with a cumulative effect. Whatever happens or does not happen in December 2012 will not affect the other elements of their discourse.

Merely speaking about 2012 does not guarantee an audience. On 12 May 2011, at the centre Die Quelle (The Source) in Bern, which offers a rich programme of all kinds of alternative spiritual messages, Renate Wildhaber presented a lecture entitled: '2011, 2012 – and Then? Introduction to the New Energy'. The lecture was listed in the programme of Die Quelle, which reaches a wide segment of the cultic milieu in the Swiss capital and beyond. But Wildhaber is an unknown name in the circuit. Despite the emphasis on 2012, few showed interest: there were only three people in the audience, including myself.

This does not mean that 2012 by itself cannot draw an audience: a lecture by representatives of a Mayan group or other kinds of exotic emissaries would attract more attention. Beside them, several authors or other figures are already well known in the cultic milieu mentioning 2012 – but what role do they play?

An example is Swiss author Erich von Däniken (b. 1935), who became famous after publishing his first book in 1968, translated into English as *Chariots of the Gods? Unsolved Mysteries of the Past* (1969). Von Däniken claims that space travellers intervened in humankind's history, leaving many traces in the monuments and mythologies of ancient civilisations. His book became a bestseller, selling millions of copies in English, and was translated into many languages. Von Däniken has since become a prolific author and speaker: his many books have been translated into 32 languages and have sold 63 million copies worldwide.[4]

The Mayan calendar was mentioned in Von Däniken's original book, but without being linked to 2012 or any date in the future. He primarily suggested that the Maya had been visited by the 'gods', i.e. space travellers, in his perspective.[5] Von Däniken could not fail to use 2012 as an additional argument for spreading his theories. In 2010 he published *Twilight of the Gods: The Mayan Calendar and the Return of the Extraterrestrials* (original German edition 2009). The book repeats his usual arguments and stresses that one thing is certain: the 'gods' will return – even if it will not necessarily be in December 2012.

Von Däniken's discourse does not need 2012 and can continue to operate perfectly well without any reference to this date. The same can be said about most of the authors building on the 2012 theme: it comes as a welcome addition, but it is not the cornerstone of their messages.

One even comes across a number of cultic milieu figures who use 2012 as a way to attract attention, while the content of their talks has little to do with the date itself. On 4 March 2012, at Lebenskraft (Lifeforce), a yearly 'fair and congress for conscience, health and spirituality' in Zurich, two lectures were listed on 2012: one by Tibetan lama Chokling Jigme Palden Rinpoche ('2012 from a Tibetan Perspective'), the other one by Armin Risi ('Paradigm Shift 2012'), who spent nearly two decades as a monk in the International Society for Krishna Consciousness and is now a lecturer and author.[6] While both lectures used 2012 as a banner in their titles, the actual content did not even mention 2012 or the Mayan calendar: Rinpoche mentioned Tibetan prophecies, but without any attempt to link them to 2012 or the fate of the world. Clearly, for both speakers, 2012 primarily allowed them to draw attention to their favourite themes.

---

[4]   According to his website: http://www.daeniken.com (accessed: 4 March 2012).

[5]   It should be added that Argüelles also had a strong interest in extraterrestrial themes and it seems quite possible that Von Däniken's theories exercised some influence.

[6]   See his website: http://armin-risi.ch/index_en.html (accessed: 4 March 2012).

More generally, one could say that this is a milieu in which many people already believe that deep changes and new orientations are required for addressing the concerns of the modern world. 2012 can come as a welcome adjunct that conveys a sense of imminence, but this does not change already existing discourses in most cases. 2012 is accepted as a topic of interest in the cultic milieu in the same way that many other themes can easily be assimilated, as long as they fit within a general pattern.

Not all speakers and authors commenting on 2012 predict sudden, visible changes in our environment on a specific date. Moreover, many of them explain 2012 as a step in a longer transition period, which somewhat deflects the notion of imminence.

One can find online videos hinting at the likeliness of terrible disasters (often including material borrowed from Hollywood movies).[7] Pete Lentini has noticed in observations about 2012 on YouTube 'that whereas the main literature on 2012 may have a reasonably good blend of the apocalyptic and the millennial, the YouTube videos that comprise part of this milieu tend to emphasize the destructive and the pessimistic' (2011: 74). Moreover, videos with 'messages for hope and rebirth in 2012' seemed to attract less interest than the others (Lentini 2011: 74). Members of the general public, especially teenagers, are more likely to come across YouTube videos than spiritual literature: it is not surprising that their perceptions of 2012 will on average have a much stronger catastrophic component. In Switzerland, as in other countries, educators report encountering young people quite frightened by the 2012 perspectives.

Most authors in the cultic milieu emphasise hope. A cleansing is inevitable, writes Diana Cooper, and the incidence of natural disasters will 'intensify especially between 2017 and 2022', but '[a]fter 2022 the disasters will stop and there will be calm' (Cooper 2009: 70, 73). Even US-based Marshall Masters, who announces that Planet X (Nibiru) will bring 'pain and destruction' and has a survivalist tenor, foresees a bright future after the turmoil:

> Yes, Planet X will cause 2012 to be a punishing time – but it will not be a punishment. Nor will it be the end of a timeline. Rather, it will be one of the most, if not the most important evolutionary events in the history of our species. There is a purpose to everything in creation. The coming pain and destruction to be wrought by Planet X in 2012 shall be a clarion call for peace and harmony …. No matter how dark the times become, always remember – the path of love reaches beyond 2012, and the path of fear ends there. Those who survive with

---

[7]   Also, a number of Christian or Muslim apocalyptic videos have been using Hollywood scenes (without mentioning where they come from) in order to stress their message: thus popular culture also contributes to shaping apocalyptic perceptions.

love will answer the call as equals, and they shall survive to become part of the most important human population to ever walk the Earth.[8]

Most of the literature and speakers encountered during field research in the Swiss cultic milieu have evidenced an emphasis on non-apocalyptic elements and a focus on a time period as much as on a precise date. German biophysicist Dieter Broers, author of a successful book on 2012, explains that on 21 December 2012 the Maya expected an event that would transform consciousness and that, after an event of such a magnitude, nothing would be the same again (2009: 21–2); later in the book, Broers writes that it is unclear if the mutation process of mankind will start or be completed in 2012 (2009: 187). Many exponents of the 2012 theme increasingly tend to stress that it will only be the beginning of a transition period that might extend over a number of years or even decades.

In his lectures, while stressing the possibility that the awaited 'return of the extraterrestrials' might be very close, Von Däniken is careful to add that there might be a margin of error of about hundred years in relation to Mayan expectations for 2012. Such caution means there is no risk that he will have to deal with a failed prophecy. Moreover, in a process typical of the cultic milieu, other explanations or new theories can always be offered while incorporating the legacy of previous themes.

Can we categorise the 2012 expectations of the cultic milieu as progressive millennialism, since most believe that human cooperation with the energies of change is needed for bringing about the New Age? As Catherine Wessinger states, progressive millennialism is 'a millennial perspective that is optimistic about human nature and the possibility of the current imperfect human society to get better' (Wessinger 2000: 332). Although it adopts an evolutionary approach, it can also include 'a sense of emergency and imminence of the arrival of the millennium' (Wessinger 1997: 53). But progressive millennialism is characterised by the absence of catastrophic scenarios: as we have seen, while some people believe in a smooth transition, others associate it with at least the possibility of disasters, sometimes understood as a necessary cleansing of the old structures. In many scenarios, this is at least partly conditional: changes in human attitudes can prevent the worst from happening. There is an open space that probably reflects the presence of both catastrophic and non-catastrophic expectations of the New Age in the roots of this milieu, in addition to its natural eclecticism. 2012 scenarios found in the cultic milieu thus include both cases of catastrophic millennialism and of progressive millennialism, plus scenarios that could probably be described as hybrid.

---

[8]   http://planetxforecast.com/h2h/index.shtml (accessed: 9 March 2012).

The 2012 theme illustrates how indigenous cultures are used as resources for answering Western uncertainties about the future.

The Maya have not been the first: a number of other indigenous cultures (including legacies of a distant, imagined Western past) are called on to address the anxieties of modern Westerners. They are assumed to retain a wisdom and spirituality that would come as a welcome balance to the doomed Western materialism and distance from nature. Thus we find a number of Mayan people and groups being invited to speak in Switzerland; in addition, travels to Mayan areas are organised by and for people involved in the cultic milieu.

In August 2011 a group of Mayan elders toured Switzerland and spoke at events that were each attended by hundreds of people (600–700 participants in Bern on 19 August, for example, around 75 per cent female). Quite remarkably, especially considering the fact that the Mayan group was unknown in Switzerland, the events were not advertised in the mainstream media (except for one article in a newspaper on the morning of one of the meetings) and the visit of the Mayan elders was made known through cultic milieu networks.

The Mayan elders (two men and two women) came from Guatemala and El Salvador. In addition to the Swiss organiser, Silvan Zülle (an active figure in the Swiss cultic milieu), they were accompanied by Joseph Giove, executive producer of the *Shift of the Ages* film project:[9] the purpose of the movie is to assist 'Wandering Wolf, Grand Elder of the living Maya … in delivering the Authentic Mayan Message to the world'. Wandering Wolf (Cirilo Perez Oxlaj) is the leader of the Mayan Elders National Council.[10] Don Cirilo Oxlaj 'stands out as the most traditional and respected of the few actual Maya teachers connected with the 2012 phenomenon' (Sitler 2011: 12). He has developed contacts around the world with other religious leaders. The group is one of the expressions of indigenous revitalisation across Latin America in the political, cultural and spiritual spheres, and more specifically of Pan-Mayan activism (see Chiappari 2002, Warren 1998). Parts of the speeches were devoted to Mayan indigenous concerns, even if this was not really what the audience had been looking for.

The Mayan elders stressed that they were bringing to the world the authentic Mayan message, in contrast with people who spend two weeks in Central America and then write a book. Regarding 2012, the elders stated that no specific date could be given and we might need to wait a few dozen years; but they confirmed that one solar period would end and a new one would start. When the time comes, everybody will know it, since we will spend several days in darkness.[11]

---

[9]   http://www. shiftoftheages.com (accessed: 4 March 2012).

[10]   A group of which Alvaro Colom, president of Guatemala from January 2008 to January 2012, is a member (and an ordained Mayan priest, although not belonging to any Mayan ethnic group).

[11]   Some statements by Wandering Wolf – who did not travel to Switzerland with the group – sound much more dramatic. In a statement released in April 2011 Oxalj declared:

We will reach a new year zero and it will be a time to celebrate, since the era of materialism will be over and there will no longer be national borders. Thus, humankind should not be afraid: 'It is a new hope, a new mankind, there will no longer be wars. We will form one mankind, full of love, peace and unity.'

The Mayan elders were not the only visitors from Central America. In Swiss esoteric bookshops one can find the German translation of a book originally published in 2008 in Spanish: *2012: The Authentic Message of the Maya for the New Age* (Nah Kin 2009). Its author is Nah Kin (Eugenia Casarin) from Mexico. She travels to different countries for seminars and lectures, such as the one I attended in Bern on 16 June 2011. The audience was much more modest than that for the Mayan elders, but Nah Kin's claims are much grander. A slide show introduced her as the 'Highest Priestess and Grandmother of the Maya', the 'Spiritual Leader for the New Era', the 'expression of an incarnated Spiritual Hierarchy', the 'Holy Lady who has created Heaven on Earth' and the 'Holy Duality with Father Kinich Ahau in the spiritual world', among other titles.

According to Nah Kin, we are coming close to the end of a 25,000-year period that will culminate in 2012. An intensive phase started in 2008, will reach its height in 2012, and will diminish from 2016. Intense solar energy is in the process of transforming into a spiritual force. In the new era, everybody needs to elevate their vibrations in order to create a unified field in which all beings will find themselves in a vibratory sphere. There is nothing to fear about 2012, but there must be acceptance of a coming cosmic leap. We are about to enter a new age of experiencing love and unity. Nah Kin puts special emphasis on the role of women in the new era. On 21 December 2012 a great ceremony will take place 'in the holy city of Uxmal, place of incomparable Divine power', as part of a 'Spiritual Planetary Summit' involving a gathering of representatives of all spiritual traditions to close the door on the past along with its paradigms and open the door to the new age.

Born in 1961, Eugenia Casarin graduated in Social Psychology at the University of Mexico. She claims to have been in touch as a teenager with the Universal Great Brotherhood, established in 1948 in Venezuela by Serge Raynaud de la Ferrière (1916–62), considered by his followers as an avatar for the Aquarian Age. She reports having been in touch with masters in different spiritual traditions (including Osho and Buddhist teachers); she also immersed

---

'We are seeing a series of events approaching us as never seen before, these events come charged with tremendous sufferings and pain. They will happen in different places. ... All this is due to the contamination. The atmosphere has lost its control. We the Maya see it with much sadness that we will see hunger and drought. Plagues will invade the fields and affect the agriculture; new illnesses will appear and will be difficult to cure. ... Our recommendation to avoid more suffering is this: No more nuclear testing, no more wars, no more mining and other explorations, no more use of chemicals. ... If we do not change, few will be the ones to survive and see the arrival of the 6th Sun', http://www.shiftoftheages. com/Maya-Message-2012 (accessed: 10 March 2012).

herself in the teachings of Ascended Masters and was active in spreading *A Course in Miracles* in Mexico between 1992 and 1997.[12]

In whatever 'authentic' Mayan message that is presented, we actually come across either indigenous revitalisation movements or products of the Central American cultic milieu, adorned with the prestige and authority of native lineage. In both cases, these are modern movements more than voices from the past: interaction with New Age messages is included.[13] They are part of what anthropologists have called the 'neo-Indian' phenomenon (Galinier et al. 2006), creatively using both ancient traditions and external inputs that they make their own – thus their messages are not merely the legacy of wise ancestors. They are also children of a globalised age, looking for interaction with spiritual figures of other traditions and sharing their views with audiences far from their home countries. Most of these groups would exist without 2012: but 2012 allows them to find an audience in other cultures – partly through the networks of the cultic milieu.

Conclusion

As we have seen, there are two types of speculations around 2012: those of the cultic milieu, from which 2012 originated, on the one hand, and echoes in popular culture, greatly helped by the Internet (including videos on YouTube), the movie *2012* and reports on 2012 expectations in the media, on the other. While the second type focuses on disasters, the first presents a more complex picture: catastrophic events, both seen as signs of the times and as cleansing, may be present, but even the reading of such events is coloured by New Age expectations and offers a revitalisation of collective hopes for a new era.

Expectations regarding 2012 match aspirations widespread in the cultic milieu, even more so at a time when the world is seen as going through turmoil. Silvan Zülle, who invited the Mayan elders to Switzerland, comments in a book that approaches 2012 as an 'awakening of mankind':

> It becomes always more manifest that this system becomes unstable. Global crises and increasing chaos point to a coming evolutionary turning point. Maybe the next change of paradigm is no longer far away. However, for that

---

[12]   Available at: http://www.kinich-ahau.org/csmaya/19012011_nahkin.html (accessed: 10 March 2012).

[13]   Sitler observes that even the teachings of Don Cirilo Oxalj mirror elements from authors such as Argüelles, for instance, the mention of a Pleiadian connection (Sitler 2011: 13) that was also mentioned during the speeches delivered in Bern. Sitler further remarks that 'cross pollination between contemporary Maya and New Age participants in the 2012 movement is inevitable', with New Agers visiting Mayan areas or settling there (Sitler 2011: 18–19).

a fundamental transformation of our consciousness and self-understanding is required. Otherwise, survival on our beautiful Earth will present increasingly greater problems (Zülle 2010: 179).

At the start of the seminar Consciousness Transformation 2012 that took place in September 2011, Zülle, acting as the convener of the meeting, reminded his audience that inherited answers to the current world problems were providing no convincing solution: the situation cannot continue as it is, but this does not mean that there will be a choice between apocalypse, on the one hand, and the ascension of humankind, on the other – more likely it will be something in between. This reflects how a number of cultic milieu figures attempt to build on the theme while exercising some level of caution.

When starting to explore meetings or lectures on 2012, one might have expected to come across people with intense millenarian beliefs. Aspirations to a New Age are strong indeed, but there are differences between them and some other types of millenarian currents: typical participants of the cultic milieu are accustomed to test and play with various ideas and messages from which they can pick what feels right for them. These ideas are not seen as infallible dogma. Moreover, the milieu provides a variety of interpretations. While it will be interesting to observe reactions after 2012 (in case the world continues to exist as it is), the attitude of most 2012ers does not seem to announce major challenges in terms of cognitive dissonance. At the end of the September 2011 seminar, a grandmother who had attended summarised her feelings to me: 'If nothing happens, we have nothing to lose. If something happens, we have everything to gain.'

References

Broers, D. 2009. *(R)evolution 2012: Warum die Menschheit vor einem Evolutionssprung steht*. Berlin: Scorpio Verlag.

Campbell, C. 1972. The Cult, the Cultic Milieu and Secularization, in *A Sociological Yearbook of Religion in Britain 5*, edited by M. Hill. London: SCM Press, 119–36.

———. 1998. Cult, in *Encyclopedia of Religion and Society*, edited by W.H. Swatos. Walnut Creek, CA: AltaMira Press, 122–3 [Online]. Available at: http://hirr.hartsem.edu/ency/cult.htm [accessed: 24 April 2012].

Chiappari, C.L. 2002. Toward a Maya Theology of Liberation: The Reformulation of 'Traditional' Religion in the Global Context. *Journal for the Scientific Study of Religion*, 41(1), 47–67.

Cooper, D. 2009. *2012 and Beyond: An Invitation to Meet the Challenges and Opportunities Ahead*. Forres: Findhorn Press.

Galinier, J. et al. 2006. *Les Néo-Indiens: une religion du IIIe millénaire*. Paris: Odile Jacob.

Hanegraaff, W.J. 1996. *New Age Religion and Western Culture: Esotericism in the Mirror of Secular Thought*. Leiden: Brill.

———. 2007. The New Age Movement and Western Esotericism, in *Handbook of New Age*, edited by D. Kemp and J.R. Lewis. Leiden: Brill, 25–50.

———. 2009. 'And End History, and Go to the Stars': Terence McKenna and 2012, in *Religion and Retributive Logic: Essays in Honour of Professor Garry W. Trompf*, edited by C.M. Cusack and C. Hartney. Leiden: Brill, 291–312.

Introvigne, M. 2000. *New Age and Next Age*. Casale Monferrato: Edizioni Piemme.

Kaplan, J. et al. 2002. *The Cultic Milieu: Oppositional Subcultures in an Age of Globalization*. Walnut Creek, CA: AltaMira Press.

Knoblauch, H. 2009. *Populäre Religion: Auf dem Weg in eine spirituelle Gesellschaft*, Frankfurt: Campus Verlag.

———. 2010. Vom New Age zur populären Spiritualität, in *Fluide Religion: Neue religiöse Bewegungen im Wandel: Theoretische und empirische Systematisierungen*, edited by D. Lüddeckens et al. Bielefeld: Transcript Verlag, 149–74.

Lentini, P. 2011. The 2012 Milieu? Hybridity, Diversity and Stigmatised Knowledge, in *2012: Decoding the Countercultural Apocalypse*, edited by J. Gelfer. Sheffield: Equinox, 60–85.

Lucas, P.C. 1992. The New Age Movement and the Pentecostal/Charismatic Revival: Distinct yet Parallel Phases of a Fourth Great Awakening?, in *Perspectives on the New Age*, edited by J.R. Lewis and J.G. Melton. Albany, NY: State University of New York Press, 189–211.

Melton, J.G. 1990. *New Age Encyclopedia*. Detroit, MI: Gale Research.

———. 2000. New Age, in *Encyclopedia of Millennialism and Millennial Movements*, edited by R. Landes. New York: Routledge, 285–8.

———. 2007. Beyond Millennialism: The New Age Transformed, in *Handbook of New Age*, edited by D. Kemp and J.R. Lewis. Leiden: Brill, 77–97.

Nah Kin. 2009. *2012: die authentische Botschaft der Maya für das Neue Zeitalter*. Munich: Sphinx.

Shearer, T. 1995. *Lord of the Dawn: Quetzalcoatl and the Tree of Life*. Happy Camp, CA: Naturegraph Publishers.

Sitler, R.K. 2011. The 2012 Phenomenon: New Uses for an Ancient Maya Calendar, in *2012: Decoding the Countercultural Apocalypse*, edited by J. Gelfer. Sheffield: Equinox, 8–22.

South, S. 2009. *2012: Biography of a Time Traveler: The Journey of José Arguelles*. Franklin Lakes, NJ: New Page Books.

Stray, G. 2005. *Beyond 2012: Catastrophe or Ecstasy*. Lewes: Vital Signs.

Sutcliffe, S.J. 2003. *Children of the New Age: A History of Spiritual Practices*. London: Routledge.

Von Däniken, E. 1969. *Chariots of the Gods? Unsolved Mysteries of the Past*. London: Souvenir Press.

———. 2010. *Twilight of the Gods: The Mayan Calendar and the Return of the Extraterrestrials*. Franklin Lakes, NJ: New Page Books.

Warren, K.B. 1998. *Indigenous Movements and Their Critics: Pan-Maya Activism in Guatemala*. Princeton, NJ: Princeton University Press.

Wessinger, C. 1997. Millennialism with and without the Mayhem, in *Millennium, Messiahs, and Mayhem: Contemporary Apocalyptic Movements*, edited by T. Robbins and S.J. Palmer. New York: Routledge, 47–59.

——. 2000. Progressive Millennialism, in *Encyclopedia of Millennialism and Millennial Movements*, edited by R. Landes. New York: Routledge, 332–3.

Zülle, S. 2010. *2012: Erwachen der Menschheit*. Fahrwangen: Silvan Zülle.

Chapter 20
Looking into the Future:
Why Prophecies Will Persist

J. Gordon Melton

During 2011, Evangelical Christians in the United States were alternately embarrassed and entertained by the series of remarks made by Christian radio owner, Harold Camping, relative to his predictions that the climatic events of history – the destruction of the world, the rapture of Christians to the heavens and Judgment Day – would occur first in May and then in October (see Duff-Brown 2011). The wealthy Camping also was able to spend several million dollars to publicise the prediction as well as advertise it on the radio station he owned. A small cadre of the embarrassed also appeared outside his establishment in the San Francisco area to protest his date-setting activity and a modest number of Christian media attacked him for ignoring Jesus' admonition, 'It is not for you to know the times or the seasons …' (Acts 1:7).

In spite of Jesus' words, as well as the experience of history in which predictions of the end have repeatedly failed, we have found would-be prophets continuing to arise, to have their moment in the sun and then to fade with the sunset – some to total obscurity and others to continue a level of leadership and respect within their religious community. In the 1970s, Baptist preacher Hal Lindsey had a best-selling book, *The Late Great Planet Earth*, in which he predicted that the founding of the State of Israel (1948) signalled the beginning of the last generation of humanity and that by 1988 (a generation being set at 40 years) Jesus would return. As of 2012, Lindsey continues to pastor a church, appear regularly on Christian television and author new books with titles such as *Faith for Earth's Final Hour* (2003).

If the history of the last century is any indication, even as we continue to study the phenomenon of end-of-the-world predictions,[1] point out the failure of past predictions and highlight the weak foundations upon which they are built, not to mention the interruption of the lives of those who accept them, we will continue to be embarrassed and entertained by further predictions in the decades ahead.

The number of such predictions that have been voiced abroad and gained a measurable audience of committed believers and additional followers at least willing to entertain the possibility of the truth of those predictions has grown

---

[1]   A base of literature on current studies in millennialism is supplied by Boyer (1994), Lewis (2000), Stone (2000), Tumminia and Swatos, Jr (2011), Wessinger (2011) and Wojcik (1999).

steadily over the last 200 years. Taken together, they, in fact, form another challenge to the secularisation theory which still seems to be hanging on in some intellectual circles in spite of the growing number of falsifications of its predictions, and there is every reason to believe that over the next generation we will begin to see the reverse of the secularised establishments that seem to have settled in parts of Europe.

But why have end-of-the-world predictions proliferated in our own days, and why should we be prepared for even more in the next generation? First, we understand that eschatology speaks to both a perennial human concern and is of the essence of the basic religious quest. Religion is built around answering the three unanswerable questions of origin, meaning and destiny – where did we come from, why are we here and where are we going? That we are part of a lost generation in a crumbling social context which is beyond our fixing and needs outside intervention to set aright, is an attractive analysis of the human state and needs only to be a-historically tied to the present moment to lay the foundation for predictions that the world is coming to a swift end. For those who feel powerless, such an understanding seems to come easily, and when presented by a social group that provides a community of like minds and hearts, finds ready recruits.

Second, we must not forget the roles that the growth of population, the building of dense urban centres, and the improvement in communication have played in not only supporting new religions (which overwhelmingly are an urban phenomenon), but in producing a growing number of potential recruits and making access to them far easier than in past generations. At the time William Miller announced the second coming for 1843 in a series of newspaper articles, the United States was home to less than 20 million people. Today it has over 300 million, the majority of whom both live in an urban centre and have immediate access to the Internet.

Third, and the point I would like to focus on most, is the growth of several new religious communities, two in England and two in the United States, which have become globally successful and have provided the intellectual underpinnings of the present prophetic movements upon which we have focused.

The first of these movements is, of course, the Millerite movement of the 1830s. Former Baptist preacher William Miller adopted a hermeneutic of the two main prophetic books in the New Testament that understood both to be an account of future history. He attempted to correlate the events he found described there with a chronology of world history. It was an interesting intellectual task, and produced a simple picture of history positing a rather recent creation and an extremely short span of human life on earth. In the Millerite scheme, the whole of history could be reduced to a single diagram that laid out God's 'Plan of the Ages' from beginning to end. Anyone could quickly come to understand the big picture.[2]

---

[2]   On Miller and the Millerites see Knight (1993) or Rowe (2008). The earlier volume by Francis D. Nichols (1944) remains an excellent source. The story of all the successive Millerite groups is found in J. Gordon Melton (2009).

Following the Great Disappointment, when Christ failed to return visibly in the 1840s, the Millerite movement splintered, and continued to spawn groups that tried to refine Miller's analysis and propose new dates, each of which subsequently failed, or like the Seventh-day Adventists found a way to justify Miller's work while settling back into a mode of waiting upon an unknown date – though one that was imminent.

Among the Millerites, a new group arose in the 1870s which began to pose a new date based upon accepting a Seventh-day Adventist approach, a beginning event that was invisible, and a future event in which the invisible will become visible. The Pittsburgh Bible Students suggested that Christ had come in 1879, that is, he had become present invisibly, and would become visibly present in a generation (understood to be 35 years). The Students looked to 1914 as the expected time, and when that date came and went, looked to 1925 and later, after changing their name to Jehovah's Witnesses, to 1945 and 1975. Both the Adventists and Witnesses have now become global groups, two of the five groups with worshipping communities in more than 200 of the world's countries, and continue to spawn splinter groups that propose new dates, the most famous being the Branch Davidians of Waco, Texas (see Chapter 14, this volume).[3]

Arising simultaneously with the Millerites were the Latter-day Saints. In the wake of their kingdom building in the last half century, we forget the millennial implication of the movement's name – Latter-day Saints. The movement was born in millennial expectations and looked for a place to build the temple, gather the saints and await the return of Christ. It would be the unintended consequences of the gathering – buying large tracts of land and block voting – that would cause the intense problems with the first generation (namely hostile neighbours) and then lead to the settled life in Utah in the present.

At the same time, however, the prophetic strain of Latter-day Saint thought has been kept alive by the many prophetic leaders it has produced and the dozens of splinter groups they have founded. The most recent wave of splinter groups emerged in the 1980s when the other Latter-day church, the Reorganized Church of Latter-day Saints (now called the Community of Christ) based in Independence, Missouri, initiated a number of changes concurrent with the loss of leadership from the family of founder Joseph Smith, Jr. Relatively little attention has been given to the Mormon apocalyptic groups apart from the several that have clashed with law enforcement over issues of violence.[4]

A late contemporary of Miller and Smith, Irish Anglican John Nelson Darby, has become possibly the most successful theoretician of end-time ideas. Once he withdrew from the Anglican Church, he developed the new approach to biblical interpretation called dispensationalism. Like Miller, Darby proposed a

---

[3]　There is a vast literature that has now developed on the Branch Davidians. Among prominent recent additions see Doyle (2012), Wright (1995) and Wright and Richardson (2011).

[4]　On Mormon millennial groups see Rich (1967) and Shields (1982).

'Plan of the Ages', that laid out biblical history and predicted its soon demise. Darbyite dispensationalism would become the essential building block of the thought world of the Brethren, a new group that eschewed any denominating name but became popularly referred to as the Plymouth Brethren and whose various divisions have become known by a variety of names.

The Brethren spread globally during Darby's lifetime, while its peculiar ecclesiology made it almost invisible on the religious landscape. In the last half of the nineteenth century, it made its way to the United States and found a convert in evangelist Dwight L. Moody. However, most Americans attracted to Darby's thought found dispensationalism attractive but chose not to become Brethren or accept Darby's ecclesiology. The Baptists, Presbyterians, Congregationalists and even a few Methodists attracted to dispensationalism would in turn come together and create a set of Prophecy conferences in which they focused on the degenerating trends they found in their denominations and looked to the next events on the horizon for the faithful.[5] This new prophetic movement would find a great spokesperson in one Cyrus I. Scofield who developed a new edition of the Bible with dispensation footnotes throughout. Published in 1909 by Oxford University Press, the *Scofield Reference Bible* became a building block of modern Fundamentalism and Evangelicalism.

Dispensationalism has become the largest group globally now focused on the imminent end of the world as we know it. In the United States, in the last generation, dispensationalism laid the foundation for the *Left Behind* series, a set of more than a dozen novels dramatising the purported events of the end time, most of which appeared on the bestseller lists and topped the religious book sales lists, and were made into movies. Among the most popular of televangelists would be John Hagee, pastor of Cornerstone Church, a mega-church in San Antonio, Texas, champion of the rights of Israel, and the author of more than a dozen books on the end time (all of which can be easily found on Amazon).

Most dedicated dispensationalists, unlike the aforementioned Hal Lindsey, do not take the final step of setting a date, stopping short at suggesting the time is near, the next decade, the next generation, during the lifetime of his/her primary audience. What they do is lay the foundation and build the walls of the prophetic structure while suggesting the outlines of the final ceiling. They create large communities in which the end times are discussed and expectancy built. Thus it is not surprising that this community repeatedly produces new date-setting prophetic leaders and groups.

And we must not forget another new highly successful millennial movement that emerged parallel to Fundamentalism – Pentecostalism. Although we generally think of Pentecostalism in terms of religious experience, speaking in tongues and spiritual healing, essential to the movement was the apocalyptic element of its first generation. When women and men began to speak in tongues, the phenomenon

---

[5]   On the Darbyite dispensationalist history in the United States see Boyer (1994), Kraus (1958), Sandeen (1970) and Weber (1979).

was viewed as an end-time event, and fulfilment of Acts 2:17, when your daughters would prophesy and young men see visions. It was a sign of the imminent coming of Christ and demanded the immediate missionary effort to get the word out to the world. Tongues appeared as a tool to convert non-Christians, a belief quickly refuted by all the missionaries who headed to specific countries whose language they believed they were now miraculously speaking. The urgency to get the word out was underscored by the devastating San Francisco earthquake of 1906.[6]

In the last 50 years, as the descendents of the original Fundamentalists and Pentecostals have merged their efforts to create contemporary Evangelicalism, their millennial roots have also been shared and cross fertilised the two communities. The expectations of an imminent return is now broadcast on cable television and radio worldwide, reaching even into those lands where no missionary dare tread.

One final note, contemporaneous with the development of modern Fundamentalism and Pentecostalism in North America, a relatively minor prophet, at least in terms of the size of his following, appeared. Aleister Crowley was a former member of the dispensational Brethren movement which he rejected as a teenager with a vengeance. However, he would, as an adult, be responsible for bringing dispensational thinking into the Western Esoteric tradition. Even as he was exploring mood-altering drugs and sex magick, he proposed a new temporal model for magical thinking to replace the essentially special model that has always dominated esoteric ruminations. He saw history divided into three eras (dispensations?) that of the Father (Osiris), the Mother (Iris) and the Son (Horus). The second era roughly coincided with the Christian era. The last era, that of thelemic magick, began in 1909 with a revelation given to Crowley, which became known as the *Book of the Law*, the Thelemic holy book.

It would be the role of Thelemic magicians to announce the arrival of the New Age, the Aeon of Horus, during which time Crowley's extreme individualistic views would come to the fore.[7] The case is yet to be made that Crowley's New Age provided the roots for the New Age that gave its name to the New Age movement of the 1970s and 1980s. However, Crowley's New Age certainly contained all of the major aspects of the new, imminent 'golden age' envisioned by the twentieth century 'New Age movement'. The Harmonic Convergence called for in 1987, and the series of date-specific New Age predictions related to this event, could be understood as a continuation of Crowley's esoteric dispensationalism.[8]

The Harmonic Convergence was but the first of a set of prophecies centred on the Mayan Calendar, initially proposed by New Age author Tony Shearer (b. 1926) who, in his 1971 book *Lord of the Dawn*, outlined a set of 22 cycles, each 52 years in length, that were launched at the day that the conquistador Cortez

---

[6]   Expectation of the end of the world in Pentecostalism has been considered by Faupel (1996). See also Riss (1987) and Yocum (1993).

[7]   On Crowley and his New Aeon, see Bogdan (2012), Richardson (2009), Suster (1989) and Weston (2009).

[8]   On millennial expectations in the Esoteric tradition see Wessinger (1988).

landed in Mexico (1519). While the Harmonic Convergence was generally seen in a very positive light, i.e. it hoped for a coming golden age, some New Age predictions also had a negative side, most notably illustrated in the prophecies of best-selling author Ruth Montgomery (1971, 1985), who saw the New Age being accompanied by the death of a fourth to a third of the world's population. The December 2012 date is, of course, the product of continued mining of the Mayan calendar puzzle.[9]

The point of this brief exercise in recent religious history has been to contextualise the many prophetic incidents at which we have looked and which will most likely continue to appear among our close neighbours in the generation ahead. They are the products of large religious communities who are day by day laying new foundations upon which new prophecies can be articulated – Christian Evangelicalism, Pentecostalism, Adventism and the Esoteric post-New Age community.

Prophecies of coming dramatic happenings are rarely falsified. They are never falsified for us who study them, because they were never true. There is a history of scholars approaching prophecies as among the worst of religious ideas, perhaps studying them in part so they could gloat a little bit at the stupid believers. Believers however, have a variety of ways of handling unfulfilled prophecies, primarily by correcting the calculations or gaining new insight about the invisible event that did occur, which allows them to go about their life.[10] Only with the advent of powerful outside forces, for example a government or a dominating religious community, do we see believers or prophets renounce their faith.[11] Those continuing communities who believed yesterday's prophecy remain in their support community today, ready to accept the next prophecy tomorrow.

---

[9]   On the 2012 prophecies and expectations see Braden (2009) and Jenkins (2009).

[10]   Most recently, for example, following the failure of his May 2012 predictions, Harold Camping suggested that the prophesised events really occurred, only in invisible ways. The earthquakes, for example, came in the form of 'man-quakes'. Mankind shook with fear from the Rapture and, he further noted, the book of Genesis describes man as made from dirt.

[11]   Again taking Camping as an example, he continued to profess his faith through his failed predictions of the 1990s and hastily recalculated the May 2012 date. He only relented, partially, after strong pressure brought on him in October 2012. Through the twentieth century, we saw the Jehovah's Witnesses survive repeated failure as did the Worldwide Church of God, The Church Universal and Triumphant and the many followers of Hal Lindsey and other conservative Evangelical Christian radio preachers.

References

Bogdan, H. 2012. Envisioning the Birth of a New Aeon: Dispensationalism and Millenarianism in the Thelemic Tradition, in *Aleister Crowley and Western Esotericism*, edited by H. Bogdan and M.P. Starr. Oxford: OUP, 89–106.

Boyer, P. 1994. *When Time Shall Be No More: Prophecy Belief in Modern American Culture*. Cambridge, MA: Belknap Press of Harvard University Press.

Braden, G. 2009. *The Mystery of 2012: Predictions, Prophecies, and Possibilities*. Boulder, CO: Sounds True.

Doyle, C. 2012. *A Journey to Waco: Autobiography of a Branch Davidian*. Lanham, MD: Rowman & Littlefield.

Duff-Brown, B. 2011. Harold Camping Avoids Press Despite End-of-Days Prediction. *Christian Science Monitor* [Online 20 October 2011]. Available at: http://www.csmonitor.com/USA/Latest-News-Wires/2011/1020/Harold-Camping-avoids-press-despite-end-of-days-prediction [accessed: 25 June 2012].

Faupel, D.W. 1996. *The Everlasting Gospel: The Significance of Eschatology in the Development of Pentecostal Thought*. Sheffield: Sheffield Academic Press.

Jenkins, J.M. 2009. *The 2012 Story: The Myths, Fallacies, and Truth Behind the Most Intriguing Date in History*. Los Angeles, CA: Tarcher.

Knight, G.R. 1993. *Millennial Fever and the End of the World*. Boise, ID: Pacific Press.

Kraus, C.N. 1958. *Dispensationalism in America: Its Rise and Development*. Richmond, VA: John Knox Press.

Lewis, J.R. 2000. *Doomsday Prophecies: A Complete Guide to the End of the World*. Amherst, NY: Prometheus Books.

Lindsey, H. 1970. *The Late Great Planet Earth*. Grand Rapids, MI: Zondervan.

——. 2003. *Faith for Earth's Final Hour*. Murrieta, CA: Oracle House Publishing.

Melton, J.G. 2009. *Encyclopedia of American Religions*. Detroit, MI: Gale.

Montgomery, R. 1971. *A World Beyond*. New York: Coward, McCann & Geohegan.

——. 1985. *Aliens among Us*. New York: Putnam's.

Nichols, F.D. 1944. *The Midnight Cry: A Defense of William Miller and the Millerites*. Washington, DC: Review and Herald.

Rich, R. 1967. *Little Known Schisms of the Restoration*. Provo, UT: Brigham Young Press.

Richardson, A. 2009. *Aleister Crowley and Dion Fortune: The Logos of the Aeon and the Shakti of the Age*. St Paul, MN: Llewellyn.

Riss, R. 1987. *Latter Rain: The Latter Rain Movement of 1948 and the Mid-Twentieth Century Evangelical Awakening*. Mississauga, ON: Honeycomb Visual Productions.

Rowe, D.L. 2008. *God's Strange Work: William Miller and the End of the World*. Grand Rapids, MI: William Eerdmans.

Sandeen, E.R. 1970. *The Roots of Fundamentalism: British and American Millenarianism, 1800–1930*. Chicago, IL: University of Chicago Press.

Shearer, T. 1971. *Lord of the Dawn: Quetzalcoatl and the Tree of Life*. Happy Camp, CA: Naturegraph Publishers.

Shields, S.L. 1982. *Divergent Paths of the Restoration: A History of the Latter-day Saints Movement*. Bountiful, UT: Restoration Research.

Stone, J.R. (ed.) 2000. *Expecting Armageddon: Essential Readings in Failed Prophecy*. New York and London: Routledge.

Suster, G. 1989. *The Legacy of the Beast: The Life, Work and Influence of Aleister Crowley*. York Beach, ME: Samuel Weiser.

Tumminia, D.G. and Swatos, Jr. W.H. (eds) 2011. *How Prophecy Lives*. Leiden: Brill.

Weber, T.P. 1979. *Living in the Shadow of the Second Coming American Premillennialism, 1875–1982*. New York: Oxford University Press.

Wessinger, C. 1988. *Annie Besant and Progressive Messianism: 1847–1933*. Lewiston, NY: Edwin Mellen Press.

——. 2011. *The Oxford Handbook of Millennialism*. New York: Oxford University Press.

Weston, P. 2009. *Aleister Crowley and the Aeon of Horus: History. Magick. Psychedelia. Ufology*. Glastonbury: Avalonian Aeon Publications.

Wojcik, Daniel. 1999. *The End of the World as We Know It: Faith, Fatalism, and Apocalypse in America*. New York: New York University Press.

Wright, S. (ed.) 1995. *Armageddon in Waco*. Chicago, IL: University of Chicago Press.

Wright, S.A. and Richardson, J.T. eds. 2011. *Saints Under Siege: The Texas State Raid on the Fundamentalist Latter Day Saints*. New York: New York University Press.

Yocum, B. 1993. *Prophecy: Exercising the Prophetic Gifts of the Spirit in the Church Today*. Ann Arbor, MI: Servant Publications.

Index

1 September 2001, 24, 96, 153, 208–9, 212
2000, 8, 18, 24, 73, 137–40, 261; *see also*
   Y2K
2012, 2–3, 9–10, 18, 21–2, 24–5, 73, 119,
   133, 221–3, 225–35, 239–52,
   255–60, 261–74, 282
   21 December, 1, 3, 15, 21–2, 221–2,
      226, 231–2, 242, 261, 266, 270,
      272, 282
   Christian criticism of, 233–4
2012 (the film), 1, 5, 133, 246, 250, 261,
   273
770 Synagogue, 33, 36

Abbasids, 90, 93
Abraham, 60, 75
Abu Bakr, 93
Adam, 7, 188, 189, 196, 204
Afghanistan, 24, 94, 96
Africa, 72, 93, 94, 95, 99, 100
Ahmandinejad, Mahmoud, 72, 98
Ahmadiyya, 95
Ajita Bodhisattva, *see* Maitreya
Al Qaeda, 96, 208
Ali, 90, 93, 94, 98
aliens, *see* extraterrestrials
Alleine, William, 50
America, *see* United States of America
amillennialism, *see* millennialism, types of
Amrah, Kaysan Abu, 90
Amsterdam, Peter, 161, 168
Anatolia, 94
Antichrist, 7, 44, 47, 91, 96–7, 157–8, 227,
   233–4
Ansar al-Mahdi, 98
apartheid, 67
Aphraates, 59
apocalypse, 5, 62, 90, 138, 139, 160, 222,
   228, 239, 248, 251, 274

apocalyptic images, 1; *see also* floods; fire;
   symbolism
   in advertising, 221n
   in film, 1, 211
   in literature, 21, 24, 96, 100
   in scripture, 46, 48, 52, 60, 62, 90
   in American culture, 228
   on YouTube, 269
apocrypha, 128
apostles, 57, 61, 63, 64, 71, 77–8
Aquarian Age, 116, 117, 118, 263, 272
Argüelles, José, 9, 15, 21–2, 221, 223,
   226–7, 229, 231–2, 234, 264–6,
   268
Armageddon, 7, 9, 19, 172, 245–6, 251,
   264
artificial intelligence (AI), 140, 141, 143,
   144, 147, 207
Ascended Masters, 3, 4, 17, 222, 223, 230,
   273
   Djwal Khul, 222
   Kuthumi, 3, 222, 255n
ascension, 3n, 198, 231, 274
Asimov, Isaac, 143
Assemblies of God, 79, 83
astrology, 125, 222, 251, 257–8
Aum Shinrikyo, 2
Australasia, 9
Australia, 10, 265
Avalokiteśvara, 123, 128
avatāras, 108
Ayyub, Sa'id, 96
Azusa Street Revival, 79, 81

Babylon, *see* symbolism
Baghdad, Iraq, 93
Bagshaw, Edward, 48
Baha'ism, 6, 97, 116
Bailey, Alice, 10, 222, 264

Bainbridge, William Sims, 155
Baker, Heidi, 86
b'ak'tun cycles, 9
Ballard, Guy and Edna, 10
Baptists, 47, 48, 50, 51, 280
Barker, Eileen, xv, 1
Barkun, Michael, ix, 2, 6, 15, 16, 17–25,
    209, 213, 227, 234
Bayly, William, 51
Beast, the, *see* symbolism
Beattie, Hugh, ix, 7, 72, 89–100
Bell, Catherine, 32–3
Bell, Christopher, ix, 5, 8, 73, 123–34
Bell Burnell, Jocelyn, 9
Bell Rock, Arizona, 3
Bengal, 112, 114n
Berg, David, 151, 152, 155, 157–61,
    166–8, 171–2, 176, 178–80
Besant, Annie, 115
Beverley, Thomas, 52
Bhaktivedanta Swami, 118
Bible, prophecy in, 19, 156, 240, 245–6;
    see also Christianity, canonical and
    non-canonical literature
    Hebrew Bible/Old Testament, 16,
        57–60, 66, 75, 197, 201
        Daniel, 45, 60, 61, 156, 199, 200,
            202, 203
        Exodus, 58–9
        Ezekiel, 156, 203
        Isaiah, 58, 66, 189, 195, 197, 200,
            201, 202
        Septuagint, The, 60
    New Testament, 57, 61, 66, 156, 278
        Acts of the Apostles, 57, 58, 76,
            281
        Corinthians, 61–2, 65, 67, 71
        First Epistle of Peter, 58
        Matthew, 58–9, 61, 156, 157, 160
        Revelation, 6, 22, 44–52, 61–3,
            96–7, 156, 157, 198, 200, 210,
            222, 228, 231, 234
        Timothy, 60
Bickle, Mike, 78n, 81, 84
black hole, 8, 146, 240, 244–5
Blavatsky, Helena, 115, 230
'blessed children', 11, 152, 185–93
Book of Mormon, The, 166–7, 172

Bön religion, 73, 123, 124, 127
Brahma Kumari, 117
Brahmans, 106–7, 109
Branch Davidians, 3, 151, 153, 209, 211,
    279
Brethren, the, 280–81
Brookhouse, Thomas, 51
Buddhism, 6, 7, 105, 106, 107n, 112, 128,
    129; *see also* Tibetan Buddhism
Bush, Vannevar, 144–6

Cain, Paul, 81
Cairo, Egypt, 81, 93
California, USA, 21, 80, 155, 166, 212,
    225, 264
    University of, 231, 247, 265
caliphs, 90–93
Calleman, Carl Johan, 221n
Campbell, Colin, 217, 227, 262
Camping, Harold, 10, 15, 18–20, 22, 24,
    25, 43, 44, 228, 250, 277, 282n
Canaan, 75
Canada, 43, 81, 85, 167
Catholicism, 44, 51, 77, 80, 176
Cayce, Edgar, 20
CERN, European Centre for Nuclear
    Research, 8, 244–5
Chabad, 33
chakras, 222, 256, 257
channelling, 4, 17, 20, 21, 130, 168–9, 177,
    191, 230, 267
charisma, 4, 34, 82, 91, 152, 171, 175–6
    routinisation of, 81, 177
charismata, 71, 76–7, 79, 82; *see also*
    glossolalia; healing
children, in prophetic movements, 11,
    161–2, 185–93
Children of God, *see* Family International
Christianity, 6, 16–17, 50, 57–69, 71–3,
    75–9, 90, 105, 114, 139, 151, 157,
    166, 175, 177, 197–8, 263; *see*
    also Catholicism; Church of Jesus
    Christ of Latter Day Saints; Eastern
    Orthodoxy; Family International;
    Protestantism; Pentecostalism
    canonical scripture, 16, 57, 60, 64–5,
        68; *see also* Bible
    Codex Sinaiticus, 62

non-canonical scripture, 16, 57, 59, 62–4
    Didache, The, 63
    Epistle of Barnabas, The, 59, 62, 66
    Shepherd of Hermas, The, 62–3, 76n
nonconformism, 16, 43–52
prophecy in, 4, 6–7, 16–17, 43–52, 57–68, 71, 75–87, 96, 156–8, 165–81, 189, 210, 228, 233–4, 245–6, 277–82; *see also* 'end times'
Church of England, 16, 44–51, 279
Church of God in Christ, 79
Church of Jesus Christ of Latter Day Saints, 77, 151, 152, 165–81, 187, 279
civil war, *see* war, civil war
China, 7, 10, 24, 161
clairvoyance, 130
Clark, Randy, 86
Clarke, Arthur C., 144, 145
class (social), 109, 111, 216n
Cleveland, Ohio, USA, 85
climate change, 18, 21, 24, 140, 147, 246; *see also* 'Earth Changes'
cognitive dissonance, 11, 15, 27–8, 30–31, 35, 39, 153, 208, 216, 217, 230, 274
Cold War, 24, 209
commitment, to new religious movements, 165, 173–5
communal living, 162, 167, 170
computers, 8, 73, 137, 138, 143, 145, 147, 148, 261
Congregationalists, 47, 49, 280
conspiracy, 96, 151, 153, 159, 207–18, 233, 234
Constantinople, 91, 92
Crowley, Aleister, 281
Crown Heights, Brooklyn, USA, 33, 36
'cultic milieu', 222, 223, 227, 229–31, 261–74
cycles of time, *see* time, cyclical

Dajjal, the, 7, 91–3, 97, 100
Dalai Lama, 124–6, 129, 131
Damascus, 90, 92

Däniken, Erich von, 268, 270
Darby, John Nelson, 7, 67, 279–80
Dawud, Muhammad Isa, 96
Dein, Simon, ix, 6, 11, 15, 27–39
demons, 80, 131; *see also rākṣasas*
Detsen, King Trisong, 123, 127–8
dharma, 72, 106–9, 111, 117, 129
    yuga dharma, 110–11
dispensationalism, *see* millennialism, types of
divination, 3, 73, 123–34, 246
Divine Principle, The, 152, 186, 188
DK Foundation, 222, 255, 258, 260
Doctrine and Covenants, 167, 168n, 169, 176, 178
Drepung Monastery, 133
Dublin, Max, 141–3, 145
dystopia, 5, 221–2, 227, 228

'Earth Changes', 15, 18, 20–25; *see also* climate change; earthquakes; floods; pole shift; volcanic eruption
earthquakes, 19, 157, 247, 281, 282n
Eastern Orthodoxy, 80
Egypt, 59, 81, 93, 95, 100
'end times', 221, 261
    in Christianity, 16, 17, 19, 44, 57, 60–62, 66–7, 139, 151–2, 155–63, 201, 210, 233, 279, 280–81
    in the conspiracy milieu, 207–18
    in Islam, 89–100
'end time disciples', 167
energy transfer, 222–3, 256–7, 260, 272
England, x–xi, 16, 43–56, 188, 278
Ephraim, 59
eschatology, 278
    apocalyptic vs. millennial, 210
    in Islam, 91
Europe, 6, 9, 24, 114, 116, 214, 225, 227–9, 244, 265, 266, 278
European Centre for Nuclear Research, *see* CERN
Eusebius, 63–4
evangelism, 65, 78n, 157, 160, 166–7, 280–81
extraterrestrials, 230, 251, 262

Fagan, Livingstone, x, 3, 153, 195–204

failed prophecy, *see* prophecy, failure of
Family International, The, 11, 151–2,
	155–63, 165–81
Family Radio/Family Stations, Inc., 2, 18,
	20
farbrengen, 37
Fatima (daughter of Mohammad), 93
Fatima, Portugal, 77
Fatimad dynasty, 93
Festinger, Leon, 15, 21, 27–31, 33, 35,
	229–30
Fifth Monarchists, 45, 47
film, 1, 15, 23, 43, 148, 207, 212–15, 228,
	271; *see also 2012* (the film)
financial collapse, 153, 157, 213, 221n
fire, 1, 114
Five Fold Ministry, 71, 78, 80
flood, 3, 8, 20–21, 28, 105n, 108, 229
'fore-telling', 11, 16, 57, 72, 82–3
'forth-telling', 11, 16, 57, 61–2, 67–8, 72,
	82–3
Fox, George, 49
France, 190
Freeman May, Abi, xi, 3, 6, 151, 155–65
Fuller Theological Seminary, 80
futurology, 73, 141–2

Gamaleddin, Muhammad, 96
Gampo, King Songtsen, 123, 127–8
Gandhi, 73, 114
Geluk (Tibetan Buddhism), 124, 126, 133
Genden Monastery, 126
Germany, 190
Gersten, Peter, 2, 3n
Gesar, 125
Ghose, Aurobindo, 114
gifts of the Spirit, 16, 17, 61, 67, 71, 76,
	78, 79, 82, 172; *see also* charismata
'global awakening', 208, 210–11, 215, 217
globalisation, 5, 116, 133, 273
glossolalia, 76, 79, 280
Gog and Magog, 89; *see also* Yajuj wa
	Majuj
Golden Age, 10, 73, 105, 115n, 118, 227,
	281, 282
González-Reimann, Luis, x, 6, 72–3,
	105–19

Google, 9–10, 240; *see also* media and
	internet
Gnostics, 76
Great Disappointment, The, 18, 279
Greco-Roman prophecy, 75
Gregory of Nazianzus, 63–4
Grossman, Wendy M., x, 8, 73, 137–49

Hadiths, 7, 89n, 90–91, 95
Hare Krishna Movement, *see* International
	Society for Krishna Consciousness
Harmonic Convergence, 9, 21, 264–6,
	281–2
Harvey, Sarah, x, 1–12
healing, 20, 61, 76, 79, 80, 87, 262, 280
Heaven's Gate, 2, 251
heretics
	Christian, 166–7
	in India, 73, 106–7, 109, 117
Hinduism, prophecy in, 71, 105–19
Hizbullah, 98–9
Hmong, 10
homosexuality, 68
Hooke, William, 49, 51
Hopi beliefs, prophecy in, 8
Huddleston, Trevor, 67
'hylozoic universe', 222, 256

I Am movement, 10, 230
I Ching, 225, 231, 232, 234, 246, 264
Icke, David, 153, 211, 213, 215, 234
Ignatius of Antioch, 64, 76n
illness, 38, 87, 125, 131, 193, 272n
illuminati, *see* New World Order
imagery, *see* symbolism
Imami/Twelvers, *see* Islam, Shia
imam, 93–4, 97–8; *see also* Twelfth Imam
immortality, 11n, 28, 146
India, 5, 10, 72, 94, 95, 112–15, 129, 265
	colonial, 113–15
	Gupta Empire, 108–9
	modern, 116–17, 119
	post-Vedic period, 105–6
	Vedic period, 105–6
inequality, 99, 208, 217
Inform, xv, 1–2, 6n, 16, 255

internet, 6, 8, 10, 15, 23, 100, 142, 143n, 158, 209–10, 222, 239, 241, 245, 249, 251, 266, 273, 278
Institute of Applied Metaphysics, 31
International Society for Krishna Consciousness (ISKCON), 118, 268
Iran, 72, 93, 94, 98–100, 116, 216
Iraq, 24, 72, 75, 90, 91, 94, 98
Isaac, 75
Ishmael, 75
Islam, 75; *see also* Mahdism
    in India, 105, 111–14
    prophecy in, 6–7, 71–2, 89–100
    Shia, 72, 92–3, 97–9, 112, 116
        Imami/ Twelvers, 93, 94, 97, 100
        Nizari Ismalism, 112–14, 116
    Sufi, 94–5
        Naqshbandi-Haqqani, 97
    Sunni, 72, 92–7, 100
Islamic Revolution in Iran, 72
Israel, 6, 33–6, 67, 75, 96, 199, 277, 280
Israfil, 92
Italy, 10

Jainism, 6, 105, 106
Jamkaran, Iran, 99
Japan, 24, 188
Jehovah's Witnesses, 279, 282n
Jerusalem, 61, 92, 199, 201, 203
Jesus, 57–61, 66, 68, 75, 111 168, 171, 188–9, 230
    return of, 6–7, 10, 89, 91–2, 94, 97, 100, 151, 155–63, 170, 233, 277
Jewish, *see* Judaism
Joel, 76
John Birch Society, 211–12
Johnston, Warren, x, 16, 43–56
Jones, Alex, 5, 153, 207–18
Jones, Bob, 81
Judaism, 27, 34, 71; *see also* Lubavitcher Hasidism
    and Christianity, 66
    festivals, 37
    Hasidism, 33, 35, 37
    Kabbala, 33
    prophecy in, 6, 34, 75
    ultra-Orthodox, 33

Judgment Day, 7, 19, 43, 92, 93, 105, 198, 200–201, 277

Kaempffert, Waldemar, 145–6
Kali-Yug, *see Yugas*, Kali
Kalki/ Kalkin, 72, 112, 114, 119
    as destroyer, 107, 112
    as rescuer, 107–9
    modern claimants, 113, 115–17
kalpa, 108, 111
Kansas City Prophets, 81; *see also* Bickle, Mike; Jones, Bob; Cain, Paul
Kanter, Rosabeth, 173
karma, 125, 234
Keach, Benjamin, 51
Kensington Temple, London, 4
Khurasan, 92, 96, 99
Khurasani, 98
kingdom
    of Christ, 44, 45, 48, 50, 51
    of God, 7, 65, 79, 80, 83, 156, 200–204
    of Heaven on Earth, 11, 60, 152, 153, 185, 189
Knollys, Hanserd, 48–9
Korea, 188–91, 193
Koresh, David, 3, 153, 198, 200n, 204
Koruna Project, Lapland, 258–60
Krishnamurti, Jiddu, 115
Kurzweil, Ray, 146
Kuthumi, *see* Ascended Masters

Laden, bin, Osama, 96, 214
LaHaye, Tim, 7, 246, 280
Large Hadron Collider, CERN, 8, 239, 240, 244–5
Larsen, Kristine, x, 9, 10, 222, 239–52
Latter Day Saints, *see* Church of Jesus Christ of Latter Day Saints
Lawson, Thomas, 49
Lead, Jane, 51
Lee, Matthew, xi, 16, 71–2, 75–87
Left Behind series, *see* LaHaye Tim
Lhasa, Tibet, 125, 131, 133
Lieder, Nancy, 232–3
Lindsey, Hal, 24, 96, 277, 280, 282n
Lubavitcher Hasidim, 11, 15–16, 27–8, 33–9
Luther, Martin, 163, 197, 265

McHyde, Tim, 233
McKenna, Dennis, 225
McKenna, Terence, 9, 221, 223, 225–7, 229, 231–2, 234, 266
Mādhyamaka, 128
magic, 144, 281
magnetic field
    of the earth, 240, 248–9
    of the sun, 243
Maguire, Andrew, xi, 16, 57–68
Mahābhārata, 106–9, 113, 115
Maharishi Mahesh Yogi, 117
mahāyuga, 108–9
Mahdism, 72, 89–100
Mahdawi, 94
Mahdi, 7, 72, 89–100, 112–13, 116
    Ahmad, Shaykh Muhammad, 95
    Fodio, dan, Uthman, 95
    Hanafiyya, al- ibn, Muhammad, 90
    Ibn Tumart, 94
    Ismail, 94
    Khomeini, Ayatollah, 97
    Muhammad, Sayyid, 94
    Mukhtar, Al-, 90, 98, 99
    Niass, Ibrahim, 95
    Nikalank/Niṣkalank, 112–13
    Qadiani, al-, Mirza Ghulam Ahmed, 95
    Qahtani, al-, Muhammad, 95
    Selim I., Sultan, 94
Maimonides, 34
'mainstreaming the fringe', 6, 15, 23
Maitreya, 7, 8, 115, 116, 128, 129
Malaysia, 10
Manu, 105n, 108
Maria (Family International), 168–70, 177–8
mark of the beast, 49, 139, 157, 159
Marrakech, 94
Martin, Dorothy, 21, 229–31
Marxism, 226
Matrix Institute, 20
Mayan
    calendar, 1, 8–10, 15, 21–2, 119, 221–2, 226–7, 231–2, 240, 242, 249, 261, 265–6, 268, 281–2
    elders (in Europe), 271–3
    prophecy, 133, 231

Mayer, Jean-François, xi, 8, 10, 223, 227, 261–74
media, 35, 37–8, 213, 215, 216n, 221
    prophecy in, 1–2, 4, 8, 10, 15, 18, 20, 23, 43, 261, 273
Mecca, 90, 92, 95, 96
Me(a)hdi Army, 72, 98
mediumship, 20, 77, 130, 191
Medina, 90, 92
Medjugorje, Bosnia-Herzegovina, 77
Melton, J. Gordon, xii, 2, 7, 11, 29, 223, 266, 277–82
Memex, 144–5
Mesopotamian prophecy, 75
Messiah, 6, 16, 27, 33–5, 75, 189–90, 192, 199, 213, 233; *see also Moshiach*
Methodist, 15, 16, 280
Middle East, 67, 94, 158, 233
militancy, 96
Millennium, the, 6–7, 44, 51–2, 80, 94, 228, 270
millennialism, 1, 11, 29, 71–2, 208, 210, 227, 277n
    amillennialism/non-millennialism, 7
    catastrophic vs. progressive, 270
    Christian/Biblical, 6
    dispensationalism, 7, 19, 67, 96, 279–81
    improvisational, 234
    post-millennialism, 7, 80
    pre-millennialism, 7, 10
    predictive vs. explanatory, 4, 30, 216–17; *see also* prophecy, types of
Miller, William, 18–20, 25, 197, 278–9
miracles, 33, 86–7, 128, 189
misfortune, 89, 125
MO Letters, 167, 176
Mohammad/Muhammad, 7, 89n, 90–93, 100, 165n, 171
Moody, Dwight, 7, 280
Moon, Heung Jin Nim, 191–2
Moon, Sun Myung (Rev), 152, 185–6, 188–93
Moore, Gordon, 146–7
monarchy, 16, 44–6, 51
Mongol, 94
Montanism, 16, 64–5, 67, 76

Mormons, *see* Church of Jesus Christ of Latter Day Saints
Morocco, 94
Moses, 38, 58–9, 92, 165n, 171, 196, 199
Moshiach, 6, 16, 27–8, 33–9
Mount Carmel, 153, 198–201
Mozambique, 86
Mujaddid, 92, 95
Muslims, *see* Islam
Muwahiddun, al-, 94

Nāgārjuna, 128
Nah Kin, 272
nanotechnology, 140–41, 144, 146
Native American beliefs, prophecy in, 8
natural disasters, 3, 6, 8, 157, 269; *see also* 'Earth Changes'
Nechung, 125
    monastery, 129
    oracle, 129, 131, 132
New Age beliefs, prophecy in, 15, 17–18, 20, 22–3, 73, 116, 133, 208, 210–11, 222–3, 227, 229, 231–4, 261–7, 272–4, 281–2
New Age movement, 8–10, 116, 222, 227, 229–31, 234, 258, 261–74, 281
New Apostolic Reformation, 71, 75, 78–87
    seven mountains of culture, 78, 80
New Jerusalem, 51, 65, 228
New World Order (NWO), 153, 207–12, 215, 233
New Zealand, 10
Newcombe, Suzanne, xii, 1–12
news, 1, 5–6, 15, 18, 22–3, 43, 78, 146, 151, 157–8, 208–9, 214, 244–5, 278
Nibiru, 232–4, 239, 248n, 269
nonmillennialism, *see* millennialism, types of
non-violence, 50, 114n
Norse mythology, 8
Nursi, Said, 97
Nyingma, 124, 127

Obama, Barack, 214, 216, 234
Ohel, 33, 38–9
Oklahoma City bombing, 209, 212, 213
One World Government, 157–8

oracles, 73, 75, 123, 125, 129–33, 152, 172, 175, 178
Origen, 60, 62n

Padmasambhava, 127–9
Pakistan, 10
Partridge, Christopher, 231
Paul, Saint, 61–3, 71, 76, 156
Pearl of Great Price, 167
Pehar, 128–9
Penden Lhamo, 125
Pentecost, 58, 75, 77, 233
Pentecostalism, xii, 16, 17, 31, 67, 71, 73, 77, 79–87, 166, 175, 280–82
Philippines, 10, 247
pilgrimage, 33, 99; *see also* ritual
Planet X, *see* Nibiru
pole shift, 21, 248–50
political change, 16, 44–7, 51–2, 72, 94, 99, 195
Poloma, Margaret, xii, 4, 16, 71–2, 75–87
popular press, 2, 7–9, 15, 23, 52, 96, 98, 138
prediction, *see* prophecy
preppers, *see* survivalists
Presbyterian, 47–50, 280
proselytisation, 28–9, 35, 39, 167
Protestantism, 7, 44, 47, 77, 78n, 79, 179, 197
Project Megiddo, 18
prophecy; *see also* 2012; Christianity; Hinduism; Islam; Judaism; New Age; Tibetan Buddhism
    definitions, 3–4, 82
    explanatory, 61, 217
    failure of, 11, 15, 21, 28–31, 81, 83, 132, 196, 208, 214, 217, 229–30, 270
    in films, 1, 43, 133, 148, 207, 212–15, 246, 250, 261, 271, 273
    mundane, 3–5, 71, 83
    in the news, 1, 10, 15, 18, 21, 22, 35, 43, 278
    persistence of, 4, 11, 15, 24, 151, 282
    in popular culture, 7–9, 23, 43, 133, 208, 221, 225, 228, 231, 273
    predictive, 16, 18, 57, 61
    ritual, in maintenance of, 27, 31–3, 84

routinization of, 11, 152
in scientific thought, 5, 8, 137–49,
    221–2, 239–52
in secular thought, 5, 8, 17–8, 71,
    137–49, 217–18, 221–2, 226–9,
    261
as social critique, 16, 45, 49, 51–2,
    153–4, 208, 217
in social science literature, 15, 21,
    27–31
textual, 57, 73, 153
    Christian scriptures as predictive of
        Christ, 57–67
theory of, 152, 165–81
    prophetic channel, 152, 177–80
    prophetic modality, 152, 177–80
prophets, 3, 4, 16, 17, 19–21, 34, 57,
    64–5, 67, 75, 77–8, 81–5, 153, 165,
    168–9, 171–2, 179, 198, 208, 277,
    281
and charisma, 4
in Christian scripture, 61–4, 76, 195,
    197, 200–203
'false', 4, 50, 63, 66, 233
secular, 142, 146
types of, 176–7, 213
pseudoscience, *see* scientific illiteracy
Purāṇa(s), 107–8, 112, 118

Qa'im, 90, 93
Qahtani, 91, 95
Quakers, 47, 49, 51, 77
Qur'an, 89–91, 100

radio, 18, 23, 27, 35, 98, 153, 158, 207,
    209–10, 212, 277, 281
Radio Frequency Identification (RFID),
    139
Raelians, 11n
Ragnarök, 8
rākṣasas, 111–13
Rāma, 110, 111, 116
Rāmāyaṇa, 111–13, 116
Ramakrishna, 114, 118
Ranters, 77
Rapture, the, 2, 15, 17–19, 43, 277, 282n

rebbe, 16, 27, 33–9; *see also* Schneerson,
    Menachem Rebbe
rebellion, 7, 45–6, 90
redemption, 27, 33, 35, 37, 49–50, 105
reincarnation, 94, 110–11
'reboot', 152, 178, 181
Red Letters, The, 222, 255n, 257–8, 260
religious economy, 171–2, 177
Restoration, English, 16, 44–8
Revelation, Book of, *see* Bible, prophecy
    in
revelation (divine), 63–5, 84, 165n,
    166–79, 191, 196, 281
Ṛg Veda, 106
ritual, 11, 16, 27, 30–33, 37–9, 77, 81–4,
    86, 106, 109, 130, 132–3, 173, 197,
    212
dance, 32, 37, 264
framing, 39
horse sacrifice, 107
performance, 31–2
pilgrimage, 33, 99
singing, 36–7, 39, 124, 173
Robertson, David G., xii, 5, 16, 153,
    207–18
Roman Catholic Church, *see* Catholicism
Rosewell, Thomas, 50
Rough, Suzanne, xii, 3, 73, 222–3, 255–60

Sadr, al-, Muhammad Baqir, 98
Sadr, al-, Muqtada, 98
Safavids, 93–4
Saint Frances of Assisi, 77
St Paul's Cathedral, London, 45
Sambala (Śambhala), 107, 112
Samyé, 128, 131
Sananda, 230
Sant tradition, 111
Santeria, 17
Satan, 7, 44, 186, 188–90, 193, 212
Saudi Arabia, 97
Scallion, Gordon Michael, 15, 20–21
Schneerson, Menachem Rebbe, 16, 27–8,
    33–9
Schneur Zalman of Liady, 34
scientific illiteracy, 9, 222, 239, 249–52

scientific thought, prophecy in, *see* prophecy, in scientific thought
science fiction, 73, 141, 143–4, 146–8, 188; *see also* Asimov, Isaac; Clarke, Arthur C.; Stross, Charles
scripture, 166–9, 176; *see also* Bible; Christianity, canonical and non-canonical scripture; Hadiths; *Purāṇa(s)*; Qur'an
  Christian, 16, 57–68, 153, 195–6, 198–9, 203–4
  Puranic, 6, 105n, 107–8, 112, 118
  Tibetan Buddhism, scriptural canon, 73, 126
Second Advent, 19, 163
Second Coming (of Christ), 7, 17, 18, 116, 170, 189, 278; *see also* Jesus, return of
secular prophecy, *see* prophecy, in secular thought
secularisation, 228, 263, 278
Sedona, Arizona, 3
Senegal, 95
Sera Monastery, 133
Seven Seals, of Revelation, 198, 200
Seventh-day Adventists, 177, 197, 279
sexuality, 11n, 68, 167, 173
Shakers, 77
Shari'ati, Ali, 97
Shaykhi, 97
Shearer, Tony, 9, 265, 281
Shepherd, Gary, xiii, 11, 152, 156, 165–81
Shepherd, Gordon, xiii, 11, 152, 156, 165–81
Sherwin, William, 48
Shils, Edward, 170
Sikh, 111, 113, 117
Singapore, 10
singing, *see* ritual
Singularity, the, 140, 146–7
Sister Thedra, 21, 229
Sitchin, Zecharia, 232–3
Smith, Joseph, 152, 165n, 166–8, 171–2, 175, 176, 178–9, 279
social change, 44, 51, 145–6, 171
social networking, 10, 143
social support, 28
solar flares, 240, 243

South Africa, 10
Soviet Union, 24
Spain, 72, 94, 100, 214
Stamford Hill, London, 33
'stigmatised knowledge', 15, 23, 227, 231–2
Stross, Charles, 144, 147–8
sub-cultures, 6, 5, 23, 262, 264
Sudan, 95, 100
suffering, 47–8, 50, 52, 72, 99, 100, 217, 272n; *see also* symbolism, suffering servants
Sufyani, 90, 92
suicide, 2, 251
supernatural, 4, 11, 78, 130, 152, 165, 171, 174–5
survivalists, 2, 137, 138, 216
Sutcliffe, Steven, 9
Switzerland, 8, 223, 261–74
symbolism, 3n, 4, 44, 188, 228
  Babylon, 46, 48–51, 61
  beast, 44, 46–50, 52, 60, 89, 92
  black flags, 89, 91
  labour pains, 50
  Queen Victoria, 113
  saints, 7, 45–6, 48–51
  seals, 195, 198, 200
  suffering servants, 58, 66
  trumpets, 49, 92, 156
synchronicity, 10
Syria, 90–92

Tagore, Rabindranath, 114
technology, x, 5, 73, 138–49, 157, 251; *see also* media
television, 2, 23, 35, 43, 145, 158, 187, 212, 221, 277, 281
terrorism, 212–13; *see also* 11 September 2001
theodicy, 5, 72, 99, 154, 208, 217
Theosophical Society, 8, 73, 115, 222
Third Wave Prophecy, 80–81, 85; *see also* Pentecostalism
Thomas Aquinas, 77
Thompson, Damian, 4, 15, 30, 138, 216
Tibetan Buddhism 5, 8, 71, 73, 123–35, 264–5, 268; *see also* Buddhism
  cycles of time, 242

divination, 123–6
    mundane vs transcendental prophecy,
        125–6
    oracles, 129–33
    scriptural canon, 126–8
    textual prophecy, 126
    treasure scripture, 127–9
time, cyclical, 6, 110–11, 225
'time wave' concept, 225, 227, 231
tongues, speaking in, *see* glossolalia
Toronto Airport Vineyard Church, 81
Toronto Airport Christian Fellowship,
    81–2, 86
Toronto Blessing, The, 79n, 80–82, 84, 86
trance, 4, 17, 20, 32, 85, 123, 130–32
Transcendental Meditation, 117
transhumanism, 11n
Tribulation, The, 6–7, 10, 161, 204
Tsongkhapa (Lozang Drakpa), 126
Tutu, Desmond, 67
Turkey, xi, 64, 95–6
Twelvers/Imami, *see* Islam, Shia
Twelfth Imam, 93, 97–100

Ubayd, Abi ibn, Al-Mukhtar, 90
UFOs, 12, 213, 229–31; *see also*
    extraterrestrials
Ultra-Orthodox, *see* Judaism
Umayyad caliphate, 90
Unification Church, xiii, 11, 151–2,
    185–94
    'blessing', 185–6, 193
    second generation, 185–94
United Arab Emirates, 10
United States of America, xii, 6–10, 15,
    19, 21, 24, 33, 35, 43, 67, 79–82,
    84, 86, 96, 99n, 118, 141, 145, 153,
    155, 159, 161, 175, 180, 188, 211,
    213–14, 221n, 225, 227–9, 230n,
    246, 251, 264–6, 273, 280–81
United Kingdom, 9, 10n, 82; *see also*
    England
USSR, *see* Soviet Union
utopias 5–6, 172, 208, 210, 217, 221–2,
    226–8, 263; *see also Śambhala*;
    New Jerusalem; kingdom

Vairocana, 127–9

Vaiṣṇavism, 108
Vedic period, 105–6, 108–9, 111
Venner, Thomas, 45–7
Vietnam, 10, 172
Vinge, Vernor, 146
violence, 45–7, 86, 153, 279; *see also* war
    and non-violence
visionary, 60, 77, 171–2, 225
Viṣṇu, 105n, 107n, 108, 110, 112
Vivekananda, Swami, 73, 114, 118
Vineyard Churches, Association of, 81–2
volcanic eruption 240, 246–7

Waco, Texas, 3, 153, 195, 198, 199–200,
    203, 209, 211, 279
Wagner, C. Peter, 78, 80
Wagner, Richard, 8
Wagner, Walter, 244–5
wars; *see also* Cold War
    civil wars 90
    Civil War (English) 16, 45
    Iraqi-Afghani War 24
    Iranian Revolution 72
    Six Day War 34
    on terrorism 213
    Vietnam War 172
Weber, Max, 4, 165, 170–71, 177
Welch, Robert, 211
Wesleyan Holiness Movement, 79
Wessinger, Catherine, 1, 115, 270, 280–81
When Prophecy Fails (1956), *see*
    Festinger, Leon
Whitesides, Kevin, 9–10
Wilcock, David, 153, 211
Wilczek, Rank, 224–5
Wilson, Andrew Fergus, xiii, 221, 223,
    225–37
Wimber, John, 81
Wither, George, 50
Witt, Steve, 84–5
women, 7, 38, 76, 82, 84, 271–2, 280
World Services, 158, 168, 172, 178

Y2K, 8, 73, 138–40, 143, 146, 261
Yajuj and Majuj, 89, 91–3
Yazid, 90
Yechi, 36
Yellowstone Caldera, 240, 246–7

Yemen, 98
Yogācāra, 128
Yudrönma, Dorjé, 125
Yuga Purāṇa, 107–8
yugānta, 108–9, 112
Yugas, 72–3, 105, 108–11
    Dvāpara, 108, 118
    length of, 208, 111, 115, 118–19
    Kali, 72–3, 108–19
    Kṛta/Satya, 72, 108–19
    Tretā, 108

Yukteswar, Swami, 118

Zaccarelli, Hani, xiii, 3, 11, 152, 185–94
zaddik, see rebbe
Zerby, Karen, *see* Maria
Zionism, Christian, 16, 67, 96, 208
Zoroastrianism, 6, 90
Zubayr, al- ibn, Abdallah, 90